"Unique and thoughtful. . . . This solid narrative of research findings—the first from a Native American perspective—is essential reading."

—C. C. Kolb, *Choice*

"Writing in the vein of scholars such as Vine Deloria Jr., Paulette Steeves's critique of the 'Clovis-first' model of peopling of the Americas both engages with and moves beyond current ideas about how and when people first came to these lands. The research presented in this book questions the ways archaeologists have traditionally constructed narratives of movement and arrival without considering Indigenous ways of knowing. This is an important and timely contribution to the field."

—Kisha Supernant (Métis), associate professor of anthropology at the University of Alberta

"Paulette Steeves decenters Western power and authority over Indigenous thought, voice, inclusion, and history. The result is an act of healing that benefits both Indigenous people and academic scholarship."

—Randall H. McGuire, Distinguished Professor of Anthropology at SUNY Binghamton University

"A timely analysis of the ethnocentric influences on past and present scientific inquiry and archaeological practice from the perspective of an Indigenous archaeologist. Steeves brings together a host of voices espousing the importance of contextual relationships in hypothesis development and archaeological analysis."

—Kathleen Holen, director of the Center for American Paleolithic Research

D0813577

THE INDIGENOUS PALEOLITHIC

OF THE WESTERN HEMISPHERE

The INDIGENOUS
PALEOLITHIC
of the WESTERN
HEMISPHERE

Paulette F. C. Steeves

UNIVERSITY OF NEBRASKA PRESS   LINCOLN

Portions of this manuscript originally appeared in the following: "Clovis and Folsom, Indigenous Occupation Prior To" and "The La Sena Site (18,440 ± 90 ^{14}C yr BP): A Pre-Clovis Site in South West Nebraska," in *Encyclopedia of Global Archaeology*, 2nd ed., edited by Claire Smith (New York: Springer, 2019); "Unpacking Neoliberal Archaeological Control of Ancient Indigenous Heritage," *Archaeologies* 13, no. 1 (2017): 48–65; "Decolonizing the Past and Present of the Western Hemisphere (the Americas)," *Archaeologies* 11, no. 1 (2015): 42–69; "Academia, Archaeology, CRM, and Tribal Historic Preservation," *Archaeologies* 11, no. 1 (2015): 121–41.

The University of Nebraska Press is part of a land-grant institution with campuses and programs on the past, present, and future homelands of the Pawnee, Ponca, Otoe-Missouria, Omaha, Dakota, Lakota, Kaw, Cheyenne, and Arapaho Peoples, as well as those of the relocated Ho-Chunk, Sac and Fox, and Iowa Peoples.

First Nebraska paperback printing: 2023

Publication of this volume was assisted by a Canada Research Chair Tier II grant jointly administered by Social Sciences and Humanities Research Council Canada, National Sciences and Engineering Research Council of Canada, and the Canada Institute of Health Research. Publication is also supported by the Algoma University Research Fund, Algoma University, Sault Ste. Marie, Ontario. Canada.

Library of Congress Cataloging-in-Publication Data
Names: Steeves, Paulette F. C., author.
Title: The indigenous Paleolithic of the Western Hemisphere / Paulette F.C. Steeves.
Description: Lincoln: University of Nebraska Press, [2021] | Includes bibliographical references and index.
Identifiers: LCCN 2020021091
ISBN 9781496202178 (hardback)
ISBN 9781496234704 (paperback)
ISBN 9781496225368 (epub)
ISBN 9781496225375 (mobi)
ISBN 9781496225382 (pdf)
Subjects: LCSH: Prehistoric peoples—America. | Paleo-Indians—America. | Paleolithic period—America. | Excavations (Archaeology)—America. | America—Discovery and exploration—Pre-Columbian.
Classification: LCC E61 .S87 2021 | DDC 970.01/1—dc23
LC record available at https://lccn.loc.gov/2020021091

Set in Garamond Premier by Mikala R. Kolander.
Designed by N. Putens.

for

Jesse Blue Steeves, 1977–99

Vine Deloria Jr., 1933–2005

Leonard Sampson, 1900s–2006

CONTENTS

TABLES

ACKNOWLEDGMENTS

This book is based on my dissertation research at SUNY Binghamton from 2008 to 2015. During this time, I had four different dissertation committees. Not everyone in academia understands or supports Indigenous voices or their counterstories that work to decolonize the academy. The ladies in anthropology offices, the silent ones who keep track of degree requirements, move papers, and get things done, they understood this. I cannot thank them enough for their winks, smiles, paper shuffling, and moral support. I thank them for putting papers where they belonged, for quietly undoing damage others did, for making sure I knew that they knew, and for having my back. I love you all so much, and I am so very grateful for your unending support.

I was not required to read published works by Indigenous scholars as an undergraduate and was only assigned one as a graduate student. However, I owe a debt of gratitude to Vine Deloria Jr. for opening my eyes and my mind to Indigenous voices within the academy. From his writing I was led to the publications and voices of many Indigenous scholars. It is their work that fueled me, that lit the fires of my mind and thus the path through research and grad school to this book. I am very grateful for the guidance and discussions of many Indigenous scholars and their like-minded peers whose works in critical Indigenous scholarship and decolonization cleared a path for those of us who follow.

I am indebted to Steve and Kathy Holen and the Denver Museum of Nature and Science for the summers of fieldwork and experience in Pleistocene archaeological sites of North America and to the Society for American Archaeology (SAA) for funding my fieldwork through the Arthur

C. Parker Award. I could not have started this research without the generous support of the Clifford D. Clark Fellowship, awarded through Binghamton University for five years of full graduate school support. Miigwech (thank you) to Dr. Andrew Merriwether, who nominated me for the Clifford D. Clark Fellowship and supported my research throughout graduate school.

My committee head, Dr. Randal McGuire, was very supportive in many ways, including offering to be my fourth committee head and reading and editing my dissertation. His support was invaluable, as was the support of my committee members, Dr. Sebastien Lacombe, Dr. Timothy McCleary, and Dr. Juanita Diaz-Cotto. One professor on my first committee, Dr. Al Dekin, was very open to listening to Indigenous voices and supported me 100 percent; he passed away before I completed my degree. However, his was one of the very few hearts that was open to inclusions of Indigenous peoples in academia, and his friendship was pivotal to my sticking it out. During my first year, I reached out to Dr. Shawn Wilson for input on my writing, and his comments were invaluable to my growth and development and learning to write like an academic rather than how a Cree elder talks, as he so kindly stated.

I would also like to thank my family and friends for their support and assistance and for always believing in me. My son Jessie Blue (1977–99) used his last discussion with me on this earth to make me promise to him, regarding my education, that I would never give up. My son Dustin helped with literature research for the database and always cheered me on and for Zion. My daughter Marina, thank you for being who you are and making me stronger and for Charlie. Thank you to my best friends, Sarah, Jen, Cindy, Shadow, and Miss Good Karma, whose unending good karma led me to the farm where I wrote my dissertation. And thank you to Jon the country veterinarian, whose kindness in offering and providing five years of monthly services free to Miss Good Karma and getting her monthly medicines sponsored saved her life and my heart and led me to Jen and Cindy. Their friendship and support, their understanding, as only academics can understand, their listening and sharing, and their numerous home-cooked dinners and unending support in so many ways were pivotal to my staying sane and staying in graduate school and thus writing this book. Many others too numerous to name supported me in many ways with letters and messages of support and with their thoughts on my work, including Elder Patrick Wood and so many others. Miigwech to all the students who supported me and who so generously gave their time to the Native American Student Association we started at SUNY Binghamton. Thank you so very much, Chi Miigwech, all my relations.

INTRODUCTION

Tansi (Hello)

My name is Paulette Steeves.

I am Cree and Metis; I have Indigenous ancestors from Canada and the United States and also ancestors from Europe.

My mother is Edna Atkinson-Steeves (Cree-Metis).

Her mother is Mary Jane Contois-Atkinson (Metis–First Nations).

Her father is James Atkinson (Cree-Metis).

My father is Paul Steeves (Native American and European).

His mother is Reva Leona Bush-Steeves (Native American and European).

His father is Alfred Steeves (Native American and European).

I come from a long line of strong women, many named in historical documents as Mary Indian.

My grandmother a few generations back was Necushin. She was Cree from Eastmain, Quebec. There she was married at a very young age to a Hudson's Bay man named George Atkinson. There are many stories about my ancestors in the oral traditions of the James Bay Cree and the books on the history of the Red River Metis.

I was born in Whitehorse, Yukon, and grew up along the Fraser River in Lillooet, British Columbia, Canada.

Colonization has torn many Indigenous communities from their traditional territories, yet we remain connected to our ancestral lands. I am currently a guest living in the heart of the traditional Anishinaabe and Metis territories in northern Ontario. However, I am from many places where my ancestors were rooted to the land: Red River, Manitoba; northern Ontario; Eastmain, Quebec; Machias, Maine; and distant lands in Europe.

Western educators in many academic institutions continue to ignore Indigenous knowledge, culture, and language, excluding everything Indigenous from the curriculum. Therefore, for many Indigenous scholars, writing is framed to privilege Indigenous knowledge. Introducing my ancestors serves cultural purposes and protocols, privileging Indigenous voices and acknowledging ancestors. "In the world today, there is a common-held belief that thousands of years ago, as the world counts time, Mongolian nomads crossed a land bridge to enter the Western Hemisphere, and became the people known as the American Indians. There is, it can be said, some scanty evidence to support the myth of the land bridge. But there is enormous wealth of proof that the other truths are all valid."[1]

There are many stories of the past; they are colored or not by the worldviews of those who tell them. In many ways, colonization in Western education has silenced Indigenous worldviews and stories of the past. There is a quote attributed to Louis Riel: "My people will sleep for one hundred years, but when they awake, it will be the artists who give them their spirit back."[2] After five hundred years of colonization, the artists, storytellers, and knowledge holders are awake, and other truths are being told. Stories have been held in Indigenous peoples' hearts and minds and held within the land for thousands of years. They rise now, bringing an enormous wealth of proof that other truths are valid.

The story I share in this book challenges dogmatic Eurocentric discussions of the history of the first people of the Western Hemisphere, the area now known as the Americas. For over ninety years, American archaeologists have argued that the first people to enter the Western Hemisphere walked across the area we know today as the Beringia landmass from the Eastern Hemisphere around 12,000–14,000 years ago.[3] This time frame is very recent on a global scale of early human migrations and is an anomaly, as hominins were present in the Eastern Hemisphere over 2 million years ago.[4] From fossil evidence, we know that *Homo erectus*, Neanderthal, Denisovan, and *H. sapiens* were very competent travelers adapting to diverse ecosystems while crossing thousands of miles of land and open bodies of water.[5] What is discussed regarding the evidence of early hominins in the Western Hemisphere has been severely constrained by academic erasure of the deep Indigenous past, an erasure of histories that cleaved Indigenous peoples' link to ancient homelands, heritage, and identity. Taiaiake Alfred and Jeff Corntassel argue: "Contemporary settlers follow the mandate provided for them by their imperial forefathers' colonial legacy, not by attempting to eradicate the physical signs of Indigenous peoples as human bodies, but by trying to eradicate their existence as peoples through the erasure of the histories and geographies that provide the foundation for Indigenous cultural identities and sense of self."[6]

Erasure of the Indigenous past is carried out in part through discussions of Indigenous peoples of the Western Hemisphere as being recent arrivals from Asia, Siberia, or France, countries and cultures that did not exist 11,000–12,000 years ago.[7] Though archaeologists discuss Pleistocene archaeological sites as being in modern nation-states, contemporary borders had no bearing on human migration and settlement during the Pleistocene. Until recent times people were not Caucasoid or Asiatic. Cultural terminologies often used by archaeologists to describe ancient human fossils are much more recent.[8]

What people have traditionally been taught about the deep Indigenous past is often framed more by what they are not taught rather than by what they are taught. Academic discussions of first people in the lands we know today as the Americas continue to be framed in agnotology, defined as "how knowledge has not come to be" and "how ignorance is produced through neglect, secrecy, suppression, destruction of documents, unquestioned tradition, and sociopolitical selectivity."[9] Educational materials framed in agnotology support colonization of the mind, teaching people to think in ways acceptable to the nation-state and not to question so-called scientific authorities.[10]

This book highlights how the histories of the Indigenous peoples of the Western Hemisphere were invented by Eurocentric academics framing the story of the Americas in a terra nullius, an empty land devoid of humanity and history. Scholars working as handmaidens of colonizing nation-states often created Indigenous peoples as recent migrants from the Eastern Hemisphere who were present for a short time before they mysteriously disappeared or became extinct.[11] They have created scenarios where contemporary Indigenous peoples' links to ancestors and lands are suspicious or nonexistent. In Western literature, Indigenous peoples were often portrayed as subhuman and a part of nature, not culture. Indigenous peoples are often discussed as simple hunter-gatherers lacking creativity, science, and intellectualism. Some Western scholars discuss areas of early civilizations in the Americas as mysterious, their former inhabitants unknown. However, precontact Indigenous peoples of the Western Hemisphere built great cities that were as old as or older and more technologically advanced than many cities of the Eastern Hemisphere.[12] Whether Indigenous peoples of Turtle Island built great cities or not, they were highly complex, sophisticated, and valued communities. The stories (archaeological sites, rock art, petroglyphs) that Indigenous peoples left on the land provide evidence that they have been here for a very long time. Many Indigenous peoples' histories are often discussed by descendant populations through oral traditions, songs, and dances, stories that acknowledge their places here since time immemorial.

In this story, I discuss hundreds of published and peer-reviewed Pleistocene archaeological site reports and lines of supporting evidence that show that it was possible for people to have been here in the Western Hemisphere for thousands of years prior to the Last Glacial Maximum (LGM, 24,000–18,000 years ago).[13] I also discuss oral traditions that tell stories of Indigenous peoples' time and place on Turtle Island. In unpacking the Indigenous past of the Western Hemisphere as framed through Western thought, I discuss a well-documented history of racism in American archaeology that has constrained and dehumanized the Indigenous past. Over the last few decades, Indigenous archaeologists and their like-minded peers have begun to carry out community-centered research with, for, and by Indigenous peoples.[14] However, North American archaeology has a long way to go to create safe spaces and open dialogues within the field.

Indigenous peoples hold commonalities in worldviews and cultural understandings, even though their cultures and worldviews are incredibly diverse. An often expressed Indigenous view of the world is that all beings are related, all have intelligence and spirit, and all are respected as relations. Richard Wagamese (Anishinaabe) has written:

> I've been considering the phrase "all my relations" for some time now. It's hugely important. It's our saving grace in the end. It points to the

truth that we are all related, that we are all connected, that we all belong to each other. The most important word is "all." Not just those who look like me, sing like me, dance like me, speak like me, pray like me or behave like me. ALL my relations. That means every person, just as it means every rock, mineral, blade of grass, and creature. We live because everything else does. If we were to choose collectively to live that teaching, the energy of our change of consciousness would heal each of us—and heal the planet.[15]

In seeking to understand the possibilities of Pleistocene land-based human migrations, I discuss mammalian migrations between the Eastern and Western Hemispheres. Mammalian migrations offer evidence of the possibilities for early human land-based migrations and an understanding of paleoenvironments on a global scale. In discussing possible time frames of a human presence in the Western Hemisphere, I consider supporting evidence through discussions of oral traditions, genetics, and linguistics, drawing on a multidisciplinary body of knowledge.

Many Indigenous people believe that knowledge gathered just for the sake of gathering is a waste of time.[16] Renee Pualani Louis, a Hawaiian scholar, argues that "research that does not benefit the community by extending the quality of life for its members . . . should not be done."[17] As discussed by Shawn Wilson, "Indigenous research is a ceremony and must be respected as such. . . . The purpose of any ceremony is to build stronger relationships or bridge the distance between aspects of our cosmos and ourselves. The research we do as Indigenous people is a ceremony that allows us a raised level of consciousness and insight into our world. Let us go forward together with open minds and good hearts as we further take part in this ceremony."[18]

In carrying out this research as a ceremony, I have learned that stories often weave through intricate webs of experiences that link back in many ways to the questions I have asked. In this, I have learned the value of silence, from which one must always be willing and ready to listen to the spirit world, to our ancestors who guide us. In my research, I have listened to the pain of people's disconnection from the land, their identities, and their past. I have listened to the spirits of ancestral sites, of which there are thousands covering the Western Hemisphere. I have listened to Indigenous elders who have informed me of the work I have been given to do. I have listened to the questions from many students who found that traditional Western archaeological stories of the initial peopling of the Western Hemisphere did not make sense to them. I have listened to the stories that archaeologists told about Pleistocene archaeological sites in the Americas, and I have wondered why some archaeologists paid a heavy price for their honesty.[19] I have listened, and through this listening, I work to rewrite the story of Indigenous peoples of the Western Hemisphere. I listened to Indigenous knowledge that arrives from many directions, and I have spent many hours weaving it through stories that have been left on the land. "Stories go in circles. They don't go in straight lines. It helps if you listen in circles because there are stories inside and in-between stories, and finding your way through them is as easy and as hard as finding your way home. Part of finding is getting lost, and when you are lost, you open up and listen."[20]

This story winds through the past, present, and future, following early humans and mammals on a global journey across time and space, unpacking the damage of Western knowledge in the present, and creating paths to places in the future where all worldviews are valued. This story is a journey of decolonization and discovery that privileges other-than-Western worldviews, respects Indigenous knowledge held in oral traditions, and honors archaeologists who have told the truth about the Indigenous past. For me, this has been an epic journey across thousands of years, unearthing histories that were previously buried beneath a dark veil of colonial oppression. Many archaeological sites have been destroyed without being recorded. Yet thousands of Pleistocene archaeological sites holding Indigenous peoples' stories of the past were kept safe within the land. Thus, there are many stories held within the land, waiting to be told.

In my dissertation defense I argued that people have been in the Western Hemisphere for over 60,000 years and likely over 100,000 years. During my doctoral research I located and studied hundreds of peer-reviewed academic publications on Pleistocene archaeological sites in both North and South America. I traveled throughout Turtle Island and visited many of these archaeological site areas. I also studied Paleolithic sites' artifact collections.

Most of these Western Hemisphere Pleistocene archaeological sites had been rejected out of hand by American archaeologists, often without a full review or a published critique. However, in recent years archaeologists have begun to reevaluate Pleistocene archaeological sites in the areas we know today as North and South America.[21] Renewed research and dating have supported some sites with evidence of a human presence prior to 11,200 years before the present.[22] At least one previously reported pre-Clovis site, the Coats-Hines-Litchy site, has been reviewed, and a new critique claims it is not an archaeological site but a paleontological location.[23]

The research I completed for this story of the Indigenous past of the Western Hemisphere included archaeological fieldwork at Pleistocene sites in the Great Plains of North America with Dr. Steve Holen. Prior to his retirement in 2014, Dr. Holen was the head archaeologist at the Denver Museum of Nature and Science. Dr. Holen and his wife, Kathleen Holen, have carried out field research and published articles and book chapters on numerous Pleistocene sites in North America, including but not limited to the La Sena site in Nebraska, Lovewell I and II in Kansas, and the Cerutti Mastodon site in Southern California.

My concerns in carrying out this research are focused on paths of healing through problematizing and rewriting the Indigenous past of the Western Hemisphere. This requires addressing Western Eurocentric stories of the Indigenous past, which are often based in conjecture, and a history of normalized embedded violence within Western knowledge production. Archaeological stories that have dehumanized Indigenous people and erased their links to their homelands are a part of ongoing intergenerational trauma, high rates of suicide, social and political disparities, and racism. In carrying out this work, I have come to realize that the past weaves through the present along paths of healing only if we do the work to clear the way.

Although I carried out this research on Pleistocene archaeological sites with a focus on relinking Indigenous peoples to their homelands in deep time, this book is for everyone. Settler populations need the tools and information to challenge what they have been taught about Indigenous histories, to unsettle their views of the past, and to inform their worldviews of the present. I titled this book *The Indigenous Paleolithic of the Western Hemisphere*, referring to the Paleolithic of the first people in the Western

Hemisphere (the Americas). It is through a very personal understanding and experience of the historic and ongoing cost of erased and dehumanized histories and colonial education that I have carried out the research for this book, a book that is as much about colonization and decolonization as it is about Pleistocene archaeological sites. In order to rehumanize the Indigenous past, it is paramount to open discussions focused on decolonizing Western knowledge production. All I ask is that you read and in reading that you listen with respect and the realization that this book and the work of many scholars I cite are based in a concern for the present and future health and well-being of all people.[24] Through critical Indigenous scholarship, this book opens spaces for discussions of the human past based on evidence from archaeology, geology, paleontology, oral traditions, linguistics, and molecular anthropology.

In chapter 1, I share my place in this story and my knowledge of Indigenous methods and theory to provide an understanding for readers who are unfamiliar with Indigenous ways of being, doing, and knowing. Chapter 2 takes a walk through the past of American archaeology and provides an informed understanding of how North America Indigenous histories came to be so severely constrained and why the Indigenous past needs to be reclaimed and rewritten. Chapter 3 is a brief journey through ancient landscapes; here you will meet up with some amazing relations, many of whom became extinct at the end of the Pleistocene. This chapter sets the stage for an understanding of possibilities of human and mammalian intercontinental migrations prior to the LGM. In chapter 4, I discuss a brief collection of early human sites in the Eastern Hemisphere and how recently discovered sites have changed our understanding of human migrations and evolution across time. In chapter 5, I introduce readers to a selection of Pleistocene sites in Turtle Island (North America) that are located throughout the continent. Short site reports help readers gain an understanding of the requirements for an archaeological site, including artifacts, stratigraphy, and dating, and a better idea of the critiques of archaeological data and research, which may often improve the analysis of a site. In chapter 6, I discuss some amazing archaeological sites in South America where the preservation of materials and artifacts is excellent. It was the Monte Verde site in Chile, after all, that opened the doors, even if by just a few thousand years, to Pleistocene archaeological research in the Americas. In chapter 7, I discuss some very intriguing supporting evidence for the presence of humans in the Western Hemisphere during the Pleistocene from linguistics, oral traditions, and molecular (genetic) research.

Some people have asked me why I carried out research in this area concerning the deep Indigenous history of the Americas. I have written a book that is likely to draw sharp words of criticism from some Western archaeologists and academics. This is the path Creator led me to walk; this is what I was asked to do. I cannot sidestep living, breathing vestiges of racism and power within the academy; I have an obligation to meet them head-on and to keep my vision resolutely fixed on clearing a path for descendant generations. I have a responsibility to the next seven generations, to all our grandchildren, to all our elders, and to all my relations to speak openly and honestly without fear. I have a responsibility to work to clear a path for the next generations who follow, to be one of many who work to remove social and political barriers to education and to all areas of life that negatively impact Indigenous people, to clarify and reaffirm Indigenous links to an ancient past, building bridges to homelands for elders, for those who lead our children.

Why does all this matter, and to whom? In chapter 8, I discuss the impacts of an erased history on all people, Indigenous voices and views, decolonizing minds and hearts, the Eighth Fire and pyroepistemology. Think *pyro-*, yes, "fire," used as an environmental technology by Indigenous people to cleanse the land and regenerate new growth. Think to cleanse the academic landscape of any dehumanizing discussion of Indigenous people, making room for regenerating new discussion in academia, or just think decolonizing education and the academy.

This book is written for all people, as everyone can benefit from critical thought and decolonization of minds, hearts, worldviews, and history. Weaving together Indigenous and Western archaeologies and knowledge has the potential, when applied in decolonizing frameworks, to address historical erasures. Work that rewrites histories and becomes the basis of an informed historical consciousness "challenges the simplifications and distortions of official history."[25] The importance of rewriting histories has been discussed by Alison Wylie: "History must be rewritten if its rationalizing consistency throughout generations of colonial domination is to be challenged."[26] This rewritten history of the early Indigenous peoples of Turtle Island is focused on reclaiming links to homelands across time and space in order to create healing in the present.

In gaining an understanding of the history and development of American archaeology, readers will come to understand the human cost of colonization and the power of education as a tool of empire, which often crafts social memories acceptable to the nation-state. My discussions of colonization and education are based on a lived experience, an experience of loss of family, language, lands, humanities, ceremonies, and safety. This story comes from the center of my heart, where hope dwells among the sadness of what may never be regained. Thus, I study and write through ceremonies of hope for all my relations, for Pimatisiwin, for decolonized spaces, to live a good life.

All my relations.

TERMINOLOGY

Western Hemisphere is used to refer to the hemispheric area now known as North and South America, as well as the associated islands of the Caribbean and the Atlantic and Pacific Oceans, the Americas.

Turtle Island is a name many Indigenous peoples of current-day North America use to identify their homelands.

Indigenous is used to refer to all first people and their descendants in the Western Hemisphere, both North and South America and all associated islands.

Pleistocene is the epoch from 2,588,000 to 11,700 years ago.

THE INDIGENOUS PALEOLITHIC

OF THE WESTERN HEMISPHERE

CHAPTER I

Decolonizing Indigenous Histories

This America
has been a burden
of steel and mad
death,
but, look now
there are flowers
and new grass
and a spring wind
rising
from Sand Creek
　　—Simon J. Ortiz (Acoma Pueblo), *from Sand Creek*

Indigenous scholars have discussed the absurdity of archaeological stories regarding time frames of initial habitation for the first people of the Western Hemisphere.[1] Archaeological discussions regarding a human presence in the Western Hemisphere before 12,000 years ago have recently begun to change; however, denial of the legitimacy of archaeological sites earlier than 12,000 years ago persists within North American archaeology. It has long been accepted that *Homo erectus*, *H. sapiens*, Denisovans, and Neanderthals were present in areas of the Eastern Hemisphere, including areas we know today as Siberia and Asia, for over 2 million years.[2] However, the typical story taught in classrooms regarding initial human migrations to the Western Hemisphere, areas we know today as North and South America, claims that the first people arrived around 12,000 years ago.[3] Regarding initial migration stories, Bill Reid (Haida) and Bill Holm have stated, "Other truths are valid."[4] Archaeologist Alan Bryan has published numerous papers on Pleistocene archaeological sites in both North and South America. He has argued that archaeological discussions on the initial peopling of the Western Hemisphere have often been based on "what might have been" and not on archaeological evidence.[5] Though denial of an earlier peopling of the Western Hemisphere has been entrenched in American archaeology, archaeologists such as Tom Dillehay, Steve Holen, Kathleen Holen, James Adovasio, Ruth Gruhn, Alan Bryan, Scotty MacNeish, Nième Guidon, Allan Goodyear, Joseph McAvoy, Lynn McAvoy, Eric Boëda, and others have supported the possibilities of earlier time frames of initial human habitation in the Western Hemisphere. Archaeologists' discussions, which focused on the possibilities of an earlier human habitation in the Western Hemisphere, have begun to change over the last twenty years. However, changes to time frames of initial migrations add only a few thousand years, suggesting people first arrived around 15,000 years ago. Archaeological discussions on Pleistocene sites have not included Indigenous knowledge drawn from Indigenous oral traditions. Holm and Reid's discourse on other truths highlights the possibilities of rewriting and recentering Indigenous histories within Indigenous knowledge. Indigenous discourses are paramount to trajectories of rehumanizing ancient and contemporary landscapes, people, and places. Rewriting the Indigenous past creates space from which to decolonize the public consciousness in the present.

In 1912 Aleš Hrdlička and his coauthors argued that "Indians" had only been in the Americas for 3,000 years.[6] Coming from the head curator of the Smithsonian Museum, his word held high authority on matters of archaeology and ancient human histories. Hrdlička's hypothesis of a very recent initial human migration into the Western Hemisphere did not stand for long. In 1908 George McJunkin, a former slave and African American ranch foreman who was out checking fences near Folsom, New Mexico, noticed large animal bones eroding out of a gully wall. He knew the bones were too large to be from modern bison or cattle. McJunkin died in 1922, but he had told his story about the big bones to many of his friends. Four years after his death, the large mammal bones McJunkin found near Folsom came to the attention of Jesse D. Figgins, a paleontologist and the director of the Colorado Museum of Natural History. Figgins was known to be a supporter of the possibilities of ice age migration across the Bering landmass. He carried out excavations near Folsom and located the fossil bones of a long-extinct bison in association with stone tools. Alfred Kidder and other archaeologists visited the site to examine the excavation and evidence, a customary practice in the validation of archaeological sites. The validity of the site brought a sea change to discussions and understanding of the Indigenous past of the Western Hemisphere. The new dates for a human presence in the Americas were based on geologically estimated extinction times of *Bison antiquus*, as carbon dating had not yet been invented. Hrdlička never visited the site. Until his death he stubbornly refused to acknowledge the evidence placing humans in the Americas 10,000 years ago.[7]

In 1927 the time frame of initial human habitation of the Western Hemisphere was radically altered by the discovery of stone tools with the fossils of a mammalian species known to have been extinct for over 10,000 years. Shortly after the discovery of the Folsom site, another site in New Mexico, Blackwater Draw, provided evidence of older stone tools and possibly mammoth hunting. The fluted stone tools found at the Blackwater Draw and Folsom sites were named Clovis after the nearby town. Clovis points were not the first fluted stone tools to be documented in North America. Prior to the discoveries at the Folsom and Blackwater Draw sites, fluted stone tools had been located in other areas known to contain mammoth remains, such as Big Bone Lick, Kentucky. In fact, three fluted points have been curated at the Cincinnati Museum of Natural History since 1817.[8] American archaeologists argued for a few years regarding the new date of 10,000 years before the present for early people in the Western Hemisphere. However, the evidence could not be denied, and 7,000 years of Indigenous history were added, more than tripling the time of humans in the Western Hemisphere. This was a human history in the Americas that Hrdlička had strongly argued against, one that inferred a humanized landscape onto land that had legally been declared terra nullius, unoccupied or uninhabited.

The first documented archaeological sites that provided the evidence for a human presence in the Western Hemisphere during the Pleistocene were just the beginning of what would become a much bigger story. Since Figgins's excavations in New Mexico, Clovis points known to date earlier than 10,200 years ago have been found at archaeological sites throughout North America.[9] In the late 1940s, Willard Libby invented carbon dating, allowing artifacts made of organic materials to be dated through an absolute method.[10] Though carbon dating did not end arguments about archaeological site dates, it did provide stronger evidence for ancient dates. Relative dating of artifacts, the order of past events, and the age of one artifact in comparison to another had been standard for decades. Clovis technologies were easily recognizable, as Clovis tools were bifacial (flaked on both sides), and they were fluted, having a wide channel running from the base toward the tip of the stone point.

Based in part on reported finds of Clovis points throughout North America, archaeologists invented a panhemispheric cultural group they named the Clovis People. Identifying all archaeological sites where Clovis tools were found as Clovis sites and discussing the Clovis People became standard in American archaeology.[11] This is very problematic, as there has never been evidence for a panhemispheric cultural group anywhere in the world. Though the identification was problematic, archaeologists discussed the Clovis People as a panhemispheric cultural group, obscuring the evidence for technological and cultural diversity on a continental scale.[12] Only recently have archaeological discussions of early stone technologies in the Western Hemisphere focused on tool technologies other than Clovis points. Charlotte Beck and George Jones have stated that Western Stemmed points have been found at sites in the Intermountain West and date to within and possibly earlier than the time frames recognized for Clovis technologies: "What has been ignored in these discussions is the presence of an early record in the region associated not with Clovis, but with different technology, the main diagnostic of which is the large, contracting stemmed projectile point."[13]

Throughout this book, I highlight other truths regarding the initial peopling of the Western Hemisphere, other truths told through an Indigenous lens woven through archaeological evidence, oral traditions, and critical thought. Recent publications have presented other truths in the form of new evidence on human evolution on a global scale and have completely changed what we know regarding early hominin evolution. Linda Tuhiwai Smith, a Māori scholar, has discussed other truths as "powerful forms of resistance that are repeated and shared across diverse Indigenous communities."[14] As archaeologists and other researchers know, our understanding of the human past on a global scale has continually evolved. Thus, knowledge of the human past has always been and remains in a continual state of growth. We should not expect our understanding of early human populations in any area of the world to remain static. Yet, the theory of initial human migrations to the Western Hemisphere remained static for over eighty years. Recent publications on archaeological sites placing humans in the Western Hemisphere earlier than 15,000 years ago have been subjected to overly critical, virulent reviews.[15] Many American archaeologists not only expect but angrily demand that the history of humans in the Western Hemisphere, remain unchanged, even though the human history of the rest of the world has recently been radically rewritten though applications of new science and archaeological research. David Turnbull has stated that "the colonizing culture has always had an interest in diminishing the length of time original inhabitants were present and in minimizing their relationship to the land."[16]

My Place in This Story

Shawn Wilson (Cree) discusses the role of relationality in Indigenous research methods in his 2008 book, *Research Is Ceremony: Indigenous Research Methods*. Wilson states that relational accountability is central to Indigenous research methods, as are respect, reciprocity, and responsibility. Therefore, I intentionally introduce myself and discuss my place in this story in part to create a relationship with readers.

Indigenous scholars often present their research as storytelling; this reflects where the storytellers are in their lives.[17] Raven Peltier Sinclair (Cree/Assiniboine/Saulteaux) has stated that "location in Indigenous research as in life, is a critical starting point."[18] In sharing details of who I am, I acknowledge my ancestors, claim my ancestry, and declare my position first as an Indigenous person and second as a researcher. In sharing my place in this story and discussing my research as relational and applied, I identify, define, and describe the elements of Indigenist research.[19]

To begin to build a relationship with the reader, I share a bit about myself and my ancestors. Links to ancestors, land, and history are important to all people. However, for people who have survived attempted genocide and forced assimilation, links to homelands are a path of reclamation, revivance, and healing. They are a detour off a colonial road to extinction, a journey from a painful past to a future of growth and renewal. Knowing and discussing links to family, identity, and culture are basic human rights, ones that are, in contemporary times, being reclaimed by thousands of Indigenous people worldwide. Margaret Kovach (Cree) has stated that a prologue in narrative writing provides the reader with information that is essential to understanding the story.[20] For non-Indigenous people unfamiliar with Indigenous ways, this creates a space for understanding.

Tansi Paulette Steeves. Hello, I am Paulette Steeves. I am a descendant of Cree and Metis people. I was born in the Yukon and grew up in British Columbia. My maternal grandfather, James Atkinson, and his ancestors are from James Bay in northern Quebec and the Metis lands of Red River and southern Manitoba. After centuries of colonization within my homelands, I am on a journey of finding my ancestors and relations and their places on the land. My grandparents came from Indigenous communities in the United States and Canada and non-Indigenous communities in Europe. In finding our ancestral families, we work our way back through time to our grandparents and their links to Indigenous communities and the land. Many people's family roots are often linked to different communities and places across time. I am from a long line of the youngest children of older parents. I do not have to count very many generations to look back to the time of the first contact between Indigenous and European people. My mother was born in 1917; her paternal great-grandparents were born between 1777 and 1780, a time when Hudson's Bay Company explorers were taking young Cree girls as wives in northern Quebec. Some of the family eventually left Eastmain, Quebec, and moved to the Red River area in Manitoba. In researching my ancestors' links to the land, I have traced my grandparents' families to many places: Red River, Manitoba; Elk Point, Alberta; Willow Bunch, Saskatchewan; Eastmain, Quebec; Machias, Maine; Lansing, Michigan; and northern Ontario. Many Indigenous people who were scattered to the winds during colonization now work to find their way home to ancestors, to each other, and to their ancestral places on the land. This process is only one piece of healing after genocide.

I was not raised in my traditional homelands or among my Cree and Metis relations. None of my grandparents lived long enough for me to know them or to be blessed by their presence and stories. However, like many First Nations and Indigenous people who experienced forced assimilation, adoption, residential schools, and erasure of identity and culture, I have found my way back to my ancestors and my identity. My family ties are linked to many communities and places on the lands of Turtle Island. My Cree and Metis grandparents and kin—Atkinson, Gunn, Swain, Flett, Contois, Caplette/Cuplete—are recorded in records of the Metis Nations of Manitoba and the Cree Nations of eastern James Bay, Quebec.[21] The Cree of northern Quebec have carried out archaeological work and discussed oral histories with archaeologists such as David Denton; my ancestors' stories are in some of these publications.[22] Some of the publications discuss my great-great-grandfather Chishaawaamishtikushiiyuu; George Atkinson Jr., a Metis trader, and his Cree wife, Winnepaigoraquai; and his parents, George Atkinson Sr., chief trader at Eastmain between 1778 and 1792, and his Cree wife, Necushin. I found online a copy of my maternal Metis grandparents' signatures on scrip payments that they signed in Manitoba that were sworn on August 17, 1875, and issued on October 2, 1876 (Matilda Gunn, scrip no. 2056, and John Atkinson, scrip no. 10931). Scrip payments were designed by the dominion of Canada to extinguish Metis title and aboriginal rights to land.

Though my family research is ongoing, I have learned a great deal about my First Nations and Native American ancestors. I also have European ancestors, some of whom arrived here with the first settlers on the *Mayflower*. One great-great-great-grandfather came to Canada with the Hudson's Bay Company and married my maternal great-great-great-grandmother Necushin in northern Quebec. Paternal genealogies of settler ancestral fathers were often well recorded. However, Indigenous histories were not well documented in the written records, and when they were, the name Mary Indian became a common identifier for Indigenous women, as most settlers did not have the ability to learn intricate and highly evolved Indigenous languages. Colonization was like a giant whirling jigsaw, decimating First Nations families across decades of violence and genocide. Now we search for shreds of jigsaw pieces to put ourselves, our families, and our communities back together into one coherent, well-formed picture. For many Indigenous people, scattered to the winds by forces of colonization, the work of reassembling identities and families becomes a path to healing, to finding a way home.

I grew up knowing I was Cree-Metis, but I was never allowed to discuss my heritage. I cannot blame my mother for raising us to silence our ancestral past; the government took her first two children from her in the early 1940s in Alberta. She was an unmarried mixed-blood woman whose mother had died when she was an infant. Though my mother told us what little she knew about our family and relations, she spent the rest of her life hiding her identity, as did my father. Hiding no more, many Indigenous people who were forced to endure attempted assimilation as children continue to find their way back to their Indigenous identities and their ancestors' places on the land.

My place in being a part of this ceremony of research and in telling this story was told to me within a discussion I had with a Salish elder named Leonard Sampson in 1988. I meet with Leonard to seek his advice just before I moved away from my home area in western Canada under great duress as a newly separated single mother of three with minimal education. Leonard told me that he and other elders in the local community who had known me since I was young had discussed my future. He stated that they had known for some time that I had a job to do that would be very difficult. Leonard was very gentle in telling me that the stress I was going through at the time was training me to deal with the even more difficult situations I would face in the future. He also stated that what I had been given to do would lead me to work that would reflect positively on future generations, not just our communities but all Indian people. What Leonard reminded me of in his talk that day was of my responsibility as an Indigenous woman to all my relations, to all beings, to the land and the water. At the time, I had no idea where I would go or what I would do. I was a single mother with three children, one terminally ill, a truck, and about twenty-six cents, and my education had ended in eighth grade. I have been given many signs over the years that this research is a part of the path that I was informed of by Leonard Sampson twenty-four years ago, though it took me as many years to understand the meaning of his message. My dissertation and my research, which focus on decolonizing Indigenous histories, may be only one path along this journey. I understand that what Leonard Sampson told me in 1988 was a guide that would lead me to many places. His counsel was and remains a constant reminder that all that we do should be focused on praxis and ceremony to make the future a better place for all our descendants. I believe that the work of many scholars across diverse academic fields that is focused on decolonizing academia will reflect positively on future generations.

Tipaachimushtuweu (She Tells a Story)

This book is written as I would tell you a story based on my experience, research, and education in both the Indigenous and Western worlds. I discuss oral traditions, archaeological sites, and ancestral landscapes where early Indigenous communities left a record of their presence on the land. This story is only the beginning, only one story of many; there are other stories told through many voices that have the power to inform our understanding of the past. If you find you get a little lost here and there in the reading, that's OK. You will find your way back, and meanings will come to you when they are meant to.

I have learned a great deal on my journey through the Indigenous past. However, discovering published literature on hundreds of archaeological sites that date earlier than 11,000 or 12,000 years ago in the Western Hemisphere was just a fraction of what I learned. The most telling lessons from my years of study and research are what I learned regarding the Western academy and the ongoing colonization of millions of minds. Through teaching, I realized that the most crucial skill you can help students to develop is the utilization and application of critical thought, teaching students to decolonize their hearts and minds. I discuss my experiences with this process as a college professor in chapter 8. Learning to think outside the Western box is facilitated through Indigenous ways of knowing, being, and doing such as oral traditions and histories woven through memories of peoples, places, and events. In learning about the ancient past, I began my research ceremony by seeking out oral traditions that hold knowledge of events and relations (all beings) across time and by becoming aware of places where Indigenous people left their stories on the land (archaeological sites).

Thousands of years ago, on Turtle Island, enormous black-winged birds known to many communities as thunderbirds flew above rivers cascading from mountain cliffs on their way to teeming seas tugged to and fro by a distant moon. It was here that the voices of many clans rose above the misting waters, escaped the dense forest canopy, and greeted each new dawn. Oral traditions told of the giant birds that kidnapped children or fought serpents to protect people, while other stories linked thunderbirds to tsunamis and storms.[23]

Fossils of different species of the genus *Teratornis*, giant birds with wingspans ranging from 12 to 18 feet (3 to 5 meters) are known from paleontological records in the Western Hemisphere. Extinct species known from the fossil record may be linked to cultural practices recorded in oral traditions and archaeological records. In Pleistocene landscapes of the Western Hemisphere, the great short-faced bears, giant sloths, mammoths, mastodons, saber-toothed cats, bison, wolves, wolverines, camels, horses, birds, fish, insects, and humans left hints of their presence and a record of their lives on the land. When these relations are remembered in oral traditions and their fossils are found within archaeological sites, we may gain an understanding of their place within Indigenous communities.

From oral traditions, I have learned how the clans' lives were woven throughout each other's hearts and essence, how one could not live without the other. Stories on the land, including archaeological sites, petroglyphs, rock art, and oral traditions, intersect at the edges of cultures, each telling stories in their own way. Oral traditions have been found to corroborate the geological, paleontological, and archaeological records of specific areas and events within the Western Hemisphere.[24] In archaeological stories of the past, oral traditions, rock art, and petroglyphs are most often ignored by many Western archaeologists in site interpretations. Far too often, what students are taught regarding Indigenous people ignores, erases, and silences Indigenous people and knowledge.[25]

There are many problematic areas of the Clovis First hypothesis of initial human migrations to the Western Hemisphere. Archaeologists who support the Clovis First hypothesis initially argued that the first people brought

Clovis stone tool technologies with them from the Eastern Hemisphere, from areas we know today as Siberia, Asia, and Europe.[26] Archaeologists have inferred that the finely crafted stone tools known as Clovis tools could not have been created by Indigenous people in the Western Hemisphere. A common theme of the Clovis First hypothesis is that hunter-gatherers likely followed herds of megafauna across the Bering landmass, then migrated south through an ice-free corridor to reach the interior of present-day North America.[27] Though archaeologists have argued for decades that Clovis tools were brought to the Western Hemisphere by people from the Eastern Hemisphere, Clovis tools have never been found outside of the Americas.[28] It is now generally accepted that Clovis fluted tool technologies developed in North America.[29] Geologists have argued that the proposed ice-free corridor from present-day Alaska to the northern Great Plains was not a viable route for human migrations early enough to account for many broadly dispersed Clovis sites.[30] "It was presumed that whatever tool the earliest Americans were using would have been an Asiatic import. That comes down to the idea that the early fluted point technology associated with the Clovis and Folsom finds should have Asiatic prototypes, but no such prototypes have been found."[31]

During the Pleistocene, many people may have traversed the lands between the Western and Eastern Hemispheres. People, after all, were traveling thousands of miles from areas we know today as Africa and the Middle East to Siberia, Russia, Spain, Australia, Java, and the Americas. Early humans most likely spent time in each new area they ventured to, getting to know the land, environment, and seasons. Human ways of being, doing, and knowing would have expanded and changed with each new ecosystem, giving rise to differences in cultural practices, subsistence strategies, and tool technologies.

However, regarding the Western Hemisphere, archaeological discussions have created the so-called Clovis People, a single panhemispheric cultural group that covered two continents with extremely diverse environments. Such oversimplified theories based on one stone tool type erase the diversity known to be present in the archaeological record, oral traditions, and linguistics. This is the same as saying that all people in the Americas who used guns in the twentieth century were a single cultural group. The "Gun

People" were a panhemispheric cultural group of hunters who caused the extinction of many species through reckless hunting practices and waged savage wars against peaceful nongun people, mailboxes, road signs, and beer bottles. In short, it takes more than one single tool type to define a cultural group. However, many academics continue to teach the so-called Clovis First hypothesis as fact and to discuss the so-called Clovis People as the first people of the Americas.

Attitudes on pre-Clovis archaeological sites have begun to change over the past twenty years; some archaeologists now discuss the legitimacy of pre-Clovis sites.[32] Others continue to deny the possibilities of earlier than Clovis sites.[33] Nonetheless, even though it should be very apparent to educators that there has never in the history of human cultures been a panhemispheric cultural group anywhere in the world, discussions on the Clovis People remain embedded in all areas of education and media.

Archaeologists' discussions of the Clovis People as a panhemispheric cultural group have been taken as truth, accepted without question, and safely embedded in social memory. Kenneth Tankersley discussed the "Clovis Cultural Complex"; he cites Otis T. Mason, who used the term "Clovis complex" in 1962 in reference to any site that produced Clovis artifacts.[34] An archaeological complex is defined as a group of artifacts and traits that regularly occur together in two or more sites within a restricted area over a period of time.[35] Colin Renfrew and Paul Bahn, following Gordon Childe, describe archaeological culture as a "constantly recurring assemblage of artifacts."[36] Childe, whose research was focused on Europe, stated: "We find certain types of remains—pots, implements, ornaments, burial rites and house forms—constantly recurring together. Such a complex of associated traits we shall call a 'cultural group' or just a 'culture.' We assume that such a complex is the material expression of what today we would call 'a people.'"[37]

In sociology and anthropology, the term *culture* is defined as both material (artifacts) and nonmaterial (symbols, language, beliefs, and values) items that are a part of society. Clearly, stone tools have been discussed as *archaeological complexes*, referring to stone tools of the same type being found in regional areas within a restricted time period. Childe referred to material culture (artifacts) as a complex of associated traits that are *assumed* to be the material expression of a people.[38] However, one stone tool type does not represent a panhemispheric cultural group of people. The term "Clovis People," used by many archaeologists, implies the existence of a panhemispheric cultural group.

Discussions of Clovis People as a distinct cultural group are not supported by literature on cultural traits (material and nonmaterial) and practices beyond the mention of Clovis tools as a technology that was used for big game hunting and animal butchering.[39] Archaeologists' discussions of the Clovis People have become so embedded in a national discourse that an archaeological site book discussing the Clovis People was assigned a Library of Congress classification number within the cultural groups and ethnographies section. Checking within an ethnographic section of the library at the University of Massachusetts at Amherst, I located books on the Cherokee, Choctaw, Chickasaw, and Chumash, followed by the Clovis People (E 99 C 815), in a section that contained books on Clovis archaeological sites. There were no books on Clovis culture because there are no Clovis People and no such thing as Clovis People's cultural practices. Cultural practices of a specific group of people are defined by subsistence practices, language, spirituality, kinship systems, music, dance, art, clothing, housing, leadership, child-rearing, material (artifacts), and other community cultural practices.

Clovis fluted tools have been found at sites throughout North America; it was likely a tool technology that was shared among many different communities of people.[40] Recently, the tenets of the Clovis First hypothesis of initial human migrations to the Western Hemisphere have been questioned by a small group of archaeologists: "After many years of debate, there has been a remarkable turn of events in the First American controversy. It is now clear that the Clovis-First version of Late-Entry Model is dead, and the field of first American studies is undergoing a significant paradigm shift."[41]

Since the Clovis First theory has been declared dead since at least 1997, I often wonder why archaeologists continue to discuss the Clovis People as if they actually had existed.[42] Acheulean handaxes have been found in areas we know today as Africa and Europe. However, archaeologists do not discuss the Acheulean People. Inventing a panhemispheric cultural group based on one tool type seems to be an archaeological practice restricted mainly to American archaeological discussions of the Western Hemisphere.

When discussing Pleistocene archaeological sites of the Western Hemisphere people are often quick to ask me, "But how did they get here, how was it possible?" Students, scholars, and others strongly impress on me their belief that it was impossible for the first people to have arrived in the Western Hemisphere prior to 12,000 years ago. It has been my experience that most people do not question the presence of people on the continent we now know as Australia over 65,000 years ago. Why would anyone doubt that early humans could have also traveled to other intercontinental or island areas before the LGM? "Everybody is willing to give humans the abilities necessary for voyaging across to Australia about 60,000 years ago. Why then would it have been impossible for them to pass from island to island along the Aleutians, just as one example? We have no justification for converting the humans who peopled the Americas to a single state of being, where they could do nothing but follow herds by land."[43]

Why do people so readily accept that early humans could have crossed open bodies of water to inhabit islands in the Eastern Hemisphere such as present-day Australia and Crete? Why would people think it was impossible to cross a short distance of approximately 51 miles of land to reach areas of the Western Hemisphere prior to 12,000 years ago? In most cases, people have told me that this is what they were taught regarding initial human migrations to the Western Hemisphere. The archaeologically invented history of the Western Hemisphere is so embedded in the literature and in academic and general discussions that it has been taken as a scientific fact and not often questioned.[44] Reporting archaeological sites with earlier than Clovis dates has been described as dangerous and career-ending. The field of Pleistocene archaeology in the Americas has been described as a battlefield, one that has often left many academic career casualties in its wake.[45] Regarding the field of American archaeology and theories of initial migrations, James Adovasio and David Pedler, who have decades of experience in the field, stated: "With the exception of a handful of obviously demented heretics and marginalized apostates, no serious archaeologist doubted that sometime around 13,000 cal BP, a small group of intrepid hunters crossed the interior of the Bering platform and arrived in the fauna-rich paradise of the unglaciated Bering Refugium."[46]

The historically embedded boundary of recent (on a global human history scale) time frames for first human migrations to the Western Hemisphere is not simply based on the archaeological record; instead, it is a political construct maintaining colonial power and control over Indigenous heritage, material remains, and history. In American and Canadian educational academies, Western knowledge production often remains deeply vested in discussions that erase and dehumanize Indigenous peoples. This epistemic violence maintains ongoing colonization and racism and has been linked to historical and ongoing social and political disparaties and discrimination within contemporary populations.[47]

Many Indigenous communities are engaged in processes of decolonization by reviving cultural traditions, languages, and knowledge and reclaiming identities and histories. Indigenous scholars and their like-minded peers have published volumes on Indigenous methodology and theory and have also shed light on the human cost of historical and ongoing colonization within the academy and Western knowledge production. I cite many Indigenous scholars such as Vine Deloria Jr. (Sioux), Shawn Wilson (Cree), Linda Tuhiwai Smith (Māori), Devon Mihesuah (Choctaw-Chickasaw), Angela Cavender Wilson (Dakota), Jody Byrd (Chickasaw), Margaret Kovach (Cree), Emma LaRocque (Cree-Metis), Sonya Atalay (Anishinaabe), and many others in this book.

In Indigenous method and theory, research results are presented as a story, and thus stories do the work of decolonization. "Stories are decolonization theory in its most natural form"; they "are resurgent moments which reclaim epistemic ground that was erased by colonialism." In processes of resistance, resurgence, and reclamation, stories lay the foundational framework for "Indigenous sovereignty and the reclamation of the material ground."[48]

Globally, first peoples who share common experiences of colonialism and contemporary struggles for sovereignty have adopted the term "Indigenous." Though it is problematic, as it collects many diverse people and communities under one identity, this paradigm turns a tool of oppression (cultural homogenization) into one of liberation (cultural unity) to support contemporary human rights struggles on a global scale, allowing collective voices and solidarity in international arenas.[49]

Throughout my academic studies and life, I have listened to many scholars, academics, and ancestors, to the voices that come to mind, and to the thoughts that question the authority of the status quo. Listening in silence to the wisdom of ancestors is a very profound way to gain an understanding of what you seek to understand. American archaeologists have traditionally been taught to not listen to oral traditions or the voices of those they study. Archaeology, however, is not entirely monolithic. In some areas of the Western Hemisphere, a few archaeologists (David Denton, for example) have worked closely with Indigenous communities, weaving their voices and knowledge through stories of the past.[50] Yet for many Western scholars, to listen to voices from outside the academy is to give up their power and control and to admit that other ways of knowing are insightful and profound. However, listening is paramount to creating knowledge of the past and present.

Weaving back through Western stories of the past exposes numerous examples of Eurocentric discussions that erased Indigenous people's connections to their ancient homelands. The histories of Indigenous people have been written by academics who have little or no firsthand experience of Indigenous cultures or worldviews. Often in Indigenous worldviews, there is no past or present or future, there is today, and for Indigenous people the past is today, and the past is tomorrow, woven through time. It's all the same.[51] Time is circular, ancestors who crossed over to the spirit world are still members of groups of people living today, and they still inhabit spirit nations and the places where they left material remains and stories on the landscape.[52]

Everything an Indian does is in a circle, and that is because the Power of the World always works in circles, and everything tries to be round. In the old days when we were a strong and happy people, all our power came to us from the sacred hoop of the nation, and so long as the hoop was unbroken, the people flourished. The flowering tree was the living center of the hoop, and the circle of the four quarters nourished it. The east gave peace and light; the south gave warmth; the west gave rain; and the north with its cold and mighty wind gave strength and endurance.[53]

In his book *Lies My Teacher Told Me: Everything Your American History Textbook Got Wrong*, James Loewen argued that American teachers have told many lies or rather left out a great deal of the past, especially aspects that did not reflect positively on the American and Canadian nations. I begin my classes each semester by telling students three things: (1) teachers may only share with them what they have been taught or been passionate enough about to learn on their own; (2) no one today is responsible for events that took place in the past, but we are responsible for learning about them so that we do not repeat negatives of the past; and (3) students have a right and a duty to challenge authority. It is in the challenging of authority that we critique colonial knowledge production and reclaim previously denied Indigenous histories and humanities. By thinking critically and by challenging Eurocentric dogmas, we reclaim our right to think, to speak, and to effect changes that reflect positively on the world. In critiquing Western knowledge production of Indigenous histories, it is essential for archaeologists to discuss and rewrite histories framed in Western ideologies of conquest that remain embedded in textbooks.

History always includes those rare people who stepped outside the box of contemporary thought and the status quo of academic discussions to follow their own paths. Archaeology is no exception; a small group of American and European archaeologists has discussed alternatives to the Clovis First hypothesis. Archaeologists such as Tom Dillehay, Allan Goodyear, James Adovasio, Ruth Gruhn, Alan Bryan, Joseph and Lynn McAvoy, Steve and Kathleen Holen, Niède Guidon, Scotty MacNeish, Jacques Cinq-Mars, Virginia Steen-McIntire, Thomas Lee, and many others have worked to highlight the past of the Americas as an unknown place and time that require a great deal more research. Despite facing certain academic bashing and potential career destruction, numerous archaeologists and geologists over the last eighty years have reported dates for archaeological sites that were earlier than 12,000 years ago. I have spent many years learning of other truths about the early peopling of the Western Hemisphere. At times I have realized possible links between archaeological sites in regional areas years after reading site reports. Thus, stories travel around and through thoughts and hearts and weave back again to bring realizations when we are meant to receive them. History is made up of stories, some written by outsiders, some by people inside their communities. For Indigenous people, their histories that became common knowledge among settler populations have been created by outsiders. When people's histories are denied and their identities and cultures dehumanized, their present and future are violated.[54] It is long past time for such discursive violence to end. I sincerely hope that this research story and discussions in this book move education and communities along paths of decolonizing minds, hearts, and worldviews and toward understanding and healing.

It is crucial to rewrite Indigenous histories, as an Indigenously informed knowledge production will challenge stereotypical colonial tropes. An Indigenous perspective creates a dialogue that forms the basis of an empowered identity from which Indigenous people can negotiate for justice and challenge erasures of identity and local histories. Archaeology has the potential when applied in decolonizing frameworks to address historical erasures in work that rewrites histories, which then become the basis of an informed historical consciousness. Histories that are written from an Indigenous perspective challenge Western-centered simplifications, erasures, silencing, and distortions of the Indigenous past.[55] Indigenous and Western scholars have acknowledged the need to rewrite history: "History must be rewritten if its rationalizing consistency throughout generations of colonial domination is to be challenged."[56] In rewriting the past, we honor and acknowledge our ancestors and the stories held within the land, stories left for descendants. Indigenous academics have a responsibility to all their relations to carry out this work of rewriting and rehumanizing the Indigenous past and decolonizing discussions, academia, and minds. The scholarship of Indigenous academics and their communities brings a much-needed sense of pride and belonging to their people, facilitating paths toward healing. It is through these gifts that Indigenous people are reclaiming their identities, heritage, history, humanity, lands, and sovereignty.

Indigenous Method and Theory

Graham Smith highlighted the need for Indigenous methodologies as an option, a "tool" available for indigenous researchers. This statement not only emphasizes the necessity of choice itself but how a lack of this methodological choice is intrinsically connected to an academy that is still colonial.

—Margaret Kovach, *Indigenous Methodologies*

Indigenous archaeology and Indigenous method and theory work to decolonize Western knowledge, to build bridges through time to places, people, and identities. Being of Cree-Metis and European ancestry and having lived in both the settler and Indigenous worlds, I speak from an informed understanding of the impacts of Eurocentric anthropological and archaeological knowledge production. In the academy, to discuss such matters is to risk being labeled anti-intellectual, because turning the critical gaze inward on anthropology is often considered taboo.[57] Such acts of Indigenous rhetorical sovereignty are often seen by the North American academic majority as detrimental, acts of anger and activism.[58] When truth-telling becomes activism and exposes the academy's dark past, oppression draws its powerful sword and slays further attempts at social justice. Indigenous rhetorical sovereignty, or speaking your mind from an Indigenous worldview in Western academic institutions, often results in the immediate activation of Western rhetorical imperialism or in Indigenous students being silenced.

For Indigenous researchers, empirical knowledge and informed understandings of oral traditions are crucial to research, as are cultural knowledge, cultural protocols, and community guidance.[59] In internalist archaeology, archaeological interpretations begin with a study of oral traditions, which are records of ancient history. Eldon Yellowhorn (Piikani) has stated, "Cultural tradition motivates fieldwork" and "appropriates the methods of archaeology to study local histories."[60] Shawn Wilson (Cree) has stated that in an Indigenous research paradigm, an individual does not own knowledge, because it is relational. Researchers answer to all their relations when doing research.[61] An Indigenous methodology includes cultural knowledge, protocols, values, and behaviors as integral parts of the methodology.[62] Empirical knowledge is a part of Western and Indigenous research, yet in Indigenous research, there are also other ways of understanding the world.[63] George Nicholas, who describes himself as an Indigenous-oriented archaeologist, agrees that there have been cases that provide corroboration between oral tradition and the archaeological record. Scholars who have supported and developed Indigenous archaeology added intellectual breadth to theoretical questioning and developments in academia.[64] This is a practice that counters historical exclusionary academic practices and works to mitigate, decolonize, inform, enrich, and expand the field.[65] Indigenous epistemologies represent an insurgency from the periphery into the center of academies, challenging the power and control of Western centers of knowledge production.

Frederick Wiseman (Abenaki) has argued that archaeological knowledge production is not neutral. It is steeped in political and colonial ideologies and has historically been controlled by non-Indigenous scholars. Wiseman further argues that control of cultural information is an essential aspect of Indigenous people's sovereignty.[66] Robert Preucel and Ian Hodder argue that Indigenous people have an inalienable right to produce knowledge about their past and present, as do all people everywhere.[67] As an academic who also has decades of experience of being a recipient of the adverse effects of colonization, I choose to frame my research as a ceremony in Indigenous method and theory. Indigenous archaeologies and methodologies critically engage with epistemic violence and embedded colonialism within academia.[68] Indigenous scholars who write from a critical pedagogy work to disrupt the structural imbalances of inequality within the academy, thereby challenging the assumed supremacy of Western epistemologies and methodologies.[69] In 2012 I coined the term "pyroepistemology," a metaphorical terminology that describes the work of critical Indigenous scholarship and the decolonizing work carried out by like-minded and informed peers and allies. For thousands of years, Indigenous people have practiced pyroregeneration, using fire to clean the land, burning away dense undergrowth and allowing the sunlight to bring new life to the earth.[70] A practice of pyroepistemology is a ceremony that cleanses the academic landscape of discussions that misinform worldviews and fuel racism. Such literary renewal clears the way for healthy growth in academic fields of thought and centers of knowledge production.[71] According to Marie Battiste (Mi'kmaq), "Whether or not it has been acknowledged by the Eurocentric mainstream, Indigenous knowledge has always existed. The recognition and intellectual activation of Indigenous knowledge today is an act of empowerment by Indigenous people. The task for Indigenous academics has been to affirm and activate the holistic paradigm of Indigenous knowledge to reveal the wealth and richness of Indigenous languages, worldviews, teachings, and experiences, all of which have been systematically excluded from contemporary educational institutions and from the Eurocentric knowledge system."[72]

Scholars have discussed research framed within Indigenous methodologies as counterstories and as powerful forms of resistance.[73] Indigenous archaeologies seek to restore the knowledge of the Indigenous past, a place that has been historically distorted, erased, and denied in anthropological knowledge production.[74] Waziyatawin Angela Wilson has stated that "Indigenous knowledge recovery is an anticolonial process." She argues that it is a project that "gains momentum from the anguish of the loss of what was and the determined hope for what will be." She further states, "It springs from the disaster resulting from the centuries of colonialism's efforts to methodologically eradicate our ways of seeing, being, and interacting with the cosmos."[75]

The recovery of Indigenous histories works to revalue Indigenous culture and history that have been denied and denigrated "and revive that which has been destroyed."[76] Kovach explains what represents an Indigenous epistemology:

> It includes a way of knowing that is fluid (Little Bear 2000) and experiential, derived from teaching transmitted from generation to generation by storytelling; each story is alive with the nuances and wisdom of the storyteller (King 2003). It emerges from traditional languages emphasizing verbs, not nouns (Cajate 1999). It involves a knowing within the subconscious that is garnered through dreams and visions (Castellano 2000). It is the knowledge that is both intuitive and quiet. Indigenous ways of knowing arise with the human world, the spirit, and the inanimate entities of the echo system (Battiste and Henderson 2000). Indigenous ways of knowing encompass the spirit of collectivity, reciprocity, and respect (Wilson 2001). It is born of the land and locality of the tribe.... These ways of knowing are both cerebral and heartfelt. As the elders say, "... If you have important things to say speak from the heart."[77]

By the 1960s, Indigenous scholars had confronted the colonizers' dehumanizing master narrative of Indigenous people and history. Vine Deloria Jr. critiqued cultural presuppositions used by Western scholars to

legitimize outmoded stereotypes of Indigenous peoples.[78] Scott Momaday discussed Indigenous knowledge in response to Western academics'
denial.[79] Michael Doxtater stated, "Scholars created an environment for
discourse from 1970 onward that was consistent with liberal democracy's
value of a deliberative, reflective process."[80] Through these newly created
discursive spaces of ideological light, Indigenous scholars began the serious
work of reconstructing their past and future. Martin Wobst stated, "We
are witnessing the emergence of a new form of archaeology, archaeology
that is informed by indigenous values and agendas."[81]

Indigenous Archaeology

Indigenous archaeology has been discussed as archaeology done with,
for, and by Indigenous people.[82] However, there is a significant difference
between "for" and "with" Indigenous people that is inclusionary of the
subject of study and archaeology "by" Indigenous people. Indigenous
archaeology and decolonizing research and discussions carried out by
Indigenous people are forms of self-determination, social and political
acts of decolonization by previously colonized people.[83] Devon Mihesuah argued that critical Indigenous scholarship is transformative and
deliberate; it is not reactive or emotive but is a scholarship that responds
to colonization.[84]

Indigenous archaeology expands Western archaeology by opening a
counterdiscourse to essentialist ideologies prevalent in histories written
from a Eurocentric gaze, and it has stimulated the intellectual growth of
the discipline.[85] The application of Indigenous knowledge to Western science has been discussed by Battiste: "Intellectual activation of Indigenous
knowledge today is an act of empowerment by Indigenous people." Battiste
further defines Indigenous knowledge as "that which is far more than the
binary opposite of Western knowledge" and concludes: "As a concept, Indigenous knowledge benchmarks the limitations of Eurocentric theory—its
methodology, evidence, and conclusions—re-conceptualizes the resilience
and self-reliance of Indigenous peoples and underscores the importance
of their own philosophies, heritage, and educational processes."[86]

Indigenous methodologies are based on Indigenous worldviews linked
to oral traditions that for thousands of years have maintained an intimate

understanding of the connection between people and living things. In many Indigenous communities, these connections are often acknowledged and expressed by the phrase "all my relations," or "we are all related."[87] In expressing an intimate connection, I am referring to an understanding of the environment and everything in it as living, feeling, thinking, animate beings imbued with spirit.[88] As such, there is mutual respect between Indigenous peoples and all their relations; the rocks, the animals, the stars, the rain, the water, the plants are all respected as relations.[89] Indigenous methodologies require researchers to situate themselves in the research and to build respectful and reciprocal relationships with the subjects of their studies.[90] Western science demands strict adherence to the gathering of empirical evidence and has, for the most part, rejected oral traditions and Indigenous knowledge.[91] Exceptions to the rejection of oral traditions may occur when specific observations within oral traditions are testable through a research regime. Eldon Yellowhorn (Piikani) has discussed a testable hypothesis: "The story of the beaver giving humans the seeds to grow their first crop is told here to illustrate the use of folklore in creating a testable hypothesis."[92] The Western scholarly bias that denies any possibility of objectivity or historical accounts of past events reflects a prejudice that is evident in contemporary archaeology's aversion to considerations of oral traditions as informative accounts.

Bagele Chilisa pointed out that in discussing Indigenous and Western paradigms, "the paradigms risk becoming essentialized along the lines of binary opposites."[93] However, rather than an essentializing discourse, the discussion of Western and Indigenous archaeology is an area of dialogue where divergent histories, epistemologies, ideologies, and philosophies may be shared to inform the past, present, and future of the field. In discussions of archaeology's colonial past, there is a need to understand how the field has developed, where it is at now, and how it may transact with Indigenous archaeology.

As Holm and Reid stated regarding stories and understandings of the Indigenous past, "There is an enormous wealth of proof that other truths are valid."[94] The truths they may be referring to include oral traditions, oral histories, petroglyphs, rock painting, Indigenous songs, and Indigenous knowledge. Other truths and other voices bring a rich body of knowledge to what we know of the past, informing educational literature and general knowledge. Regarding the Clovis First hypothesis of initial post-LGM migrations to the Western Hemisphere, archaeologists and scholars have discussed how some of the central claims, such as the presence of an ice-free corridor east of the Rocky Mountains, were accepted for decades without question: "The prominence of the ice-free corridor can be partially explained by unsubstantiated speculation and the acceptance of faulty logic by archaeologists. Dincauze noted a tendency for basic assumptions to be unexamined, data to be confused with evidence, and linking arguments to be developed poorly if at al."[95]

One thing that has become clear regarding the history of Indigenous people that archaeologists specifically should remember is that there are many worldviews in this one place, Earth. An informed intellectual realizes their ignorance of the worlds they know of but know nothing of. In challenging centuries-old dogmas of the Indigenous past that rest on a shaky frame of conjecture and bias, this book brings a new view of the Indigenous past and the Indigenous Paleolithic of the Western Hemisphere through an Indigenous lens.

Finding Home

For many years
genocide
tore us from our ancestors
from our places on the land
from our mothers and fathers and families
yet we never disappeared.

Though the invaders said we had
and they wished we would
they tried so hard to erase
our ancestors and ancestral places
our very genesis
our identities and voices.

But we never gave up
the land lives in our blood
courses through our hearts
we are returning now
to our places on the land
to our ceremonies
to our languages.

Reawakening to the voices of all our relations
echoing through our hearts and minds
calling from often distant places
memories deeply etched in rivers of blood
flowing gently through our veins
and across the lands.

We are returning and awakening
sharing ancestors' stories of places and people

where memories held within the land
held within the hearts of our ancestors
welcome us home
reviving, reclaiming, retelling
of our time and genesis on these lands
we are returning and celebrating
lighting flames of the Eighth Fire

CHAPTER 2

Unpacking Colonial Baggage

A Brief History of American Archaeology

Prehistoric archaeology, as practiced in indigenous cultures, is founded upon and underwritten by a series of deep-seated colonialist and negative representational tropes of Indigenous peoples developed as a part of European philosophies of imperialism over the last 2,500 years.

—Ian J. McNiven and Lynette Russell, *Appropriated Pasts*

Indigenous histories that are taught in most educational institutions have been framed in Eurocentric worldviews. However, recently emerging programs designed and taught by Indigenous scholars frame history in Indigenous knowledge and ways of knowing, being, and doing. In the late 1800s, anthropological discussions defined Indigenous people as uncivilized "savages." This anthropological identity denied them fundamental human rights that were commonplace in white settler society.[2] Ronald Niezen has argued that ideologies of race supremacy erase the local and paint a global homogeneous canvas of cultural uniformity and progression.[3] American archaeological discussion of first people of the Western Hemisphere, the so-called Clovis People, and "Indians" has created a canvas of panhemispheric cultural uniformity. Eurocentrically framed histories of Indigenous people represent a body of work that strips the landscape of diverse Indigenous identities, languages, and cultures. Archaeological discussions question descendant communities' connections to ancestors, rights, and sovereignty on a global scale. How archaeologists in the Americas came to discuss diverse Indigenous communities across two continents representing almost one-third of the global landmass as a single cultural group is reflected in racist academic discussions of the late 1800s.

To gain an understanding of how Indigenous people of the Western Hemisphere were dehumanized and erased by American archaeologists, we need to discuss the development of American archaeology. Jeffries Wyman, the first curator of the Peabody Museum at Harvard, was hired in 1866. His collection focus was in archaeology. By the time a new building under the directorship of Frederick Ward Putnam opened to the public in 1878, the collections had grown to number over 30,000 artifacts.[4] Universities that developed some of the first degree-granting programs in archaeology in the United States include Clark, Harvard, Chicago, and Columbia. Clark University in Worcester, Massachusetts, granted the first degree in anthropology in the United States in 1891.[5] Harvard started the first PhD program in American anthropology and archaeology in 1890 and granted its first degree in anthropology in 1894, followed by the University of Chicago in 1897, Columbia University, and the University of California at Berkeley in 1901.[6] The anthropology department at Columbia University was founded in 1896 under the direction of Franz Boas, whose student Alfred Kroeber was the first professor in the anthropology department at the University of California at Berkeley.

In the late 1800s, most archaeologists in America were not professionals; they were amateur collectors, geologists, and lawyers who were interested in human history. Anthropology and archaeology in the United States grew from organizations such as the Bureau of American Ethnology and the Peabody Museum of Archaeology and Ethnology.[7] Scholars from other fields such as geology, law, and medicine who were interested in the study of "man" became the first anthropologists and archaeologists in the Americas. Aleš Hrdlička (1869–1943) was trained as a physician and briefly studied anthropology; he was a self-taught physical anthropologist.[8] Hrdlička worked at the United States National Museum, now the Smithsonian Institution, for seven years as an assistant curator before becoming the head curator. Hrdlička and other self-taught or otherwise recognized anthropologists of the time had an impact on research and discussion in American anthropology. After writing a book titled *The Passing of the Great Race: Or, The Racial Basis of European History* (1916), Madison Grant (1865–1937), a lawyer, gained immediate popular success and became established as an authority in anthropology.[9] Grant had an avid interest in conservation and the eugenics movement. He created the racialist movement in America, which had goals that included the exter- mination of undesirables and certain racial types from the human gene pool. Grant's research provided the framework and justification for Nazi policies of forced sterilization and euthanasia. His publications are the seminal works of American racialism. Earnest Hooten (1887–1954) was a physical anthropologist and was well known for his research on racial classification. Hooten wrote a book titled *Up from the Ape* (1931), in which he described the morphological characteristics of different "primary races" and various "subtypes." He taught at Harvard for forty-one years, from 1913 to 1954, and influenced many generations of physical anthropolo- gists and future professors in the field.[10] Hooten supported the study and application of eugenics and the sterilization of those considered as unfit or criminal.[11] Lewis Henry Morgan (1818–81) a lawyer in Rochester, New York, who carried out ethnological studies of the Iroquois in New York State. Morgan argued for classification of human cultural evolution on a progressive linear scale. His scale of humans moved from savagery (primitive hunting) to barbarism (simple farming) to civilization (the highest form of society).[12] He argued that savage societies were communistic and less intelligent than those deemed civilized. Though not all anthropologists agreed with the study of eugenics, racial ideologies, or theories of linear cultural evolution, these areas of study represented the research norms within American anthropology of the time. Franz Boas taught anthropol- ogy at Columbia University, and while he published papers in physical anthropology, he eventually argued against overgeneralizations and an evolutionary cultural perspective.

Boas argued that there were many diverse cultures and that they could not be compared cross-culturally or measured on a linear evolutionary scale.[13] In arguing against a cultural evolutionary scale, Boas was critical of discussions that legitimized eugenics, racism, and discrimination. He supported a four-field approach in anthropology; that is, anthropology should include four areas of study: social-cultural anthropology, physical anthropology, archaeology, and linguistics. Boas discussed race, racial origin, and biometrics in published articles prior to rejecting biological determinism.[14]

The relationships between early archaeologists and their arguments, critiques, and actual practices would fill many volumes. Relationships in academia are never as simple as just agreeing on theories and practices. People's reputations are paramount to receiving grants, research funding, prestigious editorial positions, and leadership roles. Being right, or defending one's theories, and maintaining one's supporters and friends while remaining professional and aware of treachery are key to academic success. Hrdlička, as the head curator and physical anthropologist at the Smithsonian, held a position of power and authority that many archaeologists of the time found difficult to challenge.

Erasure of Indigenous cultures in the archaeological record was evident in the rhetoric of archaeologists tethered to national structures in the United States, such as Hrdlička. His ideologies were based on a linear evolutionary framework. He argued that whites were racially superior to Indians.[15] Hrdlička argued that Native Americans had only been in the Americas for 3,000 years, and his vehement denial of an earlier human presence in the Americas blocked further research in the field for many years.[16] Tom Dillehay has stated that Hrdlička was a "dominant and forceful individual who established a deeply rooted resistance among academics" regarding the possibility of early human sites in the Americas.[17]

As American anthropology and archaeology developed into respectable career fields, a newly educated wave of well-connected settlers graced the halls of Ivy League schools, government offices, and federal museums. At the same time, Indigenous people were being herded onto reservations and dispossessed of their lands, identities, humanity, and sovereignty.[18] Histories of Indigenous people of the Western Hemisphere were equally assailed and often erased through the knowledge production of newly sanctified archaeological experts. Archaeological experts that had a vested interest in supporting the doctrines of the nation-state.[19] Dominant archaeological discourses buried Indigenous histories in a colonial terra nullius, a land devoid of civilization.[20] Some anthropologists, specifically those who trained under Franz Boas, worked to foreground cultural differences between Indigenous communities.[21] During this time in Europe, archaeologists were exploring and discussing new ideas about the antiquity of *Homo sapiens*, an area in which studies of human evolution had previously been restricted to biblical doctrines.

In the late 1800s, a few scholars discussed the possibility of finding pre–*Homo sapiens* in the Americas.[22] This idea followed the success of geologists, paleontologists, and biologists in Europe who found Pleistocene pre–*Homo sapiens* fossil forms and Paleolithic materials. Scholars have discussed early archaeological interpretations of the material record as linked to political processes focused on the appropriation and theft of lands from Indigenous inhabitants for the expansion of the United States.[23] Anthropologists in the late 1800s and early 1900s argued that the savages of the Americas were not capable of the advanced cultural development required to construct the immense earthworks and mounds found in many areas.[24] Otis T. Mason published an article in 1880 in the *American Naturalist* in which he stated, "However long-ago man is claimed to have lived in North America, none of the relics thus far discovered, are supposed to belong to the origin of the race."[25] Had Morgan asked those he deemed to be barbaric savages what they thought, he most likely would have found that they did not see themselves as savages living in a wild, untamed land, as is evidenced in the following quote by John (Fire) Lame Deer and Richard Erodes:

> We did not think of the great open plains, the beautiful rolling hills, and winding streams with tangled growth, as "wild." Only to the white man was nature a "wilderness," and only to him was the land "infested" with "wild" animals and "savage" people. To us it was tame, Earth was bountiful, and we were surrounded with the blessings of the Great Mystery. Not until the hairy man from the east came and with brutal frenzy heaped injustices upon us and the families we loved was it "wild" for us. When the very animals of the forest began fleeing from his approach, then it was that for us the "Wild West" began.[26]

As the field of American anthropology expanded, so too did the debates on humans in the past and present. Minority voices entered the academy, and new lines of critical scholarship crept into discussions of race and identity. On a global scale, the issue of a lack of minority voices in anthropology and archaeology was highlighted by many people, including scholars such as Peter Ucko and archaeologists who supported the organizing of the World Archaeological Congress (WAC).

After the social and political crisis of World War II, when the Nazi Party made eugenics a state-sanctioned program focused on genocide, physical anthropology in the United States began to move away from a focus on race.[27] Over the last fifty years, physical anthropology has developed programs within medical anthropology, primatology, and genetics. Physical anthropology has been applied to locating and recording victims of genocide and is thus a field of study that supports Indigenous peoples who have suffered under oppression and dictatorships.

There is a long history of thefts from Indigenous burial sites throughout North and South America. Indigenous human remains and burial items that were stolen from their burial sites continue to be held by many universities and museums. Hrdlička was known to have collected Indigenous peoples' skulls from massacre sites for his research.[28] In seeking to repatriate and rebury their ancestors, Native Americans in the United States fought for legislation to have their ancestors' remains returned.[29] Native American voices pushing for human rights and the return of their ancestors' remains and sacred objects resulted in the passing of the Native American Graves Protection and Repatriation Act of 1990 (NAGPRA).[30]

Maria Pearson, a descendant of the Lakota Sioux Nation, is credited with raising awareness of the differential treatment of Native American remains and with being a catalyst for NAGPRA. In 1971 Pearson lobbied Iowa governor Robert D. Rayto to rebury the remains of a Native American woman and child that had been sent to the Office of State Archaeology. The remains of twenty-six European Americans from the same disturbed graveyard had been placed in coffins and reburied.

In 1989, the Pawnees of Oklahoma, along with other Nebraska tribes, and the Native American Rights Fund (NARF) pushed to have Native American burial and repatriation legislation passed. In 1989, Nebraska lawmakers passed the Nebraska Unmarked Human Burial Sites and Skeletal Remains Protection Act (LB 340).[31] Following the passing of LB 340, "on September 11, 1990, the remains and funerary offerings of 403 deceased Pawnee ancestors were reburied . . . at Wild Licorice Creek," which had been the Pawnees' last home prior to relocation to Oklahoma.

Prior to the passing of NAGPRA, Indigenous communities, individuals, and organizations had pushed for the protection of unmarked burial sites at both the state and federal levels. Some states had enacted unmarked gravesite protection laws prior to 1990. Behind every movement and law to protect unmarked burials stood concerned members of Native American communities. In 1987, the Smithsonian reported on the thousands of human remains in its collections. The Select Committee on Indian Affairs held hearings and found that 42.5 percent of the human remains at the Smithsonian were Native American, and another 11.9 percent were of Aleut, Eskimo, or Koniang heritage. In 1988, the Select Committee on Indian Affairs heard testimony concerning Senate Bill 187, which prompted a decision to start discussions that included Native American representatives, scientists, and communities regarding the treatment and return of human remains and cultural artifacts. In 1989, a yearlong dialogue hosted by the Heard Museum resulted in recommendations being drafted for the select committee that included a call for developing policy standards for repatriation. Eventually hearing Native American communities' concerns and sensing the need for this legislation, federal representatives met with Native American community representatives to begin talks on the drafting of repatriation legislation.

In 1989, Senator Daniel K. Inouye of Hawai'i introduced Senate Bill 978, the National Museum of the American Indian Act, which included discussions on repatriation and treatment of human remains and funerary objects held by the Smithsonian. PL 101–185, signed November 21, 1989, was combined with recommendations from the Panel for a National Dialogue on Museum Native American Relations. This became the framework for NAGPRA. NAGPRA extended the provisions of the National Museum of the American Indian Act to all federal agencies and institutions receiving federal funds.[32] NAGPRA states that human remains and funerary objects belong to lineal descendants. If no lineal descendants can be found, then the human remains and associated funerary objects belong to the tribal land or Indian tribe. The law applies only to human remains and funerary objects excavated from federal and tribal lands or currently housed in museums that receive federal funds. Unfortunately, NAGPRA does not apply to private collections or remains from private lands held by private collectors.

Decades of lobbying by Indigenous people in the United States against the destruction and collecting of burial sites and human remains resulted in the passing of NAGPRA in 1990. On November 6, 1990, George H. W. Bush signed NAGPRA, which required museums and institutions with archaeological collections to inventory human remains and objects of cultural and religious affiliation and to make the inventories available to Indigenous communities. Following the requirements of NAGPRA would be an enormous undertaking for museums and institutions holding Native American remains and objects of cultural patrimony. This undertaking slowly began after shock waves of protest; anger and grief were publicly paraded in lobbying efforts against NAGPRA by archaeologists and academics within the field.

Many archaeologists were enraged at the passing of NAGPRA. Clement Meighan stated that he feared that archaeology as a field in North America would end. Other archaeologists sought to create a working relationship with Indigenous communities and to consult with them under the guidelines and regulations of NAGPRA. Meighan saw reburying bones and artifacts as "the equivalent of the historian burning documents after he has studied them. Thus, repatriation is not merely an inconvenience but makes it impossible for scientists to carry out a genuinely scientific study of American Indian prehistory." Because of NAGPRA, he concluded, "an entire field of academic study may be put out of business."[33] In a 1996 article, Jerome C. Rose, Thomas J. Green, and Victoria D. Green stated: "The loss of these collections will be a detriment to the study of North American osteology, but the inventory and repatriation process has increased the number of skeletons studied from about 30% to nearly 100%. The availability of funds stimulated by this law produced osteological data collection and systematization unprecedented in the history of osteology. The possibility of forming partnerships between Native Americans and osteologists has the potential of producing a vibrant future for North American osteology and the new bioarchaeology."[34]

Prior to the passing of this law, many archaeologists and museums and their professional organizations rallied against the proposed act.[35] Recently, it became known that a park manager at Effigy Mounds National Monument had taken human remains from the park and stored them in his garage for decades. It is assumed he took them to protect them from being returned to an American Indian tribe through NAGPRA processes.[36]

American archaeologists who were so accustomed to helping themselves to Indigenous bodies and material cultural now faced the possibility of intense scrutiny of their traditional collecting practices in the Americas. What brought such a travesty to the bastions of colonial power and control within privileged centers of knowledge production? The Native Americans who had critiqued archaeologists' practices for decades had finally been heard.

There were petitions against NAGPRA signed by archaeologists and discussion within the professional organization against the passing of NAGPRA and eventually in support of it. In 2016, the Society for American Archaeology (SAA) published a repatriation survey analysis.[37] A total of 1,905 members of the SAA responded to the survey. One area of contention in NAGPRA has been the cultural affiliation of human remains over 2,000 years old. Regarding the question on human remains that were over 2,000 years old and if they should be repatriated under NAGPRA, 47.1 percent answered no, and 44.8 percent answered yes. Breaking down the voting to voter categories, 75 percent of no votes came from respondents in the retired category, and 70 percent of seventeen people in the avocational category voted no. In the academic category, 46 percent voted yes, and 45 percent voted no.[38] This survey was taken seventeen years after NAGPRA was passed, so it seems that some archaeologists' attitudes regarding NAGPRA have changed at a very slow pace, if at all.

There is a very clear pattern regarding Indigenous cultural items and human remains in the Americas among archaeologists. Archaeologists had to be court-ordered under NAGPRA to talk to or consult with Native Americans regarding cultural objects and ancestors' remains. Hundreds of thousands of items of cultural patrimony and human remains were taken from Indigenous lands without the consent of Indigenous communities. Indigenous groups have had to fight, to protest, and at times to be arrested in their efforts to push for repatriation legislation and the respectful treatment of their ancestors' human remains.

I worked in cultural resource management and field archaeology in North America for over five years, and it was my experience that many archaeologists refused to consult with Indigenous people about cultural sites. This was also evident in the academy; many archaeologists who taught in universities and carried out fieldwork never included Indigenous peoples' voices or knowledge of their own histories in any part of their research. Though this has recently begun to change in a few areas, it is often still the embedded norm to exclude Indigenous people and to retain power and control over their artifacts, ancestors, and histories. In discussing the development of "community archaeology," Richard Hutchings and Marina La Salle find that the field of archaeology does not always break with past practices embedded in inequality, power, and control:

> Community-Oriented Archaeology brings archaeology and archaeologists back to the center. This is a familiar problem in race discourse where, because the conversation is dominated by ethnically, and economically privileged groups, "the path of least resistance is to focus attention on themselves—who they are, what they do and say, and how they do it." Re-centering archaeology and archaeologists represent no break with past practices; indeed, it is the most common response when privilege is questioned. This is a step backward if the goal is to "move non-Indigenous archaeologists from a safe space of unassailable privilege."[39]

Archaeologists may claim to be doing Indigenous-oriented or community archaeology, but claims and actions may be very different in practice. Claims of carrying out community-oriented archaeology made by some archaeologists were discussed by Hutchings and La Salle in the above quote; they argue that some archaeologists have discussed their projects as being community centered or inclusive, yet they have not centered communities in the research. Such practices do not necessarily create or reflect change within the field. Another recent example of colonization and power and control in American archaeology is that of a group of American archaeologists who filed a lawsuit in efforts to retain ancient Native American human remains for research.

The Ancient One Explains Racism in American Anthropology

From my experiences in field archaeology and examples of how some archaeologists interact with or discuss Indigenous peoples, I would argue that colonial practices remain embedded in many areas of archaeology in North America, specifically, within areas of physical anthropology that often require human remains for research. However, physical anthropologists such as Ventura Perez at the University of Massachusetts, Amherst, have stepped outside the box to address racism and push for decolonization of research within the field. An example of bias in physical anthropology and archaeology in North America is evident in the facial reconstructions that impose European or other traits on ancient Native American remains during facial reconstructions. One example of this has been the treatment of skeletal remains that Indigenous peoples call the Ancient One and archaeologists call Kennewick Man.

The Ancient One's burial site was found after it had eroded from the banks of the Columbia River in Kennewick, Washington, in June 1996. In part because of the suspected antiquity of the Ancient One and because tribal groups expressed their intent to rebury him, as well as archaeologists erroneously stating that he looked like a Caucasoid, there was an immediate and prolonged media frenzy surrounding the case.[40] The Department of the Interior (DOI) and National Park Service (NPS), in cooperation with the Corps of Engineers, conducted a series of scientific examinations of the remains. The DOI invited eighteen scientists to conduct examinations of the Ancient One and to present their findings, which are posted on the NPS website.[41] One of the scientists was Dr. Jerome Rose, with whom I was studying at the time as an undergraduate student in anthropology at the University of Arkansas at Fayetteville. Through working with Dr. Rose, I was made aware of the importance of the case and the issues at hand. At the time, I was also in my first year of a two-year NAGPRA internship with Carrie Wilson, the Quapaw tribal NAGPRA representative. Through this internship, I became acutely aware of the importance of the return and reburial of ancestral remains for Indigenous communities. I also became aware of the roadblocks and racism many Indigenous groups faced in asserting their rights to reclaim ancestors for reburial. According to the National Park Service, the Ancient One was found to be Native American and came under the guidelines of NAGPRA.[42] The Ancient One then could be repatriated to (culturally affiliated) tribal groups requesting his return. A NAGPRA claim was filed by the Confederated Tribes of the Umatilla Indian Reservation of Oregon, along with the Confederated Tribes of the Coleville Indian Reservation of Washington State, the Yakama Nation of

Washington State, the Nez Perce Tribe of Idaho, and the Wanapums of Washington. The Ancient One was dated to 8410 ± 60 ^{14}C cal BP.[43] The National Park Service released the following report.

> We now have sufficient information to determine that these skeletal remains should be considered "Native American" as defined by NAG-PRA. The results of recent radiocarbon dating of small samples of bone extracted from the remains were given significant weight in making this determination. This interpretation is supported by other analyses and information regarding the skeletal remains themselves, sedimentary analysis, lithic analysis, an earlier radiocarbon date on a bone recovered with the other remains, and geomorphologic analysis. . . . A series of radiocarbon dates now available from the Kennewick skeletal remains indicate a clearly pre-Columbian date for the remains. . . . It is reasonable to conclude that the human remains from Columbia Park in Kennewick, WA, are "Native American" as defined by the Native American Graves Protection and Repatriation Act.[44]

After reading the reports, I found that the study provided a great deal of support for the decision made by the NPS to repatriate the Ancient One. I was not surprised, but I was disappointed in the blatant disregard of a group of archaeologists from powerful institutions who filed a lawsuit to block the repatriation so they could carry out further scientific study on the Ancient One. This group included Robson Bonnichsen (1940–2004) (Texas A&M University), C. Loring Brace (University of Michigan), George W. Gill (University of Wyoming), C. Vance Haynes Jr. (University of Arizona), Richard L. Jantz (University of Tennessee, Knoxville), Douglas Owsley (Smithsonian's National Museum of Natural History), Dennis J. Stanford (1943–2019) (Smithsonian, Department of Anthropology), and D. Gentry Steele (1941–2014) (Texas A&M University). Vine Deloria Jr. wrote that "several" of the scholars who filed a lawsuit to get access to Kennewick Man were "informally described as members of the so-called Clovis Police."[45] The Clovis Police were known to be a group of American archaeologists who adamantly denied all pre-Clovis sites that dated to earlier than 11,000 to 12,000 years ago. Recently, a few of the archaeologists Deloria referred to as the Clovis Police have accepted that there are archaeological sites in the Americas that are older than Clovis time frames. Dennis Stanford and Robson Bonnichsen have published on earlier than Clovis archaeological sites.

The group who sued to keep the remains of the Ancient One for scientific research won the lawsuit; they also released photos of forensic reconstructions of the Ancient One that were very problematic. Facial reconstructions are often presented without informing readers that soft tissue reconstructions are created through the assumed racial categories of the skulls, created by those doing the reconstructing. With ancient skulls, soft tissue is not preserved; there is no way to know the color of the skin, the texture of the hair, or the shape of the ears, mouth, or lips. These defining characteristics are assumed and may often be linked to specific groups of people on a global scale, such as Asian, African, or European. Research has been carried out and data have been gathered on cranial architecture that forensic experts use to assign unknown remains to specific groups of people, such as the size of eye sockets and nasal cavities. However, cranial features do not inform reconstruction experts as to the color of the skin, hair, or eyes or the shape of the ears or mouth. Genetics research has shown that human variation is incredibly diverse and that race is not a valid biological category for anything, including ethnic identity.[46]

In his silence, Kennewick Man speaks volumes about ongoing racism in American anthropology. The Ancient One carries a strong message that racism is active in academic circles, is still being taught and passed on, and is still negatively impacting Indigenous peoples.

The four facial reconstructions and artistic renditions of the Ancient One look very different from one another, yet they are all based on one skull. It is problematic that the reconstructions and 3D images are all so different. People like Élisabeth Daynès in Paris and Roger Nilsson of Sweden are highly regarded facial reconstruction experts, yet they were not involved in the facial reconstruction of the Ancient One. In such an important case, I would have wanted an unbiased expert who was not associated with anyone involved in the lawsuit to do a facial reconstruction. The first facial reconstruction of the Ancient One was created by James Chatters, an archaeologist, and Thomas McClelland, a sculptor. In this facial reconstruction, the Ancient One looks more like representations of people of the

Eastern Hemisphere. Facial reconstructions of the Ancient One created by artists using digital technologies reflect an Ainu or Polynesian look. What the Ancient One looked like may never be known, unless his skull, or photographs of his skull and skull cast, are sent without any identifying information to a forensic reconstruction expert who would not know where the skull came from and that person completed a facial reconstruction. Facial reconstructions were created in 1998 by James Chatters and Thomas McClelland, in 2004 by Keith Kasnot, in 2006 by Kam Mak for the cover of *Time Magazine*, and in 2015 by Douglas Owsley, Amanda Danning, and Karin Bruwelheide. The two created by Keith Kasnot and Kam Mak look similar, and both were created as an image of a contemporary Ainu or Polynesian man. The two created by archaeologists and friends at the Smithsonian look nothing alike, and both more closely resemble representations of ancient people from the Eastern Hemisphere. It is interesting to note that contemporary Indigenous males in the Americas do not often, if ever, grow full beards or mustaches, though we do not know if this would have been the case 9,000 years ago.

The first facial reconstruction, done in 1998 by archaeologist James Chatters and Thomas McClelland, a sculptor, made the Ancient One look exactly like Captain Jean-Luc Picard from *Star Trek*. Chatters argued that because the skull was narrow, it looked Caucasoid. Keep in mind the processes of evolution; we would not expect anyone today to resemble a skull from 9,000 to 8,000 years ago. Chatters discussed the Ancient One's skull as being narrow; thus, "it had to be Caucasian."[47] However, in their review, Dr. Jerome Rose and Dr. Joseph Powell stated that the skull had not been properly reconstructed. Rose and Powell reconstructed the skull and corrected the inventory and measurements originally done by Douglas Owsley of the Smithsonian Museum. On 25 February 1999, Joseph Powell and Jerome Rose checked the *Standards for Data Collection from Human Skeletal Remains* by J. E. Buikstra and D. Ubelaker (1994) inventory prepared by Douglas Owsley for accuracy: "Several changes were made, including altering the completeness scores for some bones, moving several bones from one side of the body to another, changing the numbers (L2 vs. L4) of two lumbar vertebrae, and removing one fragment of maxilla from the faunal collection from the site."[48]

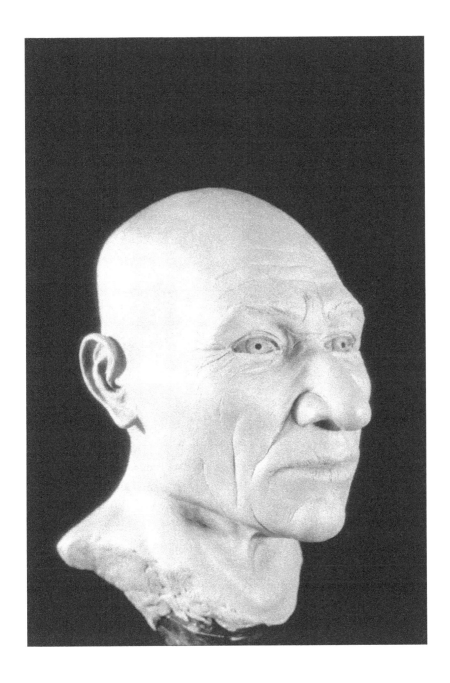

Fig. 1. Reconstruction of the Ancient One, Kennewick Man, by Jim Chatters and Thomas McClelland, 1998.

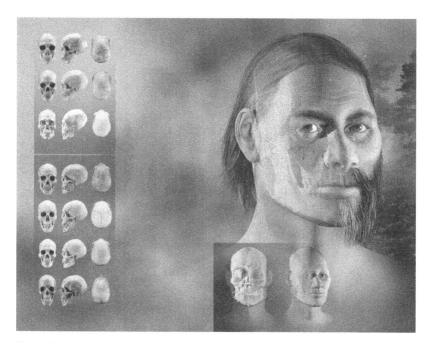

Fig. 2. Digital reconstruction of Kennewick Man by Keith Kasnot, 2004.

The facial reconstruction of Kennewick Man created by Kam Mak for the cover of *Time Magazine* in 2006 resembled a person with possibly Asian or contemporary Northwest Coast Native American features.[49] The 2004 digital rendition by Keith Kasnot made the Ancient One look like a Polynesian or Ainu male with facial hair.[50] In the 2015 version created by Douglas Owsley, Amanda Danning, and Karin Bruwelheide, the Ancient One has a full bushy beard, a trait not commonly seen among contemporary Indigenous populations of the Western Hemisphere.

I previously mentioned that I would like to see if there would be a difference if the Ancient One's face were reconstructed by someone who was not involved in the lawsuit and who saw only the skull and had no information about where it had been found. I asked an experienced forensic artist who had worked with ancient skulls and 3D reconstructions to complete a facial reconstruction from images of the skull and told her only that it was from a male who was well-built, robust, and around forty years old (figure 5). I also had a student of mine draw the Ancient One from the skull photos

Fig. 3. Reconstruction of Kennewick Man by Kam Mak, 2006.

Fig. 4. Sculptors Amanda Danning and Jiwoong Cheh, painter Rebecca Spivak, and StudioEIS collaborated in the reconstruction of Kennewick Man's appearance. Photo credit: Brittney Tatchell, Smithsonian Institution.

(figure 6). The student knew that the skull had been identified as that of a Native American male around thirty-five to forty years old and that the skull had been found in the northwestern United States.

To keep Kennewick Man for scientific research, a small group of archaeologists did everything they could to disenfranchise him from Indigenous people. Their actions and public discussions fueled fires of racism and claims of Europeans being the first Americans. Not all archaeologists who studied the Ancient One agree that he did not look like a contemporary Native American. Jerome Rose stated: "There are indications, however, that the Kennewick cranium is morphologically similar to Archaic populations from the northern Great Basin of the USA region, and to large Archaic populations in the eastern woodlands."[51]

According to Roger Downey, a week after James Chatters made a press statement regarding his views on the Caucasoid features of Kennewick Man, millions of people around the world had been informed that a 9,000-year-old European was one of the oldest skeletons ever found in North America.[52] The media frenzy and subsequent court case offer a solid example of how Western scientists' voices are privileged over Indigenous rights.

American media have sometimes framed Native Americans as anti-science and backward for wanting to rebury the Ancient One. The fight to keep Kennewick Man from being repatriated and the subsequent cost of research may have been funded in part by taxpayers and in part through funds channeled into federal institutions such as the Smithsonian, as well as the public universities where those involved in the lawsuit worked. The cost of the Kennewick lawsuit and subsequent years of research has not been publicly discussed. I did ask one of the archaeologists involved in the lawsuit about the cost of the lawyers and the court case, as well as the possible use of public funds, but I have not received a reply.

The Social and Political Power of Discourse

Political control of cultural information is critical to the survival and protection of Indigenous people's rights and sovereignty. Archaeological and historical data are not merely neutral pieces of information; they are fundamentally fouled with political and neocolonial views and ideas.

—Frederick Wiseman, *Reclaiming the Ancestors*

Fig. 5. The Ancient One, Kennewick Man, by Marcia K. Moore, 2018.

Fig. 6. The Ancient One, Kennewick Man, by Saskia Van Walsum, 2018. Courtesy of the author.

American archaeology has controlled the knowledge production of the history and heritage of the Indigenous peoples of the Western Hemisphere for decades: "Nation states or partisans thereof, control and allocate symbolic resources as one means of legitimizing power and authority, and in pursuit of their perceived nationalistic goals and ideologies. A major symbolic resource is the past."[53] Cristobal Gnecco has discussed history as a "form of the social production of knowledge which is constructed from and constitutive of social memory."[54] The importance of history in the social construction of knowledge is not a concept that has been ignored in academia but a practice that was actively applied in archaeological discussions to support the goals of the nation-state.[55] According to Deloria, "The constant drumbeat of scientific personalities who manipulate the public's image of Indians by describing archaeological horizons instead of societies, speaking of hunter gatherers instead of communities, and attacking Indian knowledge of the past as fictional mythology, had created a situation in which the average citizen is greatly surprised to learn that Indians are offended by racial slurs and insults."[56]

What is not often discussed beyond critical scholarship circles is the impact of traditional anthropological knowledge production on the people it studies. The cleaving of links between contemporary Indigenous populations and ancient homelands and links between ancient and contemporary people denies Indigenous identities and rights and fuels discrimination and social and political disparities. When their histories are destroyed and disfigured by academic writing from within colonial institutions, colonized people are often left in an empty void shattered by discussions that deny the legitimacy of their civilization before European colonization.

K. Tsianina Lomawaima, a Creek educator, has argued that in the Americas, educators have begun to create curriculum that includes Indigenous knowledge; however, educational curriculum has not been transformed.[57] What children are taught in American classrooms stretches far beyond schools. Examples of social and political disparities and racism against Indigenous people in the Americas are evident in the news on a daily basis. Thus, it seems that many non-Indigenous people in America are guided in their actions through colonial policies and educations that dehumanize Indigenous people.

Embedded and dehumanizing discussions fuel social and political disparities and discrimination linked to intergenerational and ongoing soulwounds. Soulwounds are intergenerational legacies of trauma passed on from one generation to the next.[58] Maria Yellow Horse Brave Heart (Hunkpapa / Oglala Lakota) and Lemyra Debruyn have discussed a legacy of unresolved grief and trauma that has resulted from years of colonization and massive losses of lands, culture, and human lives.[59] Legacies of intergenerational trauma have been documented among Indigenous populations after acts of colonization, including genocide, ethnic cleansing, and forced acculturation.

Academic discussions that ignore and erase Indigenous people and places remain a mainstay in processes of colonization. Erasures of histories, knowledge, and people are linked to processes of intergenerational trauma. Attempts by colonizing nation-states to eradicate Indigenous people have been ongoing for over five hundred years. This includes but is not limited to attempted physical and cultural genocide, ongoing political, social, and educational disparities, exclusion of Indigenous knowledge and history in academic curriculum, and knowledge production of Indigenous histories through a Western-only lens. Genocide was so normalized within Canada and the United States that both governments offered generous scalp rewards to settlers, paying them to kill as many Indians as possible. In fact, a two-hundred-year-old scalp law was still on the law books in Nova Scotia in 2009.[60]

Derisive discussion of Indigenous cultures of the Western Hemisphere not just are historical but remain embedded in contemporary discourse.[61] The social and political impacts of constructed Indigenous histories invented from a Western Eurocentric position work to disempower contemporary Indigenous people and fuel discrimination while creating histories and social memories that serve a dominant master narrative.[62]

Indigenous people have historically been misrepresented as uncivilized, unintellectual, and incompatible with a modern world.[63] Historic anthropological discussions of Indigenous people may be reflected in support for or against policies that may have social, legal, and economic implications.[64] The general public's perceptions of Indigenous people are most often uninformed and distorted by historical academic discourse, film, media, and popular books.[65] A recent letter to the editor of the *Nanaimo News*, published in British Columbia, is an example of the uninformed views some people have of Indigenous people. The letter, entitled "Educate First Nations to Be Modern Citizens," seriously questioned the accomplishments of First Nations communities and depicted them in the past and in contemporary times as chronic underachievers.

> It was only 12,000 years ago, or less and this should be considered; in all those years, the so-called First Nations: Never "discovered" the wheel Never had a written language Never discovered astronomy Had no science or scientific discoveries Had no mathematics Made no medical discoveries . . . Have a history that is notable only for underachievement . . . Are these people in trouble? Yes, do they need help? Yes, are they responsible enough to look after themselves and efficiently spend the billions the taxpayers give them? Certainly not.[66]

The letter was riddled with inaccurate tropes of uncivilized peoples who never invented anything worthwhile and were incapable of being modern citizens. "First Nations National Chief Shawn Atleo was outraged by the letter, saying it reflected ignorance toward his community. 'That letter—outrageous—the outside example of the deep disconnect, misunderstanding, and ignorance about First Nations people from coast to coast to coast—the kind of thinking that has created the advent of the Indian Act that led to residential schools.'"[67] Snuneymuxw chief Doug White posted his view of the letter on the Snuneymuxw blog site: "The letter and the paper that published it should be condemned in every possible way. It is the ugliest expression of ignorance and discrimination from this paper. . . . I sent it along to specialized legal counsel for advice regarding hate speech and whether a criminal prosecution should be pursued or a human rights complaint or both."[68]

The letter, printed in March 2013, sparked an immediate social media fury and protests outside of the newspaper's office in Nanaimo. The letter was apparently from a Canadian citizen responding to the Idle No More movement, which brought attention to the need to address extreme poverty among First Nations communities. The letter blamed First Nations people for their own plight and stated they had amounted and never would amount to anything.[69] First Nations leaders were cited in the press addressing the place of education in the creation and maintenance of racism: "'The foundation of racism is ignorance and fear about each other, and what we have been trying to do for many years is try and build greater understanding,' said Snuneymuxw Chief Doug White, who hopes the incident will kick start educational conferences and a change in school curricula."[70]

The letter highlighted how racist knowledge production and agnotology, a pedagogy of intentional ignorance, maintain currency in contemporary general discourses. Numerous responses to the letter discussed the historical accomplishments of Indigenous peoples in science, astronomy, mathematics, architecture, medicine, and agriculture were posted on social media sites. In a clear majority of anthropological and educational materials, Indigenous accomplishments and Indigenous worldviews remain areas that are seldom discussed. Though this has recently begun to change, colonialist discourses remain a factor in the maintenance of discrimination, racism, and reproduction of colonialism.[71] One example comes from an archaeological textbook published in 2007, Robert J. Wenke and Deborah Olszewski's *Patterns in Prehistory: Humankind's First Three Million Years*. This textbook is used in undergraduate introduction to archaeology classes and was written by two American archaeologists. Robert Wenke, an archaeologist whose scholarly focus area is Egypt and the Middle East, retired from the University of Washington, and Deborah Olszewski, whose research interests include the Middle East, Egypt, North Africa, and the southwestern United States, is an adjunct instructor at the University of Pennsylvania in anthropology. Here is an example of their discussion of an artifact: "Archaeologists analyze the archaeological record primarily in terms of artifacts which can be defined as things that owe any of their physical characteristics or their place in time and space to human activity. Thus, a beautifully shaped spear point from a 20,000-year-old campsite in France is an artifact, but so is an undistinguished stone flake some weary Native American pitched out of a Mississippi cornfield 1,000 years ago."[72] The description, which presents artifacts from France as ancient and beautiful and artifacts from Mississippi as much more recent and indistinguishable, as well as the statement identifying a "weary Indian" are highly egregious, especially as the text is often required reading for first-year undergraduate students. Archaeological discussions continue to shape public perceptions of Indigenous people. When discriminatory discussions are left unchallenged, academics and knowledge holders become a part of the problem.

Archaeologists often discuss the first people of the Western Hemisphere as being from Asia or as Asians, thereby erasing and denying their Indigenous identities. David Meltzer wrote that "they made prehistory, those later day Asians who, by jumping continents, became the first Americans."[73] Tom Dillehay stated that "Beringia was certainly used when Asians first colonized North America."[74] Initial migrations, whether 11,200 BP or earlier, took place long before Asian or Asia existed as distinct cultural or geopolitical group identifiers.[75] Geopolitical terminology applied by some archaeologists implies that thousands of years before the existence of Asians as a distinct cultural group and of Asia itself, Asians walked across the land area we know today as Beringia and instantly became Americans. Regarding the Bering Strait theory of initial migrations, Vine Deloria Jr. argued that "only rarely do scholars look at the map closely enough to see the absurdity of their claims."[76]

In discursive and legal work to rid the American landscape of Indigenous peoples, colonizers invented a hemispheric-wide terra nullius, a term that refers to a newly discovered land devoid of civilized populations.[77] European colonizers historically applied this term to Australia and the Americas to forward claims for control of land and resources.

Archaeology was not the only field in which those who advocated for human occupation of the Americas prior to Clovis dates suffered professional repercussions: "The upshot was that the question of early man in America became virtually taboo, and no anthropologist, or for that matter geologist or paleontologist, desirous of a successful career would tempt the fate of ostracism by intimating that he had discovered indications of a respectable antiquity for the Indian."[78]

Archaeologists in the United States and Canada invented the ancient Indigenous past to conform to nationalist discourses of a terra nullius discovered by Europeans and Asians. Such Eurocentric discussions of recent initial migrations on a global timescale support the nation-state's doctrines of discovery and conquest and the theft of land, resources, and ancestral remains. Archaeological knowledge of the past has traditionally been taught as truth and thus holds currency in the present within social and political institutions and in the education of the public.[79] However, much of the ancient past embedded in social memory through archaeological discourses erases Indigenous histories and identities.[80] "The appropriation of Indigenous achievements by national storytellers, all members of the elites that despised the Indians and considered themselves white, was a brutal paradox."[81]

Anthropology and archaeology faced a crisis of representation in the 1970s and 1980s, and scholars began an anthropological self-reflection. Some people in the field began to work toward a praxis that does no harm. While this is an improvement over earlier practices within the field, we have a long way to go to create open and safe spaces of equity where we teach inclusive ethical practices to do no harm. There are a growing number of Indigenous, Native American, and First Nations academic scholars focusing on practices of Indigenous archaeology and community-centered research. These practices have begun to make inroads in decentering Western knowledge in the academy. However, the Clovis First hypothesis and recent LGM initial migrations of Indigenous people into the Western Hemisphere remain entrenched in literature and academia. One area within academic knowledge production that most often remains undiscussed is that of the "deafening silence" of many anthropologists regarding the unsubstantiated Clovis First hypothesis of initial migrations into the Western Hemisphere. Thousands of academics believe in and continue to teach the Clovis First hypothesis as fact. Yet very few have openly critiqued its lack of evidence or scientific data.

In this chapter, I have presented examples of ongoing colonization within American anthropology and its impacts on Indigenous people. In discussing the impacts of Western archaeological knowledge production, I highlight the need for archaeologists to critically reflect on their practices and discussions within the field. Archaeology that ignores the damaging impacts of its past and the need to implement change in the field reproduces colonization through the power of institutional position and assumed authority. Though scholars in anthropology and archaeology have discussed the need for change in addressing the colonial past of the field, it often seems from the informed and experienced Indigenous view that not much has changed. There are a few areas of anthropology that reflect a move toward working with Indigenous people on creating safe spaces for inclusion in research and pedagogy. Examples include the World Archaeological Congress (WAC), the Society for Applied Anthropology (SFAA), and individual Indigenous academics and their like-minded peers pushing for change from within their field.

Colonization in anthropology and the subfield of archaeology has been embedded in academia for over one hundred years; it will not change quickly. Change in academia has been known to stem from demand. Thus, it may be up to students to create change and to challenge embedded "stereotypical and racist tropes" in the educational materials they are required to read and to listen to in lectures.[82] Change in the field may also be facilitated through the inclusion of minority voices and Indigenous archaeologists and scholars, though in many academies it seems archaeology remains a strictly Western endeavor unaware of the richness of knowledge that diversity in research may bring. In the academic training of archaeologists in North America, there is a vast disconnect between archaeology and teaching anything about Indigenous communities and heritage. Very few universities, if any, require students to take any courses on Native American history to earn a degree in archaeology. However, students with a bachelor's degree in archaeology become field archaeologists for cultural resource management and archaeology fieldwork in America. It is pivotal for students and faculty to become informed of First Nations, Native American, and Indigenous voices in academic literature to inform their views of Indigenous people and challenge discrimination. Stories of the past informed through Indigenous voices come alive with the richness of firsthand knowledge, knowledge of the past, knowledge of the present, and knowledge of how power and control continue to be woven through the past and present, negatively impacting Indigenous people.

Rise Up

I avoided that class
the one where
I become informant
I avoided the Western views
of me
as subhuman
I avoided discussions of white men's rights
to fondle my grandparent's bodies
still in boxes
in white men's basements
I avoided
until I learned to listen
to my ancestors
gently screaming in my mind

RISE UP
And so, I rose
like feathers on a breeze
like the blood in my professor's face
when I challenged and corrected
his Western knowledge
about me

RISE UP
Now I tell
my students
rise up
for the children
still missing
still dying
still lost

RISE UP

Demand to hear
to read
to know
to learn from
to share with
to grow with
to have hope with
me

CHAPTER 3

Relations Who Opened the Way

Seeing through New Eyes

In their discussion of Socrates's dialectics from Plato's lectures on his teachings, Robert Proctor and Londa Schiebinger stated: "Knowledge of one's ignorance is a precondition for enlightenment."[1] Proctor and Schiebinger highlight a discussion that Plato attributed to his teacher Socrates. However, it seems that in the hundreds of years that Greek philosophy has been a mainstay of study in Western education, archaeologists with their many Western educational degrees have not always caught on to discussion of the preconditions for enlightenment. For decades Western anthropologists and archaeologists have discussed communities from outside their own cultures as if they know everything about them. When anthropologists and archaeologists make claims about cultural practices or histories of communities they are not members of, they often display a lack of awareness of their own ignorance. Archaeologists do learn a great deal from the material record of early people. However, they have created unsubstantiated stories about early humans in the Western Hemisphere that became embedded in educational and general literature as facts.[2] Creative license in writing archaeologically based histories and stories of Indigenous people often runs unchecked in the Western academy. One example is the archaeological story of the so-called Clovis People. The Clovis People have traditionally been discussed by archaeologists as a panhemispheric cultural group that included the first people to live in the Western Hemisphere. However, the only place the Clovis People ever existed was in the wildest imagination of the archaeological mind. Information that would support an understanding of the possibilities of people in the deep past of the Western Hemisphere has often been left out of archaeological discussions. Discussions that highlight paleoenvironments are central to gaining an understanding of the possibilities for human and mammalian migrations across time and place. The land is the essential element linking early humans through and between places across time, and it is central to histories told through Indigenous oral traditions. Reconstructing Paleolithic landscapes links our minds, hearts, and vision to a place where ancestors walked, sang, danced, and created their lives. Research in paleoenvironments, paleobotany, and oral traditions benefits archaeological studies and provides us with a more robust understanding of the past.

A hemispheric-wide study of archaeological sites and oral traditions has the potential to add to what we know of human movements across time and space. It is essential to inform our understandings of early human technologies by studying Paleolithic collections found in many areas of the world. Archaeological studies in the Western Hemisphere have recently been carried out by archaeologists from the Eastern Hemisphere who have experience and training in Paleolithic studies, such as Jiri Chlachula.[3]

TABLE 1. Paleolithic time frames, Eastern Hemisphere

Lower Paleolithic	2,580,000 to 200,000 years ago
Middle Paleolithic	300,000 to 30,000 years ago
Upper Paleolithic	50,000 to 12,000 years ago

Source: Ambrose, "Paleolithic Technology."

Archaeologists who are experienced in Paleolithic studies add a missing dimension to Pleistocene research in the Americas. Most, if not all, archaeological programs and field schools in the United States and Canada have not focused on training students to recognize Paleolithic artifacts or technologies beyond Clovis and Folsom technologies. Training and experience in Paleolithic studies for archaeologists and students carrying out site excavations in the Western Hemisphere are paramount to furthering our understanding of the Indigenous past. Paleolithic studies would support an understanding of the intimate and detailed technological landmarks for the human production of stone tools from Paleolithic periods. A comparative study of Paleolithic tools from the Eastern and

Western Hemispheres may highlight technological similarities across time and space. There are many areas of study that are central to informing the legitimacy of Pleistocene archaeological sites, including but not limited to stratigraphy, soil studies, geology, paleobotany, oral traditions, and dating technologies. Nevertheless, if archaeologists are not open to the possibilities of an earlier human presence in a given area, then science and knowledge may not matter. Stone tools that date prior to 12,000 years ago are often accepted as produced by humans in all areas of the Eastern Hemisphere. However, similar and identical stone tools and technologies that date to older than 12,000 years ago in the Western Hemisphere are discussed as geofacts (a natural stone or piece of a stone that is often shaped through natural events and fluvial processes and that resembles a human-made artifact) and discarded.[4] Archaeologists have scientific procedures to differentiate an artifact from a geofact. Patrick Lubinski, Karisa Terry, and Patrick McCutcheon have addressed the geofact versus artifact problem through systematic and objective testing based on three criteria:

> First, [artifacts] are compared with debitage attributes typically expected of artifacts and geofacts based on published experimental and actualistic data. Second, they are compared in terms of nine of these attributes with a toolstone sample from the site excavation matrix. Third, the two possible artifacts are scored for these nine attributes and graphed against the toolstone matrix sample and two samples of flintknapped debitage assemblages. In all three comparisons, the two specimens are more like artifacts than geofacts. While this does not prove the specimens are artifacts, it at least shows they cannot be easily dismissed as the sort of geofacts typically expected in the site matrix. We argue that this distinction is an important first step in the evaluation of possible lithic artifacts.[5]

Embedded bias in archaeology regarding time frames of initial human habitation in the Western Hemisphere continues to impact archaeological interpretations of artifacts from Pleistocene sites. Outdated archaeological theories of first people of the Western Hemisphere have been critiqued by a diverse field of scholars both inside and outside of archaeology, and evidence for earlier human habitations has mounted.[6] Geologists, archaeologists, botanists, and paleontologists have added a great deal to discussions of possibilities of human migrations during the Pleistocene. To highlight the possibilities of intercontinental migrations during the Pleistocene, it is vital to study Pleistocene environments and human and mammalian migrations on a global scale. Studies of intercontinental mammalian migrations prove useful: where four-legged relations walked, so too then could two-legged.

Paleontologists have discussed numerous mammalian species that arose in the Western Hemisphere and migrated to the Eastern Hemisphere and vice versa.[7] Russell Graham stated that mammals periodically migrated across the landmass connecting the Western and Eastern Hemispheres from the Late Pliocene to the late Pleistocene.[8] The Pliocene (5.3–2.6 mya) was cooler than the Miocene (23–5.3 mya).[9] The cooling and drying of the global environment are thought to have contributed to the growth of grasslands during this time.

The growth of grasslands in both the Eastern and Western Hemispheres was a significant factor in the migration of grazing mammals and thus their predators. The fossil record informs us as to which of the four-legged clans' migrations created paths or led the way for others to follow between the Eastern and Western Hemispheres. Mammalian fossils provide evidence of many species both large and small that were drawn to make a journey from west to east and east to west across millions of years. In walking the paths created by our four-legged relations when we hike through forests and grasslands, we see the world through the eyes of another. Following animal trails through dense forests was a favorite pastime of my youth. I viewed the mountains and valleys where I grew up from the paths of deer, bears, and others. Marcel Proust, in the enduring quarrel with the baron de Charlus on the musical works by a composer named Vinteuil, expounded on the values of viewing the world through the thoughts and eyes of others as the only true path to discovery: "The only true voyage of discovery, the only fountain of Eternal Youth, would be not to visit strange lands but to possess other eyes, to behold the universe through the eyes of another, of a hundred others, to behold the hundred universes that each of them beholds, that each of them is."[10] The views espoused by Proust likely challenge many Western scholars who acknowledge only Western scientific views as valid.[11] Indigenous people were dehumanized by early

Western scholars, as they were often discussed as though they were a part of nature, not culture.[12] However, in such a vast and ecologically diverse world, Western scholars should realize that there are many ways of knowing, and a vast body of knowledge exists beyond Western thought.

Archaeologists in recent years have discussed differing views of human movement through the Western Hemisphere during the Pleistocene. Kurt Fladmark argued for ice-free traveling routes along the northern Pacific coast by boat.[13] Dennis Stanford and Bruce Bradley argued for a northern Atlantic crossing by ice from the Eastern Hemisphere to the Western Hemisphere. Their argument is based on what they see as similarities in technologies between Solutrean points found in the Eastern Hemisphere in an area now known as southern France and laurel-leaf stone tools found in present-day eastern North America.[14] Discussions of ancient migration routes are essential to furthering research in studies of human movements across time, as is knowledge held in oral traditions of Indigenous communities.

However, published research in which authors claim to have discovered the "earliest" or "first" human migrations or archaeological sites is misleading and often unsubstantiated as to their claims of earliest and or first human presence in a specific area. American archaeologists make unnecessary claims of first migrations to the Americas by "Europeans" or "Asians" and thus foreground discussions that work to disconnect contemporary Indigenous populations from their ancestral lands.[15] Discussing ancient people by applying modern continental names as identifiers creates false views of Indigenous people as Europeans or Asians during a time when such culturally distinct areas or countries did not exist. Such discussions continue to fuel misinformation and prejudice among the public and "to hold currency in essential areas of policy-making."[16] An alternative would be to discuss Pleistocene populations as Indigenous or as communities in specific directional quadrants of the Eastern or Western Hemisphere. To be able to understand the possibilities for Pleistocene migrations to or from the Western Hemisphere, it is paramount to view the evidence and time frames of human migrations on a global scale. In questioning such possibilities, I make no assumptions or predeterminations of time or place other than directional, as in Eastern or Western Hemisphere. I seek to

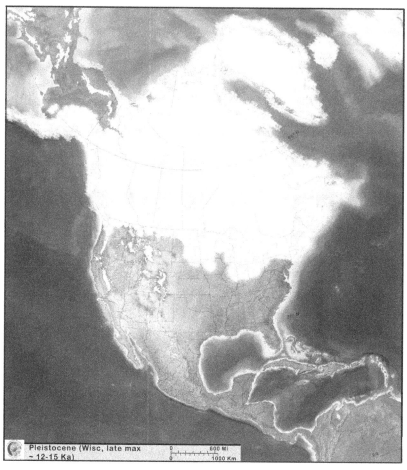

Map 1. North America, 15,000–12,000 years ago. Used with permission, Ron Blakey ©2013 Colorado Plateau Geosystems Inc.

gain an understanding of the human past and to discuss ancient human cultures on global and hemispheric scales. There are many identifiers that Indigenous people discuss in oral traditions, names for Indigenous people and places. Using a specific name that Indigenous people use to identify places and events would make much more sense than using contemporary European geopolitical identifiers to discuss Indigenous people in Indigenous lands. This would most likely be appropriate for regional or local areas. For a hemispheric area there are also names Indigenous people have used, such as Turtle Island.

Map 2. Western Hemisphere, 2 million years ago. Used with permission, Ron Blakey ©2013 Colorado Plateau Geosystems Inc.

Pleistocene Environments

During interglacial times, the Western Hemisphere was a viable landscape for the existence of humans and mammals. The environmental conditions of the continents were somewhat similar to those we see today during warm interglacial periods. Diverse populations of mammalian, avian, aquatic, and plant species covered the lands we know today as South and North America.[17] The species of plants and animals in the Americas today are very impoverished compared to the flora and fauna that were present during the Pleistocene. Mammals and humans during the Pleistocene had a greater diversity of subsistence options than they have today. As seen in map 2, the Western Hemisphere was at times almost ice-free, as it is today.

Pleistocene coastal areas where early humans and mammals left evidence of their presence on the land prior to glaciation and inundation are now submerged.[18] Understanding oxygen isotope stages (OIS) or marine isotope stages (MIS), cooler glacial and warmer interglacial stages deduced from deep sea core samples that provide oxygen isotope data, is central to understanding paleoclimates. Thus, re-creating Paleolithic landscapes and the possibilities for human and mammalian movements through time. Deep-sea cores provide evidence for Paleolithic coastlines and climates during the Quaternary (2.58 million years ago to the present). Sea-level records of glacial and interglacial periods are reflected in the oxygen isotope composition of foraminifera in deep-sea sediments.[19] Table 2 presents a general overview of glacial and interglacial events. However, during any OIS stage, there were shorter periods of smaller glacial and interglacial events, leading to periods of fluctuation of warmer and cooler cycles.

Oxygen isotope stages represent the relative amounts of ^{16}O and ^{18}O of foraminifera, which are single-celled planktonic animals that have a perforated chalky shell through which slender protrusions of protoplasm extend. They are mainly a marine animal; thick ocean-floor sediments are formed from their shells when they die. When they live in colder water, their shells precipitate more ^{18}O, reflecting a glacial period. A ^{16}O-enriched composition reflects an interglacial period.[20] Coastal landforms and the presence or absence of mammalian fossils provide evidence of sea-level history across time. Correlations of data from deep-sea cores, Paleolithic landscapes, and paleontology may provide a robust picture of sea levels across time.

In the Western Hemisphere in areas known today as North America, the Wisconsin glaciation occurred during cold periods from approximately 115,000 to 10,000 years ago, between the Sangamon interglaciation (a warm nonglacial period) and the current interglaciation.[21] Throughout the area known today as North America, the late Wisconsin glacial stage had several flow centers. Glaciation and deglaciation events, maximum and minimum, occurred at different times across the continents we know today as North and South America. During the height of the LGM, in the Western Hemisphere the maximum ice extent occurred approximately

TABLE 2. Glacial and interglacial events

Oxygen isotope stage (OIS)	Began (years before present)		
1	14,000	Warmer	Less glaciation
2	29,000	Colder	Glaciation
3	57,000	Warmer	Less glaciation
4	71,000	Colder	Glaciation
5	130,000	Warmer	Less glaciation
6	191,000	Colder	Glaciation
7	243,000	Warmer	Less glaciation

Source: Adapted from Muhs et al., "Quaternary Sea-Level History."

33,000–26,500 years ago.[22] Prior to 25,000 years ago, the area known today as Beringia was a viable migration route seasonally and between glacial events.[23] David Madsen has stated that the climate and environment of Beringia at no time during the Wisconsin glaciation reflected anything similar to modern climates in the area.[24] A warm period during the Wisconsin glaciation in Beringia was identified by P. M. Anderson and A. V. Lozhkin as the interstadial interval, which occurred between 35,000 and 33,000 years ago, when Beringia was more extensively forested.[25]

Intercontinental Mammalian Migrations

From fossil evidence, we know that mammals have traveled between the Eastern and Western Hemispheres for millions of years. This supports the use of the area known today as the Bering landmass across time as an intercontinental migration route available to all four-legged and two-legged species prior to the LGM. The order Perissodactyla is identified as odd-toed ungulates, a group that includes horses, rhinos, and tapirs. Perissodactyls evolved on the Mesozoic (252–66 million years ago) continent of Laurasia and diversified in the area we now know today as North America.[26]

Camels are even-toed ungulates within the genus *Camelus*. The northernmost-ranging camillid in the Western Hemisphere was recently discovered in the area known today as Ellesmere Island at 67° North; "dating indicated the camel existed 3.4 Ma ago."[27] The family Camelidae,

TABLE 3. Glacial/interglacial

	Beginning (years before present)	End (years before present)	Bering land area
Post LGM	19,000 cal BP	16,000 cal BP	Slower melting of ice sheets
Termination LGM	19,000 ± 250 cal BP	19,000 ± 250 cal BP	Sea level rapid sea rise 10–15 meters
LGM	22,000	19,000cal BP	Land base ice volume maximum
Late Wisconsin glaciation	24,000	14,000	Western North American entry routes blocked by ice
Middle Wisconsin glaciation	65,000	25,000	Bering land area open 45,000–75,000 years ago
Early Wisconsin glaciation	130,000	75,000	Bering land area open
Sangamon interglaciation	130,000	75,000	Bering land area open
Illinoisan glaciation	300,000	130,000	Bering land area open 180,000–132,000 years ago
Yarmouth interglaciation	750,000	400,000	
Kansan glaciation	900,000	750,000	Bering land area open
Favonian Stade interglacial	1.65 Ma	900,000	
Nebraskan glaciation	2 Ma	1.65 Ma	Open

Sources: Compiled from Yokoyama et al., "Timing of the Last Glacial Maximum," 713, 714; Ehlers and Gibbard, *Quaternary and Glacial Geology*.

which included camels and llamas, originated in the Western Hemisphere during the Eocene period and diversified during the early Miocene, giving rise to at least twenty genera. Protylopus, the earliest known camel ancestor, lived in the Western Hemisphere 50–40 million years ago.[28] Camels eventually migrated to the Eastern Hemisphere across the area known today as Beringia between 7.5 and 6.5 million years ago.[29] Camillid fossil bones have been found in many Pleistocene archaeological sites in the Western Hemisphere and have provided evidence of human use of camels possibly for food and other materials. Camels are grazers and may have been one of many species on the dinner menu of large predators such as saber-toothed cats.

Steven Wallace and Richard Hulbert have reported on the recently discovered basal species of saber-toothed cat, Megantereon, a new genus and species, *Rhizosmilodon fiteae*: "This very late Hemphillian record is the oldest for the tribe, thereby supporting a Western Hemisphere (North American) origin at least 5 million years ago (latest Miocene)."[30] Megantereon arose in the Western Hemisphere and migrated to the Eastern Hemisphere before 3.5 million years ago. Saber-toothed cat remains have been found in the fossil records of both the Western and Eastern Hemispheres. Horses also arose in the Western Hemisphere around 50 million years ago.[31] The earliest horse, Eohippus (genus *Hyracotherium*), is known from the early Eocene of present-day New Mexico.

The timing of mammalian migrations between the Western and Eastern Hemispheres is known for numerous species, yet knowledge of these events is constantly changing as new archaeological sites and paleontology sites are discovered. There is evidence of bison migrations between the Eastern and Western Hemispheres at different times during the Pleistocene. Based on their analysis of bison mitogenomes, D. Froese and colleagues have identified two bison migration events, one at 195,000–135,000 years ago and one at 45,000–21,000 years ago.[32] Migration events for bison coming from east to west include evidence for the *Bison* cf. *priscus*, the steppe bison from the Yukon, which has been dated to 130,000 years ago. The giant long-horned bison, *B. latifrons*, evolved from an earlier bison in the Great Plains. A *B. latifrons* was recently excavated from the Snowmass, Colorado, site and has been dated to 120,000 years ago. According to genetic research

Fig. 7. Saber-toothed cat. Courtesy of Mauricio Anton.

Fig. 8. Pleistocene horse. Courtesy of Mauricio Anton.

carried out by Froese and colleagues, the two morphologically distinct bison (*B. priscus* and *B. latifrons*) shared a common maternal ancestor 195,000–135,000 years ago. The authors also state that "this timing is coincident with an interval of reduced eustatic sea levels that would have enabled interchange" across the Bering land area.[33] They provide evidence for a second bison dispersal from the Eastern Hemisphere into the Western Hemisphere 42,000–21,000 years ago. Bison migrated into the Western Hemisphere most likely by grazing their way across what we know today as the Bering land area.

Mammoth fossils have been found in the paleontological record of the Western Hemisphere as early as 1.3–1.5 million years ago.[34] Mammoths first arose in the Eastern Hemisphere (Africa) and migrated throughout the Eastern and Western Hemispheres.[35] The Columbia mammoth, *Mammuthus columbi*, arose in the area we know today as North America from an earlier Eurasian species.[36]

Mammoths migrated from the Eastern Hemisphere from areas we know today as Asia to the Western Hemisphere land areas known today as North America by walking across the Bering land mass area. Mammoths are

Fig. 9. Pleistocene mammoth. Courtesy of Mauricio Anton.

known from the paleontological record of Idaho dating to 1.3–1.5 million years ago.[37] Fossil records provide evidence of biotic exchange between the Eastern and Western Hemispheres during the Pleistocene, when early hominids migrated throughout areas of the Eastern Hemisphere now known as Africa, Europe, and Asia. L. Marincovich Jr. and A. Y. Gladenkov in a study of marine bivalve taxa reported that exotic taxa signal the earliest date for the immersion of the Bering Strait at 4.8–5.5 million years ago.[38]

Imagine rhinoceroses grazing with mammoths and camels in Kansas or Nebraska; ancient fossil remains of early forms discussed as *Hyrachyus* have been found in the Western Hemisphere. For over 40 million years, rhinoceroses migrated between the Western and Eastern Hemispheres. Their fossil remains date to the middle Eocene (47.8–38 million years ago) in the Western Hemisphere. Rhinoceros fossils in Africa have been dated to the early Miocene (23.3–16.3 million years ago). According to Donald Prothero, Rhinocerotidae "were the largest mammals on the continent for 18 million years."[39] This very primitive rhinocerotoid is known from fossil records of the areas known today as Ellesmere Island, Europe, Africa, Jamaica, and Asia.[40] According to Prothero, rhinoceros likely migrated across both the Atlantic Western to Eastern Hemisphere connection and later the Pacific Beringia land area and became extinct in the Western Hemisphere at the end of the Miocene.[41] H. Wang and colleagues have reported on what they argue is a holotype of the new species from China: "Forstercooperiines are a group of primitive rhinocerotoids with a relatively large body size in the Eocene, and normally considered to be closely related to Giant Rhinos. Here we report a new forstercooperiine, Pappaceras meiomenus sp. nov, from the late Early Eocene Arshanto Formation, Erlian Basin, Nei Mongol, China. Pappaceras is the earliest known unequivocal rhinocerotoid, and the holotype of the new species."[42]

Rhinoceroses came in many shapes and sizes and were very successful in migrating across areas of the Northern Hemisphere. Though much smaller, early primates were also very successful travelers, adapting to different paleoenvironments across time. The PBS program *NOVA* posted a short video online titled "Meet Your Ancestors."[43] The *NOVA* video begins by showing a photo of a young European or European American male wearing face paint and a feather headdress. The video clips travel back in time through *Homo sapiens*, *H. habilis*, Neanderthal, *H. heidelbergensis*, australopithecine, and back to the earliest protoprimates, known from the badlands of Montana and Wyoming. According to the video, our earliest ancestors are from the Western Hemisphere from the area known today as North America. In fact, the earliest or basal protoprimate, *Purgatorius*, "has been documented in the Western Interior of North America during the first . . . few hundred thousand years of the Paleocene." The badlands of Montana, Wyoming, and Saskatchewan have provided numerous samples of Plesiadapiformes. S. G. Chester and colleagues argue that a new analysis of *Purgatorius* tarsal (ankle bone) data "supports *Purgatorius* as the most basal primate."[44] Around 65 million years ago the areas known today as North America and Asia were one landmass, called Laurasia, so there is a possibility that further evidence of Plesiadapiformes may found in Asia. J. I. Bloch and colleagues have stated that there are 120 species of Plesiadapiformes, and they are known from the Paleocene and Eocene of areas currently known as North America, Asia, Europe, and possibly Africa.[45] Though older or more basal forms may be identified in the future, it remains that one of "the oldest known placental mammals, the putative primate *Purgatorius* has been documented in the Western Interior of present-day North America."[46]

Distributional and fossil evidence suggests that protoprimates originated within areas currently known as North America.[47] Later Eocene

(56–33.9 million years ago) primate fossils came mainly from the Western Hemisphere (the areas we know today as Western North America and Western Europe), and some are also known from Asia, but they have yet to be found in present-day areas of Africa or South America. Richard Fox and Craig Scott have published on a newly discovered and the oldest member of *Purgatorius* from Saskatchewan in 2011: "Here we describe *Purgatorius coracis* n. sp. from the Ravenscrag Formation, at the Rav W-1 horizon, Medicine Hat Brick and Tile Quarry, southwestern Saskatchewan. This horizon occurs within C29R, making *P. coracis* the earliest known primate while strengthening the evidence that plesiadapiforms, and hence primates, originated and underwent their initial evolutionary diversification in North America."[48]

The earliest members of *Purgatorius ceratops* date from the late Cretaceous (145–66 million years ago) and early Paleocene (66–56 million years ago) and are found exclusively in present-day North America.[49]

Bloch and colleagues stated that "the origin of primates represents the first clear step in the divergence of humans from the rest of Mammalia, yet our understanding of this important period in evolutionary history remains limited."[50] Recruiting future researchers to any given field requires that they are introduced to a specific field of study. I hope to encourage students to consider studies and research in the paleontology of the Americas; it is a fascinating area of study that informs our worldview of the deep past. I always ask students in my classes on the human past where humans arose, and they correctly state Africa. I then ask them which mammals humans evolved from, and they correctly answer primates. I then ask them where primates or the basal primate arose, and they answer incorrectly, Africa. Students and faculty alike are shocked to learn that the currently oldest known most basal form of protoprimates is known from the fossil records of areas we know today as Montana, Wyoming, and Saskatchewan. For a very long time, educational materials regarding North America have erased important events linked to the continents of the Western Hemisphere. However, it is clear that on a global scale, there has always been two-way traffic of all our relations, all two-legged, four-legged, winged, finned, and rooted relations. There is substantial evidence for important evolutionary events leading to the rise of primates

Fig 10. *Purgatorius.* Courtesy of Doug Boyer.

taking place in the Western Hemisphere in the area we know today as North America.

Human interactions with extinct and extant mammalian species have provided a great deal of evidence supporting earlier dates of human presence in the Western Hemisphere. In American archaeological studies of first people, there has historically been a focused discussion of Indigenous people in the Western Hemisphere as big-game hunters. Though we do see some evidence of big-game hunting in the archaeological record, a lot is missing from these discussions. In a chapter included in a major publication, *The Quaternary Period in the United States* (2004), David Meltzer addressed problematic issues in past perspectives of the peopling of North America. Meltzer critiqued Paul Martin's 1967 "Clovis hunter overkill" hypothesis, pointing out the following issues, which remain to be resolved:

1. the absence of widespread archaeological evidence of human hunting of megafauna
2. the complete lack of any association of Clovis artifacts with animals other than mammoth and mastodon
3. uncertainty about when extinctions occurred

4. more than half the megafauna genera in question did not have ^{14}C dates, which indicates that they have survived into the Clovis time period
5. recent research of isotopic geochemistry on human bone and studies of Clovis site faunal collections shows that late Pleistocene people exploited a greater variety of plant and animal resources than were traditionally believed
6. applying new criteria to a renewed understanding or previously designated Clovis megafauna to kill sites leaves only fourteen of seventy-five North American sites with "secure and unambiguous evidence of human hunting"
7. there are no unequivocal kill sites for thirty-three of the thirty-five genera of large mammals that went extinct near the end of the Pleistocene[51]

Tyler Faith and Todd Surovell have added to the discussion, highlighting the small number of genera that vanished during Clovis times: "The majority (29 genera), including mastodons, saber-toothed cats, and giant ground sloths, became globally extinct at that time, whereas a handful (6 genera) vanished from North America while continuing to persist elsewhere."[52]

Our understanding of the distant human past can be completely changed through research, technology, and open minds. One example is the work of Ventura Perez, a physical archaeologist at the University of Massachusetts at Amherst. Perez's research on ancient bird bones changed the dates of early human presence on the island of Madagascar from 2,400 to 4,000 years ago to 10,500 years ago.[53] Perez and colleagues identified anthropogenic modification (cut marks) on directly dated elephant bird bones that predate all other archaeological evidence of a human presence on Madagascar by 6,000 years.[54]

Many Paths

It requires a lot of courage to produce your own, new ideas, to have new eyes on science, or even redefine old truths.

—Kistian Overskaug, "Homage to Marcel Proust"

Homo habilis is argued to have been present in the area we know today as Africa 2.1 million years ago, and *H. erectus* was in the area we know today as Asia as early as 1.9 million years ago.[55] As map 2 of the Western Hemisphere (North America) at 2 million years ago shows, it was a vast, open, unglaciated area and a viable landscape for the survival of humans and animals. I am not saying that *H. erectus* or archaic *H. sapiens* did or did not migrate to the Western Hemisphere. I am saying that any two-legged or four-legged mammal could have migrated east to west or west to east over what we know today as the Bering land area during the Pleistocene prior to the LGM 24,000 to 11,000 years ago. Since the environmental history shows that a viable landmass area was available for most of the last 100,000 years and for a greater part of the last 65 million years, one has to question why discussions have not traditionally mentioned the possibilities of earlier than LGM hominin migrations to the Western Hemisphere. The most likely answer to this is that an understanding of the past has been informed through political bias linked to historical processes of colonization.[56] That includes not only colonization of the land and the Indigenous people but also colonization of the minds of all people through public and general education.[57]

Based on the environmental evidence, it would not have been impossible for hominins to have migrated intercontinentally between the Eastern and Western Hemispheres as early as 130,000 years ago or even much earlier. In other words, environmental and ecological data support the possibility of earlier initial migrations. It was never "impossible" for humans to have arrived in the Western Hemisphere much earlier than 11,000–15,000 years ago. There are numerous archaeological sites that date to prior to the LGM. Research by L. Bourgeon, A. Burke, and T. Higham in 2017 on fossil collections from Blue Fish Caves in the Yukon Territory provides evidence for a human presence at 24,000 cal BP (19,650 ± 130 cal BP).[58] At the Monte Verde II site in southern Chile, Tom Dillehay has reported dates of 18,500–14,500 cal BP years and possibly human occupation dated to 33,000 years before present at Monte Verde I.[59] James Adovasio, J. Donahue, and R. Stuckenrath have carried out extensive research and testing on materials form the Meadowcroft Rockshelter site in Pennsylvania,

reporting that the earliest dates for human occupation may have occurred around 16,770 years ago.[60]

In American archaeology, there is a history of complacency and silence that supported the Clovis First hypothesis of initial migration after 12,000 years ago, allowing it to be accepted as fact in all areas of academic and general discourses.[61] The environmental record shows that the most challenging and difficult time to have tried to migrate across the area known today as the Bering land area was during the late Wisconsin 25,000 years ago and later during the LGM. As there are numerous archaeological sites in both North and South America that date prior to 25,000 years ago in the Western Hemisphere, we should then be open to considering earlier time frames for initial human migration into the Western Hemisphere.

Riddle Me This

Riddle me this
Rhinoceros said
My cousins in the West
have all gone dead

Horse stopped grazing
he could not believe
his ears.
Also, mine
he sighed
dropping a giant tear

Crow crooned to them
with his saddest lilt
giant raptors
are no more
after lands
of the West
became
the closing door

Boa hissed
in angry
tones.
So many relations
lost to dust
their bones
become
two-leggeds'
lust

Riddle me this
Elephant said
will anyone know
why they all
went dead
In a thousand years
maybe more
will the riddles
be known
of closing doors.

CHAPTER 4

Minds Wide Open

Changing Human History on a Global Scale

In seeking to understand the possibilities of Pleistocene archaeological sites and hominin migrations on a global scale, it is essential to ask where and when in the past there is evidence for the emergence of modern human behavior. Developing visual stories such as maps of human movements across time and space on a global scale informs the questions we ask and the stories we tell. Studies of Eastern Hemisphere archaeological sites provide a picture of human technologies and practices that are found in the archaeological record dating to the Pleistocene. Archaeological understandings of human technologies from the Pleistocene have traditionally been based on stone and bone tools, faunal remains, use of fire, exotic biota and materials, ornamentation such as the use of red ocher, mortuary practices, and cave art. Advancements in science now provide more precise dating of artifacts and bone. This has challenged our understanding of the human past and supported the rewriting of early human history on a global scale. An example would be the intricately carved sophisticated bone tools from Katanda in Zaire that date to approximately 90,000 years ago.[1] The range for early hominins has expanded in time and space as scientists reevaluate archaeological sites and collections and apply genetic studies to the identification of fragmented fossil remains.

Johannes Krause and his colleagues have reevaluated hominid remains from Okladnikov Cave and Teshik Tash in Uzbekistan and the Altai region of southern Siberia. They found that the fossil remains carried mtDNA of the Neanderthal type; this pushed the habitation range for Neanderthals 2,000 kilometers farther east.[2] Krause and colleagues have stressed that their research results raise the possibility that Neanderthals may have been

TABLE 4. Modern human behavior

Social reproduction	Groups composed of family units that includes males and females
Unit cooperation	Males and females cooperate in bringing up offspring
Group cooperation	Family units cooperate to obtain resources
Subsistence	Meat hunting, fishing, plant gathering
Omnivorous diet	Dependence on meat eating: more than 40 percent of energy comes from eating meat
Tools	Dependence on tools for survival
General community space home base	Spatial adaptation, home bases
Complex thinking	Planning and forethought, anticipation of future needs, symbolism and abstract thought
Communication	Articulated phonetic language
Locomotion	Committed terrestrial bipedalism

Source: Adapted from Dominguez-Rodrigo, *Stone Tools and Fossil Bones*.

present farther east in the areas we know today as Mongolia and China. The dates for the Neanderthal fossils (teeth) from Okladnikov Cave and Teshik Tash in Uzbekistan and the Altai region of southern Siberia are 37,750 ± 750 and 43,700 ± 1,100/1,300 cal BP.

This research and other similar projects expand our knowledge of early human movements during the Pleistocene in areas of the Eastern Hemisphere we now know as China, Mongolia, and Siberia. Archaeologists have recently provided evidence of sites on the island of Crete that imply open-water crossing by hominins prior to 100,000 years ago.[3] Our knowledge of early human technologies may be significantly expanded in the coming years as archaeologists further clarify the possibilities of early human migrations across land and open bodies of water. Table 4 summarizes the principal elements of human behavior compared to nonhuman primate behavior as determined by Manuel Dominguez-Rodrigo, a professor at and the codirector of the Institution for Human Evolution in Africa.

Dominguez-Rodrigo stated that his comparison is "based on analogical reasoning, which cannot be uncritically applied to the past."[4] To argue for a modern human presence at an archaeological site, evidence of one or more human traits must be present in the material record. Many of Dominguez-Rodrigo's traits for modern human behavior are, in fact, found in the material record of Pleistocene archaeological sites on a global scale. Anthropologists argue that modern human culture consists of learned and shared behaviors and beliefs.[5] A few examples of material remains that provide evidence of modern human behavior include but are not limited to artifacts such as stone and bone tools, hearths, wooden implements, remnants of structures, intentional burials, and rock art.

Pleistocene Sites of the Eastern Hemisphere

Our understanding of human migrations throughout the Eastern Hemisphere during the Pleistocene has been greatly expanded over the last twenty years. Numerous sites spanning the continents across 2 million years in some areas have been discussed in published literature. What we know of early human migrations on a global scale now includes evidence of migrations across open bodies of water during the Pleistocene.[6]

T. F. Strasser and his colleagues have reported on Pleistocene sites containing Paleolithic artifacts in the Plakias region of southwestern Crete that date to early in the late Pleistocene.[7] The presence of Paleolithic sites on Crete dating earlier than 100,000 years ago is evidence of *Homo sapiens* successfully making open-water crossings. Based on recent archaeological evidence from Madjedbebe, a rockshelter in northern Australia, archaeologists have stated that people were in Australia prior to 65,000 years ago.[8] On the web page of the Australian Museum, the pride of claims to Pleistocene ocean crossings to the continent by early humans is evident: "The settlement of Australia is the first unequivocal evidence of a major sea crossing and rates as one of the greatest achievements of early humans."[9]

Archaeological reports provide evidence that humans were utilizing some form of open-water transport much earlier than previously thought.[10] Therefore, we must remain open to the possibility that early humans may have been using open-water transport to gain access to areas of both the Eastern and Western Hemispheres. Nièda Guidon and B. Arnaud have discussed the possibilities of open-water crossings: "Everybody is willing to give humans the abilities necessary for voyaging across to Australia about 60,000 years ago. Why then would it be impossible for them to pass from island to island along the Aleutians, just as one example? We have no justification for converting the humans who peopled the Americas to a single state of being, where they could do nothing but follow the herds by a land route."[11]

Discussions of the human settlement of island areas support an argument that modern humans as early as 100,000 years ago had developed the knowledge and technological skills required to build watercraft.[12] The map of archaeological sites in the Eastern Hemisphere, with a small sample of sites across time and space, presents a picture of hominins in areas we know today as Africa at 2.1 million years ago and in Eurasia as early as 1.85–2.5 million years ago.

There are archaeological sites outside of Africa that date to over 1.8–2.0 million years ago that provide evidence of lithic technologies and use of fire. The evidence shows that modern humans and early hominins (humans and archaic groups more closely related to humans than chimpanzees) had the

TABLE 5. Open-water crossings during the Pleistocene

Flores, Southeast Asia, 800,000 years ago	Possible evidence for limited seafaring by *Homo erectus*[1]
Australia, New Guinea, 60,000–40,000 years ago	The oldest sites in Suhul are the earliest evidence for planning maritime voyaging, involving multiple sea crossings, some up to 90 km long[2]
Crete, Greece	*Homo sapiens* remains with poorly documented context; calcareous breccia in which bones were cemented dated by Pa/U to 51,000 ± 12,000 BP; colonization of Crete apparently required several short sea crossings
Bismarck Archipelago, Melanesia, 35,000 years ago	Shell middens, fishing, and seafaring at several sites dated from 15,000 to 35,000 years ago, with voyages up to 140 km long[3]

Sicily, Italy, 30,000 years ago	Aurignacian assemblage from Mediterranean Island possibly involving a sea crossing[4]
Ryukyu Islands, Japan, 32,000–15,000 years ago	Human skeletal remains found in Yamashita-cho and other caves on Okinawa and other islands; involved voyages of ca. 75–150 km[5]
Kozushima Island, Japan, 25,000–20,000 years ago	Upper Paleolithic peoples on Honshu crossing a 50 km wide channel to obtain obsidian[6]
Melos Island, Greece, 13,000 years ago	Travel across ca. 24 km of open water to obtain obsidian for mainland trade[7]
Admiralty Islands, Melanesia, 12,000 years ago	Settlement of Manus Island required 200 km voyage[8]
Cyprus, 10,000 years ago	Occupation of Aetokremnos site, Akrotiri Peninsula on southwest coast of Cyprus[9]
Channel Islands, California, 11,000–10,000 years ago	Boat and marine resource use by coastal Paleoindian groups, with sea crossings of at least 10 km[10]
Southeast Alaska and British Columbia, 10,000–9,000 years ago	Presence on islands indicates a maritime lifestyle and seafaring capabilities[11]

Sources: Adapted from Erlandson, "Anatomically Modern Humans," updated and expanded by the author. See also Ferentinos et al., "Early Seafaring Activity"; Kuzmin, "Obsidian"; Nakagawa et al., "Pleistocene Human Remains"; Sondaar, "Faunal Evolution"; Strasser et al., "Dating Palaeolithic Sites"; Tsutsumi, "The Dynamics of Obsidian Use."

1. Morwood et al., "Fission-Track Ages"; Sondaar et al., "The Human Colonization"; Bednarik, "The Initial Peopling."
2. Groube et al., "A 40,000-Year-Old Human Occupation Site"; Roberts, Jones, and Smith, "Thermoluminescence Dating"; Thorne et al., "Australia's Oldest Human Remains."
3. Allen and White, "The Lapita Homeland"; Fredericksen, Spriggs, and Ambrose, "Pamwak Rockshelter."
4. Chilardi et al., "Fontana Nuova di Ragusa"; Cherry, "The First Colonization."
5. Matsu'ura, "A Chronological Review."
6. Oda 1990.
7. Cherry, "The First Colonization."
8. Allen and Kershaw, "The Pleistocene–Holocene Transition."
9. Cherry, "The First Colonization."
10. Johnson et al. 2002; Oar, *The Prehistory*.
11. Davis 1989; Fedje and Christensen, "Modeling Paleoshorelines."

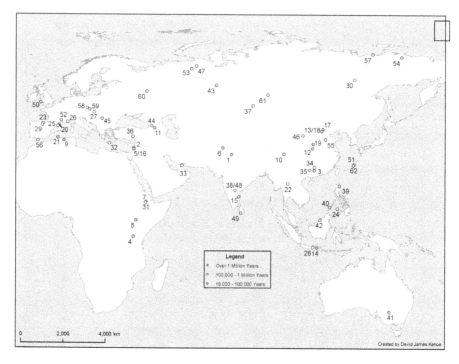

Map 3. Eastern Hemisphere Pleistocene sites. Cartography by David James Kehoe.

1. Masol
2. Yiron
3. Shangchen
4. Olduvai Gorge
5. Erq El–Ahmar
6. Riwat
7. Kadar
8. Koobi fora
9. Ain Hanech
10. Longuppo Cave
11. Dmanisi
12. Gongwangling
13. Goudi
14. Mojokerto
15. Attirampakkam
16. Ubeidiya
17. Majuangou III
18. Xiaochangliang
19. Xihoudu
20. Sima del Elefante
21. Barranco Leòn
22. Lampang
23. Gran Dolina
24. Mata Menge
25. Vallparadís
26. Terra Amata
27. Vertesszölös
28. Ngandong
29. Sima de los Huesos
30. Diring Yuriakh
31. Herto
32. Crete
33. Jebel Faya
34. Fuyan Cave
35. Liujiang
36. Skhul
37. Kara-Bom
38. Jwalapuram
39. Callao Cave
40. Tabon Cave
41. Lake Mungo
42. Niah Cave
43. Irtysh River
44. Bondi Cave
45. Peştera cu Oase
46. Shuidonggou
47. Mamontovaya Kurya
48. Laibin
49. Batadomba-lena
50. Paviland
51. Ryukyu Island
52. Chauvet Cave
53. Byzovaya
54. Berelekh
55. Zhoukoudian
56. Gorham's Cave
57. Yana rhs
58. Krems Wachtberg
59. Dolni Vestonice
60. Sungir 3
61. Pokrovka 2
62. Minatogawa

technology and knowledge to successfully travel great distances through diverse ecological zones as early as 1.8–2.0 million years ago.[13] Scholars have accepted that *Homo erectus* and archaic *H. sapiens* were present in the Eastern Hemisphere 2 million years ago. The search for early human sites across the Eastern Hemisphere has been ongoing for over a hundred years. In the Western Hemisphere, a few twentieth-century archaeologists have pursued research on early human sites. However, Pleistocene archaeology has only recently been considered as a possibility in the Western Hemisphere, and the field still faces overly aggressive denials of earlier sites.

Some Eastern Hemisphere archaeological sites contained thousands of artifacts and hundreds of animal fossils, yet others contained very few material remains. However, even one small fragment of bone or one artifact can entirely change our understanding of human evolution and migrations. Some of the sites on the following charts have been deemed controversial, and others are accepted. New technologies in dating allow scientists to reevaluate older sites and collections with more precise results; there are many sites on a global scale that would benefit from further testing and dating of collections and soils. By adding a site to the list of archaeological sites in the Eastern Hemisphere in the appendix, I am not arguing that they are not in need of further research. With all that we know regarding embedded racism and bias in anthropology and recent research that expands our knowledge of human evolution, we need to be open-minded regarding our understanding of the human past on a global scale not just in the Eastern Hemisphere but in the Western Hemisphere as well.

New Evidence of Ancient Human Migrations

For as long as scholars have studied human evolution, there have been competing hypotheses of initial human migrations out of the Eastern Hemisphere (Africa) and the evolution of modern humans. There are two main theories of modern human evolution: the out-of-Africa theory and the multiregional theory. Allan Wilson at the University of California at Berkeley and R. L. Cann argue for a mitochondrial African Eve, the mother of all modern humans. Wilson and Cann's Eve theory required the extinction of all archaic hominins outside of Africa and a complete replacement of hominins on a global scale by an exodus of Eve's descendants migrating out of Africa around 70,000 years ago.[14]

The following tenets have been proposed for the replacement hypothesis of modern human evolution:

1. a single origin of modern humans in Africa
2. an exodus out of Africa around 60,000 to 70,000 years ago
3. reproductive isolation from archaic *Homo sapiens*
4. the extinction of all other archaic *H. sapiens* on a global scale

This is a very simple explanation for the evolution of modern humans, far too simple, in fact. Nothing, it seems, is simple about human evolution. Genetic studies in the 1990s supported the replacement hypothesis.[15] As we now know, the reasoning of molecular scientists in this instance was flawed.[16] From recent DNA research, we now know that there was gene flow between *Homo sapiens*, Neanderthals, and a yet to be found archaic hominin.[17] New evidence from the Eastern Hemisphere, from the area known today as Asia, places modern humans outside of the area known today as Africa at a much earlier date. W. Liu and colleagues had dated forty-seven modern human teeth to between 80,000 and 120,000 years old.[18] The human teeth were found during excavations at Fuyan Cave in Daoxian, China. The dates for Fuyan Cave provide evidence supporting the presence of modern humans in the area we know today as Asia over 80,000 years ago and thus contradicts the out-of-Africa replacement theory of modern human evolution.

Some researchers who strongly supported the out-of-Africa hypothesis of modern human evolution also supported genetic analysis. However, while genetics can be very useful in informing us of the possibilities of human evolution, there are many lines of evidence to include in our considerations of the human past. Fossil remains, artifacts, soil studies, geology, demography, linguistics, paleobotany, dating sciences—all represent evidence that may provide support in clarifying migration patterns of early humans. In fact, genetics has recently provided the nasty little facts that have disproven the overly simplistic hypothesis of modern human evolution.

The multiregional hypothesis of human evolution included the tenet that hominins originated in Africa and then migrated to and evolved in many areas of the Eastern Hemisphere: "Multiregional evolution is a model to account for the pattern of human evolution in the Pleistocene. The underlying hypothesis is that a worldwide network of genetic exchanges, between evolving human populations that continually divide and reticulate provides a frame of population inter-connections that allows both species-wide evolutionary change and local distinctions and differentiation."[19]

Recent research has shown that archaic *Homo sapiens* and modern humans did, in fact, share genes. We now know that Neanderthals are among us, genetically speaking at least. Evidence from DNA has informed us that some modern humans carry Neanderthal genes.[20] Neanderthal sites in the Eastern Hemisphere range between areas we now know as Europe beginning around 400,000 years ago and Asia around 150,000 years ago and as far as southern Siberia.[21] Neanderthals had distinct morphological features, including a much larger cranial capacity and protruding brow ridges that defined them from other hominins, including modern humans. Scholars have discussed modern human morphology as evidence both for and against the flow of genetic materials between Neanderthal and anatomically modern humans.[22] Recent genetic research supports arguments that modern humans did interbreed with Neanderthals: "It is important to note that although we detect a signal compatible with gene flow from Neandertals into ancestors of present-day humans outside Africa, this does not show that other forms of gene flow did not occur. . . . For example, we detect gene flow from Neandertals into modern humans but no reciprocal gene flow from modern humans into Neandertals."[23]

Richard Green and his colleagues argued that Neanderthal were the closest evolutionary relatives to present-day humans and that Neanderthals did share genetic materials with modern *Homo sapiens*. *H. sapiens* and Neanderthal territories overlapped possibly as early as 300,000 years ago.[24] From the recent evidence of previously unknown hominins in present-day Georgia, we now know that Denisovans also shared genetic materials with *H. sapiens*. Denisovan Cave is in the area now known as southern Siberia along the present-day Russian border with Kazakhstan and Mongolia. Paleontologists, archaeologists, and geneticists have found evidence of Denisovans, Neanderthals, and *H. sapiens* in a three-room cave. Along with fragments of fossil remains, they found sophisticated stone tools and bone artifacts. Swedish geneticist Svante Pääbo of the Max Planck Institute for Evolutionary Anthropology has stated that "the multiple instances of gene flow now documented among hominin groups show that modern humans were part of what one could term a 'hominin metapopulation'—that is, a web of different hominin populations, including Neanderthals, Denisovans and other groups, who were linked by limited, but intermittent or even persistent, gene flow."[25]

The recent discovery of Denisovan fossil remains in a cave in Siberia and the subsequent successful extraction of ancient DNA have completely transformed what we know about the human past. Some modern humans carry genetic materials of Neanderthals; others Denisovans; and yet others may carry the DNA of an ancestral group known only from DNA. Pääbo discussed the findings regarding the Neanderthal and *Homo sapiens* genetic admixture. He summed it up very nicely:

> While most of the human gene pool shows origins in Africa, approximately 1–3% of the genomes of all people outside sub-Saharan Africa show Neanderthal ancestry (Prufer et al. 2014). In addition, up to 5% of the genomes of people in Oceania were contributed by another group, the Denisovans, distant relatives of the Neanderthals who have been identified based on a genome sequence from a bone found in southern Siberia (Meyer et al. 2012). The analysis of high-quality genomes of a Neanderthal, a Denisovan and present-day humans has yielded evidence for at least three additional instances of gene flow: one from Neanderthals into the ancestors of many present-day groups in Asia, one from Neanderthals into Denisovans, and one into Denisovans from an unknown hominin that diverged at least a million years ago from the human lineage. Also, gene flow from Denisovans to people in mainland Asia is likely to have occurred, and unpublished work shows that early modern humans mixed with Neanderthals when they arrived in Europe (Q. Fu, M. Hajdinjak, and S.P., unpublished observations). These results show that the modern human gene pool and the gene pools of Neanderthals, Denisovans and other extinct hominins were open systems that allowed the exchange of genes among the groups when they met. This may have had advantages for the ability of modern humans to adapt to new environments as they spread across Eurasia.[26]

The archaic hominin fossil record has always been sparse.[27] Modern human morphology is more gracile than that of archaic *Homo sapiens*, smaller and less pronounced brow ridges, a clear division between the left and right brow ridges, a smaller mandible, and differences in dental size and structure. There would possibly be a great deal more to inform our understanding of human evolution if further intermediary modern human fossils from 200,000 to 400,000 years ago are discovered. However, there are still many gaps in our knowledge about the evolution of modern humans and their ancestors within the genus *Homo*.[28]

Discussions on modern human morphology and evolution have been dominated by two lines of thought. Did modern human morphology emerge rapidly 200,000 years ago among earlier *Homo sapiens* in areas we now know as Africa, or did modern human morphology evolve gradually over the last 400,000 years?[29] The DNA analysis of contemporary humans and fossil remains of their ancient ancestors suggest that our lineage diverged from Denisovans and Neanderthals around 500,000 years ago.[30] Previously, paleontologists argued over whether modern humans evolved very rapidly or if the process was much longer and we had yet to find evidence of divergence in the fossil record. Jean-Jacques Hublin and his colleagues recently published a report on fossils from Jebel Irhoud, Morocco.[31] The Jebel Irhoud site has been known since 1961, when fossil remains were found at the site along with Mousterian tools, and the remains were assumed to be Neanderthal. The age for the site was previously estimated to be 40,000 years old.[32] In 1968 a subadult jaw was excavated from the site and dated to 160,000 years old.[33] Advances in dating technologies have shown that the site is at least twice as old as previously thought. Hublin and his colleagues reported dates from their recent excavations and from a previously excavated bone from the site and came up with a date of 350,000–280,000 years old.[34] Hublin and colleagues argue that the fossils from Jebel Irhoud align with "early or recent anatomically modern humans and a more primitive neurocranial and endocranial morphology in combination with an age of 315 ± 34 thousand years."[35] The new research by Hublin and colleagues supports a theory of a gradual evolution of modern humans across time as opposed to a rapid event at 200,000 years ago, providing evidence that the evolution of modern humans was a hemispheric-wide (Africa) event.

One ugly fact of research is that science often provides new data that slay older "set-in-stone" truths.

The archaeological record provides evidence of hominin dispersal between areas of the Eastern Hemisphere now known as Africa and into Asia as early as 2.4 million years ago. Access to island areas that may have required watercraft technologies is inferred prior to 100,000 years ago. Mammalian fossil records provide evidence that interglacial periods were windows of opportunity for intercontinental migrations across millions of years. Mammals and humans were in the northern areas of the Eastern Hemisphere 72,000 and possibly over 300,000 years ago. Early modern humans were very capable of traveling over great distances, adapting to diverse environments, and creating technologies to survive in harsh climates. There is no reason to assume that it would have been impossible for humans to travel between the Eastern and Western Hemispheres during the Pleistocene.

Regarding the Western Hemisphere, archaeologists in America were expected to not look for earlier than Clovis age sites, as they did not exist. Those archaeologists who published pre-Clovis dates (11,200 years BP) for archaeological sites were seen by their peers to be committing academic suicide. Though the status quo in American archaeology denied earlier than Clovis sites for decades and was supported by the silence of the majority, we now know they were wrong in many ways. It is essential to discuss the paleontological fossil record, paleoenvironmental data, the global history of human movements and technologies, oral traditions, paleoecology, and the history of racism and ongoing colonialism in North American archaeology. It is from these discussions that we decolonize our worldviews and create a space of decolonization of knowledge production and rewrite human history.

CHAPTER 5

Pleistocene Sites in North America

The Presence of the Past

The shards of the past insinuate themselves into what we see, and don't see, value, and don't value, subtly informing every gaze, every movement, every decision. The privileges we enjoy, or don't enjoy, the inequities we fail to notice, or rail against, are the individual legacies of our shared pasts. Thus, a proper acknowledgment of history is basic to an understanding of the present circumstances of our societies. If we are to create a better future, the past has to be embraced, in both its accomplishments and its failures.

—Claire Smith and Gary Jackson, "Decolonizing Indigenous Archaeology"

Archaeological sites are histories held in the land, places where ancestors left us stories about their lives. Many archaeological sites are discovered inadvertently during the construction of roads, buildings, dams, and pipelines. Other sites are discovered when academic archaeologists specifically search for sites in areas of high probability or are informed of a possible site within their area of interest. All archaeological sites must meet specific criteria to be accepted as legitimate sites.

Scientific criteria are described by James Adovasio and Jake Page as

1. Undeniable artifacts or osteological remains that are unmistakably human.
2. An indisputable context such as direct stratigraphic association with extinct Pleistocene faunal remains.
3. A valid and reliable control over chronology . . . which meant an undisturbed stratigraphy.[1]

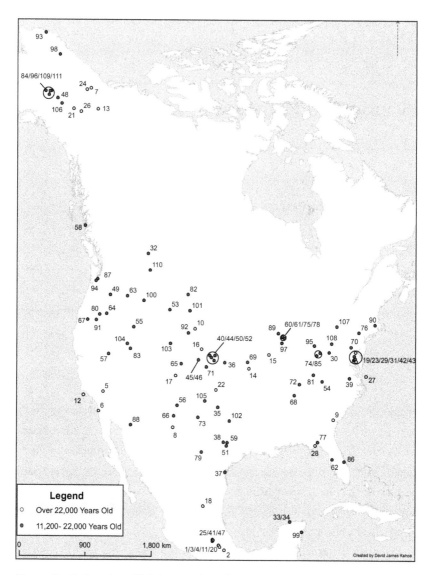

Map 4. North American Pleistocene sites. Cartography by David James Kehoe.

1. El Horno
2. Hueyatlaco
3. El Mirador
4. Texacaxco
5. Calico
6. Cerutti
7. Old Crow
8. Pendejo Cave

9. Topper
10. Schulz
11. Toluquilla
12. Santa Rosa Island Woolly Mammoth
13. Bonnet Plume
14. Miami Mastodon
15. Frye

16. New Nebraska
17. Villa Grove
18. Rancho La Ampola
19. Miles Point
20. Caulapan
21. Jack Wade Creek
22. Burnham
23. Oyster Cove

24. Bluefish Caves II
25. Tlapacoya
26. Dawson
27. Cinmar
28. Wakula Springs
29. Cators Cave
30. Meadowcroft
31. North Paw Paw Cove
32. Varsity Estates
33. El Tunel
34. El Toro
35. Cooperton
36. Lovewell II
37. Petronilla Creek
38. Gault
39. Cactus Hill
40. La Sena
41. Los Rayez La Paz
42. Crane Point
43. Parsons Island
44. Hamburger
45. Selby
46. Dutton
47. Santa Isabel Iztapan
48. Broken Mammoth Clovis
49. Rimrock Draw Rockshelter
50. Shaffert
51. Debra Friedkin
52. Jensen

53. False Cougar Cave
54. Saltville
55. Wilson Butte Cave
56. Lucy
57. Smith Creek Cave
58. Heiltsuk Nation Territory
59. Levi
60. Mud Lake
61. Fenske
62. Little Salt Spring
63. Coopers Ferry
64. Fort Rock Cave
65. Lamb Springs
66. Hermits Cave
67. McMinnville
68. Coats-Hines
69. Shriver
70. Shoop
71. Kanorado
72. Johnson
73. Lubbock Lake
74. Burning Tree
75. Hebior
76. Dutchess Quarry Cave
77. Page Ladson
78. Schafer
79. Bonfire Shelter
80. Paisley Caves
81. Cloudsplitter Rockshelter

82. Lindsay
83. Bonneville Estates
84. Swan Point
85. Eppley Rockshelter
86. Vero Beach
87. Manis
88. Lehner
89. Chesrow
90. Sands of the Blackstone
91. Cougar Mountain Cave II
92. Agate Basin
93. Nogabahara
94. Ayer Pond Orcas Island
95. Firelands Ground Sloth
96. Moose Creek
97. Perry Mastodon
98. Mesa
99. Eve of Naharon
100. Jaguar Cave
101. Mill Iron
102. Aubrey
103. Union Pacific Mammoth
104. Danger Cave
105. Miami
106. Healey Lake Village
107. Lamb
108. State Road Ripple
109. Walker Road
110. Whally Beach
111. Owl Ridge

The majority of sites I discuss in this chapter have met or exceeded the scientific criteria required for archaeological sites and have been published in peer-reviewed journals and books. Some sites have one of the above three criteria that may be questionable or problematic and would benefit from further excavations, dating, or testing. A few sites may have been excavated decades ago prior to the invention of carbon dating, and site dates are based on a geological time frame. Finally, some sites are in an initial stage of investigations, and others may no longer be viable for further testing due to flooding or destruction. However, many archaeologists, geologists, and their peers have dedicated thousands of hours to excavating, recording, dating, and writing up their understandings and interpretations of these sites; they are all worthy of mention and discussion. Recently, archaeological sites that were initially rejected as legitimate pre-Clovis sites (earlier than 11,200 years BP) by archaeological authorities have been reevaluated and are now accepted as legitimate pre-Clovis sites. Some previously denied pre-Clovis sites are now recognized as earlier sites of human habitation and listed on the United States National Register of Historic Places (NRHP).[2]

If an archaeologist finds that artifacts, dating, or stratigraphy is problematic at a given archaeological site, then a critique of the site may be published in a peer-reviewed journal. If the critique is deemed to have merit, the archaeologist who initially excavated and reported on the site may answer the critique or carry out further testing to clarify the problematic areas addressed in the critique. When critiques are based on an informed understanding of the site data and research, they offer further insights and lead to the publication of improved data. Further testing of archaeological sites may pinpoint problematic areas of testing and dating or refute any critiques that were published.

However, in the Western Hemisphere, Pleistocene sites that date to earlier than Clovis age sites or earlier than 11,200 years ago have often been denied as legitimate archaeological sites without an informed or published critique. For decades there has been a practice in American archaeology of dismissing all sites with older than Clovis dates. Often, a pre-Clovis site is denied by archaeologists who have never visited the site or studied the site artifacts. It may be that from published data, an archaeologist finds some aspect of the testing to be problematic. That can be enough to carry out further research and discussions that lead to retesting of a site or site area. Archaeologists have often disagreed on the legitimacy of dating, stratigraphy, and artifacts of sites.[3] However, the arguments against pre-Clovis sites are often unsubstantiated, as they are, for the most part, merely opinions and not published scientific critiques presenting evidence. Tom Dillehay has discussed the arguments against pre-Clovis sites as invented: "In their haste to defend the Clovis First model, they fantasized floods and other natural events to explain the association of the different cultural traits often found at non-Clovis sites, or, worse they invent mistakes in the analysis of those sites to give them cause for dismissing them. What this all boils down to is the politics of science and the replacement of one paradigm by another."[4]

No one book could include a full discussion of all pre-Clovis sites that have been recorded in North and South America; that discussion would fill numerous volumes. However, it is vital to begin to frame our understanding of Pleistocene archaeological sites in the Western Hemisphere on a hemispheric scale. Many Pleistocene sites in the Americas that date to earlier than 11,000–12,000 years ago contain stone or bone tools with remains of extinct megafauna. Other sites where the stratigraphy is questioned or deemed problematic are in areas where archaeological sites of the same age have been recorded. Thus, in looking at the bigger picture of Pleistocene sites in regional areas, we must remain mindful of how humans arrived in those areas. If there is one site in an area of a specific age, there are likely others as humans took time to cross the land and left evidence of their presence and travel across the land.

Clovis age sites containing distinctive bifacial fluted stone tools are argued to date between 11,200 and 10,800 ^{14}C BP and have been documented throughout North America.[5] A few Clovis tools have been found in Mexico and northern South America.[6] The Paleoindian Database of the Americas (PIDBA) is an online website of late Pleistocene and early Holocene sites. As of 2009 there have been "30,000 projectile points, attribute data on over 15,000 artifacts, and image data on over 6,000 points from across North America" listed in the database.[7] There are thousands of artifacts distributed across Canada, the United States, and Mexico that attest to human presence in the Western Hemisphere prior to 10,000 years before present. However, there has been a long-standing reluctance on the part of archaeologists to accept that humans were in the Western Hemisphere prior to the accepted time frames for Clovis technologies, or prior to 11,000–12,000 ^{14}C BP.[8] In their 2016 book, *Strangers in a New Land: What Archaeology Reveals about the First Americans*, James Adovasio and David Pedler list only six pre-Clovis sites as legitimate. Tom Dillehay discussed over forty sites as pre-Clovis in his book *The Settlement of the Americas*. James Dixon briefly discussed over ninety sites that have reported pre-Clovis dates in his book *Bones, Boats, and Bison*. It is not possible that there are thousands of Clovis archaeological sites and fluted point finds dating to between 10,800 and 11,200 ^{14}C BP and only six or even forty archaeological sites dating to earlier than 11,200 ^{14}C BP. There are thousands of archaeological sites dating between 6,000 and 11,000 years ago in the Western Hemisphere. It should not be a surprise, then, to any archaeologist that there are, very minimally, hundreds of sites dating to earlier than 11,000 years before present.

It is highly unlikely that there is only one pre-Clovis archaeological site in any given regional or local area. If there is one pre-Clovis archaeological site in a regional area, there may be numerous pre-Clovis sites in that area that have not yet been discovered or reported. I say there may be because early humans traveled across the land; there is no evidence of people flying around from place to place during the Pleistocene. People traveled on foot, they stopped and camped, and they spent time hunting, gathering, fishing, birthing, dying, and living on their way to and between areas. People did not fall out of a plane and land at a specific area where we know there is a Pleistocene archaeological site; they traveled to the area on foot. To listen to archaeologists in denial of Pleistocene sites with older than Clovis dates, you would be led to believe that people had magically arrived there without leaving any trace of their travels and then mysteriously disappeared.

Many Indigenous communities were written into extinction through archaeological stories of disappearing cultures and people.[9] Large communities of people do not just disappear; they may leave one location for numerous reasons, such as drought, conflict with neighboring groups, environmental change, and catastrophic events. Humans evolve and adapt cultural practices. In discussing Indigenous communities as having mysteriously disappeared, archaeologists erase them from the land and create a scenario of questionable ancestral links to contemporary Indigenous people.

When Indigenous communities are discussed as having disappeared, it seems they were magical. Indigenous people just disappeared from the landscape without a trace at the exact date the archaeologists conjured up for their story. Or, as my sister Carrie Wilson, a Quapaw tribal NAGPRA representative, told me, "It's like archaeologists think we were dropped off by little green men from a spaceship—like we just fell out of the sky right before the French arrived."[10] Quapaw towns such as Kappa, Tourima, and

Osotouy were well-established when Europeans first arrived, and Quapaw communities flourished along the western side of the Mississippi River in the area we now know as Arkansas. In 1998, when I was a student at the University of Arkansas at Fayetteville, the Quapaw tribe was denied NAGPRA cultural affiliation in their efforts to repatriate ancestral remains from their traditional territories. This changed due to a great deal of hard work and perseverance by Carrie Wilson and the Quapaw tribal elders. The repatriation work was supported in part through research that the Quapaw asked me to consider and that I carried out with the support of a Student Undergraduate Research Fellowship (SURF). Out of respect for the Quapaw, I will not further discuss this research here; the project was reported in my undergraduate honors research thesis. The Quapaw were successful in their NAGPRA claim and repatriated and reburied hundreds of their ancestors.

The archaeological sites I discuss in this chapter represent many ancestral communities that are directly related to contemporary Indigenous people. The connections between ancient and contemporary people will be further discussed in chapter 7. Disappearing Indian stories are prevalent in American archaeological and historical literature. It is important to remember, however, that even though Indigenous people are the world champions at hide-and-seek, people do not just disappear or become extinct. Indigenous people left their stories on the land, and they left hints of their travels to new areas. When people are facing danger and aggression from hostile groups or, as in the case of the European invasion of the Western Hemisphere, facing genocide, they often flee their traditional territories and hide to survive. In discussing the fallacies of unsupported archaeological stories of disappearing Indians and the Indigenous past, Vine Deloria Jr. and other Indigenous scholars and their like-minded peers have carried out the critical work of challenging archaeological conjecture embedded as truth in historical and educational literature.[11]

I have read hundreds of reports of pre-Clovis archaeological sites in present-day North and South America. For every Pleistocene archaeological site that has been reported, there are most likely many more that have not yet been discovered. As I stated earlier, though, some archaeologists insist that Indigenous people are recent arrivals on a global scale of time and thus had to have fallen out of the sky to cover almost a third of the global landmass in a short time span. I am betting that Indigenous people had other ways of traveling.

There are pre-Clovis archaeological sites in the middle of the Amazon and the middle of Nebraska. In every single place, people left their histories on the land. There are many more stretching across thousands of miles from the east to the west coast and from north to south. What I am implying is that for an Indigenous group to be in the Amazon or eastern Brazil over 22,000 or 50,000 years ago, they most likely had to have walked there and in doing so left their stories on the land in many areas on their way to, say, Pedra Furada in Brazil or Monte Verde in Chile, or to Meadowcroft Rockshelter in Pennsylvania or the Cerutti site near San Diego, California, which is dated to minimally 130,000 years ago. Archaeologists should not be surprised when they find a pre-Clovis site because they know that people did not fall out of the sky or arrive in spaceships. They know that if there is one site of a certain age in a specific area, there are likely other sites of the same age within the same region. Archaeologists are well aware of the time required to cross the land with a family during the Pleistocene while learning what to eat, how to avoid predators, and how to adjust to weather patterns and seasons. In the Western Hemisphere, there was a lot of land to cross between the far north of North America and the distant south of South America and from the east to the west of both North and South America. Discussions of early human sites would benefit from a more vibrant body of knowledge. Archaeologists could accomplish this by talking to the descendants of first people, a required starting point, as it is their history we are discussing and recording. Looking at the past through a hemispheric view of reported archaeological sites and realizing there had to be many sites between and beyond currently known locations of reported pre-Clovis sites would illuminate paths to understanding.

When I was formalizing my dissertation research plan in 2010, I began to create a list of published, peer-reviewed archaeological reports of Western Hemisphere sites older than the earliest dates for Clovis technologies (11,200 ^{14}C BP). To support knowledge production and to develop an informed understanding of the possibilities of the initial peopling of the Western Hemisphere, it is imperative to maintain a broad hemisphere-wide perspective and to consider multiple and varied models of human migration and adaptation.[12] Since I began to build the original database (the Indigenous Paleolithic Database of the Americas, https://tipdba.com/; see also the appendix), I have found publications on hundreds of Pleistocene archaeological sites in the Western Hemisphere (the Americas). Since 2010 at least six of the sites in the database have been reevaluated and republished: the Coats-Hines site in Tennessee, the Manis Mastodon site in Washington State, the Page-Ladson site in Florida, the Topper site in South Carolina, and Blue Fish Caves in the Yukon. The sites have been redated and reevaluated and present evidence that supports the initially reported pre-Clovis dates. Coats-Hines and the Manis site are now listed on the NRHP. There are forty-four North American pre-Clovis sites listed on the NRHP dating from 11,000 BC to 40,000 BC to in perpetuity, to possibly older than 40,000 BC.[13] All sites nominated and accepted to the National Park Service (NPS) listing as National Historic Landmark (NHL) or National Register of Historic Places (NRHP) status must meet strict archaeological criteria for site components, dating, stratigraphy, and recordation as defined by NPS archaeologists.

Keeping an Open Mind

It is essential for archaeologists to keep an open mind, as so often we are shown that we did not know what it was we thought we knew. Scholars such as Alan Bryan have made this clear: "Diffusion from America to Japan would be just as possible as diffusion in the opposite direction."[14] Jiri Chlachula has argued that Pleistocene research in the Americas is limited by a lack of experience and training in Paleolithic studies and stone-flaking techniques. Chlachula has highlighted the fact that there is an "absence of rigorous scientific data-supported arguments addressing the body of well-reported Pleistocene culture records."[15] Chlachula stated that in European archaeology, Pleistocene studies are carried out in a multidisciplinary framework of Quaternary (2.58–0.012 million years ago) research, unlike North American archaeology, which has not traditionally addressed the need for Quaternary geology and sciences in the study of early human sites. Many Pleistocene sites in the Western Hemisphere have unique features and components, and some share similar technologies, such as fishtail points or ivory tools. Most of the archaeological sites that I have reviewed fall between 11,200 and 44,000 years ago. I also reviewed the literature from earlier sites, such as the Cerutti Mastodon site (formally named the Hwy 54 Mastodon site), the Calico site in California, and Hueyatlaco-Valesqueo sites in central Mexico. The following brief discussions of sites are meant to provide readers with a view of the archaeology and the material record of pre-Clovis sites in North America. South American sites are discussed in chapter 6. I compiled these brief reports to provide a view of archaeological data and artifacts gathered during excavations and testing at pre-Clovis sites.

Archaeological site dates are listed as they are reported in published articles and books. Archaeological sites are listed as either radiocarbon years before present, denoted as ^{14}C BP, or thousands of years before present based on the dating from artifacts or organic materials or cal BP for calibrated dates. Recently, archaeologists have begun to correct radiocarbon dates to arrive at more precise dates. Carbon in the atmosphere has not remained the same across time. Thus, according to the changes in the amount of carbon in the atmosphere, radiocarbon dates have been calibrated and are denoted as calibrated years before present (cal BP).[16] According to R. W. Reimer and colleagues, "It is now well known that ^{14}C years do not directly equate to Calendar years (de Vries 1958; Stuiver and Suess 1966; Reimer et al. 2009) because atmospheric ^{14}C concentration varies through time due to changes in the production rate, caused by geomagnetic and solar modulation of the cosmic-ray flux, and the carbon cycle. Hence, a Calibration is required, which, to be accurate and precise, should ideally be based on an absolutely dated record that has carbon incorporated directly from the atmosphere at the time of formation."[17]

Table 6 compares ^{14}C BP to cal BP. However, I report dates as they are reported by the archaeologists who completed the research on the site, so some dates are listed as cal BP and some as ^{14}C BP.

Paleolithic Sites in North America

Y. V. Kuzmin and S. G. Keats have discussed their results of a study of Siberian Paleolithic population demography based on reported radiocarbon dates for archaeological sites. Their results were very informative and

TABLE 6. A Comparison of ^{14}C BP to cal BP

Radiocarbon age (^{14}C BP)	Mean calibrated age (cal BP)
12,000	13,810
13,000	15,540
14,000	16,990
15,000	18,220
16,000	19,330
17,000	20,500
18,000	21,790
19,000	22,880
20,000	24,060
21,000	25,350
22,000	26,200
23,000	27,330
24,000	28,010

Source: Adapted from Adovasio and Pedler, *Strangers in a New Land*.

presented an example of a bigger picture when viewing human populations across time and space: "We can now try to establish the overall patterns of population dynamics, i.e., changes through time in the intensity of human occupation. This can bring us toward an understanding of the relative size of human populations, although we are fully aware of the fact that it is a first degree of approximation in Paleolithic demography."[18]

To create a view of human populations in the Western Hemisphere during the Paleolithic requires a database of archaeological sites that includes evidence of artifacts, provenience, soil stratigraphy, and radiocarbon dates. The Indigenous Paleolithic Database of the Americas will be online in late 2020. As there have been hundreds of Pleistocene sites dated and reported in the academic literature, there is a distinct possibility for many students and researchers to carry out research in Pleistocene population demography of the Western Hemisphere.

The Paleolithic (Old Stone Age) is defined for the Eastern Hemisphere and begins when it is presumed the first stone tools were made millions of years ago, though the dates for the earliest stone tools are contested, as researchers have found stone tools that date to over 3 million years ago, before the appearance of hominins.[19] Clovis tool technology in the Western Hemisphere is argued to span approximately four hundred years, from 10,800 to 11,200 ^{14}C BP.[20] However, Clovis sites have been reported at early and later dates than 11,200–10,800 years ago. Thus, the time frames for Clovis technologies, though relatively short, are perhaps somewhat longer than four hundred years. Archaeologists have not discussed Pleistocene sites in the Americas as Paleolithic, yet there are many archaeological sites with stone tools that are as old as Paleolithic sites in the Eastern Hemisphere. A comparative study of Paleolithic tool technologies, both stone and bone, found at pre-Clovis sites in the Western Hemisphere would inform research in studies of what the "American Paleolithic" might look like and would create a body of data for further reference.[21] Eldon Yellowhorn (Piikani) has discussed the need for changes in terminologies used in archaeology to better fit with emerging world archaeology: "Terms such as prehistory and archaic were created to describe the material cultural assemblages in the Western hemisphere. However, as a global perspective becomes more common in archaeology, there is a need to adopt terms that have meaning for audiences around the world.... Replacing Paleoindian with Upper Paleolithic, archaic with Epipaleolithic, and Woodland with Neolithic achieves the object of placing aboriginal people on an equal basis with other early peoples elsewhere in the world."[22] Yellowhorn was referring specifically to "the development of chronological taxonomies for the Northern Plains."[23] However, he makes a valid point regarding the need to adopt terms that place Indigenous technologies and histories on a recognizable world scale. Hemispheric and regional studies of technologies across time and place in the Western Hemisphere are needed if we are to challenge outdated stereotypes embedded in naming and taxonomies within American archaeological discussion of the Indigenous past.

Archaeologists in North America created a time frame discussed as Paleoindian, as distinct from the Paleolithic of the so-called Old World. However, Indigenous people of the Western Hemisphere are not Indians. The identifier "Indian" is discussed as having been first used by Christopher Columbus, who mistakenly thought that he had reached eastern Asia.[24] While the term "Indian" is embedded in North and South American media, literature, law, education, politics, and Indigenous humor, some people are offended by the term. Dr. Michael Yellow Bird (Mandan, Hidatsa, and Arikara) prefers the term "Indigenous peoples" or "First Nations peoples" to either "American Indian" or "Native American." He has discussed both "American Indian" and "Native American" as "oppressive, counterfeit identities."[25] Archaeologists should be aware that the identifier of Paleo-Indian used to frame specific archaeological technologies and times is drawn from a mistake made by a perpetrator of genocide against Indigenous people. Thus, in using the term "Paleo-Indian," archaeologists have drawn from one mistake made by a European who got lost in 1492 and then built on it. This is not at all scientific or acceptable. Mi'kmaq scholar Donald Julien has reminded archaeologists and others that "Paleo" is not our name.[26] As the term "Paleolithic" (Old Stone Age) is used to identify and define human stone and bone tool technologies across time and space in the Eastern Hemisphere, I use it to define specific tool technologies in the Western Hemisphere, as Yellowhorn suggested the term "Paleolithic" is recognizable on a world scale. A specific time frame of tool technologies across time and space for the Western Hemisphere has yet to be defined through a study of material collections.

Archaeological data published to date have the potential to frame the Paleolithic of the Americas. There are stone and bone tool technologies that are well known from archaeological sites dated to the Late Paleolithic, such as Clovis and Western Stemmed technologies dating between 10,000 and 12,000 years ago. There are also archaeological sites with stone and bone tool technologies that date from 12,000 years ago to over 20,000 years ago. Defining the Indigenous Paleolithic through studies of material collections from archaeological sites in the Americas would be a significant endeavor and may provide a study area for numerous students, though it would be a formidable task. The published data on stone and bone tool technologies for sites across the Americas exist, and the Indigenous Paleolithic may, in the near future, be defined in part on technologies across time and space. This allows for the Western Hemisphere to be acknowledged on a global scale as having a Paleolithic and holding evidence of a human presence at earlier dates than previously accepted.

The following site reports represent a small selection of Paleolithic sites in North America. The brief discussions of pre-Clovis archaeological sites highlight the data and publications across the last ninety years. Not all archaeological site publications are listed, as some sites have been discussed and reviewed in numerous publications. I wanted to present a brief selection of sites and site data to allow the reader to understand what it is that archaeologists focus on in their work of collecting data and legitimizing (or not) archaeological sites. There are many other areas to consider, such as the number of samples from a site that were dated: some sites have over two hundred samples dated, while some have fewer than ten. Stratigraphy (the analysis of the order and position of layers of archaeological remains) of the site must be well recorded and artifacts recorded in situ. Geological studies are critical to the understanding of archaeological sites across time, and numerous archaeological site reports include an in-depth discussion of the geological formations of a site area. Geological soil profiles for some areas are well known, as are natural events that may have impacted soil stratigraphy of a site area.

Depending on the location and site preservation, archaeologists may discuss the paleobotany, plant phytoliths, vertebrate fossils, exotic materials, deposition of soils, mammalian dung fungus, coprolites, bone breakage patterns, stone flaking patterns, presence of hearths or fire-hardened clay, fire-cracked rock, burned animal bones, ocher or plant pigments, human and animal proteins in soils, DNA in soils, marine shell deposits, geological processes, and more.In these brief site reports, I include a discussion of the material record of a site, the dates of each site, and publications related to the site. Some of the sites have been nominated and listed on the NRHP. NRHP designations for archaeological sites provide a protected status, which is great but which also hampers possible future research and/or excavations at a site area.

A Sample of Paleolithic Sites in North America

Site	Dating	Location	Artifacts	Reference
Coats-Hines, NRHP	12,869 12,050 ± 60 ^{14}C BP	Williamson County, Tennessee	Thirty-four stone artifacts Mastodon remains	Deter-Wolf, Tune, and Broster 2011

References for all sites are listed in the appendix.

The Coats-Hines site, also known as the Coats-Hines-Litchy site, was initially denied as being a legitimate pre-Clovis site. The site was inadvertently discovered in 1977 during the construction of a golf course in Tennessee. After excavations in 2010 and reevaluation of the site, the Coats-Hines site was accepted as a legitimate pre-Clovis site in 2011 and earned a spot on the NRHP. In 2018, Jesse W. Tune and colleagues published a new report on the Coats-Hines-Litchy site, reassessing earlier site reports and once again denying the site as a legitimate pre-Clovis site. I also have discussed concerns regarding this site and previously stated that the site requires further testing, study, and definition as to possible site type. I discuss the Tune article in the critique section at the end of this mini site report.

Within Tennessee, Kentucky, Alabama, and the surrounding areas, there are many sites that have been dated to over 11,000 years before present. Therefore, that people were present in the area of Coats-Hines between 11,000 and 13,000 years ago is not surprising. The Coats-Hines archaeological site (40WM31 in the Tennessee Division of Archaeology database) is in northern Williamson County, Tennessee. Construction of the Crockett Springs Golf Course in 1977 disturbed the area, which contained mastodon A.[27] Tennessee Division of Archaeology archaeologists collected materials from the site in 1977 and 1994. The lithic artifacts from the 1994 excavation were found in direct association with fossil remains of mastodon B.[28] Microscopic examination of the thoric vertebra bones from mastodon B revealed distinctive linear V-shaped cut marks. In 1995 Emanuel Breitburg and John Broster argued that the cut marks were consistent with marks created by stone tools, signifying intentional butchering rather than natural processes or predator gnawing.[29]

Even though archaeologists found lithic artifacts with the mastodon remains at Coats-Hines, this does not in itself support the claim for a butchering site. M. D. Cannon and D. J. Meltzer argued: "Simple co-occurrences of artifacts and bone cannot be treated as if they reflected human consumption of animals."[30] The Coats-Hines site is problematic in that no unbroken or whole projectile points were found at this site. However, Breitburg et al. have argued that the recovered tools are "known from only Paleoindian kill or task-specific butchering sites."[31] As the tools are fragmentary and the collection small, it would be difficult to substantiate such a claim. The presence of bone modifications that include a V-shaped cut mark is not satisfactorily explained. How is the cut mark any different from the "many scratches evident on the specimens pictured in the reports"?[32] The excavators of the Coats-Hines site assume a mastodon butchering site, yet they do not discuss the possible human utilization of numerous other species found in the assemblage, such as turtles, which are known to have been present in other Pleistocene sites. I have not found any in-depth discussions of spiral fracturing of a mammoth or other bone from the Coats-Hines assemblage; this raises concerns about claims of butchering, as bone marrow and bone were valuable resources. The Coats-Hines site may offer opportunities for further research. However, the claims of this site being a mastodon butchering site based on the evidence presented are problematic and require further study and discussions of the assemblage. The Coats-Hines site did provide evidence of human technology on stone tools, but further evidence is required to clarify the site type. Though the site was discussed in 2011 by Aaron Deter-Wolf, Jesse W. Tune, and John B. Broster as a mammoth butchering site, one of the coauthors of the 2011 article, Jesse Tune, now argues in Tune and colleagues (2018) that Coats-Hines is a paleontological site and that the majority of the flakes and artifacts are geofacts. It will be interesting to see if archaeologists who carried out excavations at Coats-Hines prior to 2018 will respond in publications defending their earlier work or if they will agree with Tune and colleagues. The Coats-Hines site presents a very good example of the difficulty of assessing archaeological sites that have been recorded and excavated across many years, including both salvage and planned excavations, and assessing small collections of stone artifacts in fluvial settings.

There is no question as to the presence of humans in the areas between the Great Smoky Mountains in the east and the Mississippi River in the west prior to 11,000 years ago, as there have been numerous archaeological sites reported and published.

The Coats-Hines site is not the only pre-Clovis site in the region; there are many sites in the Southeast in all directions from the Coats-Hines site that date between 11,000 and 15,000 ^{14}C BP.

Site	Dating	Location	Artifacts	References
Topper	6,670 ± 70 54,700 ^{14}C BP	South Carolina	40,000 artifacts	Adovasio and Pedler 2016; Goodyear 2009

The Topper site is in South Carolina in Allendale County along the Savannah River. In 1986 Allan Goodyear identified an intact archaic occupation, and in 1998 he discovered an intact Clovis occupation below the archaic-level deposit.[33] The pre-Clovis level was as much as 2 meters (6 feet) below the Clovis level. Mike Waters and his colleagues from Texas A&M University carried out geological and archaeological studies of the site beginning in 1999. The Topper site's Clovis level was dated to 13,200 ^{14}C BP and the pre-Clovis level to as early as 54,700 ^{14}C BP.[34] Professional archaeologists were skeptical and did not accept the validity of the pre-Clovis level at the Topper site. However, Douglas Sian, a University of Tennessee graduate student, carried out testing on the pre-Clovis artifacts from the Topper site. In his 2015 doctoral dissertation, Sian argued that the pre-Clovis artifacts were human-made and that some artifacts showed signs of use through edge polish, striations, edge damage, and plant and animal residue on tools. He concluded that the pre-Clovis artifacts were found in situ.[35]

Site	Dating	Location	Artifacts	Reference
Little Salt Spring	13,450 ± 190 12,030 ± 200 ^{14}C BP	Florida	Wooden stake, bone, shell, and stone artifacts Hearths and fire-hardened clay Antler projectile point Wooden boomerang	Clausen et al. 1979

Little Salt Spring is an underwater site in southwestern Florida. The site was initially thought to be nothing more than a shallow pond until divers discovered the opening to a sinkhole at the base. Little Salt Spring is a shallow water-filled basin on top of a 60-meter-deep water-filled cavern. Think about the shape of a Champagne glass with a stem around 60 meters tall and a 12-meter-deep basin-shaped glass on top of the stem. The basin-shaped depression of the pond is approximately 12 meters deep, sloping 25 degrees from the land surface.[36] The site was used by Indigenous people approximately 12,000–9,000 years ago and from 6,800–5,200 years ago. During the later time period, the sinkhole was also used as a mortuary site. When people lived at or near the site 12,000 years ago, it was an abundant source of freshwater and food. Evidence suggests that many people used the site for thousands of years. The site was used by people when water levels were much lower and surface water may not have been as available in the general area.

Freshwater would have drawn numerous animals to the sinkhole, and once an animal went down 26 meters to a ledge to drink, it may not have been able to climb back up. The lower water level and the basin-shaped pond leading to the edge of the sinkhole acted as a natural trap.[37] Little Salt Spring site has provided numerous artifacts and evidence of human interaction with extinct vertebrates in the Southeast. The collapsed shell of an extinct species of giant land tortoise, *Geochelone crassiscutata*, was found impaled with a sharp wooden stake, and fire-hardened clay was found beneath the tortoise carapace, suggesting that it was killed and cooked in situ. Other extinct fauna directly associated with the land tortoise included two smaller members of the same species of tortoise, an extinct box turtle, an extinct ground sloth, extant species of freshwater turtle, diamondback rattlesnake, rabbit, land tortoise, and wood ibis. A short distance away from the remains of the giant land tortoise, portions of a young mammoth or mastodon and an extinct bison were found.[38] There are other sites in Florida as old as and older than Little Salt Spring, including Page-Ladson and Warm Mineral Springs. Artifact and fossil preservation at some sites in Florida have shown to be excellent regarding organic artifacts made of wood and bone; this is due to the anaerobic environments of some submerged wet site areas.

Site	Dating	Location	Artifacts	Reference
Page-Ladson	14,550 cal BP	Florida	Stone tools Projectile points Mastodon bone	Halligan et al. 2016

Page-Ladson is one of a growing number of sites that have been discussed as problematic and not accepted as evidence of earlier than Clovis time frames for a human presence in North America. The site recently benefited from further excavations and testing, which supported the original dates. Page-Ladson is a submerged site 9 meters deep within a midchannel sinkhole along the Aucilla River in Florida.[39] The site was initially investigated between 1983 and 1997. Artifacts recovered during the initial excavations included eight stone tools and associated mastodon remains with butchering marks on the bone. The initial findings and age of the site were challenged, and it was discussed as problematic and not accepted as a legitimate pre-Clovis site. J. J. Halligan and colleagues reinvestigated the site and confirmed the original findings and date in their 2016 paper. They reported recovering six stone artifacts from undisturbed sediments. The deposits that held the artifacts also contained the remains of extinct mammals, including camelid, bison, and mastodon. In reexamining a mastodon tusk from the original excavations, they confirmed earlier reports that marks on the tusk were made by humans during the extraction of the tusk from the alveolus. Halligan stated that "the record of human habitation in the Americas between 14,000–15,000 Cal ^{14}C BP is sparse but real."[40] I agree that the record of human habitation is real, but I do not agree that it is sparse. There are hundreds of Pleistocene sites in the Americas older than 15,000 ^{14}C BP, or 13,000–12,000 radiocarbon years ago; many are published in academic peer-reviewed papers.

Site	Dating	Location	Artifacts	Reference
Manis Mastodon	13,860– 13,763 cal BP	Washington State	Bone point in mastodon rib Flaked cobble spall	Waters et al. 2011

The Manis Mastodon site was discovered accidentally between 1977 and 1979 by a landowner excavating a pond. The remains of a single mastodon (*Mammut americanum*), including two 3-meter-long tusks, were recovered ex situ from screenings of the back dirt and in situ from the pond area.[41] The Manis Mastodon site was not initially accepted as a legitimate pre-Clovis site. However, based on new research by M. R. Waters and colleagues, the Manis site has recently been accepted as a valid pre-Clovis site. The primary artifact recovered was an osseous bone point fragment embedded in a mastodon rib. A flaked stone cobble spall was also recovered.[42] According to Waters and colleagues, DNA analysis and radiocarbon dating were carried out on mastodon bone from the site. The mastodon bone was spirally fractured and showed signs of butchering, including flakes having been removed from a long bone fragment. A high-resolution CT scan was used to document that the 3.5-centimeter-long object was embedded 2.5 centimeters into the mastodon rib and was shaped to a point.

Many places where Indigenous people have left their stories on the land tell us about their interactions with proboscideans (mammoths and mastodons) and another megafauna. Some sites, such as the Manis site, provide direct evidence of hunting; other sites provide evidence of humans collecting the dense bones of deceased proboscideans, likely for making tools. The bone tip point found embedded in the Manis mastodon shows that humans were using mastodon bone from previous kills or finds to make points for hunting megafauna. The Manis mastodon was not excavated in situ. It was accidentally disturbed by a backhoe, and later in-situ mastodon bone was recorded and excavated. However, thanks to a well-documented record of the find, curation of the mastodon remains, and applications of modern scientific research, Waters and colleagues were able to support the legitimacy of the site without stratigraphy and with only one artifact. They stated that the site dates to 800 years before known dates for Clovis technologies.

Paisley Caves is yet another site that was rejected as a legitimate pre-Clovis site and has now been supported by more recent excavations and testing. The site was initially investigated by Luther Cressman, founder and chair of the University of Oregon Department of Anthropology from 1938 to 1940.[43] Cressman recorded artifacts associated with the remains of

Site	Dating	Location	Artifacts	Reference
Paisley Five Mile Point Caves	Cave 5, 14,850–14,110 ^{14}C BP Cave 2, 13,560–13,380 ^{14}C BP	Oregon	Coprolites Human DNA 3,800 lithic artifacts, including Western Stemmed points Hearths	Adovasio and Pedler 2016

extinct fauna, camel, horse, and bison beneath layers of pumice, volcanic material from an eruption of Mount Mazama.[44] Cressman's interpretation of the site was rejected, and the site was ignored by archaeologists until 2002, when Dennis Jenkins at the University of Oregon took an interest in the site. As with many archaeological site areas in both North and South America, Paisley Caves is not just one site in one cave but is a series of caves and sites. The oldest evidence of a human presence came from Caves 2 and 5, where the stratigraphy was documented with over 180 radiocarbon dates.[45] Dennis Jenkins and colleagues reported that chronological control is documented through 203 radiocarbon dates dating from 16,000 cal BP to historical times.[46] One of the oldest dates is recorded from butcher cut mountain sheep bone dating to 12,380 ± 70 ^{14}C BP calibrated to 14,248 (14,591) 14,933 cal BP.[47] Paisley Caves contained stone tools, extinct faunal remains, and human coprolites, supporting an earlier than Clovis human presence in the Western Hemisphere. The best-documented feature was recorded in Cave 5 and has been described as a bone pit that included bones of camel and horse, butchered bones of mountain sheep, human coprolites, human hair, and debitage flakes. This reinvestigated archaeological site is an excellent example of what can be done when adequate funding and support are received for research on older than Clovis sites. Dennis Jenkins discussed receiving the support from at least thirty-six major institutional funders, private donors, and professional services for the research and excavations at Paisley Five Mile Point Caves.[48]

Regarding the evidence of human DNA from coprolites at Paisley Caves, A. Sistiaga and colleagues argue that the coprolites are from an herbivore and are not human.[49] However, Jenkins and his colleagues found stone tools within the same site area and are standing by their evidence and dates for the Paisley Caves.

Site	Dating	Location	Artifacts	Reference
Meadowcroft Rockshelter	21,980–17,250 ^{14}C BP Hearths, 26,210–21,090 ^{14}C BP Possible cultural origin	Pennsylvania	20,000 artifacts 2 million animal and plant remains 150 fire pits 30 storage pits 33 fire floors	Adovasio and Pedler 2016

Meadowcroft Rockshelter was located in 1955 by the landowner, Albert Miller, who protected the site area and brought it to the attention of James Adovasio at the University of Pittsburgh in the 1970s.[50] Adovasio led a multidisciplinary project and field school at the site from 1973 to 1978 and in 1994 and 1995. Meadowcroft Rockshelter is one of many sites that has produced evidence of long-term human occupation of an area through the recordation of numerous cultural levels across time. Adovasio and Pedler reported ten cultural levels in excavations that extended to almost 5 meters in depth. The cultural material found below the Clovis level is discussed, as the Miller complex has been bracketed by radiocarbon dates above and below the level 15,160–11,250 ^{14}C BP to 17,580–13,060 ^{14}C BP, respectively. Archaeologists often name archaeological sites and tool assemblages after the landowners who own the land on which the sites are located. Albert Miller's family owned the property that Meadowcroft Rockshelter is located on. Miller protected the site and informed James Adovasio about it. Miller lanceolate projectile points are bifacial but not fluted. Miller points have been found in other areas off the Cross Creek drainage, not far from the Meadowcroft Rockshelter. The Miller stratum contained a distinctive Miller bifacial point, which was found in situ on the living floor of stratum IIA. Similar points discussed as Miller specimens have been found at nearby sites at the Krajacic site and the Mugnai Farm, both of which are located in the Cross Creek drainage, not far from the

Meadowcroft Rockshelter site, but they were not recovered from a directly dated stratigraphic context. Possible cultural materials were found in older deposits at Meadowcroft, including hearths dating to 21,980–17,250 ^{14}C BP and 18,360–13,220 ^{14}C BP. The Miller level is underlain by possible cultural material that dated to 26,210–24,140 ^{14}C BP and 25,040–21,090 ^{14}C BP. Adovasio and Pedler discuss this oldest possible cultural level as very tentative.[51] People were living at Meadowcroft Rockshelter at minimally 15,000 ^{14}C BP and possibly much earlier.

In 1987 *American Antiquity* published a critique by Kenneth Tankersley, C. A. Munson, and D. Smith regarding problematic radiocarbon dating at Meadowcroft Rockshelter due to the possible presence of coal.[52] In 1992 Tankersley and Munson once again reiterated their concerns in a published critique of the Meadowcroft radiocarbon dates based on the possibility that the dates might be contaminated by anthropogenic-derived coal or coal by-products.[53] Adovasio, J. Donahue, and R. Stuckenrath responded to the critiques and put the matter to rest in an article titled "Never Say Never Again: Some Thoughts on Could Haves and Might Have Beens," published in *American Antiquity*. Adovasio and his collogues carried out further testing related to concerns raised in critiques of the dates for the Meadowcroft Rockshelter site. They successfully answered all critiques regarding concerns about the possible contamination: "There is no evidence whatsoever for particulate or nonparticulate contamination of any part of the Meadowcroft Rockshelter radiocarbon chronology."[54]

Site	Dating	Location	Artifacts	References
Cactus Hill	21,930–18,490 ^{14}C BP 18,530–18,080 ^{14}C BP 21,930–18,490 ^{14}C BP	Virginia	5,000 lithic flakes 600 artifacts Hearth	Adovasio and Pedler 2016; McAvoy and McAvoy 1997

The Cactus Hill site is in Virginia along the Nottaway River. The earliest cultural deposits at the Cactus Hill site were discovered beneath an intact Clovis horizon. The site was located in an exposed wall of an open pit sand mine in the 1980s and tested in 1988 by Joseph McAvoy of the

Nottaway River Survey. Joseph and Lynn McAvoy excavated the Cactus Hill site, collecting over 500,000 stone flakes and over 600 diagnostic artifacts, as well as finding stone tools below a Clovis level. However, in an interview they shared the following sentiments about their experience: "The McAvoys have already invested more time and money defending their dates and conducting new tests than they had ever imagined, says Joe McAvoy. And although he thinks that the antiquity of the site has been established, the effort has been stressful. If he were to do it all over again, he sometimes thinks, he wouldn't dig so deep."[55]

Archaeological excavations were carried out between 1993 and 2002. The excavation was led by Joseph McAvoy and Michael Johnson of the Fairfax County Parks Authority and the Archaeological Survey of Virginia. The dates for the earliest artifacts at Cactus Hill are similar to those at Meadowcroft Rockshelter, which is approximately 450 kilometers northwest of Cactus Hill.[56] The site was not accepted by prominent archaeologists as a legitimate pre-Clovis site and was ignored in discussions of early human sites in North America. Critics of the site mentioned the small number of artifacts in the lowest pre-Clovis level as problematic. However, as we see from the data of the Manis site, which was recently legitimized based on one artifact, a smaller number of artifacts is not a reasonable critique from which to deny the legitimacy of a site.

Multiple lines of evidence have supported the radiocarbon dating of the pre-Clovis level at Cactus Hill. The Clovis and pre-Clovis cultural levels at the Cactus Hill site were separated by 7–15 centimeters of sand.[57] To test for the chronological integrity of the site, J. K. Feathers and colleagues used optically stimulated luminescence (OSL) to date the sand grains of the pre-Clovis level. OSL is used to date the last time quartz sediments were exposed to light and may potentially identify the mixing of sand grains of different depositional ages within a cultural level. OSL can potentially inform archaeologists if there has been postdepositional bioturbation or mixing of soil and sand between cultural levels. Artifacts found within a cultural level are most likely the same age as the soils they rest in unless there is evidence of bioturbation of the soils. Studies of the stratigraphy of a site are paramount to understanding possible bioturbation or postdepositional events that may have facilitated the downward displacement of artifacts. The O S L testing of the cultural-level sands at the Cactus Hill site supported the radiocarbon dates and the stratigraphic integrity of the cultural levels: "At Cactus Hill, the agreement between several lines of evidence—from archeology, sedimentology, pedology, botany, radiocarbon, and luminescence—is critical in not only understanding the formation of the site but in evaluating the merit of each piece of evidence on its own."[58]

The Cactus Hill site was recently listed by Adovasio and Pedler as a legitimate pre-Clovis site in their 2016 publication, *Strangers in a New Land.*

Site	Dating	Location	Artifacts	Reference
Hebior Mammoth	15,170–14,670 ^{14}C BP 15,040–14,270 ^{14}C BP AMS	Wisconsin	Butchered mammoth remains Lithic artifacts	Adovasio and Pedler 2016
Schaefer Mammoth	15,150–14,630 ^{14}C BP 14,630–14,030 ^{14}C BP	Wisconsin	Butchered mammoth remains 2 lithic artifacts	Adovasio and Pedler 2016

The Hebior and Schaefer Mammoth sites are located to the west of southern Lake Michigan and were discovered accidentally through work on water diversion projects in southern Wisconsin. The Schaefer site was initially discovered in 1964 and was investigated in 1992–93 by Daniel Joyce, an archaeologist with the Kenosha Public Museum, and the Great Lakes Archaeological Research Center.[59] Archaeological investigations at the Hebior site were carried out by the Great Lakes Archaeological Research Center and began in 1994.[60] At the Schaefer site, the mammoth bones exhibited multiple cuts and wedge marks and had been sorted into piles. This is consistent with human action.[61] Both the Hebior and Schaefer sites have benefited from a regional and multidisciplinary research interest with published papers by numerous authors on human-induced bone taphonomy, paleoenvironment, glacial chronology and lithostratigraphy, water level fluctuations in the Lake Michigan basin, paleoenvironments, and archaeology. There are two other mammoth butchering sites nearby, the Mud Lake (47KN246) and Fenske (47KN240) sites, which are just south and southeast of the Hebior and Schaefer sites. From the research, it is clear that in the area that is known today as southern Wisconsin, at the Schaefer and Hebior sites humans were hunting and butchering mammoths after glaciers had retreated to the north. The time frames of these two sites are consistent with being earlier than Clovis time frames.

Site	Dating	Location	Artifacts	References
La Sena Site	18,440 ± 90 ^{14}C BP	Nebraska	Spirally fractured mammoth limb bone	Holen 2006; Holen and May 2002

The La Sena Mammoth site is in southwestern Nebraska. Bureau of Reclamation archaeologists Bob Blasing and Brad Coutant discovered the site in 1987 during a routine shoreline survey.[62] The La Sena site has benefited from an interdisciplinary multiyear study directed by Dr. Steve Holen. Excavation at La Sena took place over eleven years, from 1987 to 1998. The analysis of the La Sena site was supported by archaeological excavations, dating, geoarchaeological studies, microfaunal and paleo-ecological analyses, a paleoenvironmental reconstruction based on opal phytolith analysis, and a study of fossil land snails as indicators of paleo-climate. On a regional scale, there are several sites in the area with similar dates and artifacts, as well as megafauna remains. Pleistocene sites close to La Sena include but are not limited to Lovewell I in Kansas, dated to 18,250 ± 90 ^{14}C BP; Lovewell II in Kansas, dated to 19,530 ^{14}C BP; and the Dutton site in Colorado, dated to 16,330 ± 320 ^{14}C BP. The artifacts at the La Sena site include spirally fractured limb bones of an adult Columbian mammoth (*Mammuthus columbi*). The spiral fracture of the limb bone indicated that the bones were broken relatively recently after the animal's death. The femur segments "exhibited impact points," an indication that "humans were responsible for the bone breakage."[63]

Steve Holen has argued that the presence of spirally fractured mammoth limb bones, dynamic loading points, and bone flaking from in situ deposits at both La Sena and Lovewell sites could be representative of human modification of mammoth bone.[64] proboscidian bone is known to have been used by humans as a resource for tools and bone marrow and is known from the archaeological record of the middle Pleistocene of the Eastern Hemisphere.[65] In North America, pre-11,200 ^{14}C BP communities utilized proboscidean bone to manufacture bifacial tools, shafts, projectile points, and shaft wrenches.[66] The procurement of bone for tool manufacture would require the reduction of mammoth limb bones into large flakes or cores, which would require striking with a hammerstone.[67] The taphonomic studies from La Sena were compared with "naturally induced fracture patterns on modern elephant bone."[68] Holen argued that both carnivore gnawing and trampling could be eliminated as factors in mammoth limb bone fracturing and flaking at La Sena and Lovewell based on this evidence.

Gary Haynes and Katherine Krasinski have stated that arguments for human breakage of proboscidian bone have not been perfectly supported. They further argued that modified mammoth remains in the Americas "do not indicate a Pre-Clovis human presence." The authors offer no citation or reference to support some of their statements, such as "crania may be picked up by curious elephants and broken" and "a single elephant's foot placed upon a bone may create one mark." In critiquing the La Sena and Lovewell sites' fossil mammoth bone collection, Haynes and Krasinski state that the mammoth remains do not have visible marks from anvils or hammerstones, yet hammerstone and impact marks have been recorded, discussed, and photographed on mammoth limb bone from both sites.[69]

There has not been an overall comparative analysis or an overall report on all mammoth bone breakage at mammoth fossil sites in the Americas. However, Haynes and Krasinski state that "most if not all the modifications on North American Pre-Clovis mammoth bones can be more parsimoniously attributed to non-human taphonomic processes," although they provide no citation for this information.[70] To back up this statement with scientific data would require an extensive study of all North American sites that contain fractured mammoth bone. However, as far as I know, as of the time of writing this book, no such study has been published. Therefore, I would argue that Haynes and Kransinski's argument failed to support their critique of the La Sena site.

The Debra L. Friedkin site in central Texas, also known as the Buttermilk Creek Complex (BCC), is dated to 13,200–15,500 years ago. The Buttermilk

Site	Dating	Location	Artifacts	Reference
Debra L. Friedkin	15,500– 13,200 BP OSL	Texas	15,528 lithic artifacts 56 tools	Jennings and Waters 2014

Creek site area is comprised of two sites, the Debra L. Friedkin site and the Gault site; the BCC cultural levels overlie a Clovis cultural horizon.[71] The two sites are separated by only 250 meters and may represent one larger site area. Site investigation and excavations began at the Debra L. Friedkin site in 2006 and continued to 2011. During the 2007–9 field seasons, 15,528 lithic artifacts were recovered. Thirty-six were described as stone tools, and the remainder were described as macro- and microdebitage, fragments, shatter, and flakes. T. A. Jennings and M. R. Waters argue that the BCC tool assemblage differs from Clovis tools but that Clovis lithic assemblage "could be from Friedkin BCC lithic technology."[72]

Juliet Morrow and colleagues wrote a critique of the BCC in 2012 that was published in the *Journal of Archaeological Science*.[73] Jennings and Waters stated that the concerns regarding site context and dating had been addressed in detail by Driese and colleagues, Jennings, Keen, and Lindquist and colleagues.[74] Jennings and Waters answered the second part of the critique regarding the stylistic interpretation of the artifacts in their 2014 paper published in *American Antiquity*.[75]

Site	Dating	Location	Artifacts	Reference
Cerutti Mastodon	130,700 ± 9.4 (MIS 5)	California	Spirally fractured mastodon bone Hammer-stones	Holen et al. 2017

The Cerutti Mastodon site in Southern California, previously known as the Hwy 54 site, is just a few miles northeast of San Diego. The site and over one hundred other sites within a short area of the State Hwy 54 route were accidentally discovered during a road extension project; the site was excavated in 1992–93. The Cerutti Mastodon site contains evidence of human technology and activity on mastodon bone.[76] Thomas Demere,

Richard A. Cerutti, and Paul C. Majors analyzed the site area and found that spirally fractured bone was concentrated around two large stones, a pattern that is similar to that recorded at two experimental replication sites in Tanzania. The project was initially funded by the public; however, the unusual taphonomy of the specimen and the threat of destruction and loss due to highway construction required further funding, which was provided by the National Geographic Society (NGS 4971–93), the California Department of Transportation (Caltrans, contract 11C841 to the San Diego Natural History Museum), and a gift from John and Christie Walton of National City, California.

I visited the former site area and studied the artifact collection at the San Diego Museum of Man in 2011. I obtained a copy of the Caltrans report on the site and included a discussion of it in my 2015 dissertation. In 2017 S. R. Holen and colleagues published the dating results from mastodon bone minimally 130,000 years old.[77] Numerous Pleistocene age sites located in Southern California and central Mexico were reported from 1960 to 1980. All of them have been denied as legitimate archaeological sites and relegated to archaeological obscurity. Holen and his colleagues spent years studying the materials from the Cerutti Mastodon site prior to publishing their findings in 2017, as they knew they would face certain denial of the site's dates and human-induced bone modification. The article was published in *Nature* and faced an immediate firestorm of criticism from American archaeologists.

Every archaeological site in the Americas that has published dates older than 11,000–12,000 years has faced sharp critiques from numerous archaeologists, regardless of the evidence for the site's antiquity. The Cerutti site report was published in a very well respected and highly read scientific journal, *Nature*, and drew immediate critiques from a number of archaeologists. Gary Haynes stated that the stratigraphy of the site needed clarification regarding possible bone breakage from construction equipment. Haynes also stated, "Another problem is the absence of reputable archaeological traces of such a long-distance dispersal into North America by unknown hominins from Asia."[78] However, there is substantial evidence in hundreds of archaeological sites in the archaeological record of the Americas that proves that hominins migrated long distances from the Eastern

Hemisphere to the Western Hemisphere. Long-distance intercontinental hominin dispersal is known to have occurred on a global scale during the Pleistocene, and there is no absence of reputable archaeological traces of long-distance hominin dispersal into the Western Hemisphere. There are very few recorded archaeological sites in the published literature that date to over 100,000 years before present in the Americas. This is due in part to bias and denial in the field over the last one hundred years. Those few archaeologists who did report on earlier than 12,000-year-old sites faced overly aggressive critiques and ostracism. Long-distance dispersal into the Americas has never been questioned, as long as it took place after 12,000 years ago and agreed with outmoded and unsubstantiated recent initial human migrations theories. Holen and colleagues replied to Haynes's critique with a solid scientific explanation for every point he raised regarding the question of possible bone breakage by heavy equipment: "This notion can be discounted primarily because most of the relevant CM fragments were found coated in thick crusts of pedogenic carbonate clearly showing that breakage occurred thousands of years ago."[79]

The critiques of the Cerutti site were fast and furious. Many were authored by longtime pre-Clovis site deniers such as Haynes, and to address them all would require an extended volume. Critiques and question are a part of archaeology and can provide valuable insights that improve archaeological site evidence. However, Holen and colleagues were well aware of the critiques they would face when publishing on a site that dates to over 115,000 years beyond accepted times frames of human occupation of the Western Hemisphere. The knowledge of the critiques they would face was with them every day, and they were very diligent in every aspect of their research and testing of the Cerutti site materials.

Critiques of earlier than 11,000–12,000-year-old archaeological sites in the Americas are often written by archaeologists who have not studied the site area or materials, as noted by Ruth Gruhn regarding the Cerutti site. Gruhn stated in her review of the Cerutti site: "I may be the only professional archaeologist to have visited the Museum and actually looked at the site material; I understand that as yet none of the site's critics have done so." Regarding critiques of possible bone breakage by heavy equipment, Gruhn stated: "My examination of the broken bone fragments in the Cerutti Mastodon Site collection indicates that the hypothesis of breakage by modern heavy machinery is invalid, as a thick precipitate of soil carbonate on the broken surfaces proves that the breakage was indeed very ancient. The site remains an anomaly in present modeling of the initial peopling of the Americas."[80]

I studied the original site records and materials for my dissertation, and I did find that the evidence provided a good case for further testing and research. This is what archaeology and scientific procedure are about. On a global scale, discussions on human evolution that have been unquestioned for decades have recently been challenged and falsified. No one should expect that archaeological theories of early human habitation anywhere in the world will not change. New knowledge, open minds, technology, and science are enriching what we know about the human past on a global scale, the Americas included.

Site	Dating	Location	Artifacts	References
Bluefish Caves	24,070– 23,170 ^{14}C BP	Yukon Territory	100 lithic artifacts, including exotic chert Culturally modified bone	Adovasio and Pedler 2016; Bourgeon, Burke, and Higham 2017; Cinq-Mars 1979

Bluefish Caves is comprised of three small cave sites that were investigated from 1977 to 1987 by Jacques Cinq-Mars, who worked for the Archaeological Survey of Canada.[81] This is another site that was initially rejected as a legitimate pre-Clovis site by the archaeological community and has now been supported as a legitimate earlier than Clovis site through a reanalysis of the materials from the original excavations. Materials from the site include 36,000 faunal specimens. The materials were recently reexamined, and a small percentage of the bones was found to bear marks consistent with butchering.[82] There are numerous pre-Clovis sites in the Yukon and Alaska, including Old Crow, which is in the same general area as Bluefish Caves.

L. Bourgeon, A. Burke, and T. Higham studied 36,000 mammal bones from the Bluefish Caves site and stated: "Our Taphonomic analysis indicates that wolves, lions and, to a lesser degree, foxes were the main agents of bone accumulation and modification, but that humans also contributed to the bone accumulation in both caves, particularly confirming earlier Taphonomic studies."[83] Bourgeon and her crew carried out a substantial study of the materials from Bluefish Caves and confirmed that the initial investigations by Cinq-Mars were correct: humans were present at Bluefish Caves over 19,000 ^{14}C BP.

In their recent book, Adovasio and Pedler discuss Bluefish Caves as a controversial archaeological site.[84] They cited a recent study that found human cut marks on only two bones out of 6,000 specimens. However, no matter how small the collection of bones with cut marks, they still represent a human presence at a given time.

Site	Dating	Location	Artifacts	References
Valsequillo Reservoir: El Horno, El Mirador, Texacaxco, Hueyatlaco	23,000–over 200,000	Mexico	Lithics, tools and flakes Butchered mammal bone Human and animal footprints Engraved bone Human skulls	Irwin Williams 1978; Szabo, Malde, and Irwin-Williams 1969; Steen-McIntyre and Malde 1970; Steen-McIntire, Fryxell, and Malde 1981; Camacho 1978

Numerous sites have been located along the Valsequillo Reservoir in central Mexico. The modern reservoir was built in the 1940s and mirrored a Pleistocene lake. Extensive multidisciplinary research has been conducted at the archaeological sites surrounding and close to the Valsequillo Reservoir for over sixty years. Arguments have raged for and against the earliest dates. To compile the research and data on the archaeological sites in this area would take a lifetime and volumes of books. However, the archaeological area should not be missed in any study with a focus on early humans in the

Western Hemisphere. There are numerous archaeological sites in the area, including El Horno, El Mirador, Texacaxco, and Hueyatlaco. The dating at many of the sites has been extensive and includes geological studies, studies of deposited volcanic ash layers, and studies of diatoms. Diatoms are single-celled photosynthetic organisms that produce mineralized cell walls called thecae.[85] Diatoms are silicified and may be found in soils dating to hundreds of thousands of years ago. If you are interested in microscience and the microarchaeological record viewed via scanning electron microscopes, this is a field for you. Microarchaeology, in the archaeological record of a site, includes the presence of diatoms, phytoliths, and organic or silicified remains that are beyond the visible archaeological record yet may be highly informative. Paleo microspecies identification has been carried out to support the early dates at the Valsequillo Reservoir sites.

The archaeological record of the Valsequillo Reservoir began in the 1930s, when Armenta Camacho documented over one hundred sites with extinct mammal remains and evidence of a human presence in the area south of Puebla.[86] The evidence for human interaction with extinct species in the area included butchering marks on bone, engravings, green bone fractures, and a large jaw with an embedded flint point. Species of mammals found within the area include dire wolf, bison, horse, camel, antelope, glyptodont, peccary, short-faced bear, and saber-toothed cat.

The Hueyatlaco archaeological site was dated to 250,000–275,000 years old by U/Th and fission track dating on butchered bone associated with stone tools. (Fission track dating is a radiometric dating technique. Uranium-bearing minerals and glasses are analyzed for tracks left by fission fragments. Fission tracks are heat sensitive; thus, the technique has the ability to capture the thermal evolution of rocks and minerals. Uranium-thorium dating is based on detection by mass spectrometry of the decay of chain of $[^{234}U]$, the parent, and $[^{230}Th]$, the daughter. Uranium-series dating uses the radioactive decay of uranium to calculate an age. This dating method can be used for samples such as bones, teeth, and carbon sediments that can retain uranium and thorium.) Dates on butchered mastodon tooth fragments at El Horno agree with this age. The soils from the area where stone artifacts were found at Hueyatlaco were rich in diatoms and held taxa that became extinct during the end of the Sangamon interglacial 80,000 years ago. Cynthia Irwin-Williams denied the early dates for Hueyatlaco and argued for a maximum date of 23,000 years.[87] The evidence from the Valsequillo Reservoir sites includes stone tools associated with extinct fauna that dates much earlier than Clovis, minimally 23,000 years before present. Irwin-Williams and colleagues argued that the stone tools could not have been used at Valsequillo more than 200,000 years before they are known to form the archaeological record of the Old World or before the appearance of *Homo sapiens*.[88] Archaeologists now know more about *H. sapiens* and stone tools than they did in 1969. The most sophisticated stone tools to date have been found in Australia and date to over 60,000 years ago, and *H. sapiens* was present in some areas of the world prior to 100,000 years ago and possibly as early as 300,000 years ago.[89] There has been a great deal of controversy over the dating of the Valsequillo Reservoir sites. However, archaeological excavations and research have shown that humans were indeed interacting with extinct mammals in this area during the Pleistocene. The sites and the area are undoubtedly worthy of further research.

The southwestern area of the United States and central Mexico stand out as areas where numerous sites dated between 22,000 to over 200,000 years ago have been reported. As we learn more about the presence of early *Homo sapiens* and advanced stone tools on a global scale, specifically in areas outside of the so-called Old World, earlier sites and advanced technologies in present-day areas such as Australia and the Americas may not be so controversial.

The Calico site is the only site I know of that Louis S. B. Leakey, the famous British archaeologist who was born in Kenya, worked on in North America. Leakey supported the early dates for the Calico site and discussed the lithic tools as human-made. Many other archaeologists have disagreed with him, including Gary Haynes.[90] Leakey and his contemporaries who worked at the site responded to the site critiques by carrying out further research and testing.[91] Investigations began at the Calico site in 1964 under grants from the National Geographic Society. In initial excavations, 170 specimens of lithic materials were found in an undisturbed stratigraphy. Leakey argued that there was a "definite selectivity in respect of materials from which the flakes and other artifacts had been made."[92] At the time,

Site	Dating	Location	Artifacts	References
Calico NRHP	200,000 ^{230}Th/^{234}U 40,000–20,000	Pleistocene Lake Manix, California	Lithic artifacts and tools Hearth	Leakey et al. 1968; Leakey 1979; Simpson 1979; Duvall and Venner 1979; Payen 1982; Simpson and Patterson 1984; Bischoff et al. 1984; Simpson et al. 1986; Leland et al. 1987; Bischoff et al. 1981; Gruhn and Young 1980

geologists who examined the alluvial fan where the site is located estimated the fan was between 40,000 and 120,000 years of age. J. L. Bischoff and colleagues concluded that at the deepest level, the site had an age of 200,000 years before present.[93] The levels that contained possible lithic artifacts were dated, and the results were published in 1981. Uranium-series dating was carried out on carbonates that coated cobbles from the lower level of the deposits, and this resulted in a date of 200,000 ± 20,000 years before present.

One of the critiques of the Calico site is an argument that the lithic flakes were not made by humans but by natural causes.[94] L. W. Patterson and colleagues responded to this critique in a detailed study of 13,677 lithic flakes from five units at the Calico site; they found that highly repetitive patterns known to be products of human flint knapping were present on the lithics from Calico.[95] Lithic flakes were found in clusters within the excavation area; clusters are typically found in areas where humans were making stone tools or reducing materials for later tool manufacture.

Patterson and colleagues argued that natural forces are not capable of simulating the patterns of human manufacture of lithic materials. Natural forces are not selective as to material type, and if one type of stone is broken by nature in a given area, then all types of stone of similar sizes would be expected to be broken similarly within a given area. Ruth Gruhn and David Young published a critique of James Duvall and William Venner's critique of Leland Patterson and colleagues' work: "Duvall and Venner's paper on the lithic materials from the Calico Site of California is a classic example of the misuse of statistical analysis in support of a bias." Gruhn and Young further stated: "Duvall and Venner's use of statistics do not support their conclusion that the Calico is not an archaeological site and the Calico tools are not artifacts. Their entire statistical exercise does not answer the question one way or another. It was largely a fruitless exercise because the only way to decide if a rock was naturally flaked or a man-made tool is to conduct a minute analysis of the flake scar morphology in an attempt to understand the underlying processes responsible for the flaking."[96]

The Calico site has been discussed by archaeologists as controversial and has resulted in numerous publications both for and against the legitimacy of the site. The investigators of the Calico site were familiar with ancient deposits and human-made artifacts. The Calico site would benefit from further excavation and research. The area is now bounded to the north by a military base, and access to some areas is restricted. This area of ancient Pleistocene lakes is rich in archaeological and paleontological remains. Other older sites have been reported in Southern California, including the Cerutti site, which is 170 miles southwest of Calico; it was recently dated to minimally 130,000 years before present. If the lithics from Calico are human-made, the site may have been a materials procurement site or tool workshop site. It would be ideal to support further excavations and research in this area, where Pleistocene lakes once graced the land and provided a viable habitat for mammals and humans. However, as mentioned by Leakey and Patterson and colleagues, it is challenging to obtain funding for controversial archaeological sites.[97] The Calico site is listed on the National Register of Historic Places. There are permanent buildings on the site, and members of a group, Friends of Calico Early Man Site, are involved with activities at the site, which is now managed by the National Park Service.

A new archaeological site, Chiquihuite cave, in the Astillero mountains of Mexico was announced in the academic press just as this book was in production. The cave has been dated to 26,500 years ago. The primary investigator, Ciprian Ardelean, has suggested that people had to be in the Western Hemisphere prior to 30,000 years ago.[98] Thus, the number of archaeological sites dating to earlier than 12,000 years before present that will be listed in the Indigenous Paleolithic Database of the Americas continues to grow.

A list of Pleistocene archaeological sites for North and South America is included in the appendix.

Eyes Wide Shut

It can be said that for the last century, many archaeologists in North America viewed the deep past with eyes wide shut. If most archaeologists had opened their eyes and viewed the published archaeological record of the Americas, they could not possibly have supported the tenets of the Clovis First hypothesis of postglacial initial human migrations into the Western Hemisphere. However, over the last thirty years, some American archaeologists have conceded that initial migrations to the Western Hemisphere were likely earlier than 12,000–13,000 years ago.[99] A great deal of research on early human sites in the Western Hemisphere remains to be done. However, due to the embedded dogma of the Clovis First hypothesis, funding for research to study controversial earlier sites has been slow to develop.[100] Canada may be ahead in this area of research funding, as in 2019 I was awarded a Canada Research Chair Tier II in Indigenous History Healing and Reconciliation with a research grant of $500,000 to continue my research on the Indigenous Paleolithic of the Western Hemisphere.

Mapping Pleistocene sites in the Eastern and Western Hemispheres paints a picture of human occupation across diverse environmental niches as early as 130,000 ^{14}C BP and possibly earlier than 200,000 ^{14}C BP in the Western Hemisphere. There are human technologies that are common to both the Eastern and Western Hemispheres, including stone tool manufacture, bone tool manufacture, plant gathering, hunting of game, fishing, use of natural materials such as shells for adornment, and oral traditions, which are present in a majority of cultures on a global scale. One future area of study that may add to our understanding of Pleistocene human migrations and sites would be to carry out a comprehensive comparison of technologies and cultural traits present in the material record of sites in both the Eastern and Western Hemispheres. As all early people had oral traditions, it would be interesting to study possible similarities in oral traditions that relate to specific Pleistocene species or geological events in both the Eastern and Western Hemispheres.

One point remains clear, and that is that much work remains to be done. Earlier dates of human occupation are beginning to be accepted. Thus, for students and future researchers, there are many opportunities in Paleolithic studies of the Western Hemisphere. According to R. S. MacNeish, "It is not correct to tentatively accept a few of these earliest sites and then act as if only the ones more recent than 12,000 years are worthy of analysis. . . . One just cannot reach any sort of conclusions on these subjects if one ignores all of the early man data before 10,000 B.C. Either there was man in the New World before 12,000 years ago or there wasn't—as the doctor said, 'You can't be just a little bit pregnant!'"[101]

Old World: -60,000

The diggers among old bones have an ax to grind, a stone to chip. Archeology is a child of conquest, a follower of armies, conceived in the looting of treasures from other people's graves, born under colonial flags, with a story to tell. The archeology of colonial masters finds evidence to put us in our places, to put them on their thrones. If what they find contradicts the story of their unique superiority, then the evidence is wrong. How can it be that the people they have enslaved built cities, studied the stars, were scientists and artists? How can it be that the empty lands they imagine have been waiting to be claimed were not empty at all? They insist that Turtle Island is a new world, that human cultures barely scratched the wild surface of all that real estate. That it is all raw material. They have an official account, and they're sticking to it. The bones and stones keep talking back, but anyone who listens is ridiculed. They have to keep saying it was simple; it was recent. No matter that humans have been settling continents, walking over isthmuses for hundreds of thousands of years, traveling oceans for forty thousand, the experts keep saying it couldn't have happened here, not in America, the source of so much wealth. They say we stumbled across the land bridge at the worst possible time, a single culture with a single style of tool making, 13,500 years ago, which in the world of old things is just the other day. But there are hundreds of mouths scattered across this earth, all speaking, all saying older, older, older. Saying it could have been a hundred thousand years ago, it could have been sixty thousand, but it was very much longer ago than that, when we climbed up out of a hole in the ground, left a cave, emerged from a shell, fell out of the sky, and began to shape this old American world.

—Aurora Levins Morales, *Remedios*

CHAPTER 6

Pleistocene Sites in South America

Landscapes of Richness and Diversity

Recent archaeological discoveries in the highlands of Peru have extended the pre-history of the New World in two significant respects. First, the finds themselves indicate that we must push back the date of man's earliest known appearance in South America from the currently accepted estimate of around 12,000 B.C. to perhaps as much as 20,000 B.C. Second and even more important is the implication, in the nature of the very early Andean hunting cultures now brought to light, that these cultures reflect Old World origins of even greater antiquity. If this is so, man may have first arrived in the Western Hemisphere between 40,000 and 100,000 years ago.

—Richard S. MacNeish, "Early Man in the Andes"

The archaeological record of Central and South America attests to a fantastic diversity of cultures and great civilizations across time. It has been my experience in teaching in higher education that students are aware of world greats on a global scale. When I ask students what they know about pyramids and mummies and where the oldest mummies and the most significant pyramids are found, they answer Egypt. They answer Egypt because that is what they have been taught, that great things in the deep past happened in many places, but not in the Americas. Most students are surprised to learn that the oldest record of mummification is not found in Egypt but in North and South America. The Spirit Cave mummy was found in a cave in Nevada and was wrapped in rabbit fur. The burial dated to 9415 ^{14}C BP. The Chinchorro mummies have been found throughout areas of the Atacama Desert of northern Chile; The oldest mummies date to around 7,000 years ago.[1] The Atacama Desert is one of the driest regions on earth and thus provides a high level of preservation for organic materials.

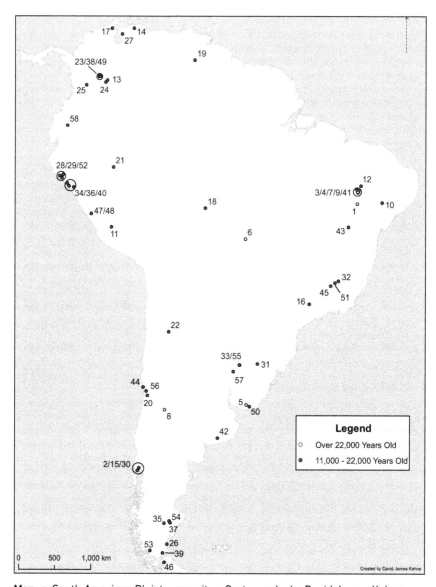

Map. 5. South American Pleistocene sites. Cartography by David James Kehoe.

1. Toca da Esperança
2. Monte Verde I
3. Pedra Furada
4. Vale da Pedra Furada
5. Arroyo Vizcaíno
6. Santa Elina
7. Sítio do Meio

8. Atuel
9. Tira Peia
10. Morro Furado
11. Pikimachay
12. Caldeirão de Rodriguez
13. Pubenza
14. Muaco

15. Chinchihuapi Locality and Monte Verde new data
16. Alice Böer
17. Rancho Peludo
18. lt Ji-Paraná-Rolim de Moura
19. lt Brazil
20. Quebrada El Membrillo

21. Huargo Cave	33. rs q-2	46. Tres Arroyos
22. Cueva Cacao	34. Huaca Prieta	47. Pachamachay
23. Sueva	35. Los Toldos	48. Telarmachay
24. Tequendama	36. Guitarrero Cave	49. Tibito
25. El Jordán	37. El Ceibo	50. Urupez
26. Piedra Museo aep-1	38. El Abra II	51. Lapa Vermelha
El Puesto Rockshelter	39. Cueva del Medio	52. El Palto
27. Taima-Taima	40. La Cumbre	53. Cueva Sofia 1
28. Complejo Paiján	41. Garrincho	54. Cerro Tres Tetas
29. Quirihuac	42. Arroyo Seco Sitio 2	55. rs-168
30. Monte Verde II	43. Lapa do Boquete	56. Tagua-Tagua II
31. rs 1 50	44. Quereo I	57. El Tigre
32. Santana do Riacho	45. Lapa Mortuária	58. San José

People have lived in the Atacama Desert and northern coastal areas of Chile for over 10,000 years, relying mainly on fishing as a food source. Hundreds of archaeological sites have been discovered along the rugged coastal area of Peru and Chile, some dating back to the late Pleistocene and early Holocene. Archaeological sites include but are not limited to Quebradas Tacahuay Quebrada Jaguay (the Ring Site) and Quebrada Los Burros in Peru 11,000–9,000 B C, or 13,000–11,000 years ago.[2]

Mummification in Egypt is thought to have begun around 4,600 years ago.[3] Recently, archaeologists dated textiles thought to have been used to wrap bodies for mummification to 1,500 years earlier in Egypt. However, as the bodies were not with the curated materials, this is a tentative change of early mummification dates for Egyptian mortuary practices. It may be that further research into mummification practices in Egypt will push back the currently known date for elaborate burials. But for now, the oldest known complex and elaborate practices of mummification of human remains are those of the Chinchorro people of Chile. The Chinchorro people's mortuary practices of mummification and the Spirit Cave mummification and burial reflect Indigenous people's cultural practices of respect and care for ancestors and ancestral remains. Though early Indigenous people are most often described by archaeologists as highly mobile hunter-gatherers, evidence from the Chinchorro region indicates that people maintained year-round residences along the coast of northern Chile.[4] The archaeological record provides evidence of abundant resources in many coastal areas, large shell mounds, and extinct mammal remains, including marine mammals. Chemical analysis of human bone from the area shows a diet highly reliant on plant, animal, and marine resources.[5]

According to Cristóbal Gnecco and Javier Aceituno, Pleistocene studies in American archaeology has been conducted in large part from the "standpoint of eco-functional theory," described by Gnecco and Aceituno as "a process whereby humans adapted to a basically unknown environment using a limited cultural repertoire, salient among which were bifacial hunting weapons and tools."[6] For decades archaeologists assumed that all Indigenous people across the Americas were highly mobile hunters who pursued big game mammals with bifacial stone tools.[7] However, such generalizing theories of ancient human subsistence practices discussed on a hemispheric scale beg to be critically reevaluated.[8] Archaeologists have recently begun to discuss the problems inherent in such claims, as they are aware that on a continental scale, there were vast ecological differences that would have facilitated diverse economies.[9] Traditional theories of subsistence patterns framed in environmental reductionism have recently been questioned, allowing a broader view of early human cultures and spaces.[10]

Some archaeologists in the Americas have discussed mounting evidence of a generalist economy.[11] Discussions of a generalist economy during the Pleistocene expand the traditional archaeological view of hunter-gatherers following megafauna and subsisting on diets heavily reliant on big game. By "generalist economy," I am referring to the use of plant foods, roots, nuts, eggs, seeds, small game, fish, and birds, as well as larger game animals. Contrary to dogmatic stories of hunter-gatherers stalking herds of megafauna across the tundra, evidence from numerous archaeological sites indicates that early people in the Western Hemisphere practiced a broad-spectrum foraging and hunting economy, including much smaller game animals.[12] According to Tom Dillehay and Jack Rossen, subsistence diversity and cultural complexity would most likely require a more significant time depth of humans in the New World than was previously recognized.[13]

The landmass area of the Western Hemisphere represents over one-quarter, or 28 percent, of the global landmass. North America covers 9.355 million square miles (24.23 million square kilometers), or 16 percent of the global landmass. South America covers 6.89 million square miles (17.81

million square kilometers), or 12 percent, of the global landmass.[14] Therefore, from the ecological diversity of the Western Hemisphere, we can expect to see a reflection of cultural diversity. Humans based their ways of being, doing, and knowing—their culture—in part on their environments and the knowledge they developed of the flora, fauna, land, and resources within their territories.

Numerous Pleistocene archaeological sites have been reported in South America, and archaeologists have begun to discuss possible regional areas.[15] In a 2009 report, J. Steel and G. Politis discussed their work on dating Pleistocene archaeological sites in Argentina. They discussed the possible dispersal times that would be required to reach Argentina from a northern point during the Pleistocene. They argued that dates for the earliest South American sites in their sample should be at least 1,500–2,400 years after initial entry from a northern location and reported that one site in their sample, Cerro Tres Tetas, is 12,000 kilometers from Edmonton on a great circle route. The authors suggest that human occupation in North America would have to predate 11,000 ^{14}C BP and that perhaps there are older sites in North America yet to be discovered. Steel and Politis highlight meaningful discussions regarding sites of roughly the same age (10,000–12,000 years ago) that are missing from many archaeological site reports. Regarding the human dispersal times required to populate a hemispheric area, they stated: "We are aware of no plausible demographic model that would predict the contemporaneous first archaeological appearance at such widely separated locations of a population expanding from a single initial dispersal event."[16]

It is clear from the reported dates of South American Pleistocene sites that the picture of human dispersal across the Americas is far more complicated than previously believed. Given that there are sites in North America that predate 40,000–200,000 years ago, archaeologists need to consider other possibilities in their discussions and research into the initial peopling of the continents. Given the size and ecological diversity of the Americas, a much longer time frame than a few hundred years is required for people to have had time to move across and adapt to new environments prior to the time when the archaeological signature shows people in areas throughout North and South America.

There are archaeological sites within South America that may be considered as possible regional areas, where a cluster of sites dates to within a few hundred or few thousand years of each other. This is to be expected, as people were mobile and did not utilize just one resource or one site area. Archaeologists in Brazil have reported on numerous sites in and close to the area of Serra da Capivara National Park, located in the state of Piauí, northeastern Brazil. Serra da Capivara National Park is a UNESCO heritage site. Information on the UNESCO web page for the park provides a view of the reported human presence, including rock art sites and archaeological sites: "Over 300 archaeological sites have been found within the park, the majority consisting of rock and wall paintings dating from 50,000–30,000 years Before Present. Many of the numerous rockshelters in the Serra da Capivara National Park are decorated with rock paintings, some more than 25,000 years old. The analyses and dating of the evidence and artefacts found in the Serra da Capivara National Park serve to confirm the millennial presence of human beings on the American continent and the importance of the heritage."[17]

Analysis and dating of calcite veneer found on the paintings at the rockshelter called Toca da Bastiana in Serra da Capivara National Park have resulted in dates prior to 36,000 years ago.[18] These early dates correspond to radiocarbon dates for the Pedra Furada archaeological site, also in Serra da Capivara National Park. Pleistocene archaeological sites in and close to the park include Pedra Furada, Vale da Pedra Furada, Toca da Tira Peia, Toca da Pena, Baxao da Esperenca, and Sítio do Meio.[19] Farther to the south of this area, Pleistocene archaeological sites reported include Lapa do Boquete, Lapa dos Bichos, Santana do Riacho, Lapa Vermelha, Largo Santa, and Alice Boer. To the north is Pedra Pintada, and to the west is Santa Elina.

In a 2008 paper, A. Kinoshita and colleagues stated: "On the overall, the region, that was declared a Human Heritage site by UNESCO, has up to the present 940 archeological sites registered by the National Institute for the Historical and Artistic Heritage Instituto do Patrimônio Histórico e Artístico Nacional IPHAN. Among those sites, 45 were already excavated and the data collected show a continuous human occupation since at least 100,000 yr BP."[20]

Stories on the Lands of South America

Brazil

Site	Dating	Location	Artifacts	References
Pedra Furada	55,575 ± 5,865 53,120 ± 3,965 32,160 ± 1,000 31,700 ± 830	Brazil	Lithic artifacts Hearths Rock paintings	Santos et al. 2003; Delibrias and Guidion 1986

Pedra Furada is located in Serra da Capivara National Park in northeastern Brazil. It was located by a French and Brazilian archaeology team in 1973. The archaeological site is within the area of a rockshelter situated 20 meters above the floor of the valley of Pedra Furada.[21] The initial investigation at the site focused on recording and dating rock art at Pedra Furada, which is only one of the hundreds of rock art sites in the region. The Pedra Furada archaeological site contained stone tools and well-formed hearths in levels dated at 25,000 ^{14}C BP.[22] Given that the earliest date accepted by a majority of American archaeologists for a human presence in the Western Hemisphere was around 11,000–12,000 ^{14}C BP, the site was very controversial.

Archaeological research in the area and at the Pedra Furada site continues with the recent investigation at a new site, Toca da Tira Peia, just meters away that was dated to 20,000 calendar years before present.[23] Excavations at Pedra Furada exposed hearths with abundant charcoal in levels with stone tools. Thermoluminescence (TL) measurements on the hearthstones demonstrated that the stones from the hearth were heated independently from the stones found outside the hearths, thus supporting a human presence at the site.[24] There have been published critiques of the Pedra Furada site.[25] However, the initial investigators and a second generation of archaeologists to investigate the site defend the original assessment of the Pedra Furada and continue to investigate sites in the area, providing evidence of a human presence prior to 20,000 ^{14}C BP.[26]

In 2014 Kinoshita and colleagues discussed the dating results from two teeth of a fossil cervid, *Blastocerus dichotomus*, that were found in a well-defined stratum in proximity to human remains at the site of Toca do

Serrote das Moendas, Piauí, Brazil.[27] The cervid teeth were dated by electron spin resonance (ESR). The authors report the independent testing of the dates and the capping layer of the level at three labs as follows: "The ages obtained for the teeth were 29 ± 3 ka and 24 ± 1 ka. The concretion layer capping this stratum was dated by optically stimulated luminescence (OSL) of the quartz grains to 21 ± 3 ka. As these values were derived independently in three different laboratories, using different methods and equipment, these results are compelling evidence of early habitation in this area."[28]

Kinoshita and colleagues argue that the remains were found in situ and that the sedimentology did not show a disturbance. They allow that "determining a possible burial is more problematic."[29] The authors argue that the evidence of human remains in an in situ stratigraphic level with the fossil remains of an animal that is portrayed in numerous rock art panels (the cervid *Blastocerus dichotomus*) supports the evidence for a human presence in northeastern Brazil 24,000 years ago. Nième Guidon and G. Delibrias had initially reported dates of 30,000–32,000 years ago based on charcoal from a hearth and a fragment of rock art that has dislodged from a wall and was found in a deep level of the Pedra Furada site.[30] They later recanted their claim after critiques called the dating into question and they revised the dates for the rock painting at the site to around 12,000 years ago.[31] The debate on the age of rock art in northeastern Brazil has recently been resurrected by S. Watanabe and colleagues, who reported dates of over 36,000 years ago. Watanabe's dates for early rock art agree with the dates of human presence reported for the Pedra Furada site.[32] M. W. Rowe and K. L. Steelman published their research from rock art at the same site and other sites and stated that their research contradicts Watanabe's findings: "The EPR and TL ages cannot be used as conclusive evidence to support very early human occupation in Brazil near Pedra Furada until this controversy is resolved. Our results do not negate the possibility of human occupation in the area as early as 35 ky ago, but those radiocarbon-dated paintings surviving on rock shelter walls are not of that extreme antiquity. Once again, and most dramatically, these studies point to the necessity of independent studies in dating rock art."[33]

A. M. Pessis and N. Guidon discussed the difficulties in dating rock art panels; they argued that ages could vary depending on where samples for dating are collected from within each panel.[34] While rock art dating is problematic, it may provide evidence supporting a human presence in a given area. R. G. Bednarik has denied the early rock art dates reported by Nìède Guidon and colleagues for the sites in northeastern Brazil. However, in a lecture paper he stated, "Older paintings may have existed, and at least some of the pigment traces reported from the floor deposit seem authentic."[35] At Toca do Baixao do Perna I, another site excavated by Guidon, numerous red paintings are at least 10,000 years old.[36] There are thousands of rock art and petroglyph sites in North and South America that are very deserving of further study, and for every rock art site there is a distinct possibility of locating associated archaeological sites. Wherever humans were creating rock art, they were most likely living either temporarily or seasonally and leaving traces of their lives and activities within the land.

Site	Dating	Location	Artifacts	Reference
Vale da Pedra Furada	29,365–28,553 cal BP 28,100–28,600 cal BP	Brazil	Several thousand artifacts 294 tools Hearths	Boëda et al. 2014

Vale da Pedra Furada is an open-air site in the São Raimundo Nonato region in close proximity to Serra da Capivara National Park. It was located in 1998 during a survey to test for archaeological sites within the regional area of Boqueirão da Pedra Furada.[37] The Vale da Pedra Furada site was dated to 29,365–28,553 cal BP and 28,100–28,600 cal BP. Given the harsh critiques of the nearby Pedra Furada archaeological site, the chronology study "employed both radiocarbon and luminescence techniques; radiocarbon dates were obtained on charcoal, multi-grain and single-grain OSL ages on sedimentary quartz grains."[38] Based on their research and studies of the lithic artifacts at the site, C. Lahaye and his coauthors argued that the comparison of 294 artifacts identified by technical traits set them apart from naturally broken stone.[39] Conclusions drawn from the lithic comparisons and testing led the authors of the study to confidently argue that the lithic artifacts from the Vale da Pedra Furada site were undeniably of human origin. Evidence of human use of stone tools included signs of butchering activities and sawing and scraping on wood and hide. Optically

stimulated luminescence (OSL) ages reported by Lahaye and colleagues highlight internal consistency and agreement with previously reported OSL and radiocarbon ages for the cultural levels at the site and are in chronological order stratigraphically. The earliest dates are found at the base of the excavations, and most recent dates are near the uppermost level. Vale da Pedra Furada is one of four recent site that have been investigated in the area and that support a pre-20,000 ^{14}C BP human presence. F. Parenti has argued that the Vale da Pedra Furada and the Pedra Furada sites are two areas of one site, as they are as close as 70 meters apart.[40]

Site	Dating	Location	Artifacts	Reference
Toca de Tira Peia	20,000 ±1,500 BC	Brazil	113 lithic artifacts 35 tools Burned pebbles	Lahaye et al. 2013

The Toca da Tira Peia site is located close to Serra da Capivara National Park in northeastern Brazil near the Pedra Furada site. In 2008, three test pits were excavated at the site.[41] In 2009, OSL sampling and further excavations were carried out. During excavations in 2010 and 2011, dozens of lithic artifacts were unearthed. Lahaye and colleagues argue that the lithic artifacts are indisputably human-made and report that the artifacts were found in situ. Some artifacts had been refitted. The Toca da Tira Peia site is evidence of new data and a renewed understanding that can result from archaeologists working with their eyes and minds wide open. The French and Brazilian archaeological team investigated the regional area in and around the Pedra Furada site in 2008 and reported on new sites that support the controversial dates of the Pedra Furada site. As I stated earlier in this book, where there is one site of a specific age, there have to be others, because people did not fly from place to place. The area of northeastern Brazil holds a rich record of a human presence prior to 20,000 years ago that includes a vast collection of hundreds of rock painting sites and evidence of human technology, including fire hearths and stone and bone tools at many archaeological sites.

Site	Dating	Location	Artifacts	Reference
Sítio do Meio	29,365–28,553 cal BP 28,100–28,600 cal BP	Brazil	Lithic tools Hearths	Boëda et al. 2016

The archaeological site of Sítio do Meio is located in Sierra Captiva National Park close to the Pedra Furada site. The Sítio do Meio site includes rock paintings similar to those at Pedra Furada and hundreds of other sites in the area. N/ède Guidon discovered the Sítio do Meio archaeological site in 1973; the site was excavated between 1978 and 2012.[42] Charcoal fragments near the base of the lowest cultural level provided dates between 23,000 and 25,000 ^{14}C BP. Eric Boëda led renewed excavations at the Sítio do Meio site in 2012 and 2013 and reported spectacular discoveries, including a rock superstructure that "cannot be attributed to a natural deposition."[43] Boëda and his team reported finding charcoal-rich horizons with associated artifacts; dating provided dates between 20,280 ± 450 and 25,170 ± 140 ^{14}C BP.

Site	Dating	Location	Artifacts	Reference
Alice Boer	14,200 ± 1,150 ^{14}C BP	Brazil	Hundreds of artifacts, including bifacially flaked stone tools	Beltrao et al. 1983

The Alice Boer archaeological site is located in São Paulo State, Brazil. M. Beltrao and her colleagues reported nineteen cultural levels in excavations carried out to a depth of 4 meters, all of them containing chert artifacts.[44] Beltrao examined the tools and found that many of them had been pretreated thermally with fire before being knapped. A charcoal sample from level 10 was dated to 14,200 ^{14}C BP. Beltrao selected eight chert samples for thermoluminescence dating; the TL ages ranged from 2190 ^{14}C BP for level 1 to 11,000 ^{14}C BP for level 8. The increase in TL ages correlated with stratigraphic depth. Beltrao concluded that early humans were in Brazil by 14,000 years ago and likely much earlier. Tom Dillehay has mentioned issues with the site's dating and stratigraphy and highlighted the possibility of disturbance by fluvial action, as the site was in a buried terrace where stratigraphy can be mixed by flooding.[45] The Alice Boer site has provided burned cherts that dated to 11,000–14,000 ^{14}C BP; this is indicative of the early human use of the area. However, the site would benefit from further excavations and testing.

Venezuela

Site	Dating	Location	Artifacts	Reference
Taima-Taima	14,200 ± 300 12,980 ± 85	Falcón State, Venezuela	El Jobo point Anvils, pounders, axes, and knives	Bryan and Gruhn 1979

The Taima-Taima archaeological site in northern Venezuela was first excavated by José Cruxent in 1962.[46] Ruth Gruhn and Alan Bryan, archaeologists from the University of Calgary, and Claudio Ochsenius, the founder of the Centro de Investigaciones del Paleo-Indio y Cuaternario Sudamericano (CIPICS), joined Cruxent to further investigate the Taima-Taima site in 1976. During excavations, the midsection of an El Jobo point was found in situ in the right pubic area of a mastodon skeleton. Ochsenius and Gruhn reported a utilized jasper flake in direct association with the mastodon.

Ochsenius and Gruhn argued that the El Jobo point found in the pubic cavity of a mastodon skeleton dated to minimally 13,000 ^{14}C BP at the Taima-Taima site, shattering the long-standing concept of the Clovis complex as the initial and earliest migration into the "New World." Radiocarbon dates were run at two labs and were statistically identical: the Smithsonian lab reported 12,980 ± 85, and the Birmingham lab 12,960 ± 200 ^{14}C BP and 13,030 ± 170 ^{14}C BP. The dates were identical to dates from the bone in the same cultural level: 13,010 ± 280 ^{14}C BP.[47] The dates were based on twigs that had been sheared on the ends, evidence of chewing, and the stomach contents of the mastodon. Critiques of the Taima-Tiama site were raised by Thomas Lynch and Vance Haynes in response to Alan Bryan's discussion of the site.[48] Bryan responded to the critiques and discussed the stratigraphy and dating of the site in detail in a number of publications.[49] Extinct fauna recovered from the Taima-Taima include Proboscidea, Gomphotheriidae, *Haplomastodon*, *Stegomastodon*, Equidae, *Equus*, *Hippidion*, *Glyptodon*, Mylodontidae, *Glossotherium*, Carnivora, Ursidae, Felidae, and Artiodactyla.[50] The basal oldest level of the site contained the disarticulated and butchered bones of a mastodon.[51] In their publication on the Taima-Taima site, Cruxent and Ochsenius discuss three sites in the Coro area that provide evidence of El Jobo points and extinct fauna: Mauco, Tiama-Taima, and Cucuruchu.[52]

Colombia

Site	Dating	Location	Artifacts	Reference
Tibitó	11,740 ± 110	Colombia	120 lithic artifacts Mastodon remains Horse remains in association with charcoal Bone and antler artifacts	Urrego 1981

The Tibitó site is in the central highlands of Colombia north of Bogotá; it was investigated by Gonzalo Correal Urrego in 1980.[53] The Tibitó site was found by a local workman who informed Correal Urrego of the possible site. The pollen profile for the site placed the occupation within the Guantiva Interstadial and supported the radiocarbon dates 11,740 ± 110 ^{14}C BP. Tom Dillehay discussed the site as a possible butchering locality on the banks of a marsh and reported that some of the bones showed evidence of cutting, burning, and possible marrow extraction. It is important to note that Dillehay discussed this archaeological site as being in an area of low energy and mentioned that the site was located in an "undisturbed geological layer overlaid by recent sediments."[54] Thomas Lynch critiqued the site for not having projectile points, and Ruth Gruhn discussed this, relating a lack of projectile points at the site to the nature of the Abriense lithic industry, bifacial points are rare, on the Bogatá savanna.[55] Ruth Gruhn noted that at the time the site's date was almost a millennium too early for the postulated arrival of Paleoindians in South America from the North. Thomas Dillehay has discussed the Tibitó site as "one of the oldest known and most widely accepted sites of early human occupation in Colombia."[56] Other Pleistocene sites have been reported in Colombia, including El Abra II (12,400 ± 160 ^{14}C BP), Pubenza (13,280 ± 100–17,790 ± 120 ^{14}C BP), Tequendama I (28,890 ± 840–10,130 ± 150 ^{14}C BP), and Sueva (11,740 ± 110–10,090 ± 90 ^{14}C BP).[57]

Peru

Site	Dating	Location	Artifacts	Reference
Pikimachay	25,000–11,000 ^{14}C BP	Peru	Lithic tools Hundreds of artifacts Thousands of pieces of debitage Hundreds of faunal bones Thermo-fractured rocks	MacNeish 1979

Pikimachay Flea Cave is located on the side of a mountain 2,850 meters above sea level in the Ayacucho area of central Peru. Richard Scotty Mac-Neish located the cave during a survey in 1967. MacNeish stated that when he first noticed the cave and hiked up to it, he found "261 artifacts that seemed to be mainly preceramic and the collection included every kind of projectile point I had ever seen in Peru."[58] Investigations at Pikimachay Cave began in 1967, and formal excavations began in 1969. Pikimachay is a large cave with three rooms. The mouth of the cave is 40 feet high in places and 175 feet wide.[59] MacNeish recorded eleven stratigraphic zones, and in the process of excavations, he had his workmen remove tons of boulders from the previous rockfall within the cave to reach the lower levels. The oldest zones of the cave (I1, I, J, and K) contained seventy-three lithic artifacts, one hundred flakes, and ninety-six megafauna bones. MacNeish named the stratigraphic levels or zones of the cave by separating them into what he described as phases. Zones H1 and H were the two levels that were overlying or just above the lowest and presumably oldest four zones; these are known as the Ayacucho Complex. A radiocarbon date taken from the bones of sloth from zone H returned dates of $14,150 \pm 180$ ^{14}C BP ($17,221–16,560$ cal BP).[60]

The reports on Pikimachay garnered numerous critiques.[61] However, the Ayacucho Complex, dated by extinct mammalian bone found in association with stone and bone artifacts, has been accepted by most archaeologists.[62] The lower and oldest zones of the cave (older than $20,000$ ^{14}C BP) have not been accepted as having provided irrefutable proof of a human presence. The stone tools from zone H at Pikimachy were studied by Leon Canales and Yataco Capcha, who found that the collection of lithic tools was the result of human workmanship.[63] The lithic artifacts from the lower zones of Pikimachay cave are, however, deserving of further study, as we have learned a great deal more about early lithics in South America since the reports on Pikimachay were published. MacNeish and his field team did locate other preceramic archaeological locations in the area, including Jayamachay and Pepper Cave; he reported finding at least five hundred sites representing human occupations across time on his initial survey of the Ayacucho area.[64]

Chile

Site	Dating	Location	Artifacts	Reference
Monte Verde II Monte Verde I	14,600 cal BP	Llanquihue Province, Chile	MV II Lithic artifacts Charcoal Clay-lined fire pits Human footprints Meat and animal hides Wood Architectural remains MV I Lithic artifacts 26 stone tools Burned features	Dillehay et al. 2008

Monte Verde is an open-air site in Chile where excavations were led by Thomas Dillehay beginning in 1977. Initial investigations produced numerous types of artifacts, including butchered mastodon bones, clay-lined hearths with charcoal, burned plant food, and stone tools. Preservation of organic artifacts at the site such as wood and animal hides was high, as the site was buried beneath a muddy bog. Dillehay wrote that he assumed the Monte Verde site would date to between 10,000 and 11,000 ^{14}C BP and that he and his colleagues were "startled, however, when the radiocarbon dates on the bone, charcoal from fire pits, and wooden artifacts consistently yielded dates of more than 12,000 years ago."[65] According to Dillehay, the dates were impossible, because he had been taught to believe and never questioned the paradigm of the Clovis cultures as the first people in the Americas around 11,200 years ago. Dillehay and his colleagues faced sharp critiques for their analysis of the site, artifacts, and dating by what Dillehay described as die-hard Clovis loyalists. The research team at Monte Verde spent ten years excavating and analyzing materials from the site. Dillehay is one of the few archaeologists who openly agree with Vine Deloria Jr. regarding his comments on the absurdity and inadequate explanations of the Clovis First hypothesis.

Dillehay wrote that a research team of over sixty scientists had studied artifacts excavated from two areas of the site: Monte Verde II, dating to 12,500 ^{14}C BP, and Monte Verde I, dated to around 33,000 years. Monte Verde I, a buried location, is located in a different area of the site from Monte Verde II.

Monte Verde is unique in that the artifacts are so varied and well-preserved and include medicinal plants and plant food such as wild potatoes, living structures, wooden stakes, animal hides, meat, stone tools, and food storage pits, which were found within the areas of structures. Some of the plant medicines found at Monte Verde are the same species that Indigenous people of the region, the Mapuche people, use today. Half of the plants were local, and half of the plants were imported from the coast, over 70 kilometers to the west. One plant was from an area 700 kilometers to the north. The Monte Verde site provides irrefutable evidence of humans in southern South America, and due to the excellent preservation of organic materials, it also provides an in-depth look into the culture of early humans, whose stories on the land give us an amazing view of their ways of knowing, being, and doing.

Argentina

Site	Dating	Location	Artifacts	Reference
Arroyo Seco 2	12,170–11,180 ^{14}C BP	Argentina	Lithic tools Butchered mammalian bone 44 human skeletons, 8000–6300 ^{14}C BP	Politis et al. 2016

Arroyo Seco 2 archaeological site is located in the Pampa region of Argentina and is an open-air multicomponent site.[66] Other Pleistocene sites that are reported in this area include El Abra and Cerro La China and, farther south, Tres Tetas and Los Toldos. The site artifacts include lithic tools and associated remains of both extant and extinct fauna, including modern llama and the extinct megamammals *"Megatherium americanum* giant sloth, *Equus neogeus* Hippidion sp Horse, *Toxodon platensis* hoofed mammal, *Glossotherium robustus* ground sloth and *Paleolama wedelli* Llama ancestor."[67]

In a 1986 report on the site, F. Fidalgo and colleagues reported lithic tools, mammalian bone, elaborate human burials with powdered ocher, drilled canid-tooth ornaments, and burial items.[68] The forty-four human burials were later dated to between 8000 and 6300 ^{14}C BP and discussed as having been cut into and intruding into the lower level.[69] The lowest levels of the site contained lithic tools and the remains of helically fractured mammalian bone.[70]

The Arroyo Seco 2 artifacts collection has been restudied and redated. Mammalian specimens for dating were chosen based on the presence of fracture patterns that were deemed to be cultural modifications associated with marrow extraction.[71] The mammalian bone was excavated from a level that contained unifacial lithic tools.[72] J. Steel and G. Politis, in their argument for cultural modification of the mammalian bone, stated that "the open setting of the site on a low loess dune, is viewed by the investigators as inconsistent with a natural accumulation of such a diversity of mega-mammals."[73] The new dates obtained on animal bone by Steel and Politis reported as 12,155 ± 70 ^{14}C BP on *Megatherium* bone are consistent with two other labs' previous dating of the specimen and inconsistent with a younger date on the same specimen reported by a third lab. That younger date is now rejected by the authors.

In a recent genetic study focused on the demographic evolution of early humans in the Southern Cone of Argentina, S. I. Perez and colleagues suggest that the colonization and demographic human expansion took place earlier than accepted.[74] Their genetic research, which considered the known archaeological sites of the area, suggests that Patagonia was peopled between 17,000 and 14,000 cal BP. Patagonia is the southernmost area in South America, and what we know from the archaeological record is most likely not complete. However, this area holds great promise for further research as more sites benefit from renewed investigations and archaeologists focus on regional areas rather than just single sites.

An Ancient and Diverse Landscape

South America is a landmass of immense geological and environmental diversity, including rainforests, mountain ranges, sea coasts and islands, and deserts and plains, and it includes a robust archaeological record dating from the Pleistocene. The archaeological Pleistocene record of South America and the work of dedicated archaeologists such as Tom Dillehay have hammered the final nail in the coffin of the Clovis First hypothesis of initial human migrations into the Western Hemisphere. Prior to the acceptance of the Monte Verde site, South America provided an archaeological record that vastly predated the Clovis time frames and fueled fires of debate and heated discussions about the denial of early humans in the Western Hemisphere.

Much of the archaeological research in South America has been carried out by scholars from countries other than North America, and this may be in part a reason why it has for so long been a place where some archaeologists such as Nièllide Guidon and others carried out research with their minds and eyes wide open. A few American and Canadian archaeologists have reported on numerous pre-11,000 ^{14}C BP sites in South America, including Scotty MacNeish, Alan Bryan, Ruth Gruhn, and Tom Dillehay. Archaeologists can no longer deny a site's dates, stratigraphy, or artifacts on conjecture alone, as was done in previous decades in the Americas. As Pleistocene archaeology in South America grows and expands we may in the future learn a great deal more regarding stories on the land, the archaeological record left by the ancestors of Indigenous people. It is hopeful and most beneficial that archaeologists in South America are now researching regional areas, seeking for and finding linked Pleistocene archaeological sites and artifact assemblages, though this work may take decades to complete.

CHAPTER 7

Genetics, Linguistics, Oral Traditions, and Other Supporting Lines of Evidence

Many Ways to Know

The study of early humans in the Western Hemisphere (the Americas) has been of interest to scholars and invading settlers ever since 1590, when Jesuit missionary José de Acosta theorized an Asian origin of the first people.[1] Archaeologists and geneticists have argued for single initial human migration into the Western Hemisphere during the end of the Late Glacial Maximum (LGM).[2] However, the archaeological record of the Western Hemisphere does not agree with post-LGM initial human migrations, as numerous archaeological sites predate 12,000–15,000 years before present. Nor do Indigenous peoples' oral traditions agree with genetically framed stories of the Indigenous past, as many oral traditions state that Indigenous people have been here on Turtle Island (North America) since time immemorial.[3] There is no consensus regarding theories based on genetic studies of initial human migrations into the Western Hemisphere. As more genetic research is carried out, even though the data set is problematically small, the theories of initial peopling of the Western Hemisphere have grown and expanded. Some recent molecular research has been very holistic and promising. However, some molecular research remains very problematic regarding claims of genetic links between ancient (12,600 years ago) human populations and all contemporary Indigenous populations of the Western Hemisphere.[4] The molecular data that would represent all Indigenous people of the Western Hemisphere do not exist, as the genetic sampling collected and recorded from Indigenous people of the Western Hemisphere accounts for less than 1 percent of the overall historical and contemporary populations of Indigenous people.[5] Statements regarding human migrations based on genetics that do not discuss the sample size are often highly misleading.

Molecular Anthropology

Molecular research does not provide the physical or cultural evidence required to confirm the presence of a story on the land (an archaeological site). One might ask, then, Why is it even mentioned? Molecular research can provide evidence that informs an understanding of links between ancient and contemporary Indigenous people. However, discussions that are based in genetic research into the initial peopling of the Western Hemisphere can be misconstrued and manipulated by researchers to fit specific paradigms of human migrations. In academia, it is the responsibility of researchers to discuss problematic areas of research and to publish discussions so as to problematize scientific claims and open new discussion to further research in a given field. Thus, I highlight problematic claims and analysis regarding molecular anthropology so as to generate questions and bring a renewed focus to research discussions. As so few DNA samples have been collected, and so little (genetically) is known of the Indigenous peoples of the Western Hemisphere, no claims to have discovered a founding initial ancestor or population can be soundly supported.

The genetic research on the Anzick child burial is an important addition to an emerging body of data that links ancient populations to contemporary Indigenous people in the Americas.[6] M. Rasmussen and colleagues have presented data derived from skeletal remains that were initially disturbed by a bulldozer. These remains were looted from the Anzick site in Montana and then returned thirty years later. Thus, the Anzick site had been previously thought to be too problematic to provide reliable data. The authors' in-depth research and discussion, which are careful in their use of identifiers and language, are an improvement over previously published literature in the field. However, the article's central arguments contain statements that are inconsistent with the published literature on the Anzick Site. Rasmussen and colleagues state that the remains were found in direct association with Clovis tools. However, the Anzick artifacts and the Anzick child remains were not excavated or collected by archaeologists from an in situ deposit in direct association with Clovis tools. The burial and stone tools were disturbed by a bulldozer, and the site was looted and thus not recorded in situ or with a direct association between the burial and artifacts.[7] A construction worker, Ben Hargis (now deceased), who was removing soil with a front-end loader, accidentally discovered the Anzick site in 1968. Hargis and his wife, Faye, and their friend Calvin Sarver and his wife, Mary, all returned later in the day and collected artifacts and the partial remains of a human. L. Larhen reinvestigated the Anzick site in 1999; he persuaded Faye Hargis-Case and Calvin Sarver to visit the site area with him to recall where the artifacts and the human remains had been located. This was over thirty years after the initial disturbance and looting of the site.[8]

There are many problematic areas that are often undiscussed in reports of genetic analysis and inferences of population demography, specifically regarding the initial peopling of the Western Hemisphere. I was therefore happy to read a recent paper authored by Leonardo Arias and colleagues, who addressed problematic areas within genetic research today.[9] Arias and his coauthors discussed their results, which suggested that Indigenous links to land (rivers) and place were more important than language and family in understanding the genetic structuring of descendant populations in the Northwest Amazon. Arias and colleagues discussed the following areas of genetic research:.

1. Recent developments in sequencing technology allow the determination of complete mtDNA genomes at the population level and thus enable unbiased insights into the maternal history of human populations.
2. Available studies of complete mtDNA genomes from Native Americans have been restricted to a limited number of individuals carrying particular haplogroups, or to archaeological remains from different time periods.
3. These studies have primarily focused on inferences about the peopling of the continent, the number of migrations, the divergence times, and changes in the effective population size through time.[10]

Some scholars within the field of human genetics have argued that there are several problems and biases associated with sampling strategies in genetic research.

1. A "bottleneck erased the signals of ancient demographic history from recent Native American mtDNA pool, and conclude that the proposed early expansion and occupation of Beringia is an artifact caused by the misincorporation of non–Native American haplotypes."[11]
2. Scientists have genetically sampled only a few tenths of a percent of the entire living Native American population and less than a hundredth of a percent of the deceased Native American populations.[12]
3. Reference bias has the potential to cause minor but significant differences in the results of downstream analyses, such as population allele sharing, heterozygosity estimates, and estimates of archaic ancestry.[13]

Arias and colleagues, who are from the Max Planck Lab, discussed their research project in very clear terms: "In this study, we use complete mtDNA sequencing in a large and representative sample of populations covering the extant ethnolinguistic diversity from NWA [the Northwest Amazon] to reconstruct their maternal history, as well as to determine their genetic diversity and to make inferences about the origins of this diversity. Finally, we aim to investigate the impact of prehistoric population dynamics and cultural interactions on the structure of the genetic variation observed among present-day NWA populations."[14] The results of the study by Arias and colleagues create counterdiscourse regarding Indigenous diversity in the Northwest Amazon previously made by authoritative voices emanating from institutions such as the Smithsonian, long seen as experts on Amazonian history.

Contrary to the view of NWA as a pristine area inhabited by small human populations living in isolation, our data support a view of high diversity and contact among different ethnolinguistic groups; movement along rivers has probably facilitated this contact. Additionally, we provide evidence for the impact of cultural practices, such as linguistic exogamy, on patterns of genetic variation. Overall, this study provides new data and insights into a remote and little-studied region of the world . . . [that] contains tremendous biological, linguistic, and cultural diversity, which likely reflects the heterogeneity of the landscape, especially the complex and extensive network of rivers found in this area.[15]

Antonio Torroni and colleagues have reported on Native American mitochondrial haplogroups. They identified four mtDNA haplotypes (A, B, C, and D), which they traced back to Asian populations.[16] Mitochondrial DNA is inherited maternally. According to D. Andrew Merriwether, "A haplotype is any pattern of linked polymorphisms."[17] There is no recombination in mtDNA that allows for any polymorphisms found in mtDNA from an individual to be grouped together into a pattern called a haplotype. The circular mtDNA molecule has a 16,560 nucleotide sequence. A haplotype may be a single continuous stretch of mtDNA, or it may be a collection of restriction fragment length polymorphisms (RFLPs). In 1998 Michael D. Brown and colleagues discussed a fifth haplogroup, X, found in North America and Europe: "It has been inferred that ⊠97% of Native American mtDNAs belong to one of four major founding mtDNA lineages, designated haplogroups 'A'–'D.' It has been proposed that a fifth mtDNA haplogroup (haplogroup X) represents a minor founding lineage in Native Americans."[18]

R. S. Malhi and his colleagues analyzed the DNA from two mid-Holocene (5,000 years BP) individuals from the Charlie Lake Site in north-central British Columbia and identified mitochondrial DNA haplogroup M.[19] The M haplotype is common in East Asia, but this study was the first time haplogroup M had been reported in an Indigenous population in the Western Hemisphere. M is a macrohaplogroup that includes C and D in Indigenous populations of North America. Haplogroup M and its sister haplogroup N are descendants of haplogroup L3. This study provides evidence that there is more to learn regarding the founding haplogroups of Indigenous people of the Western Hemisphere: "This discovery broadens existing views of the colonization of the Americas. Researchers studying mtDNA of contemporary populations may have ignored evidence of additional founding haplogroups because it did not fit the prevailing five-founder model for the peopling of the Americas. In addition, studies of ancient DNA in the Americas may have misidentified authentic evidence of additional founder lineages as contamination and, as such, failed to report the results."[20]

Regarding the small percentage of genetic sampling for the Western Hemisphere and the likelihood that there is much greater genetic diversity than presently discussed, Malhi and colleagues stated: "Global genetic surveys suggest that Native American populations exhibit greater amounts of inter-population genetic differentiation relative to populations in other continental regions (Rosenberg et al., 2002). This large amount of inter-population genetic differentiation combined with the paucity of sampling in many regions in the Americas, makes it likely that significant undocumented genetic structure still exists in the Americas."[21]

In their paper, Leonardo Arias and colleagues discussed the genetic diversity identified in a study of ethnolinguistic groups in the Northwest Amazon: "The mtDNA data revealed that NWA populations have high genetic diversity with extensive sharing of haplotypes among groups. Moreover, groups who practice linguistic exogamy have higher mtDNA diversity, while the foraging Nukak have lower diversity. We also find that rivers play a more important role than either geography or language affiliation in structuring the genetic relationships of populations."[22]

According to B. H. Kashani and colleagues, mitochondrial genomes from Native Americans expanded from four to fifteen maternal founding lineages. The authors stated that not much is known regarding some of these lineages, leaving a gap in our knowledge of founding populations.[23]

Among geneticists, there is no consensus on the proposed number of possible founding populations or initial migrations into the Western Hemisphere. Some geneticists argue for a single founding population migration hypothesis.[24] The proposed two-migrations hypothesis is supported by others in the field.[25] The three-migrations hypothesis is proposed and supported by Joseph Greenberg and colleagues based on evidence from linguistics, genetics, and dental morphology.[26] A four-wave migration has also been discussed by a group of geneticists in numerous publications.[27]

R. H. Ward and colleagues carried out molecular research with samples from a population of Nuu-Chah-Nulth peoples from the Pacific Northwest; the study revealed a "substantial level of mitochondrial diversity for a small population, 28 lineages defined by 26 variable positions."[28] Other interesting results were reported by Carlos Lalueza and colleagues on ancient DNA extracted from bones and teeth of sixty individuals.[29] The individuals represented four extinct human populations from Tierra del Fuego: Selknam, Yamana, Kaweskar, and Aonikenk. "The results revealed the complete absence of two of the four primary mitochondrial haplotype groups present in contemporary Amerinds, namely A and B. In contrast, haplogroups C and D were found in all but one sample with frequencies of ~38% and 60%. These results, together with the decreasing incidence of group A in more southerly latitudes in the American continent and the absence of cluster B above 55° North in America and Asia, argue that the first settlers entering America 21,000–14,000 years ago already lacked both mtDNA lineages."[30]

Numerous initial migrations have been suggested by Torroni and colleagues and by Shields and colleagues.[31] Torroni and colleagues argue that as Na-Dene carry only haplogroup A and Amerinds carry four lineages, this supports the argument for independent migrations from the Eastern Hemisphere to the Western Hemisphere. In opposition to theories of multiple founding migrations, proponents of a single founding migration hypothesis posit the existence of variants of the major founding mtDNA lineages.[32] This has been discussed as evidence of a single wave of migration into the New World.[33] Luca Cavalli-Sforza, a faculty member at Stanford and a population geneticist, when discussing the many debates over the timing of initial migrations into the Western Hemisphere stated: "The archaeology of America is more like a battle field than a research topic. Given the circumstances, I suppose it's reasonable to be cautious. Only if I were forced to bet, I would prefer older dates."[34]

There is no overall consensus for when initial migrations occurred or numbers of migrations among geneticists discussing the peopling of the Western Hemisphere. Geneticists Douglas Wallace and Antonio Torroni have argued that the overall age of three of the four mtDNA Amerindian lineages dated to 21,000–42,000 years.[35] Wallace and Torroni allowed that at the time, it was unclear where the founder effect that led to these mtDNA lineages occurred in areas of the Eastern Hemisphere now known as Siberia or Beringia. While molecular evidence is invaluable to studies of the human past, it presents an incomplete picture of Indigenous populations of the Western Hemisphere. Given the tiny fraction of Indigenous groups' DNA that has been studied, we cannot conclude the number of founding haplotypes or timing of initial migrations. Geneticists have provided informative molecular data for Western Hemisphere populations they have studied. However, they have a long way to go to even come near to having a comprehensive body of data that will inform us of the overall molecular view of the human past of the Western Hemisphere.

Geneticists have discussed the known Native American populations as having a low genetic diversity and greater differentiation than other continental populations.[36] However, they have allowed that the datasets for genetic diversity in the Americas have been constrained by very small sample sets.[37] There are many reasons for the lack of DNA sample sets for Indigenous populations of the Americas.

1. Postcontact disease and attempted genocide have resulted in estimated losses of the overall Indigenous population of the Western Hemisphere being as high as 95 percent.[38]
2. Research projects and funding may be constrained by preconceived notions of late post-LGM migrations.
3. Many contemporary Indigenous communities have no desire or need to share their genetic histories and are understandably wary of sharing anything so sensitive with European American researchers, in part due to the misuse of genetic materials and data.

A geneticist may frame their discussion of the possibilities of Native American genetic diversity on incredibly small sample datasets and on constrained archaeological views regarding initial habitation of the Western Hemisphere. What geneticists and researchers know regarding initial migrations and Indigenous people of the Americas has, in part, been framed by Eurocentric archaeological discussions and archaeologists who are vested in a field that has a long and well-documented history of dehumanizing Indigenous people and minimalizing their history. This is an archaeological praxis that continues today, evidenced by the fact that some geneticists and archaeologists argue for the Beringia Standstill Hypothesis, which is based on initial migrations around 15,000 years BP. However, this hypothesis is not supported by archaeological evidence.[39] There are a few examples of researchers who are just beginning to lift the lid off that box of complicit minimization of all things Indigenous within the Americas. In a recent study, B. Llamas and colleagues identified eighty-four haplotypes previously unknown from any other population study. They sequenced ninety-two "whole mitochondrial genomes from pre-Columbian South American skeletons dating from 8.6 to 0.5 ka years ago. None of the 84 haplotypes identified from ancient samples are represented in the existing genealogy of global human mitochondrial diversity . . . or in the literature. Although modern Native American genetic diversity is not well characterized, this result clearly illustrates the importance of sampling pre-Columbian specimens to fully measure the past genetic diversity and to reconstruct the process of the peopling of the Americas."[40] The authors highlighted what has been long discussed as a near-extinction event and a genocide of 90–95 percent of precontact Indigenous people in the Americas due to European colonization: "All of the ancient mitochondrial lineages detected in this study were absent from modern data sets, suggesting a high extinction rate. To investigate this further, we applied a novel principal components multiple logistic regression test to Bayesian serial coalescent simulations. The analysis supported a scenario in which European colonization caused a substantial loss of pre-Columbian lineages."[41] Though a small sample set was tested for this genetic research project, it provided eighty-four previously unknown haplotypes. Given that the current haplotypes known for the Western Hemisphere represent a tiny percent of the contemporary and precontact populations, it is likely that the genetic view of people in the Western Hemisphere may greatly expand in the future.

Geneticists acknowledge that there are significant issues within the field regarding studies of Indigenous people of the Americas, including small sample sets, problems with setting the molecular clock for American populations, and disagreements on the number of founding populations. It seems rather like trying to build and ride a bicycle with only the handlebars. You have a steering mechanism, a horn, and an idea but nothing to attach them to. Undaunted, you ride the bicycle and honk the horn anyway, making the bike look as good as you can. Your imagination plays a significant role here. I appreciate the work of researchers, especially when it lifts lids of closed boxes of biased thought and moves understandings of the human past in positive directions. Genetics can be a tool that Indigenous people can use and has supported community-centered work in repatriation, health, and linking contemporary communities with their ancient ancestors across time and place. Regarding the peopling of the Western Hemisphere, geneticists would benefit from listening to and gaining an understanding of oral traditions and genesis stories and from becoming informed of the ancient time frames held within those stories and within the archaeological record of Turtle Island. Kim TallBear has discussed tribally driven participatory research (TDPR) as having the potential to create a genetics research program governed by Indigenous people.[42]

Linguistics and Time

The unmistakable testimony of the linguistic evidence is that the New World had been inhabited nearly as long as Australia or New Guinea, perhaps some 35,000 years. Genetic unity for "Amerind" is incompatible with the chronology demanded by the linguistic facts.

—Johanna Nichols, "Linguistic Diversity and the First Settlement of the New World"

Johanna Nichols has discussed rates of language spread at low and midlatitudes and considered coastal and interior routes of migration and settlement. She posits that the fastest rate would have required an initial entry date of 26,000 years ago into the Western Hemisphere. Nichols argued that considering languages from Alaska to Chile at an average rate of language spread would have taken 50,000 years, requiring an entry date of 60,000 years. She stated that interior rates of language were somewhat faster, but even so, it would have taken at least 30,000 years for the average rate and over 20,000 years for the fastest rate to have reached the unusually high diversity of languages that have been recorded in the Western Hemisphere. Earlier linguists such as Joseph Greenberg created a linguistic lumping model that fit the diversity of Western Hemisphere Indigenous languages into the time frame of the Clovis First hypothesis, allowing for only three founding linguistic stocks.[43] Nichols argued that these scenarios assume a "tenfold discrepancy in the rate of linguistic differentiation" and further stated that "unless researchers can demonstrate different input conditions . . . we have no business assuming that a tenfold discrepancy" is a valid explanation to account for the diversity of languages in the Western Hemisphere.[44]

The number of Indigenous languages previously spoken in the Western Hemisphere may never be known due to the rapid population declines after contact. Minimally, 85–95 percent of the Indigenous population was wiped out post-1492.[45] The languages we know of may represent only a fraction of the precontact Indigenous people's languages. In the study of languages, the oldest group reachable by what Nichols describes as the comparative method is called the stock—calculating the known number of language stocks of Amerinds.[46] Nichols stated that there are about 50 for North America, 14 for Mesoamerica, and over 80 for South America.[47] Minimally, there are 144 language stocks or language families in the Americas.

TABLE 7. Linguistic Stocks

Area	Stock low	Stock high	Language families
North America	42	51	69
Mesoamerica	14		14
South America	80	90	115
Africa	5	14	25
Ancient Near East	>6		
Northern Eurasia	15	14	26
Australia	?	20	11
New Guinea	27		>60
Siberia	8	7	10
Europe	3		9

Source: Adapted from Nichols, "Linguistic Diversity," 514–18.

Keep in mind that researchers point out that inland routes from the areas we know today as Beringia and North America were blocked by glacial ice from 24,000 to about 15,000 years ago.[48] Nichols discusses the timing required for such a high linguistic diversity based on one or more initial migrations: for Amerindian languages to have evolved from a single genetic lineage would have required at least 50,000 years.[49] However, if Indigenous language families evolved from only a few lineages, then 20,000 years would have been needed to move even a few languages from Siberia or Asia throughout the Western Hemisphere. Evidence from linguistic studies suggests that for such an unusually high diversity of languages to have developed, people would have initially migrated to the Western Hemisphere prior to 30,000 years before present. Nichols argues that there is no obstacle to pushing back the time frame of initial habitation of the Western Hemisphere to at least 20,000 and perhaps 40,000 years ago.

Oral Histories in Deep Time

Indigenous scholars and communities are working to undo colonial misreading of their oral traditions. American scholars have collected and published many oral traditions; however, their understanding of the intricacies of cultural meanings was nonexistent, and thus volumes of misinterpreted oral traditions line the shelves of modern libraries. Indigenous peoples tell stories of the past and present of a vibrant world in which all things have life and are respected.[50] Oral traditions are not merely stories or histories. They are living intergenerational experiences of respectful cohabitation, where humans considered themselves to be only one of many beings in a sacred landscape: "Oral histories cannot be validated by the standard systems of a literate society. It would be unfair to judge the spiritual beliefs, the emotions and dreams of a culture based on oral traditions with tools that do not give much weight to matters that are of great importance to one culture and not in another."[51]

In seeking to gain a deeper understanding of Paleolithic archaeological sites in the Americas, we need to consider and include oral traditions and Indigenous people's knowledge of lands, flora, and fauna. American archaeologists would benefit from an understanding of Indigenous oral traditions, languages, worldviews, and epistemologies. There are vast differences between Western and Indigenous perceptions of who and what form a society and family. To interpret oral tradition requires more than a Native informant. It requires academics to step outside the colonial mainframe and become open to understanding other realities, to surrender their authority, power, and preconceived notions of "others." Oral traditions hold knowledge based on centuries of intimate experiences viewing everything on the land as relations.[52] Western knowledge of Indigenous landscapes is most often impoverished, as it is based on very recent and shallow history and understanding based on an etic (outsider) perspective. That is improvised when compared to the thousands of years of experience and knowledge held by Indigenous people who have a firsthand experience of Indigenous landscapes across thousands of years. Joe Watkins has discussed the difference between Western archaeologists and Indigenous people and scholars, in the interpretation of artifacts: "While artifacts are tangible relics of the past the way they are viewed by Indigenous populations and archaeologists is tempered by cultural differences. Archaeologists tend to focus on the physical, technological or esoteric attributes of an artifact, while Indigenous populations tend to focus on the ritual or social importance of the artifacts."[53]

A holistic archaeological discussion would consider the physical, technological, and esoteric attributes and the ritual or social meaning of the artifacts. Indigenous scholars are uniquely situated to create knowledge in a holistic framework as they are informed through both Indigenous and Western ways of knowing. Indigenous archaeologists can be outsiders among Indigenous communities of which they are not members, but they may be aware of commonalities in worldviews and cultural protocols across Indigenous communities.

Traditional Knowledge of Pleistocene Environments and Species

There are oral traditions of Pleistocene species and representations in rock art and petroglyphs. I have reviewed the literature of oral traditions that specifically discuss interactions between Indigenous people and extinct species such as mammoth and mastodon in the area of the La Sena site near Medicine Creek, along the Ohio and Pomme de Terre Rivers, north and west of the Coats-Hines site, and in other areas of the Western Hemisphere. One such area is that of the Columbia Plateau. A paper authored by the staff of the Cultural Resources Protection Program, Department of Natural Resources, Confederated Tribes of the Umatilla Indian Reservation

Joor Story

(CTUIR) discusses oral traditions, a pictograph, and a dance that are based on the story of a battle between the great god Coyote, king of the gods, and the king of the elephants.

According to Tribal Elders, this story was handed down from the great god Coyote directly to an old Chieftain, whose wisdom was beyond any other members of the tribe, and who had the good of man in his heart. The story relates the happiness of the Cayuse people in the land along the Umatilla. Then there was plenty to eat, venison, wild berries, salmon, birds, and roots. One day, as the hunters were tracking game, they saw all the animals fleeing to the south in great fright. The earth beneath them began to tremble and trees began to fall, then vast shapes came into view. These great things were waving snake-like shapes in front of them and making terrible trumpeting sounds as they crashed through the forest. The strange creatures tore huge trees from the canyon tops and hurled them into the valley below. The warriors were brave, but as the creatures came closer they fled in panic to higher ground. The creatures took possession of the land and plunged into the Umatilla River. They tossed water high in the air and churned the current into mud until the frightened salmon threw themselves on the banks to die or were trampled beneath their great feet. The Cayuse fled to the River of the North [Columbia River?] and spread the news of the strange demons that had turned the Umatilla River into a sluggish creek of mud and destroyed the land. The salmon were dead, the deer scattered, berries and roots had been uprooted and eaten by the creatures.

Coyote had been watching from his high mountaintop and had seen the beasts coming from the North to wreak havoc on the Umatilla River. He knew they had been sent by an evil spirit to harass the Cayuse. He came to the aid of his children and confronted the elephant herd, demanding that they leave the land of the Cayuse. In fear of Coyote's power, the herd obeyed and returned north. The salmon soon returned to the river, the land healed, and the people were content and fed again. However, in the Northland, the king of the herd brooded, remembering the lush grass and the cool river where he had bathed. He slipped away on a dark night and returned to the land of the Cayuse. Coyote saw the elephant had returned and confronted him again. The King of the elephants refused to leave, testing Coyote's authority, and threatening to send for the rest of the herd. Coyote was insulted by the elephant's impudence and cursed the bull, saying that he would stand upon this spot forever, through winter's cold and summer's heat. He would be a warning to any animal that may come into the land to harm the Cayuse. The elephant would be chained to the mountainside in solid rock, "to suffer forever and forever the pangs of remorse and the pain of great disobedience to the god Coyote of the Cayuse" (Searcey 1986, 6). To this day, there is a name in the local Sahaptin dialect, K'alallii, which means big, furry monster. Also, an old song and dance is known among the people of the CTUIR that coincides with K'walalliz'. The dancers stomp slowly and heavily along like a great herd of elephants, swaying and singing as they go.

It is of great interest to note, in conjunction with this story, that there is a site on the Umatilla Indian Reservation known as the Mammoth Site (temporary number 96UMoIPA). Two mammoth teeth were uncovered during construction of the Wildhorse Resort Golf Course.[54]

Ashley Montagu wrote about an Osage tradition of a battle between the great beasts that inhabited the area and others that had traveled to the area from the east via the Mississippi and Missouri Rivers.[55] According to Osage oral history, there were so many angry beasts that the people could no longer travel and hunt safely. The Osage story tells of a fierce battle between the two groups of giant beasts, which left many of them dead. After the battle between the beasts was over, the Indians burned many of the animals as an offering to the Great Spirit. The place of the battle became a sacred spot, as the Osage had been spared and could once again travel and hunt safely. Every year after that, the Indians brought a yearly sacrifice to the site in thanks to the Great Spirit for their safety. When settlers began arriving in the area, the Osage protected the site and challenged the settlers' attempts to disturb the ground and desecrate it. However, the federal government forced the Osage onto reservations a considerable distance from the site, and settlers soon moved in and began to disturb the sacred site area.

The legend can be connected with historical events. In the early 1800's at Big Bone River, white settlers digging out a spring discovered some huge bones, which they linked to the local Osage lore about the Battle of the Monsters. In 1806, Georges Cuvier received news of the bones of Mastodons in Osage lands; he even acquired a Mastodon molar from Big Bone River, sent to Paris by the American naturalist Benjamin Smith Barton, who obtained it from an "intelligent voyageur." There were thousands of Mastodon bones along the "riviere des Indiens Osages," wrote Barton, many of the skeletons were buried in a standing position, and many were well preserved in peaty bogs. . . . The Mastodon molar from Osage territory is currently in the Museum of Natural History in Paris.[56]

According to Adrienne Mayor, Albert Koch from the St. Louis Museum was "spurred on by the Osage legend, and the settlers find."[57] Koch continued to dig in the areas of the Big Bone and Bourbeuse Rivers, and at Kimmswick, he discovered many fossils of *Mastodon americanus* and collected hundreds of teeth and tusks. According to Ashley Montagu, Koch claimed in 1839 that he had unearthed arrowheads and mammoth bone at several Missouri sites.[58] Paleontologists of the time dismissed his claims; however, in the 1960s, new work confirmed his earlier findings.[59] Excavations at the Kimmswick site support Koch's discussions of finding mammoth remains and stone tools at the location the Osage identified in oral traditions as a commemoration site where there had been a battle between great monstrous beasts.[60]

Mnemonic Paths through Time

Many oral histories contain mnemonic pegs to places and events through time and space.[61] Montagu's discussion of the Osage history demonstrates two profound possibilities. First, oral histories may be transferred intergenerationally across thousands of years, and second, oral histories can inform us of events in the deep past.[62] Catastrophic environmental events such as volcanic eruptions have been documented in oral traditions of cultural histories. Katherine Cashman and Shane Cronin have stated that oral traditions of volcanic and catastrophic events contain data that can extend the geological interpretation of the frequency and reoccurrence of hazardous events.[63] Cashman and Cronin highlight research that shows that worldwide there are many oral histories that have been proven through geological study to be documentation of ancient and historical catastrophic events.

The reluctance of many academics to consider oral traditions in archaeology is often based in settler academics' lack of knowledge of Indigenous cultures. David Pendergast and Clement Meighan concluded from their investigations of archaeological sites and oral traditions that accurate information may be preserved across several hundred years.[64] Pendergast and Meighan argued that historical information might broaden and substantiate understandings of archaeological sites. As archaeologists, we seek to create a holistic understanding of the past; we should be considering and incorporating all forms of knowledge relating to research areas.

A few academics who have discussed links between oral histories and archaeological sites have also discussed the evidence of the past, which is presented in oral traditions.[65] "The land is more than a backdrop . . . or a location, it is a sustainer, speaker, and archive for Indigenous stories."[66] Haunani-Kay Trask has argued that "Indigenous stories . . . rest within the culture, which is inseparable from the land."[67] Aman Sium and Eric Ritskes discuss the place of Indigenous knowledge production as a tool of decolonization because it is "disruptive of Eurocentric norms of objectivity and knowledge."[68] Indigenous knowledge and traditions centered within academia work to decolonize embedded colonial practices of exclusion of other ways of knowing. Indigenous traditions place Indigenous people at the center of their own histories, illuminating complex, rich, and multi-layered levels of intellectualism across time and space. Oral traditions and legends are known to have existed in every culture and have been accepted by some scholars as histories holding facts of the past in Asia, Africa, and Europe. Some archaeologists do not consider the possibilities of finding facts or historical accounts of events, people, and places in oral traditions; instead, they recolonize research and history: "Oral tradition does not provide us with a series of data which stand by themselves. It is more like a prism which becomes richer as our abilities improves [sic] to view it from a variety of angles. The question is not whether a particular tradition reflects the way a particular individual views the world, but whether it broadens the world-view of the listener."[69]

Memories

Our ancestors are in our hearts, minds, and souls
they remain with us always
and their memories
of places on the lands
of ceremonies
of pimatisiwin
live within us
course through our veins
as we work to reclaim, revive, and relink our descendants to their lands
the places of their ancestral birth
the places where blood and memories run free

CHAPTER 8

Reawakening, Resisting, Rewriting

Confronting Soulwounds along Paths to Healing

> The problem is that constant efforts by governments, states, societies, and institutions to deny the historical formations of such conditions have simultaneously denied our claims to humanity, to having a history, and to all sense of hope. To acquiesce is to lose ourselves entirely and implicitly agree with all that has been said about us. To resist is to retrench in the margins, retrieve what we were and remake ourselves.
> —Linda Tuhiwai Smith, *Decolonizing Methodologies*

> Archaeologists are acutely aware of the possible implications of the earlier peopling of the Americas, which reflects on contemporary issues of identity, ancestry, and ownership of the past and present.
> —David Meltzer, *First Peoples in a New World*

Discussions on the unsubstantiated claims of the Clovis First hypothesis of initial human migrations to the Western Hemisphere have arisen in academic literature and the general media.[1] Critical discussions regarding the Western view of the histories of first peoples are a crucial area of study, for what remains undiscussed remains unchallenged and hidden. Critical scholarship and discussions refuse to allow colonial violence to continue unabated and to allow false doctrines of Indigenous people's histories to go unchallenged. Contemporary colonial violence against Indigenous people is normalized in literature and remains embedded in many forms throughout education, institutions, and the general media: "The Western worldview permeated throughout academic institutions serves to minimize, marginalize, undermine, and smother the worldviews of Indigenous peoples in a toxic cloud of racism, sexism and, capitalism. When Indigenous and

Western worldviews meet under these conditions of conflict, resistance emerges on both sides. The Western worldview systematically prevails because their values are backed up by the Government, enforced by their laws and perpetuated by the dominant society."[2]

To stay silent is to allow violence and colonialization to continue. It is essential to rewrite Indigenous histories that continue to erase diversity and humanity, such as the Clovis First hypothesis of initial migrations into the Western Hemisphere.[3] Archaeologists discuss sites in the Western Hemisphere where Clovis fluted tools and associated artifacts have been discovered as sites that were inhabited or used by the "Clovis People." Anthropologists and archaeologists are aware of the fact that one tool type does not define a culture, specifically, not a panhemispheric culture. Contemporary archaeologists continue to discuss the "Clovis People," and, as I said earlier, no such cultural human group ever existed beyond the wildest imagination of the archaeological mind. Indigenous histories framed by Western academics are often accepted as fact by the general population; they are not exposed for what Vine Deloria Jr. called the absurdity of their claims.

Disagreements between archaeologists over the peopling of the Americas have been so fierce that the field has been described as a battleground and an archaeological badlands. It is a battleground that is, unfortunately, littered with unnecessary academic casualties. In 1991 Niède Guidon, a prominent South American archaeologist, asked for an end to the "cold war of Americanist archaeology," calling for those who support pre-Clovis sites and those who do not to "seek collaboration" and the necessary evidence for "building a cultural sequence."[4]

Archaeological goals are to understand the human past; however, it is evident that we cannot possibly understand anything if we deny it exists before we even look for it. The absence of evidence is not evidence of absence. However, the absence of questioning and open minds is evidence of hubris, agnotology, and neocolonial praxis. Archaeologists focused on Pleistocene studies of the Americas and initial human habitations are currently inching back in time, accepting initial human migrations at around 15,000 cal BP.[5] However, discussions of initial migrations at 15,000 or even 18,000 years ago still ignore the evidence for a much earlier habitation of the Western Hemisphere.

In seeking to gain an understanding of initial human migrations, archaeologists need to consider possible time frames for people to have migrated throughout the Western Hemisphere and to have become intimately familiar with the landscape: "No matter how fast was the process of human peopling, several generations of people interacting with the environments, and with the local climates, would be needed to be successful in so many regions. These people have to understand the new environment and then transform it as a result of its exploitation. The variety of habitats exploited ca. 10,000 BP also suggests that the history of the human expansion into South America was not simple and that a number of theoretical and practical issues should be considered."[6]

Time frames much greater than 12,000–18,000 years may have been required to have settled an area that accounts for over one-quarter or minimally 28 percent of the world landmass. As there are hundreds of Pleistocene sites that date to earlier than 14,000 years ago, I do not find the archaeological signal of early humans in the Western Hemisphere to be sparse at all. I do find that archaeological discussion that denies a human presence in the Western Hemisphere prior to 14,000 years ago is often political and dehumanizing and not based on the archaeological record.

Dehumanizing discussions of Indigenous people embedded in educational and general literature and media maintain colonial tropes and festering racism. Maria Yellow Horse Brave Heart and Lemyra Debruyn (1998) have discussed a legacy of unresolved grief and trauma that has resulted from years of colonization and massive losses of lands, culture, identities, and human lives. Legacies of intergenerational trauma have been documented among Indigenous populations after acts of colonization, including genocide, ethnic cleansing, and forced acculturation.[7] The ongoing denial of Indigenous people links to an ancient time and place in the Western Hemisphere and also affects the worldviews and education of non-Indigenous people, distorting their views of history.

Archaeological reports may be impressive in their discussions and applications of science and multidisciplinary research. However, very few archaeologists ever mention or acknowledge the colonial history of archaeology or the social and political aspects linked to an archaeological discussion of the Indigenous Paleolithic of the Americas. Archaeologists who have reported on pre-Clovis sites older than 11,000–12,000 years ago have been viciously academically bullied while the majority of American archaeologists remained silent. Archaeologists who reported on Holocene sites, dating after 10,000 years ago, were not often subjected to overly aggressive critiques. The same archaeologists whose research on Holocene sites is not questioned, when working on Pleistocene sites are suddenly doing work that is highly problematic when they report on earlier than 11,000–12,000-year-old sites: "One may wonder how 'highly qualified' teams can carry out excellent interdisciplinary work in the Holocene levels, and then suddenly to be unable to recognize the stratigraphic details, the signs of climatic change and the paleontological evidence, the moment they come to the Pleistocene. In another example, Guthrie (1984) declares that 'Beringia is the only realistic route for human entry to the New World,' but he gives no explanation of what exactly 'realistic' means. Why should this have been the only route?"[8]

There is nothing wrong with a well-substantiated critique of archaeological reports and data; critiques may benefit an archaeological site interpretation. However, there is a decades-old practice of attacking any archaeologist who reports on sites that may link Indigenous people to the lands of the Western Hemisphere prior to 12,000–15,000 years ago.

In their focus on the peopling of the Americas, archaeologists ask many questions, including questions regarding the paleoenvironment, where people came from, and how they traveled to specific areas. The priority of questions regarding the possibilities of early human sites in the Americas would benefit from new directions of inquiry. How can anyone research where people came from and how they got there when they deny a priori evidence of how long people have been in a specific area? The questions archaeologists ask and the research focus need to shift to gain an informed understanding of how long people have been in the Western Hemisphere. What good are genetic or any models of initial migrations into a continental landmass area when you ignore the earliest evidence of human habitation?

Decolonizing Minds and Hearts

The stories of the past that we are taught throughout our primary and secondary education color our worldviews of ourselves and others. A view of how people see the world or, rather, are taught to see the ancient Indigenous past of the Western Hemisphere was recently provided to me through an essay assignment I gave in two Anthropology 100 classes. I was impressed by the honesty and clarity of the essays. Many students stated that they were taught that Christopher Columbus discovered the Americas; however, they were not taught much at all about the Indigenous people who were here before 1492.

Though students were not asked, they offered this information in a reflection of their primary and secondary school education regarding Indigenous people of the Americas. Out of 256 students, 58 stated they were taught that Christopher Columbus discovered the Americas, and 116 stated they were not taught much about Native Americans. Students were asked to discuss their worldviews and knowledge of Indigenous people and if what they had learned in the course might expand or alter their understanding about the Indigenous past and their views of Indigenous people of the Americas.

1. 175 students stated that an expanded view of time that includes earlier initial migrations into the Western Hemisphere would change their worldviews of Indigenous people of the Americas.

2. 61 students stated that they previously had high regard and/or respect for Indigenous people. Thus, their worldview would not change.

3. 217 out of 256 students stated that an expanded view of the past of Indigenous people in the Americas, that is, an understanding of an earlier time of initial habitation, would support the human rights of Indigenous people.

4. 39 students refrained from answering the question.

American archaeology has controlled the knowledge production of the history and heritage of Indigenous people of the Western Hemisphere for over a century. Academic scholars have discussed their understanding of the past as a tool of power and authority, identity erasure, and the loss of human rights. The impact of archaeological knowledge production on Indigenous peoples has been discussed by a few American archaeologists who recognize that the archaeological record used to interpret and construct the past has power in the present.[9]

The relations amongst traditional knowledge, Native voices, and archaeological work are structured by inequalities that affect the lives and ongoing resistance of indigenous communities and emerging nations. This suggests that archaeological studies in Indian country should always be critical: confronting silences, building new approaches that are collaborative and grounded, and recovering counterfactual histories to challenge neocolonialist discourse.[10]

Nation-states or partisans thereof, control and allocate symbolic resources as one means of legitimizing power and authority, and in pursuit of their perceived nationalistic goals and ideologies. A Major symbolic resource is the past.[11]

Reclaiming Histories

When we choose to grapple with wrong and bias within the historic narrative, we restore our own humanity.

—Julie Cajune, *Montana Tribal Histories*

To allow that Indigenous people were present in the Western Hemisphere over 14,000 years ago is to solidify their claims to Indigeneity and to support Indigenous ownership of the past, cultural identity, and links to homelands and material heritage. American archaeologists' reluctance to consider earlier initial migrations reflects a neocolonial practice of maintaining the historical erasure of an ancient Indigenous presence in the Western Hemisphere. Erasure of the deep past denies Indigenous people a place in world history that accords them full humanity.[12] It also denies knowledge of the past that is known from oral traditions and the material record. Linda Tuhiwai Smith discussed knowledge of the past as being crucial for Māori pride, growth, development, identity, and cultural survival.[13]

I began this journey, this ceremony of research, by asking questions regarding the paleoenvironmental possibilities of Pleistocene migrations and of the evidence for pre-Clovis sites in the Western Hemisphere. From what I have learned, I argue that there is a vast body of evidence that supports initial migrations to the Western Hemisphere much earlier than the accepted dates for Clovis technologies 11,200–10,800 years ago. The paleoenvironmental record does not suggest that pre–Late Glacial Maximum migrations were ever an impossibility. The environmental record and the record of mammalian migrations between the Eastern and Western Hemispheres informs us that the area we know today as the Bering landmass was available for dry-land migrations at different times during the Pleistocene, prior to the LGM.[14] However, it was not likely a viable land crossing during the LGM of 23,000–18,000 years ago due to the glacial environment.

Throughout this research process, I became familiar with the published literature of hundreds of Pleistocene age archaeological sites and the decades-long, overly aggressive denial of an earlier Indigenous presence. After reading numerous accounts of academic bashing and the history of a priori dismissal of pre-Clovis sites, I began to question why such a violent denial of earlier sites existed in a field where the main goal has always been the pursuit of knowledge of the human past. From what I have learned and experienced in American archaeology, I argue that the academic denial over the legitimacy of pre-Clovis sites reflects a neocolonial practice of maintaining the erasure of an ancient Indigenous presence in the Western Hemisphere. I agree with Vine Deloria Jr. that this erasure denies Indigenous people a place in world history that accords them full humanity and denies knowledge of the past, which is known from oral traditions and the material record.

Archaeology is a science that seeks to investigate anomalous data to learn on a global scale of early human histories and cultures. Regarding the Western Hemisphere, the question becomes, Why? Why was finding or discussing possibilities of earlier archaeological sites in the Western Hemisphere a forbidden and academically dangerous pursuit in American archaeology, and why for such a long time were earlier sites automatically deemed as "controversial" and denied? Why did so many American archaeologists not question or critique the aggressive blocking of academic pursuits and the apparent need to test an untested Clovis First hypothesis? Why the silence and complicity in a field that claims to be built on open dialogue and discovery of the human past? The answers are not complicated, as there is a well-documented, long-standing, and violent history of colonialism that dehumanized Indigenous people, relegating them to New Worlds of cultural infancy dominated by foreign Old World empires.

Thus, in discussing Indigenous histories, I would encourage scholars to contemplate their possible mimicking of the colonizers' language, which is deeply embedded in a violent praxis of erasure and dehumanization of Indigenous peoples. Cleansing our minds and language of colonial narratives can be visualized as an Indigenous ceremony of decolonizing the mind. In academic discussions, it is important not to re-create the erasure of Indigenous diversity, which is evident in archaeological discussions such as the discussions regarding the so-called Clovis People. As I stated earlier, no such cultural group ever existed but in the wildest imagination of the archaeological mind.

In my journey through the anthropological and Indigenous past, I came to understand that discussion of these areas and decolonization of knowledge production matter for many reasons. First and foremost, this research matters for what it restores to all Indigenous people of the Western Hemisphere, a public consciousness of a human presence in the Pleistocene prior to 25,000 years ago and likely before 130,000 years ago.[15] This research matters in that it brings to the public an understanding of Indigenous people's ancient links to the lands of the Western Hemisphere. This research matters because of the opportunities it opens for Indigenous communities and all students and scholars in the field and for the paths it opens to decolonizing the past and present. It matters in that it gives the public a path to decolonize their worldviews of the past and thus challenge discrimination in the present. It matters most profoundly for the questions it raises about processes of Indigenous erasure and dehumanization in knowledge production and how rewriting and rehumanizing the past reflect positively on the present and the future.

Decolonizing Archaeology

Although some American archaeologists now concede that initial migrations into the Western Hemisphere were earlier than 11,000–12,000 years ago, ongoing denial and hegemonic practices in American archaeology continue to be limiting factors, restraining research on Indigenous sites in the Western Hemisphere.[16] Hegemonic practices include but are not limited to the following:

1. identity politics, such as identifying ancestral and descendant Indigenous peoples of the Western Hemisphere as "Asians" rather than as Indigenous to the Western Hemisphere;[17]
2. scientific colonialism, which persists in archaeology;[18]
3. unbalanced power in managing heritage and controlling access to the archaeological record;[19]
4. the exclusion of minority scholars in archaeology . . . which sustains privileged access to interpretations of the past and bestows ideological power on the dominant culture;[20]
5. academic imperialism, discussed by Bagele Chilisa as "the unjustified and ultimately counterproductive tendency in intellectual and scholarly circles to denigrate, dismiss, and attempt to quash alternative theories, perspectives, or methodologies."[21]

The record of Pleistocene sites in the Western Hemisphere and our current knowledge of global intercontinental hominid and mammalian migrations across millions of years should be cause for further research. Though some archaeologists have accepted the legitimacy of pre-Clovis sites, the false doctrine of minimalized time frames for initial migrations to the Western Hemisphere has persisted for over eighty years as archaeological fact and remains cemented in academic and general discourses. In fact, archaeologists have for the most part been reluctant to accept dates that are more than a few thousand years older than Clovis. Though this has changed, the degree of change among archaeologists and anthropologists is relatively small. According to a 2012 survey of archaeologists carried out by Amber Wheat, many archaeologists do not support the legitimacy of pre-Clovis sites, or they had no opinion.[22] Wheat conducted a survey that included 132 respondents, mainly archaeologists, a few genetic anthropologists, and scholars in ecology and geology. Wheat invited survey participation from individuals who researched on or published on the peopling of the Americas. Survey questions included the acceptance or rejection of five well-published pre-Clovis sites. Only one site was accepted by most respondents. Monte Verde was accepted by approximately 65 percent of the respondents as a valid pre-Clovis site. Four other sites, including Paisley Caves, Topper, Cactus Hill, and Meadowcroft, had an acceptance rate of approximately 8–28 percent and a rejection rate of approximately 10–48 percent, while those who neither agreed nor disagreed ranged between 20 and 52 percent. Monte Verde is the youngest of the sites at 12,500 years BP and has a rock-star record of artifacts and scientific research. The dates for Paisley Caves are supported by human DNA. Meadowcroft has an excellent record of all required archaeological evidence, and Adovasio and colleagues successfully answered all critiques of the site. The Topper site has now been supported by further research on the pre-Clovis tools. In 1997 Adovasio and Pedler declared that the Clovis First version of the peopling of the Americas was dead; however, in 2012, as Wheat's survey shows, it was still very much alive.[23] Wheat's survey suggested that pre-Clovis sites are not accepted even when they have published data on all required aspects of an archaeological site and answered all critiques: "After many years of debate, there has been a remarkable turn of events in the First American controversy. It is now clear that the Clovis-First version of Late-Entry Model is dead, and the field of first American studies is undergoing a significant paradigm shift."[24]

It has been my experience when discussing Pleistocene archaeological sites in the Western Hemisphere with academic and cultural resource management archaeologists that many are quick to refute the legitimacy of a pre-Clovis site: they often state that there are few sites and that they are not legitimate sites. However, after further engaging these scholars, I find that most are not familiar with the literature of the sites they had deemed controversial, including their locations and their published archaeological records. Controversial, when assigned to archaeological sites that do not fit the politicized paradigms of colonial oppression, "controversial" when vocalized to delegitimize ancient Indigenous cultures, that controversial, is a Western political construct of colonial oppression, not a science. In the American academy, it was indeed dangerous to discuss a belief in the legitimacy of pre-Clovis sites. For decades, this was a profoundly limiting factor to further research in the field. Archaeologists often remained silent regarding numerous earlier sites and even today are reluctant to openly discuss their research on earlier sites. Archaeologists who have published on earlier sites did so with trepidation and the reality of facing severe scrutiny, academic bashing, and a loss of research funds.[25] Within archaeology today, academic bias and control of the Indigenous past remain a limiting factor over funding for research on Pleistocene sites in the Americas.

The evidence of highly civilized and extremely diverse cultures of Indigenous people in the Western Hemisphere has been known to American archaeologists for decades.[26] American archaeology's colonial past and linkages between knowledge production and political policy-making have been known and discussed for decades. Regarding possibilities of earlier Pleistocene migrations, the silence of scholars strolling academic halls with their eyes wide shut often remains painfully deafening. However, as academics, we have a responsibility to publish knowledge that is substantiated through data and research, to challenge dogmatic tropes that are unsubstantiated, and thereby to carry out work that may improve the human condition. We are charged with creating safe academic spaces from and through which to discuss the human past.

The three sites I reviewed for my dissertation research represent much more than a material collection of artifacts as defined in time and space by archaeologists. They are places of power and memory that speak to an Indigenous presence in the Western Hemisphere earlier than 11,000–12,000 years ago. They are a testimony to the fallacy of politically grounded academic practices, which are now being critiqued and decolonized. The Monte Verde site was denied as being a legitimate site for years, until it became somewhat safe to publish research on sites that were just slightly older than Clovis. The artifacts and knowledge on the site did not change the initial findings or dates of the site. The only thing that changed was the political and academic arena, which now allows for only slightly earlier sites to be discussed as legitimate. The La Sena site, dated to over 18,000 years ago, is located in southern Nebraska. Other Pleistocene sites with the fossil remains of mammoths have also been found in the Great Plains area. That Indigenous people in this area were harvesting mammoth bone for tool making and or marrow is no surprise; this has been suggested or argued for at numerous sites throughout North America.[27]

The Hwy 54 site, now known as the Cerutti Mastodon site, represents opportunities for archaeologists to apply archaeological sciences to informing the record of Pleistocene sites in the Western Hemisphere. Possible ongoing research includes testing of materials for residual analysis, which may inform the time frames for the site.[28] Given that a mammoth tusk was excavated from a vertical position in Pleistocene soils, spiral fracturing and impact points were identified on mammalian bone, and the materials from the site were recently dated to over 130,000 years ago, the Cerutti site is deserving of funding and further research.[29]

Indigenous Voices and Views

Indigenous critiques of Western knowledge, science, and education are based on firsthand experience of the negative social and political impacts of ethnocentric interpretations and cognitive imperialism. Marie Battiste (Mi'kmaw) has argued that both aboriginal and nonaboriginal people accept that knowledge liberates one's mind and ultimately has value for society as a whole.[30] Battiste discussed Western education and cognitive imperialism as a form of cognitive manipulation that is used to disclaim non-Western knowledge bases. She further argued that the maintenance of cognitive imperialism is legitimized through one language, one culture, and one frame of reference. Cognitive imperialism in anthropology has traditionally produced Indigenous histories based on Eurocentric assumptions of the past, which continue to fuel discrimination and agnotology in the present: "Culture has to be studied and written about by aboriginal people to allow space for aboriginal conscience, language, and identity to flourish without Eurocentric or racist interpretation."[31]

In work to repair the damage of cognitive imperialism, Indigenous scholars have begun to critique and rewrite knowledge of the past and present from an informed view based in intimate firsthand knowledge of their own histories and the history of anthropology: "Native intellectuals have both a right and an obligation to challenge the colonial dominance of our history, whether it be social-cultural, poetical, artistic, linguistic or legal."[32]

Indigenous people on a global scale have united in efforts to control their respected lifeways and communities while universally seeking to challenge structures of discrimination and inequality.[33]

Pyroepistemology and Healing: The Eighth Fire

Further research of Pleistocene archaeological sites and initial migrations to the Western Hemisphere emancipated from historical and political boundaries and the rhetoric of a discipline embedded in processes of colonial nation-building may enrich the archaeological record and expand the global history of human migrations. A few archaeologists have discussed problems within American archaeological practices. Ian Hodder discussed the need for a reorientation within American archaeology, stressing that there needs to be an understanding that the discipline is alienated from Native people. He further states that for archaeology to be meaningful, an understanding of the Indigenous past needs to become an objective of research.[34]

Eduardo Duran addresses the path of critical inquiry as one that leads to a liberation discourse and new narratives of healing.[35] Beyond a beginning of healing discourses, Duran reaches into the very heart of academia and reminds us this is not just a healing for those impacted by colonial histories. Critical scholarship of our field is a path to liberating ourselves and the academy.

Decolonizing Indigenous histories rebuilds bridges to ancestral places and times, which American archaeology burned in political fires of power and control. Indigenous critical theory exposes a past that American archaeology buried beneath the dark mire of colonial terra nullius. Scholars have documented improvements in Indigenous communities' well-being after a revival of Indigenous languages and cultural practices. This well-being was reported as a decline in youth suicide rates and an increase in higher education rates. All aspects of a community's culture, including their histories, ancient past, and links to homelands, are essential to individual and community identity and well-being.[36] This is a reflection on the possible well-being effects of a renewed and decolonized history that highlights Indigenous voices in knowledge production. Reclaiming and sharing our cultures, stories, and histories serves many purposes, including a political act of decolonization of the past and present. For the Cree, the importance of preserving and sharing their culture is discussed in the following quotes regarding Aanischaaukamikw, the museum of Cree culture.

Aanischaaukamikw is the physical expression of something the Cree Elders have challenged us to see for a long time, the reclaiming of the ways of Aanscha, the passing-on and protecting of our legends, our stories, and our way of life.

The presence of Aanischaaukamikw will allow us to share the best we have with the world, offering unique lessons in cultural diversity to Canada and other nations; presenting our ways of biodiversity, sustainable activity, and ecology; fostering better understanding of aboriginal needs, values and perspectives; and reinforcing the enormous value of cultural linkage and exchange.[37]

In educating the public about their heritage and cultures, Indigenous scholars highlight humanity that colonially constructed histories erased. Through Indigenous discourses and reclaiming their histories, identities, knowledge, and lifeways, Indigenous people work to heal their communities and create knowledge and energy that have the power to transform social, political, and public consciousness. In community and academic work that becomes a part of informing and transforming public consciousness, social and political discrimination and racism are confronted and challenged. In seeking to challenge and transform embedded racism and discrimination, academics and Indigenous communities work to make the world a better place for everyone. It is imperative that scholars include in knowledge production a discussion of anthropological discursive tactics of erasure. Through remembering and sharing past events that reflect on contemporary relationships, we honor all our ancestors, and we honor the creation of safe spaces in centers of knowledge production.[38]

There are discussions within the field that speak of an emerging archaeology that is informed by Indigenous values and a call to rethink Western method and theory, to decolonize it. Open discussions on the past of American archaeology highlight the critical need for self-reflection within the field and a rethinking of methodological and theoretical frameworks within which the field had located its work on Indigenous cultures. However, beyond rethinking theory and method, American academics need to reflect on their place within settler populations and the ongoing wielding of power that keeps subaltern voices outside the periphery of academic bastions of unfreedoms: "We are committed to complicating and transgressing the disciplinary and epistemological boundaries of established academic discourses on native Peoples."[39]

Shifting boundaries in American anthropology and archaeology highlight decolonizing scholarship, which traverses pathways between the center and periphery of academia, exposing links between knowledge production and oppression. Social and political impacts of constructed histories invented from a Western Eurocentric gaze worked to disempower contemporary Indigenous people and fuel discrimination while creating histories and social memories to serve a dominant master narrative. Challenging and critiquing a dominant master narrative works to foreground a need to transform academia through decolonization of practice and thought. The Clovis First hypothesis limits an Indigenous presence in the Western Hemisphere to recent time on a world history scale and disassociates, disenfranchises, and dispossesses Indigenous people from their ancestral past. The education of the dominant populace, designed through policies of Indigenous erasure, has influenced racial and discriminatory practices that affect Indigenous peoples at all levels of social and political life.[40] Through a newly informed understanding of earlier initial habitations and possible links between ancient and contemporary Indigenous populations, the general public may begin to become informed of the diverse civilizations that are Indigenous to the Western Hemisphere. An Indigenously informed knowledge production of earlier habitations and the presence of diverse and complex Indigenous people may challenge discrimination among the general population: "Regarding the harm is done, it is the responsibility of the current generation of archaeologists and anthropologists to begin to mitigate past wrongs and to put in place ethical procedures that ensure that we maximize benefits to indigenous people and minimize harm."[41]

Scholars have discussed the need for decolonizing the academy and knowledge production.[42] Indigenous scholars' discussions guide me in unraveling a tangled nest of politics, denial, and bias that has for so long disconnected Indigenous peoples from their birthright, their history, and their deep past and ancient connections to the land: "Transgression is the root of emancipatory knowledge and emancipatory knowledge is the basis of revolutionary pedagogy."[43]

Archaeological discussions of the Indigenous past of the Western Hemisphere are a product of dominant ideologies based in a colonial past and are not based on the known archaeological record. I argue that the historically embedded boundary of recent post-LGM time for first migrations to the Western Hemisphere is not based on the archaeological record but is a political construct maintaining neocolonial power and control over Indigenous heritage, the material remains, and history. Discussion on this within the field is paramount to opening a dialogue that will create safe intellectual spaces from within which to enact positive change.

A traditional practice of caring for the land in many Indigenous areas, pyroregeneration burns away old dense forest cover and allows the sunlight to bring new life to the earth. Pyroregeneration is a ceremony of cleansing and rebirth. This is a fitting metaphor for the critical scholarship of colonial knowledge production and epistemologies of agnotology. In 2012 I coined the word "pyroepistemology" to describe critical Indigenous scholarship and decolonization of discussions of the Indigenous past and present. The fire, being critical Indigenous scholarship, flames away through critical discussions layers of biased colonial thought to allow room for new frames of knowledge to take hold in academia. Pyroepistemology is one flame of many that fuel the Eighth Fire, thus bringing the healing smoke of Indigenous knowledge as the wind that fans the flames and transgresses a dehumanizing Eurocentric knowledge production. Discussing academic history will guide us along one path of many that lead to the Eighth Fire, where cleansing smoke offers opportunities for healing through rituals of respect and reciprocity.

Discussion facilitates a movement toward emancipation, self-determination, and decolonization. This is a discursive transformation, telling and sharing as a process of decentering Western power and authority over other histories. Many Indigenous and Indigenous-oriented scholars have begun to tell stories that in an academic sphere become the basis for challenging political and social boundaries, for shifting historical paradigms, a movement toward the telling of truths or possibilities in a safe intellectual space. What I hope to have accomplished in this book, if nothing else, is to open a discourse on the need for archaeologists to reexamine some of the assumptions that form Paleolithic research in the Western Hemisphere and to reflexively consider the impacts of their work on Indigenous populations.

Understanding the possibilities and deep time frames for the initial peopling of the Western Hemisphere speaks to a much deeper meaning than a date or a time frame; it speaks to the possibilities of decolonizing the history of Indigenous peoples. It speaks to the possibilities of a greatly expanded academic field for current and future students, thus moving American archaeology into a place with a global view of the human past. Decolonizing the field allows for other ways of knowing and knowledge to be incorporated into the essence of a holistic discipline, where scholars from all walks of life are safe to think and discuss epistemologies, methodologies, and worldviews. Further research into the American Paleolithic emancipated from political boundaries and rhetoric of a discipline embedded in processes of colonization may enrich the archaeological record and expand the global history of human migrations while offering archaeologists and anthropologists the opportunity to begin to mitigate past wrongs of their predecessors and decolonize their field.

To summarize my research focus, I sought to gain an understanding of the evidence for and environmental possibilities of Pleistocene human migrations to the Western Hemisphere prior to 11,000–12,000 years ago. To complete this research, I traveled a road through my connections to the land and the impacts of cleaved and disrupted connections to place and past. I came to understand that political and social disparities, including high rates of suicide among Indigenous populations, are intimately tied to historical anthropological knowledge production of dehumanization and erasure. I walked paths of immense loss justified through archaeological discussions denying the civility, intellect, humanity, and heartbeat of Indigenous nations. As a member of a colonized Indigenous population, I have a very personal and intimate understanding of erasure and loss. This may be considered by some as a limitation of this research. However, I argue it is more of an in-depth enlightenment based on a personal and intimate understanding of the impacts of colonization and policies of erasure, genocide, and ethnocide. This research has led me to understand this is a place and a path that millions of Indigenous people experience daily. Reflecting on this, I argue that it is essential to open academic discussions and awareness of the impacts of historical and contemporary knowledge production on colonized populations: "Our history works this way; everything is connected. In order to understand where you are going and how to get there, you must know where you are now; in order to understand that, you must know where it is you have been."[44]

I hope to have brought attention to the need to transform contemporary epistemological processes of structural violence evident in archaeological discourses of Indigenous histories, a scholarship that remains embedded in and re-creates colonial violence. The social and political significance of the research addresses the need for a discursive space in academia that recognizes the benefits of a decolonized history of the Indigenous people of the Western Hemisphere through decentering Western power and authority over history, voice, and inclusion. That research would also address the need for transforming contemporary epistemological processes of structural violence and historical Western educational agendas of erasure through common goals based on informed views of the colonial past and neocolonial present.

For many if not all Indigenous people, there is no separation between the past and the present; all time and all history are crucial to their culture and well-being. Therefore, rupturing the connections between the present and the past, contemporary and ancestral people, and the people and the land as American archaeology has done has been a very violent and destructive historical event. For many first people, Indigenous identities weave threads of primordial memories through space and time and acknowledge connections to ancestors and sacred homelands. A denial of ancient ancestral connections to the land remains a part of what is at the heart of lingering intergenerational trauma and individual and community illness. American archaeology has an ethical and moral duty to unerase histories and identities that its academic predecessors erased through violent discursive processes of knowledge production.

The existence of stories on the land, archaeological sites older than 12,000–15,000 years ago, and ancestral connections between ancient first peoples and contemporary Indigenous communities are empowering to Indigenous people. The existence of hundreds of ancestral sites in the Pleistocene creates a dialogue from which Indigenous people can challenge erasures of histories. It foregrounds their Indigenous identities and their links to the land and empowers them in seeking justice. To allow that Indigenous people have been present in the Western Hemisphere for a much greater time is to support Indigenous ownership of the past and present, their lands and material heritage. To accept that Indigenous peoples have been in the Western Hemisphere for over 60,000 years and possibly prior to 100,000 years ago is to put them on equal footing with areas of the so-called Old World.

Based on my research across the last twenty-four years, I argue that people have been present in the Western Hemisphere for over 130,000 years and possibly earlier. However, whether first peoples have been here for 15,000 years or over 130,000 years, the first people and their descendants are Indigenous to the continents of the Western Hemisphere and have been so for thousands of years. This land is where their cultures and lifeway were born; this is where they are from. I argue that in knowledge production of the Indigenous past, there is a vast body of material evidence that academics ignore a priori, mainly due to embedded Eurocentric histories that erased an ancient Indigenous presence. I argue that an ongoing denial of human antiquity in the Western Hemisphere is not due to a lack of archaeological evidence. I find it is based on the colonial history of American anthropology and archaeology and remains a construct of power and control over Indigenous heritage, material remains, history, and humanity.

There is a human cost woven throughout Eurocentric histories that have erased and marginalized Indigenous pasts and peoples. As histories are rewritten, people, places, and communities are revived from the dark depths of a colonial terra nullius. The human cost of denied histories is thus acknowledged, discussed, and rewoven into stories that highlight the antiquity and humanity of the Indigenous people of the Western Hemisphere. Indigenous people have been here in the Western Hemisphere since time immemorial, they have always known this, and it is discussed in many first people's oral traditions. For Indigenous people, forever may mean from their physical creation or from the beginning of their cultural identities in a specific place, "an emergence into a precise cultural identity."[45] Indigenous people have an inalienable right to tell their history and their stories in their own voice and their own ways of knowing. Indigenous discourse challenges academic hegemony that maintains traditional privileging of non-Indigenous written sources in knowledge production of the Indigenous past.[46]

For Indigenous people, there is no past. It is one with the present, so when their past is denied, so is their history, humanity, and present. It is essential for Indigenous people that their ancient ancestral links to these lands are acknowledged, that they are known and discussed as Indigenous peoples of the Western Hemisphere, the keepers and protectors of the land where their ancestors came to be. It is time for pyroepistemology, time to burn colonial rhetoric that dehumanizes Indigenous people and denies their deep history in the Western Hemisphere. Time to fan the flames of the Eighth Fire, a place of peace for all people, both settlers and Indigenous. When this begins in earnest, the winds of Indigenous knowledge will carry a healing smudge from the Eighth Fire to cover the earth and all her people.

All My Relations

In a thousand dreams, I embrace our ancient past
Flying with ancestors winged and not
Soaring close to our mothers' skin we inhale the essence of life
Gathering the tears of thousands of scattered seeds of colonial violence
Picking up the shattered hearts while embracing the children now crossed
    over
Whispering to the leaders, this way, this way, along the good red road
Almost there, keep on, never idle, smile and know, we are always with you
Healing smoke of the eighth fire now arises
And soon, very soon, justice and peace will prevail for all.

APPENDIX

Pleistocene Sites and References

This list of Pleistocene sites represents a small fraction of the possibilities for future Paleolithic research in the Western Hemisphere. Many of the site collections may be available for further study, and new excavations may be feasible at some site areas. The inclusion of a site on this list does not mean that the site is not controversial or that it does not warrant further work. Some archaeological sites need a great deal more research. Many of the sites in the database have all the required components for being designated an archaeological site. Archaeological sites with all the required evidence are often in areas with sites that require further research. The majority of sites predate Clovis time frames (11,200 years BP); a few are younger and/or within the Clovis time frames. Archaeological sites with Clovis technologies may also contain unidentified or other stone tool technologies. Though Clovis technologies are discussed as being bracketed between 10,800 and 11,200 years BP, sites with older dates that contain Clovis technologies have also been reported. The database of pre–Clovis age archaeological sites in North and South America is not complete. There have been many more sites discussed in both academic and gray literature (unpublished cultural resource management reports), and new sites are being reported every year.

There was an available land route between the Eastern and Western Hemispheres for much of the last 100,000 years during interglacial events. The Eastern Hemisphere has provided archaeological evidence of an early human (hominin) presence for over 2.4 million years. Thus, we should remain open to the possibilities of an earlier human presence in the Western Hemisphere. This is not a complete list of all the sites that predate 11,200 years BP or 13,100 cal BP in both North and South America; instead, it is a very minimal number. There are most likely sites that have been published in diverse language publications in South America that I have not yet accessed. There are also new sites that have been reported but not yet published; thus, they are not included in my database. This list is just a starting point that represents the possibilities of studying early human history on a local, regional, or hemispheric scale.

Eastern Hemisphere Archaeological Sites

	Site dates	Site name	Area	References
1	2.6 Ma	Masol	India	Sao et al. 2016
2	2.4 Ma	Yiron	Israel	Ronen 2006
3	2.12–1.26 Ma	Shangchen	China	Zhu et al. 2018
4	2.0–1.7 Ma	Olduvai Gorge	Tanzania	Leakey, Tobias, and Napier 1964; Leakey 1971
5	2.0–1.7 Ma	Erq El-Ahmar	Israel	Ron and Levi 2001
6	2.1–1.9 Ma	Riwat	Pakistan	Dennell, Rendell, and Hailwood 1988
7	2.33 Ma ± 0·07	Kadar	Ethiopia	Kimbel et al. 1996
8	1.9–1.95 Ma	Koobi Fora KNM-ER 62003	Kenya	Leakey et al. 2012
9	1.95–1.77 Ma	Ain Hanech	Algeria	Sahnouni et al. 2002
10	1.96–1.78 Ma	Longgupo Cave	China	Wanpo et al. 2005
11	1.85–1.78 Ma	Dmanisi	Georgia	Ferring et al. 2011
12	1.62 ± 0.06 Ma	Gongwangling	China	Zhu et al. 2015
13	1.66–1.36 Ma	Goudi	China	Gao et al. 2005
14	1.49 ± 0.13 Ma	Mojokerto	Indonesia	Morwood et al. 2003
15	1.5 ± 0.07 Ma	Attirampakkam	India	Pappu et al. 2011
16	1.4–1.0 Ma	Ubeidiya	Israel	Gaudzinski 2004
17	1.7 Ma	Majuangou III	China	Liu et al. 2014
18	1.36 Ma	Xiaochangliang	China	Zhu et al. 2001

19	1.27 Ma	Xihoudu	China	Bar-Yosef and Wang 2012
20	1.2–1.1 Ma	Sima del Elefante	Spain	Carbonell et al. 2008
21	1.4 Ma	Barranco León	Spain	Toro-Moyano et al. 2013
22	800 ± 0.3 ka	Lampang	Thailand	Pope et al. 1986
23	>780 ka	Gran Dolina	Spain	Falguères et al. 1999
24	900–800 ka	Mata Menge	Indonesia	Morwood et al. 1999
25	980–950 ka	Vallparadís	Spain	Martinez et al. 2014
26	300 ka	Terra Amata	France	De Lumley 1969
27	500 ka	Vertesszölös	Hungary	Fluck and McNabb 2007
28	100–27 ka	Ngandong	Java	Yokoyama et al. 2008
29	300–200 ka	Sima de los Huesos	Spain	Arsuaga et al. 1997
30	370–270 ka	Diring Yuriakh	Siberia	Waters, Forman, and Pierson 1999
31	160–154 ka	Herto	Ethiopia	Clark et al. 2003
32	125 ± 5 ka	Crete	Greece	Strasser et al. 2011
33	127 ± 16 ka	Jebel Faya	UAE	Armitage et al. 2011
34	120–80 ka	The Fuyan Cave	China	Liu et al. 2015
35	139–111 ka	Liujiang	China	Shen et al. 2002
36	135–100 ka	Skhul	Israel	Grün et al. 2005
37	43 ka	Kara-Bom	Siberia	Zwyns et al. 2012
38	77 ± 6–74 ka	Jwalapuram	India	Petraglia et al. 2007
39	66.7 ± 1 ka	Callao Cave	Philippines	Mijares et al. 2010
40	47 ± 11–30.5 ka	Tabon Cave	Malaysia	Détroit et al. 2004
41	50–46 ka	Lake Mungo	Australia	Bowler et al. 2003
42	46–34 ka	Niah Cave	Malaysia	Barker et al. 2007

43	45 ka	Irtysh River	Siberia	Fu et al. 2014
44	39 ka	Bondi Cave	Georgia	Tushabramishvili et al. 2011
45	36–34 ka	Peştera cu Oase	Romania	Trinkaus, Moldovan, and Bilgar 2003
46	29–24 ka	Shuidonggou	China	Madsen et al. 2001
47	37.4–34.4 ka	Mamontovaya Kurya	Russia	Pavlov, Svendsen, and Indrelid 2001
48	112–44 ka	Laibin	China	Shen et al. 2007
49	36 cal BP	Batadombalena	Sri Lanka	Perera et al. 2011
50	26 ka	Paviland	Wales	Aldhouse-Green and Pettitt 1998
51	29,000–28,000 cal BP	Ryukyu Islands Pinza-Abu	Japan	Takamiya et al. 2019
52	32.4 ka 29.7	Chauvet Cave	France	Valladas et al. 2001
53	28.6 ka	Byzovaya	Russia	Heggen, Svendsen, and Mengerud 2010
54	14–13 ka	Berelekh	Siberia	Pitulko et al. 2004
55	29–24 ka	Zhoukoudian	China	Ticmci, Hedges, and Zhenxin 1992; Norton and Gao 2008
56	28 ka	Gorham's Cave	Gibraltar	Finlayson et al. 2006
57	28.5–27 ka	Yana River Valley	Siberia	Basilyan et al. 2011
58	28.6–27 ka	Krems Wachtberg	Austria	Einwögerer et al. 2009
59	27–25 ka	Dolni Vestonice	Czech Republic	Trinkaus and Svoboda 2006
60	26.4 ka	Sungir 3	Russia	Kuzmin et al. 2004
61	27.74 ± 150	Pokrovka 2	Russia	Akimova et al. 2010
62	18.25 ± 650	Minatogawa	Japan	Baba and Narasaki 1991

References for Eastern Hemisphere Sites

Akimova, E., T. Higham, I. Stasyuk, A. Buzhilova, M. Dobrovolskaya, and M. Mednikova. 2010. "A New Direct Radiocarbon A M S Date for an Upper Palaeolithic Human Bone from Siberia." *Archaeometry* 52 (6): 1122–30.

Aldhouse-Green, S., and P. Pettitt. 1998. "Paviland Cave: Contextualizing the 'Red Lady.'" *Antiquity* 72 (278): 756–72.

Armitage, S. J., S. A. Jasim, A. E. Marks, A. G. Parker, V. I. Usik, and H. P. Uerpmann. 2011. "The Southern Route 'out of Africa': Evidence for an Early Expansion of Modern Humans into Arabia." *Science* 331 (6016): 453–56.

Arsuaga, J. L., I. Martinez, A. Gracia, J. M. Carretero, C. Lorenzo, N. Garcia, and A. I. Ortega. 1997. "Sima de los Huesos (Sierra de Atapuerca, Spain): The Site." *Journal of Human Evolution* 33 (2–3): 109–27.

Baba, H., and S. Narasaki. 1991. "Minatogawa Man, the Oldest Type of Modern *Homo sapiens* in East Asia." *Quaternary Research (Daiyonki-Kenkyu)* 30 (3): 221–30.

Barker, G., H. Barton, M. Bird, P. Daly, I. Datan, A. Dykes, L. Farr, et al. 2007. "The 'Human Revolution' in Lowland Tropical Southeast Asia: The Antiquity and Behavior of Anatomically Modern Humans at Niah Cave (Sarawak, Borneo)." *Journal of Human Evolution* 52 (3): 243–61.

Bar-Yosef, O., and Y. Wang. 2012. "Paleolithic Archaeology in China." *Annual Review of Anthropology* 41:319–35.

Basilyan, A. E., M. A. Anisimov, P. A. Nikolskiy, and V. V. Pitulko. 2011. "Wooly Mammoth Mass Accumulation next to the Paleolithic Yana R H S Site, Arctic Siberia: Its Geology, Age, and Relation to Past Human Activity." *Journal of Archaeological Science* 38 (9): 2461–74.

Bowler, J. M., H. Johnston, J. M. Olley, J. R. Prescott, R. G. Roberts, W. Shawcross, and N. A. Spooner. 2003. "New Ages for Human Occupation and Climatic Change at Lake Mungo, Australia." *Nature* 421 (6925): 837–40.

Carbonell, E., J. M. Bermúdez de Castro, A. Parés, G. Pérez-González, A. Cuenca-Bescós, Ollé, M. Mosquera, et al. 2008. "The First Hominin of Europe." *Nature* 452 (7186): 465–69.

Clark, J. D., Y. Beyene, G. Wolde Gabriel, W. K. Hart, P. R. Renne, H. Gilbert, A. Defleur, et al. 2003. "Stratigraphic, Chronological and Behavioural Contexts of Pleistocene *Homo sapiens* from Middle Awash, Ethiopia." *Nature* 423 (6941): 747–52.

De Lumley, H. 1969. "A Paleolithic Camp at Nice." *Scientific American* 220 (5): 42–51.

Dennell, R. W., H. Rendell, and E. Hailwood. 1988. "Early Tool-Making in Asia: Two-Million-Year-Old Artefacts in Pakistan." *Antiquity* 62 (234): 98–106.

Détroit, F., E. Dizon, C. Falguères, S. Hameau, W. Ronquillo, and F. Sémah. 2004. "Upper Pleistocene *Homo sapiens* from the Tabon Cave (Palawan, the Philippines): Description and Dating of New Discoveries." *Comptes Rendus Palevol* 3 (8): 705–12.

Einwögerer, T., M. Händel, C. Neugebauer-Maresch, U. Simon, P. Steier, M. Teschler-Nicola, and E. M. Wild. 2009. "¹⁴C Dating of the Upper Paleolithic Site at Krems-Wachtberg, Austria." *Radiocarbon* 51 (2): 847–55.

Falguères, C., J. J. Bahain, Y. Yokoyama, J. L. Arsuaga, J. M. Bermudez de Castro, E. Carbonell, J. L. Bischoff, and J. M. Dolo. 1999. "Earliest Humans in Europe: The Age of TD6 Gran Dolina, Atapuerca, Spain." *Journal of Human Evolution* 37 (3–4): 343–52.

Ferring, R., O. Oms, J. Agustí, F. Berna, M. Nioradze, T. Shelia, M. Tappen, et al. 2011. "Earliest Human Occupations at Dmanisi (Georgian Caucasus) Dated to 1.85–1.78 Ma." *Proceedings of the National Academy of Sciences* 108 (26): 10432–36.

Finlayson, C., F. G. Pacheco, J. Rodríguez-Vidal, D. A. Fa, J. M. G. López, A. S. Pérez, G. Finlayson, et al. 2006. "Late Survival of Neanderthals at the Southernmost Extreme of Europe." *Nature* 443 (7113): 850.

Fluck, H., and J. McNabb. 2007. "Raw Material Exploitation at the Middle Pleistocene Site of 27. Vertesszölös, Hungary." *Lithics: The Journal of the Lithic Studies Society* 28:50–64.

Fu, Q., H. Li, P. Moorjani, F. Jay, S. M. Slepchenko, A. A. Bondarev, P. L. F. Johnson, et al. 2014. "Genome Sequence of a 45,000-Year-Old Modern Human from Western Siberia." *Nature* 514 (7523): 445–49.

Gao, X., Q. Wei, C. Shen, and S. Keates. 2005. "New Light on the Earliest Hominid Occupation in East Asia." *Current Anthropology* 46 (S5): S115–S120.

Gaudzinski, S. 2004. "Subsistence Patterns of Early Pleistocene Hominids in the Levant: Taphonomic Evidence from the 'ubeidiya Formation (Israel)." *Journal of Archaeological Science* 31 (1): 65–75.

Grün, R., C. Stringer, F. McDermott, R. Nathan, N. Porat, S. Robertson, L. Taylor, et al. 2005. "U-Series and ESR Analyses of Bones and Teeth Relating to the Human Burials from Skhul." *Journal of Human Evolution* 49 (3): 316–34.

Heggen, H. P., J. I. Svendsen, and J. Mangerud. 2010. "River Sections at the Byzovaya Palaeolithic Site: Keyholes into the Late Quaternary of Northern European Russia." *Boreas* 39 (1): 116–30.

Kimbel, W. H., R. C. Walter, D. C. Johanson, K. E. Reed, J. L. Aronson, Z. Assefa, C. W. Marean, et al. 1996. "Late Pliocene Hominid Oldowan Tools from the Hadar Formation (Kada Hadar Member), Ethiopia." *Journal of Human Evolution* 31 (6): 549–61.

Kuzmin, Y. V., G. S. Burr, A. T. Jull, and L. D. Sulerzhitsky. 2004. "AMS ¹⁴C Age of the Upper Palaeolithic Skeletons from Sungir Site, Central Russian Plain." *Nuclear Instruments and Methods in Physics Research Section B: Beam Interactions with Materials and Atoms* 223:731–34.

Leakey, M. G., F. Spoor, M. C. Dean, C. S. Feibel, S. C. Antón, C. Kiarie, and L. N. Leakey. 2012. "New Fossils from Koobi Fora in Northern Kenya Confirm Taxonomic Diversity in Early *Homo.*" *Nature* 488 (7410): 201–4.

Leakey, L. S., P. V. Tobias, and J. R. Napier. 1964. "A New Species of the Genus *Homo* from Olduvai Gorge." *Nature* 202 (4927): 7–9.

Leakey, Mary Douglas. 1971. *Olduvai Gorge: Volume 3, Excavations in Beds I and II, 1960–1963*. Vol. 3. Cambridge: Cambridge University Press.

Liu, C. R., G. M. Yin, C. L. Deng, F. Han, and W. J. Song. 2014. "ESR Dating of the Majuangou and Banshan Paleolithic Sites in the Nihewan Basin, North China." *Journal of Human Evolution* 73:58–63.

Liu, W., M. Martinón-Torres, Y. J. Cai, S. Xing, H. W. Tong, S. W. Pei, M. J. Sier, et al. 2015. "The Earliest Unequivocally Modern Humans in Southern China." *Nature* 526 (7575): 696–99.

Madsen, D. B., L. Jingzen, P. J. Brantingham, G. Xing, R. G. Elston, and R. L. Bettinger. 2001. "Dating Shuidonggou and the Upper Palaeolithic Blade Industry in North China." *Antiquity* 75 (290): 706–16.

Martínez, K., J. Garcia, F. Burjachs, R. Yll, and E. Carbonell. 2014. "Early Human Occupation of Iberia: The Chronological and Palaeoclimatic Inferences from Vallparadís (Barcelona, Spain)." *Quaternary Science Reviews* 85:136–46.

Mijares, A. S., F. Détroit, P. Piper, R. Grün, P. Bellwood, M. Aubert, G. Champion, et al. 2010. "New Evidence for a 67,000-Year-Old Human Presence at Callao Cave, Luzon, Philippines." *Journal of Human Evolution* 59 (1): 123–32.

Morwood, M. J., F. Aziz, P. O'Sullivan, D. R. Hobbs, and A. Raza. 1999. "Archaeological and Palaeontological Research in Central Flores, East Indonesia: Results of Fieldwork 1997–98." *Antiquity* 73 (280): 273–86.

Morwood, M. J., P. O'Sullivan, E. E. Susanto, and F. Aziz. 2003. "Revised Age for Mojokerto 1, an Early *Homo erectus* Cranium from East Java, Indonesia." *Australian Archaeology* 57 (1): 1–4.

Norton, C. J., and X. Gao. 2008. "Zhoukoudian Upper Cave Revisited." *Current Anthropology* 49 (4): 732–45.

Pappu, S., Y. Gunnell, K. Akhilesh, R. Braucher, M. Taieb, F. Demory, and N. Thouveny. 2011. "Early Pleistocene Presence of Acheulian Hominins in South India." *Science* 331 (6024): 1596–99.

Pavlov, P., J. I. Svendsen, and S. Indrelid. 2001. "Human Presence in the European Arctic Nearly 40,000 Years Ago." *Nature* 413 (6851): 64–67.

Perera, N., N. Kourampas, I. A. Simpson, S. U. Deraniyagala, D. Bulbeck, J. Kamminga, J. S. Perera, et al. 2011. "People of the Ancient Rainforest: Late Pleistocene Foragers at the Batadomba-Lena Rockshelter, Sri Lanka." *Journal of Human Evolution* 61 (3): 254–69.

Petraglia, M., R. Korisettar, N. Boivin, C. Clarkson, P. Ditchfield, S. Jones, J. Koshy, et al. 2007. "Middle Paleolithic Assemblages from the Indian Subcontinent before and after the Toba Super-Eruption." *Science* 317 (5834): 114–16.

Pitulko, V. V., P. A. Nikolsky, E. Yu Girya, A. E. Basilyan, V. E. Tumskoy, S. A. Koulakov, S. N. Astakhov, et al. 2004. "The Yana RHS Site: Humans in the Artic before the Last Glacial Maximum." *Science* 303:52–56.

Pope, G. G., S. Barr, A. Macdonald, and S. B. Nakabanlang. 1986. "Earliest Radiometrically Dated Artifacts from Southeast Asia." *Current Anthropology* 27 (3): 275–79.

Ron, H., and S. Levi. 2001. "When Did Hominids First Leave Africa? New High-Resolution Magnetostratigraphy from the Erk-El-Ahmar Formation, Israel." *Geology* 29 (10): 887–90.

Ronen, A. 2006. "The Oldest Human Groups in the Levant." *Comptes Rendus Palevol* 5 (1–2): 343–51.

Sahnouni, M., D. Hadjouis, J. Van Der Made, A. Canals, M. Medig, H. Belahrech, Z. Harchane, and M. Rabhi. 2002. "Further Research at the Oldowan Site of Ain Hanech, North-Eastern Algeria." *Journal of Human Evolution* 43 (6): 925–37.

Sao, C. C., S. Abdessadok, A. D. Malassé, M. Singh, B. Karir, V. Bhardwaj, S. Pal, et al. 2016. "Magnetic Polarity of Masol 1 Locality Deposits, Siwalik Frontal Range, Northwestern India." *Comptes Rendus Palevol* 15 (3–4): 407–16.

Shen, G., W. Wang, H. Cheng, and R. L. Edwards. 2007. "Mass Spectrometric U-Series Dating of Laibin Hominid Site in Guangxi, Southern China." *Journal of Archaeological Science* 34 (12): 2109–14.

Shen, G., W. Wang, Q. Wang, J. Zhao, K. Collerson, C. Zhou, and P. V. Tobias. 2002. "U-Series Dating of Liujiang Hominid Site in Guangxi, Southern China." *Journal of Human Evolution* 43 (6): 817–29.

Shlemon, R. J., and F. E. Budinger Jr. 1990. "The Archaeological Geology of the Calico Site, Mojave Desert, California." *Geological Society of America, Centennial Special* 4:301–13.

Strasser, T. F., C. Runnels, K. Wegmann, E. Panagopoulou, F. Mccoy, C. Digregorio, P. Karkanas, and N. Thompson. 2011. "Dating Palaeolithic Sites in Southwestern Crete, Greece." *Journal of Quaternary Science* 26 (5): 553–60.

Takamiya, H., C. Katagiri, S. Yamasaki, and M. Fujita. 2019. "Human Colonization of the Central Ryukyus (Amami and Okinawa Archipelagos), Japan." *Journal of Island and Coastal Archaeology* 14 (3): 375–93.

Tiemei, C., R. E. M. Hedges, and Y. Zhenxin. 1992. "The Second Batch of Accelerator Radiocarbon Dates for Upper Cave Site of Zhoukoudian." *Acta Anthropologica Sinica* 11 (2): 112–16.

Toro-Moyano, Isidro, Bienvenido Martínez-Navarro, Jordi Agustí, Caroline Souday, José María Bermúdez de Castro, María Martinón-Torres, Beatriz Fajardo, et al. 2013. "The Oldest Human Fossil in Europe, from Orce (Spain)." *Journal of Human Evolution* 65 (1): 1–9.

Trinkaus, E., O. Moldovan, and A. Bilgar. 2003. "An Early Modern Human from the Peştera cu Oase, Romania." *Proceedings of the National Academy of Sciences* 100 (20): 11231–36.

Trinkaus, E., and J. Svoboda, eds. 2006. *Early Modern Human Evolution in Central Europe: The People of Dolní Věstonice and Pavlov.* Vol. 12. Oxford University Press on Demand.

Tushabramishvili, N., D. Pleurdeau, M. H. Moncel, T. Agapishvili, A. Vekua, M. Bukhsianidze, B. Maureille, et al. 2011. "Human Remains from a New Upper Pleistocene Sequence in Bondi Cave (Western Georgia)." *Journal of Human Evolution* 62 (1): 179–85.

Valladas, H., J. Clottes, J. M. Geneste, M. A. Garcia, M. Arnold, H. Cachier, and N. Tisnerat-Laborde. 2001. "Paleolithic Painting: Evolution of Prehistoric Cave Art." *Nature* 43 (479).

Wanpo, Huang, Russell Ciochon, Gu Yumin, Roy Larick, Fang Qiren, Henry Schwarcz, Charles Yonge, et al. 1995. "Early *Homo* and Associated Artefacts from Asia." *Nature* 378 (6554): 275–78.

Waters, M. R., S. L. Forman, and J. M. Pierson. 1999. "Late Quaternary Geology and Geochronology of Diring Yuriakh, an Early Paleolithic Site in Central Siberia." *Quaternary Research* 51 (2): 195–211.

Yokoyama, Yuji, Christophe Falguères, François Sémah, Teuku Jacob, and Rainer Grün. 2008. "Gamma-Ray Spectrometric Dating of Late *Homo erectus* Skulls from Ngandong and Sambungmacan, Central Java, Indonesia." *Journal of Human Evolution* 55 (2): 274–77.

Zhu, R. X., Kenneth A. Hoffman, Richard Potts, C. L. Deng, Y. X. Pan, Bin Guo, C. D. Shi, et al. 2001. "Earliest Presence of Humans in Northeast Asia." *Nature* 413 (6854): 413–17.

Zhu, Z., R. Dennell, W. Huang, Y. Wu, S. Qiu, S. Yang, Z. Rao et al. 2018. "Hominin Occupation of the Chinese Loess Plateau since about 2.1 Million Years Ago." *Nature* 559 (7715): 608.

Zhu, Z. Y., R. Dennell, W. W. Huang, Y. Wu, Z. G. Rao, S. F. Qiu, J. B. Xie, et al. 2015. "New Dating of the *Homo erectus* Cranium from Lantian (Gongwangling), China." *Journal of Human Evolution* 78:144–57.

Zwyns, N., E. P. Rybin, J. J. Hublin, and A. P. Derevianko. 2012. "Burin-Core Technology and Laminar Reduction Sequences in the Initial Upper Paleolithic from Kara-Bom (Gorny-Altai, Siberia)." *Quaternary International* 259:33–47.

North American Archaeological Sites

	Site name	Site dates (^{14}C or other)	Area	References
1	El Horno (Valsequillo)	>280,000 ^{230}Th	Mexico	Steen-McIntire, Fryxell, and Malde 1981; Szabo, Malde, and Irwin-Williams 1969
2	Hueyatlaco (Valsequillo)	245,000 ± 40,000 ^{230}Th/^{234}U	Mexico	Steen-McIntire, Fryxell, and Malde 1981; Szabo, Malde, and Irwin-Williams 1969

3	El Mirador (Valsequillo)	Cultural level stratigraphically below Hueyatlaco and Texacaxco	Mexico	Irwin-Williams 1978
4	Texacaxco (Valsequillo)	200,000 Stratigraphic position is somewhat lower (earlier) than Hueyatlaco	Mexico	Camacho 1978; Irwin-Williams 1978
5	Calico	200,000 ^{230}Th/^{234}U 120–40 ka	CA	Bischoff et al. 1981; Leakey, Simpson, and Clements 1968; Shlemon and Budinger 1990
6	Cerutti Mastodon	130,700 ± 9.4 ^{230}Th	CA	Holen et al. 2017
7	Old Crow	25 ka 42 ka ± 1,200	YT	Cinq-Mars, J. and Morlan 1999; Morlan et al. 1990
8	Pendejo Cave	55,000 38,820 14,875	NM	MacNeish and Liddy 2003; Adovasio and Pedler 2016
9	Topper	20–15 ka >50 ka 15,200–14,800 ka 54,700 ka	SC	Goodyear 2005; Adovasio and Pedler 2016
10	Schulz	39,350 ± 770 37,567 ± 590	SD	Holen and Holen 2014
11	Toluquilla	38,000 ± 8,570 OSL	Mexico	Gonzalez, Huddart, and Bennett 2006
12	Santa Rosa Island Woolly Mammoth	37,000 29,700 ± 3,000 16,700 ± 1,500 12,500 ± 250	CA	Orr and Berger 1966
13	Bonnet Plume	36,900 ± 300	YT	Hughes et al. 1981

14	Miami Mastodon	35,900 ± 900	MO	Hamilton 1996;
		35,773 ±. 251		Holen and Holen
		34,000 ± 1600		2014
		(IRSL)		
15	Frye	35,000–40,000	IL	Munson and Frye
		Stratigraphic		1965
16	New Nebraska	33,590 ± 450	NE	Holen and Holen
				2014
17	Villa Grove	33,405 ± 340	CO	Holen and Holen
				2014
18	Rancho La	33,300 ± 2,700	Mexico	Lorenzo and
	Amapola	38–21 ka		Mirambell 1986;
				Sanchez 2001
19	Miles Point	27,240 ± 230	MD	Lowery et al. 2010
		21,490 ± 140		
		Miles Point Loess		
		25–41 ka		
		MIS 3		
20	Caulapan	30,600 ± 1,000	Mexico	Szabo Malde, and
		21,850 ± 850		Irwin-Williams
				1969
21	Jack Wade Creek	29,700 ± 240	AK	Morlan and Cinq
				Mars 1982
22	Burnham	26,000	OK	Wyckoff 1990
23	Oyster Cove Point	18–25 ka	MD	Wah, Lowery, and
		Tilghman soil		Wagner 2014
24	Bluefish Caves II	19,650 ± 130	YT	Adovasio and
				Pedler 2016;
				Bourgeon, Burke,
				and Higham 2017;
				Cinq-Mars 1979
25	Tlapacoya III	24,000 ± 4,000	Mexico	Mirambell 1978
26	Dawson	23,900 ± 470	YT	Harington 1975;
	Hunker Creek	11,350 ± 110		Harington and
				Morlan 1992

27	Cinmar (not in situ)	22,760 ± 90 23,000	VA	Stanford and Bradley 2012
28	Wakulla Springs Lodge	22,500–11,600	FL	Rink, Dunbar, and Burdette 2012
29	Cators Cove Supporting paleosols dates on pre-Clovis sites on the Delmarva Peninsula	22,050 ± 100 18–25 ka Tilghman soil	MD	Wah, Lowery, and Wagner 2014
30	Meadowcroft Rockshelter	21,980–17,250 Hearths 26,210—21,090 Possible cultural origin	PA	Adovasio and Pedler 2016
31	North Paw Paw Cove and South Paw Paw Cove	21,116 ± 251 15,590 ± 60– 21,490 ± 140 Tilghman soil	MD	Lowery et al. 2010
32	Varsity Estates	21,000 15,000–13,000	Alberta	Chlachula 1994; Bryan and Gruhn 2007
33	El Tunel	21,000–11,000	Mexico	Gonzalez, Silvia and Huddart 2008
34	El Toro	21,000–11,000	Mexico	Gonzalez,Silvia, and Huddart 2008
35	Coopertown	21,000–17,000	OK	Anderson 1975
36	Lovewell II	19,570 ± 60	KS	Holen and Holen 2014
37	Petronila Creek	18,560 ± 280 18,180 ± 130	TX	Lewis 2009
38	Gault	18,500 ± 1,500 OSL	TX	Williams et al. 2018
39	Cactus Hill	21,930–18,490 18,530–18,080	VA	McAvoy and McAvoy 1997; Adovasio and Pedler 2016
40	La Sena	18,440 ± 90	NE	Holen 2006; Holen and May 2002

41	Los Reyes La Paz	18,280 ± 160	Mexico	Cook 1975
		14,770 ± 280		
42	Crane Point	15,590 ± 60–	MD	Lowery et al. 2010
		21,490 ± 140		
		Tilghman soil		
43	Parsons Island	23,149 ± 267 cal BP	MD	D. Lowery personal communication 2020 Lothrop et al. 2016
		20,525 ± 341 cal BP		
		17,133 ± 88		
44	Hamburger	16,480 ± 60	KS	Holen and Holen 2014
45	Selby	16,330 ± 320	CO	Holen and Holen 2012
		11,710 ± 150		
46	Dutton	16,330 ± 320	CO	Holen and Holen 2012
		11,710 ± 150		
47	Santa Isabel Iztapan	16,000	Mexico	Hester 1960
		11,003 ± 500		
48	Broken Mammoth	11,770–11,280	AK	Hamilton and Goebel 2005
		15,830 ± 70		
		Possible scavenging of older ivory tusks		
49	Rimrock Draw Rockshelter	15,800	OR	Henderson 2016
50	Shaffert	15,600 ± 60	NE	Holen and May 2002
51	Debra L. Friedkin	15,500–13,200 OSL	TX	Jennings and Waters 2014
52	Jensen	14,830 ± 230	NB	Holen and Holen 2014
53	False Cougar Cave	14,590 ± 300	MT	Bonnichsen et al. 1986
		1,690 ± 90		
		Human hair 10,530 ± 140		
54	Saltville	14,510 ± 80	VA	McDonald 2000
55	Wilson Butte Cave	14,500 ± 500	ID	Gruhn 1961; Dixon 1999
		10,230 ± 90		

56	Lucy	14,300 ± 650 Mammoth date Recorded as Folsom and Sandia	NM	Agenbroad 2005; Reitze 2016; Roosa 1968; Dawson and Judge 1969
57	Smith Creek Cave	14,220 ± 650 9280 ± 160	NV	Goebel 2007
58	Heiltsuk Nation Territory	14,000–13,600 cal BP, also supported by oral traditions	BC	Jodry and Santoro 2017
59	Levi Clovis and pre-Clovis	Zone I Pre-Clovis Zone II Clovis 13,750 ± 410	TX	Alexander 1982
60	Mud Lake	13,530 ± 50 Not in situ	WI	Overstreet and Kolb 2003
61	Fenske	13,510 ± 50 Not in situ	WI	Overstreet and Kolb 2003
62	Little Salt Spring	13,450 ± 190	FL	Clausen et al. 1979
63	Coopers Ferry	16,560–15,280 cal BP	ID	Davis et al. 2019
64	Fort Rock Cave	13,200 ± 720	OR	Cressman 1977; Bedwell 1973
65	Lamb Springs	13,140 ± 1,000	CO	Dixon 1999
66	Hermits Cave	12,900 ± 350	NM	Rubin and Alexander 1958
67	McMinnville	12,890 ± 70	OR	Stenger 2012
68	Coats-Hines	12,869 ± 60 OCR	TN	Deter-Wolf, Tune, and Broster 2011
69	Shriver	12,855 ± 1,500 >13,000	MO	Reagan et al. 1978
70	Shoop	12,750	PA	Adovasio and Pedler 2016
71	Kanorado	12,670 ± 35	KS	Holen and Holen 2012
72	Johnson	12,660 ± 970 11,980 ± 110	TN	Barker and Broster 1996
73	Lubbock Lake	12,650 ± 250	TX	Holliday et al. 1983

74	Burning Tree	12,620 ± 90 11,720 ± 110	OH	Haynes 2015
75	Hebior	15,170–14,670 15,040–14,270 AMS	WI	Adovasio and Pedler 2016
76	Dutchess Quarry Cave	12,580 ± 370	NY	Kopper, Funk, and Dumont 1980
77	Page-Ladson	14,550 cal BP	FL	Halligan et al. 2016
78	Schaefer	15,150–14,630 14,630–14,030	WI	Adovasio and Pedler 2016
79	Bonfire Shelter	12,430–11,330	TX	Adovasio and Pedler 2016
80	Paisley Five Mile Point Caves	Cave 5 14,850–14,110 Cave 2 13,560–13,380	OR	Adovasio and Pedler 2016
81	Cloudsplitter Rockshelter	12,360 ± 400 12,000 ± 400	KY	Cowan et al. 1981
82	Lindsay	12,330 ± 50 11,925 ± 350	MT	Agenbroad 2005; Rutherford, Wittenburg, and Wilmeth 1979
83	Bonneville Estates	12,390 ± 40 10,970 ± 60	NV	Goebel 2007
84	Swan Point	14,490–14,050	AK	Adovasio and Pedler 2016
85	Eppley Rock Shelter	10,743	OH	Steele 2010
86	Vero Beach	12,130 ± 70 Mammoth date 7,500 artifacts Mammoth carving min. 13,000 ka	FL	Agenbroad 2005; Adovasio et al. 2019; Purdy et al. 2011
87	Manis Mastodon	13,860–13,763 cal BP	WA	Waters et al. 2011
88	Lehner	13,770–13,560 12,910–12,710	AZ	Adovasio and Pedler 2016

89	Chesrow	12,000–10,000 Calumet II beach ridge 11,400–11,000	WI	Overstreet 1993; Joyce 2006
90	Sands Blackstone	11,990 ± 60	MA	Leveillee 2016
91	Cougar Mountain Cave II	11,950 ± 350 Terminal Pleistocene	OR	Bedwell 1973; Rosencrance et al. 2019
92	Agate Basin	11,840 ± 130	WY	Frison and Stanford 1982; Agenbroad 2005
93	Nogahabara	11,815 ± 70	AK	Holmes et al. 2008
94	Ayer Pond, Orcas Island	11,760 ± 70	WA	Kenady et al. 2010
95	Firelands Ground Sloth	11,740 ± 35 13,738–13,435 cal BP	OH	Redmond et al. 2012
96	Moose Creek	11,730 ± 250	AK	Pearson 1999; Powers and Hoffecker 1989
97	Perry Mastodon	11,700 ± 60 13,710–13,410 cal BP	IL	Neïburger 2011
98	Mesa	11,700–9,700	AK	Kunz and Reanier 1995
99	Eve of Naharon	11,670 ± 60	Mexico	González et al. 2008
100	Jaguar Cave	11,580 ± 250	ID	Plew et al. 1982
101	Mill Iron	11,570 ± 170 11,340 ± 120	MT	Agenbroad 2005; Frison 1978; Haynes 1987
102	Aubrey (Proto-Clovis)	11,565	TX	Haynes 2015
103	Union Pacific Mammoth	11,560 ± 60 11,000–10,000	WY	Haynes, Surovell, and Hodgins 2013
104	Danger Cave	11,453 ± 600 11,151 ± 570	UT	Jennings 1957

105	Miami	11,415 ± 125 11,400–10,500	TX	Holiday et al. 1994
106	Healy Lake Village	11,410–11,090	AK	Cook 1996
107	Lamb	11,400 ± 100	NY	Gramly 1999
108	State Road Ripple	11,385 ± 140	PA	Goreczny 2017
109	Walker Road	11,330 ± 80	AK	Hamilton and Goebel 2005; Goebel, Powers, and Bigelow 1991
110	Whally Beach	11,350 ± 80	AB	Kooyman et al. 2001
111	Owl Ridge	11,300	AK	Hamilton and Goebel 2005

References for North American Sites

Adovasio, J. M., C. A. Hemmings, F. J. Vento, J. S. Duggan, and J. H. Higley. 2019. "What We Learned at the Old Vero Site (8IR009), Vero Beach, Florida: 2014–2017." *Paleo-America* 5 (3): 231–61.

Adovasio, J. M., and D. Pedler. 2016. *Strangers in a New Land: What Archaeology Reveals about the First Americans*. Richmond Hill ON: Firefly Books.

Agenbroad, L. D. 2005. "North American Proboscideans: Mammoths; The State of Knowledge, 2003." *Quaternary International* 126:73–92.

Alexander, Herbert L. 1982. "The Pre-Clovis and Clovis Occupation at the Levi Site." In *Peopling of the New World*, edited by Jonathan E. Erickson, R. E. Taylor, and Rainer Berger. Los Altos CA: Ballena Press.

Anderson, A. D. 1975. "The Coopertown Mammoth: An Early Man Bone Quarry." *Great Plains Journal* 14 (2): 140–73.

Barker, Gary, and John B. Broster. 1996. "The Johnson Site (40DV400): A Dated Paleoindian and Archaic Occupation in Tennessee's Central Basin." *Journal of Alabama Archaeology* 42 (2): 97–153.

Bedwell, S. F. 1973. *Fort Rock Basin: Prehistory and Environment*. Eugene: University of Oregon Press.

Bischoff, J. L., R. J. Shlemon, T. L. Ku, R. D. Simpson, R. J. Rosenbauer, and F. E. Budinger Jr. 1981. "Uranium-Series and Soil-Geomorphic Dating of the Calico Archaeological Site, California." *Geology* 9 (12): 576–82.

Bonnichsen, R. 1979. *Pleistocene Bone Technology in the Beringian Refugium*. Mercury Series, Archaeological Survey of Canada no. 89, 1–280. Ottawa: National Museums of Canada.

Bonnichsen, R., R. W. Graham, T. Geppert, J. S. Oliver, S. G. Oliver, D. Schnurrenberger, et al. 1986. "False Cougar and Shield Trap Caves, Pryor Mountains, Montana." *National Geographic Research* 2 (3): 276–90.

Bourgeon, L., A. Burke, and T. Higham. 2017. "Earliest Human Presence in North America Dated to the Last Glacial Maximum: New Radiocarbon Dates from Bluefish Caves, Canada." *PLoS ONE* 12 (1): e0169486.

Bryan, A. L., and R. Gruhn. 2007. "A Revised Chronology for the Varsity Estates Site, Calgary, Alberta." *Canadian Journal of Archaeology / Journal Canadien d'Archéologie* 31:79–103.

Camacho, J. A. 1978. *Vestigios de labor humana en huesos de animales extintos de Valsequillo, Puebla, México*. Puebla: Gobierno del Estado de Puebla.

Chlachula, J. 1994. "Varsity Estates, a Palaeo-American Site in Southwestern Alberta, Canada (1990–1992 Investigations)." *Anthropologie* 32 (8): 101–27.

Cinq-Mars, J., and R. E. Morlan. 1999. "Bluefish Caves and Old Crow Basin: A New Rapport." In *Ice Age Peoples of North America: Environments, Origins, and Adaptations of the First Americans*, edited by Robson Bonnichsen and Karen L. Turnmire, 200–212. Corvallis: Oregon State University Press, Center for the Study of the First Americans.

Clausen, C. J., A. D. Cohen, C. Emiliani, J. A. Holman, and J. J. Stipp. 1979. "Little Salt Spring, Florida: A Unique Underwater Site." *Science* 203 (4381): 609–14.

Cook, A. G. 1975. "Dos artefactos de hueso en asociación con restos pleistocénicos en Los Reyes La Paz, México." *Anales del Museo Nacional de México* 4:237–50.

Cook, J. P. 1996. "Healey Lake." In *American Beginnings: The Prehistory and Palaeoecology of Beringia*, edited by C. F. West and B. S. Robinson. Chicago: University of Chicago Press.

Cowan, C. W., H. E. Jackson, K. Moore, A. Nickelhoff, and T. L. Smart. 1981. "The Cloudsplitter Rockshelter, Menifee County, Kentucky: A Preliminary Report." *Southeastern Archaeological Conference Bulletin* 24:60–76.

Cressman, L. S. 1977. *Prehistory of the Far West: Homes of Vanished Peoples*. Salt Lake City: University of Utah Press.

Davis, L. G., D. B. Madsen, L. Becerra-Valdivia, T. Higham, D. A. Sisson, S. M. Skinner, D. Stueber, et al. 2019. "Late Upper Paleolithic Occupation at Cooper's Ferry, Idaho, USA, ~16,000 Years Ago." *Science* 365 (6456): 891–97.

Dawson, J., and W. J. Judge. 1969. "Paleo-Indian Sites and Topography in the Middle Rio Grande Valley of New Mexico." *Plains Anthropologist* 14 (44): 149–63.

Deter-Wolf, Aaron, Jesse W. Tune, and John B. Broster. 2011. "Excavations and Dating of Late Pleistocene and Paleoindian Deposits at the Coats-Hines Site, Williamson County, Tennessee." *Tennessee Archaeology* 5 (2): 142–56.

Dixon, E. J. 1999. *Bones, Boats and Bison: Archeology and the First Colonization of Western North America*. Albuquerque: University of New Mexico Press.

Frison, G. C. 1978. *Prehistoric Hunters of the High Plains*. Vol. 1. New York: Academic Press.

Frison, G. C., and D. J. Stanford. 1982. *The Agate Basin Site: A Record of the Paleoindian Occupation of the Northwestern High Plains*. New York: Academic Press

Goebel, T. 2007. "Pre-Archaic and Early Archaic Technological Activities at Bonneville Estates Rockshelter: A First Look at the Lithic Artifact Record." In *Paleoindian or Paleoarchaic? Great Basin Human Ecology at the Pleistocene/Holocene Transition*, edited by Kelly E. Graf and David N. Schmitt, 156–84. Salt Lake City: University of Utah Press.

Goebel, T., R. Powers, and N. Bigelow. 1991. "The Nenana Complex of Alaska and Clovis Origins." In *Clovis: Origins and Adaptations*, edited by Robson Bonnichsen and Karen L. Turnmire, 49–79. Corvallis: Center for the Study of the First Americans, Oregon State University.

González, A. H. G., C. R. Sandoval, A. T. Mata, M. B. Sanvicente, W. Stinnesbeck, J. Aviles O., M. de los Ríos, and E. Acevez. 2008. "The Arrival of Humans on the Yucatan Peninsula: Evidence from Submerged Caves in the State of Quintana Roo, Mexico." *Current Research in the Pleistocene* 25:1–24.

Gonzalez, S., D. Huddart, and M. Bennett. 2006. "Valsequillo Pleistocene Archaeology and Dating: Ongoing Controversy in Central Mexico." *World Archaeology* 38 (4): 611–27.

Gonzalez, Silvia, and David Huddart. 2008. "The Late Pleistocene Human Occupation of Mexico." In *Memoria de Simposio Internacional de FUMDHAM*.

Goodyear, A. C. 2005. "Evidence of Pre-Clovis Sites in the Eastern United States." https://scholarcommons.sc.edu/cgi/viewcontent.cgi?referer=https://www.bing.com/&httpsredir=1&article=1026&context=sciaa_staffpub.

Goreczny, A. 2017. "Uncovering the Middle Archaic in Pennsylvania: Studies from State Road Ripple Site (36CL0052)." Master's thesis, Indiana University of Pennsylvania.

Gramly, R. M. 1999. *The Lamb Site: A Pioneering Clovis Encampment*. Buffalo NY: Persimmon Press.

Gruhn, R. 1961. *The Archaeology of Wilson Butte Cave South-Central Idaho*. Occasional Papers of the Idaho State College Museum, no. 6. Pocatello: Idaho State College.

———. 1965. "Two Early Radiocarbon Dates from the Lower Levels of Wilson Butte Cave, South Central Idaho." *Tebiwa* 8:57.

Halligan, J. J., M. R. Waters, A. Perrotti, I. J. Owens, J. M. Feinberg, M. D. Bourne, B. Fenerty, et al. 2016. "Pre-Clovis Occupation 14,550 Years Ago at the Page-Ladson Site, Florida, and the Peopling of the Americas." *Science Advances* 2 (5): e1600375.

Hamilton, T. D., and T. Goebel. 2005. "Late Pleistocene Peopling of Alaska." In *Ice Age Peoples of North America: Environments, Origins, and Adaptations of the First Americans*, edited by Robson Bonnichsen and Karen L. Turnmire, 49–79. 2nd ed. Corvallis: Oregon State University Press, Center for the Study of the First Americans.

Hamilton, T. M. 1996. "The Miami Mastodon, 23SA212." *Missouri Archaeologist* 54:79–88.

Harington, C. R. 1975. "A Bone Tool Found with Ice Age Mammal Remains near Dawson City, Yukon Territory." *Arctic Circular* 23(1): 1–5.

Harington, C. R., and R. E. Morlan. 1992. "A Late Pleistocene Antler Artifact from the Klondike District, Yukon Territory, Canada." *Arctic* 45 (3): 269–72.

Haynes, C. V., Jr. 1987. "Clovis Origin Update." *Kiva* 52 (2): 83–93.

Haynes, C. V., Jr., T. A. Surovell, and G. W. Hodgins. 2013. "The UP-Mammoth Site, Carbon County, Wyoming, USA: More Questions Than Answers." *Geoarchaeology* 28 (2): 99–111.

Haynes, G. 2015. "The Millennium before Clovis." *PaleoAmerica* 1 (2): 134–62.

Henderson, J. L. 2016. "Digital Technology and a New Era for Archaeology: Cooper's Ferry, Idaho." Senior thesis, Western Oregon University.

Hester, J. J. 1960. "Late Pleistocene Extinction and Radiocarbon Dating." *American Antiquity* 26 (1): 58–77.

Holen, S. R., T. A. Deméré, D. C. Fisher, R. Fullagar, J. B. Paces, G. T. Jefferson, J. M. Beeton, et al. 2017. "A 130,000-Year-Old Archaeological Site in Southern California, USA." *Nature* 544 (7,651): 479–83.

Holen, S. R., and K. Holen. 2012. "Evidence for a Human Occupation of the North American Great Plains during the Last Glacial Maximum." In *IV Simposio Internacional el hombre temprano en America*, edited by J. Concepción Jiménez López, Carlos Serrano Sánchez, Arturo González González, and Felisa J. Aguilar Arellano, 85–105. Mexico City: Instituto Nacional de Anthropologia and Historia.

———. 2014. "The Mammoth Steppe Hypothesis: The Middle Wisconsin (Oxygen Isotope Stage 3) Peopling of North America." In *Paleoamerican Odyssey*, edited by K. E. Graf, C. V. Ketron, and M. R. Waters, 429–44. College Station: Texas A&M University Press.

Holen, S. R., and D. W. May. 2002. "The La Sena and Shaffert Mammoth Sites." In *Medicine Creek: Seventy Years of Archaeological Investigations*, edited by Donna C. Roper, 20–36. Tuscaloosa: University of Alabama Press.

Holen, Steven R. 2006. "Taphonomy of Two Last Glacial Maximum Mammoth Sites in the Central Great Plains of North America: A Preliminary Report on La Sena and Lovewell." *Quaternary International* 142:30–43.

Holliday, V. T., C. V. Haynes Jr., J. L. Hofman, and D. J. Meltzer. 1994. "Geoarchaeology and Geochronology of the Miami (Clovis) Site, Southern High Plains of Texas." *Quaternary Research* 41 (2): 234–44.

Holliday, V. T., E. Johnson, H. Haas, and R. Stuckenrath. 1983. "Radiocarbon Ages from the Lubbock Lake Site, 1950–1980: Framework for Gul Tural and Ecological Change on the Southern High Plains." *Plains Anthropologist* 28 (101): 165–82.

Holmes, C. E., B. A. Potter, J. D. Reuther, O. K. Mason, R. M. Thorson, and P. M. Bowers. 2008. "Geological and Cultural Context of the Nogahabara I Site." *American Antiquity* 73 (4): 781–90.

Hughes, O. L., C. R. Harington, J. A. Janssens, J. V. Matthews Jr., R. E. Morlan, N. W. Rutter, and C. E. Schweger. 1981. "Upper Pleistocene Stratigraphy, Paleoecology, and Archaeology of the Northern Yukon Interior, Eastern Beringia 1. Bonnet Plume Basin." *Arctic* 34 (4): 329–65.

Irwin-Williams, C. 1978. "Summary of Archaeological Evidence from the Valsequillo Region, Puebla, Mexico." In *Cultural Continuity in Mesoamerica*, edited by David L. Browman, 7–22. The Hague: Mouton.

Jennings, J. D. 1957. *Danger Cave*. Vol. 22. Salt Lake City: University of Utah Press.

Jennings, T. A., and M. R. Waters. 2014. "Pre-Clovis Lithic Technology at the Debra L. Friedkin Site, Texas: Comparisons to Clovis through Site-Level Behavior, Technological Trait-List, and Cladistic Analyses." *American Antiquity* 79 (1): 25–44.

Jodry, M. A., and C. M. Santoro. 2017. "Walking Closer to the Sky: High-Altitude Landscapes and the Peopling of the New World." *Quaternary International* 461:102–7.

Joyce, D. J. 2006. "Chronology and New Research on the Schaefer Mammoth (? *Mammuthus primigenius*) Site, Kenosha County, Wisconsin, USA." *Quaternary International* 142:44–57.

Kenady, Stephen M., Michael C. Wilson, Randall F. Schalk, and Robert R. Mierendorf. 2010. "Late Pleistocene Butchered Bison Antiquus from Ayer Pond, Orcas Island, Pacific Northwest: Age Confirmation and Taphonomy." *Quaternary International* 233 (2): 130–41.

Kooyman, B., M. E. Newman, C. Cluney, M. Lobb, S. Tolman, P. McNeil, and L. V. Hills. 2001. "Identification of Horse Exploitation by Clovis Hunters Based on Protein Analysis." *American Antiquity* 66 (4): 686–91.

Kopper, J. S., R. E. Funk, and L. Dumont. 1980. "Additional Paleo-Indian and Archaic Materials from the Dutchess Quarry Cave Area, Orange County, New York." *Archaeology of Eastern North America* 8:125–37.

Kunz, M. L., and R. E. Reanier. 1995. "The Mesa Site: A Paleoindian Hunting Lookout in Arctic Alaska." *Arctic Anthropology* 32 (1): 5–30.

Leakey, L. S. B., R. D. Simpson, and T. Clements. 1968. "Archaeological Excavations in the Calico Mountains, California: Preliminary Report." *Science* 160 (3831): 1022–23.

Leveillee, A. 2016. "Sands of the Blackstone: A Paleo-Indian Site in the Narragansett Bay Drainage." Public Archaeology Laboratory. October. https://www.palinc.com/sites /default/files/publications/Sands%20of%20the%20Blackstone-Leveillee.pdf.

Lewis, C. R. 2009. "An 18,000-Year-Old Occupation along Petronila Creek in Texas." *Bulletin of the Texas Archaeological Society* 80.

Lorenzo, J. L., and L. Mirambell. 1986. "Preliminary Report on Archeological and Paleoenvironmental Studies in the Area of El Cedral, San Luis Potosí, México." In *New Evidence for the Pleistocene Peopling of the Americas*, edited by A. L. Bryan, 107–13. Orono ME: Center for the Study of Early Man.

Lothrop, J. C., D. L. Lowery, A. E. Spiess, and C. J. Ellis. 2016. "Early Human Settlement of Northeastern North America." *Paleoamerica* 2 (3): 192–251.

Lowery, D. 2020. Smithsonian Institution, personal communication, email.

Lowery, D. L., M. A. O'Neal, J. S. Wah, D. P. Wagner, and D. J. Stanford. 2010. "Late Pleistocene Upland Stratigraphy of the Western Delmarva Peninsula, USA." *Quaternary Science Reviews* 29 (11–12): 1472–80.

MacNeish, Richard S., and Jane G. Liddy, eds. 2003. *Pendejo Cave*. Albuquerque: University of New Mexico Press.

McAvoy, J. M., and L. D. McAvoy. 1997. "Archaeological Investigations of Site 44SX202, Cactus Hill, Sussex County, Virginia (No. 2)." Department of Historic Resources.

McDonald, J. N. 2000. "An Outline of the Pre-Clovis Archaeology of SV-2 Saltville, Virginia, with Special Attention to a Bone Tool Dated 14,510 yr BP." Jeffersoniana 9. Martinsville: Virginia Museum of Natural History.

Mirambell, L. 1978. "Tlapacoya: A Late Pleistocene Site in Central Mexico." In *Early Man in America from a Circum-Pacific Perspective*, edited by A. L. Bryan. Occasional Paper No. 1, Department of Anthropology, University of Alberta, Canada.

———. 1980. *Tlapacoya: A Late Pleistocene Site in Central Mexico.* N.p.

Morlan, R. E., and J. Cinq-Mars. 1982. "Ancient Beringians: Human Occupation in the Late Pleistocene of Alaska and the Yukon Territory." In *Paleoecology of Beringia*, edited by David M. Hopkins, 353–81. New York: Academic Press.

Morlan, R. E., D. E. Nelson, T. A. Brown, J. S. Vogel, and J. R. Southon. 1990. "Accelerator Mass Spectrometry Dates on Bones from Old Crow Basin, Northern Yukon Territory." *Canadian Journal of Archaeology / Journal Canadien d'Archéologie*, 75–92.

Munson, P. J., and J. C. Frye. 1965. "Artifact from Deposits of Mid-Wisconsin Age in Illinois." *Science* 150 (3704): 1722–23.

Neiburger, E. J. 2011. "UPDATE: A New Date for the Perry Mastodon." *Central States Archaeological Journal* 58 (3): 130–31.

Orr, P. C., and R. Berger. 1966. "The Fire Areas on Santa Rosa Island, California." *Proceedings of the National Academy of Sciences of the United States of America* 56 (5): 1409.

Overstreet, D. F. 1993. *Chesrow: A Paleoindian Complex in the Southern Lake Michigan Basin.* Milwaukee WI: Great Lakes Archaeological Press.

Overstreet, D. F., and M. F. Kolb. 2003. "Geoarchaeological Contexts for Late Pleistocene Archaeological Sites with Human-Modified Woolly Mammoth Remains in Southeastern Wisconsin, USA." *Geoarchaeology: An International Journal* 18 (1): 91–114.

Pearson, G. A. 1999. "Early Occupations and Cultural Sequence at Moose Creek: A Late Pleistocene Site in Central Alaska." *Arctic* 52 (4): 332–45.

Plew, Mark G., and Max G. Pavesic. 1982. "A Compendium of Radiocarbon Dates for Southern Idaho Archaeological Sites." *Journal of California and Great Basin Anthropology* 4 (1).

Powers, W. R., and J. F. Hoffecker. 1989. "Late Pleistocene Settlement in the Nenana Valley, Central Alaska." *American Antiquity* 54 (2): 263–87.

Purdy, B. A., K. S. Jones, J. J. Mecholsky, G. Bourne, R. C. Hulbert Jr., B. J. MacFadden, et al. 2011. "Earliest Art in the Americas: Incised Image of a Proboscidean on a Mineralized Extinct Animal Bone from Vero Beach, Florida." *Journal of Archaeological Science* 38 (11): 2908–13.

Reagan, M. J., R. M. Rowlett, E. G. Garrison, W. Dort, V. M. Bryant, and C. J. Johannsen. 1978. "Flake Tools Stratified below Paleo-Indian Artifacts." *Science* 200 (4347): 1272–75.

Redmond, B. G., H. G. McDonald, H. J. Greenfield, and M. L. Burr. 2012. "New Evidence for Late Pleistocene Human Exploitation of Jefferson's Ground Sloth (*Megalonyx jeffersonii*) from Northern Ohio, USA." *World Archaeology* 44 (1): 75–101.

Reitze, W. T. 2016. "Folsom on the Edge of the Plains: Occupation of the Estancia Basin, Central New Mexico." *PaleoAmerica* 2 (2): 109–15.

Rink, J. W., J. S. Dunbar, and K. E. Burdette. 2012. "The Wakulla Springs Lodge Site (8WA329): 2008 Excavations and New OSL Dating Evidence." *Florida Anthropologist* 65 (1–2): 5–24.

Roosa, W. B. 1968. "Data on Early Sites in Central New Mexico and Michigan." PhD dissertation, University of Michigan.

Rosencrance, R. L., G. M. Smith, D. L. Jenkins, T. J. Connolly, and T. N. Layton. 2019. "Reinvestigating Cougar Mountain Cave: New Perspectives on Stratigraphy, Chronology, and a Younger Dryas Occupation in the Northern Great Basin." *American Antiquity* 84 (3): 559–73.

Rubin, M., and C. Alexander. 1958. "U.S. Geological Survey Radiocarbon Dates IV." *Science* 127 (3313): 1476–87.

Rutherford, A. A., J. Wittenberg, and R. Wilmeth. 1979. "University of Saskatchewan Radiocarbon Dates VIII." *Radiocarbon* 21 (1): 48–94.

Sanchez, M. G. 2001. "A Synopsis of Paleo-Indian Archaeology in Mexico." *Kiva* 67 (2): 119–36.

Stanford, D. J., and B. A. Bradley. 2012. *Across Atlantic Ice: The Origin of America's Clovis Culture*. Berkeley: University of California Press.

Steele, J. 2010. "Radiocarbon Dates as Data: Quantitative Strategies for Estimating Colonization Front Speeds and Event Densities." *Journal of Archaeological Science* 37 (8): 2017–30.

Steen-McIntyre, V., R. Fryxell, and H. E. Malde. 1981. "Geological Evidence for Age of Deposits at Hueyatlaco Archaeological Site, Valsequillo, Mexico." *Quaternary Research* 16:1–17.

Stenger, Alison T. 2012. "Pre-Clovis in the Willamette Valley." PhD dissertation, Institute for Archaeological Studies.

Szabo, B. J., H. E. Malde, and C. Irwin-Williams. 1969. "Dilemma Posed by Uranium-Series Dates on Archaeologically Significant Bones from Valsequillo, Puebla, Mexico." *Earth and Planetary Science Letters* 6 (4): 237–44.

Wah, J. S., D. L. Lowery, and D. P. Wagner. 2014. "Loess, Landscape Evolution, and Pre-Clovis on the Delmarva Peninsula." In *Pre-Clovis in the Americas: International Science Conference Proceedings Led at the Smithsonian Institution, Washington, DC*, 32–48. Washington DC: CreateSpace Independent Publishing Platform, Smithsonian Institution edition.

Williams, T. J., M. B. Collins, K. Rodrigues, W. J. Rink, N. Velchoff, A. Keen-Zebert, A. Gilmer, et al. 2018. "Evidence of an Early Projectile Point Technology in North America at the Gault Site, Texas, USA." *Science Advances* 4 (7): eaar5954.

Wyckoff, D. G. 1999. "The Burnham Site and Pleistocene Human Occupation of the Southern Plains of the United States." In *Ice Age Peoples of North America: Environments, Origins, and Adaptations of the First Americans*, edited by Robson Bonnichsen and Karen L. Turnmire, 340–61. Corvallis: Oregon State University, Center for the Study of the First Americans.

Wyckoff, D. G., B. J. Carter, W. Dort Jr., G. R. Brakenridge, L. D. Martin, J. L. Theler, and L. C. Todd. 1990. "Northwestern Oklahoma's Burnham Site: Glimpses beyond Clovis." *Current Research in the Pleistocene* 7 (6): 63.

South American Archaeological Sites

	Site name	BP unless otherwise noted	Area	References
1	Toca da Esperança	295,000 ± 780 (geological) 200,000–300,000 ^{230}Th/^{234}U 295–204 ka	Brazil	Beltrao et al. 1987; Dillehay 2000
2	Monte Verde I	33,370 ± 530 Base of MV 7	Chile	Dillehay 2000
3	Pedra Furada	55,575 ± 5,865 53,120 ± 3,965 32,160 ± 1,000 31,700 ± 830	Brazil	Santos et al. 2003; Guidon and Delibrias 1986
4	Vale da Pedra Furada	35–27	Brazil	Boëda et al. 2016
5	Arroyo del Vizcaíno	27 ± 0.45–30.1 ± 0.6	Uruguay	Fariña et al. 2014
6	Santa Elina	27,000 ± 2,000 ^{230}Th/^{234}U 23,120 ± 260	Brazil	Vialou et al. 2017
7	Sítio do Meio	28,100–28,600	Brazil	Boëda et al. 2016
8	Atuel	23,490 13,100	Argentina	MacNeish 1978
9	Toca de Tira Peia	20,000 ± 1,500 BC 15,100 ± 1,200 BC	Brazil	Lahaye et al. 2013
10	Morro Furado	21,090 ± 420 18,570 ± 130 16,200 ± 290	Brazil	Kipnis 1998; Dillehay 2000
11	Pikimachay	25,000–11,000	Peru	MacNeish 1979
12	Caldeirão de Rodrigues	17,000 ± 400	Brazil	Guidon 1986; Dillehay 2000

13	Pubenza	17,790 ± 120 16,460 ± 420	Colombia	Dillehay 2000; Van der Hammen and Urrego 2001
14	Muaco	16,375 ± 400 14,300 ± 500	Venezuela	Rouse and Cruxent 1963; Gnecco and Aceituno 2006
15	Chinchihuapi Locality and Monte Verde new data	19,000–14,500	Chile	Dillehay et al. 2015
16	Alice Böer	14,200 ± 1,150	Brazil	Beltrao et al. 1983, 1974
17	Rancho Peludo	13,915 ± 200 6,130 ± 90 2,325 ± 80	Venezuela	Rouse and Cruxent 1963; Gnecco and Aceituno 2006
18	LT Ji-Paraná-Rolim de Moura	13,720 ± 160	Brazil	Meggers and Miller 2003
19	LT Brazil	13,660 ± 430	Venezuela	Meggers and Miller 2003
20	Quebrada El Membrillo	13,500 ± 65	Chile	Jackson, Méndez, and De Souza 2004; Dillehay 2000
21	Huargo Cave	13,460 ± 700	Peru	Cardich 1973, 1978; Cardich and Izeta 1999
22	Cueva Cacao	13,300	Argentina	Aschero, Martínez, and Powell 2013
23	Sueva	=11,740 ± 110	Colombia	Dillehay 2000
24	Tequendama	12,500–10,100 ka	Colombia	Dillehay 2000; Urrego and Van der Hammen 1977
25	El Jordán	12,910 ± 60	Colombia	Aceituno et al. 2013
26	Piedra Museo AEP-1 El Puesto Rockshelter	12,890 ± 90	Argentina	Miotti and Salemme 1998
27	Taima-Taima	14,200 ± 300 12,980 ± 85	Venezuela	Bryan and Gruhn 1979

28	Complejo Paiján	12,845 ± 280	Peru	Ossa 1978; Dillehay 2000
29	Quirihuac	12,745 ± 350	Peru	Ossa 1978; Dillehay 2000
30	Monte Verde	18,500—14,500	Chile	Dillehay et al. 2015
31	RS 1 50	12,770 ± 220	Brazil	Miller 1987; Dillehay 2000
32	Santana do Riacho	12,760 ± 70 Human bone collagen 18,000 ± 1,000 Charcoal	Brazil	Neves et al. 2003
33	RS Q-2	12,690 ± 100	Brazil	Miller 1987; Dillehay 2000
34	Huaca Prieta	14,500	Peru	Dillehay et al. 2017
35	Los Toldos	12,600 ± 600	Argentina	Cardich 1978
36	Guitarrero Cave	12,560 ± 360 10,000–9,000	Peru	Lynch 1980; Dillehay 2000
37	El Ceibo	Similarities in technologies and extinct fauna to level 11 at Los Toldos 12,600	Argentina	Cardich et al. 1987; Cardich et al. 1982
38	El Abra II	12,400 ± 160	Colombia	Dillehay 2000; Urrego 1986
39	Cueva del Medio	12.3–9.5 ka 12,390 ± 180	Chile	Borrero and Franco 1997; Borrero 1996
40	La Cumbre	12,360 ± 700 10,535 ± 280	Peru	Ossa 1978; Borrero 1996
41	Garrincho	12,210 ± 40	Brazil	Guidon et al. 2000
42	Arroyo Seco Sitio 2	12,170–11,180	Argentina	Politis et al. 2016
43	Lapa do Boquete	12,070 ± 170 9,350 ± 80	Brazil	Prous 1986; Dillehay 2000
44	Quereo 1	11,600–11,400 11,400 12,000 ± 195	Chile,	Dillehay 2000; Núñez et al. 1994; Núñez et al. 1983

45	Lapa Mortuária	12,000–11,000 Human remains	Brazil	Neves and Hubbe 2005
46	Tres Arroyos	11,880 ± 250	Argentina	Borrero et al. 1998
47	Pachamachay	11,800 ± 930	Peru	Rick 1980; Dillehay 2000
48	Telarmachay	12,040 ± 120	Peru	Dillehay 2000
49	Tibito	11,740 ± 110	Colombia	Urrego 1986; Dillehay 2000
50	Urupez	11,690 ± 80	Uruguay	Nami 2008
51	Lapa Vermelha	25,000–15,300 15,300–11,600 11,960–10,200 Human remains	Brazil	Dillehay 2000; Laming-Emperaire 1979
52	El Palto	11,650	Peru	Dillehay 2000
53	Cueva Sofia 1	11,570 ± 60 10,910 ± 260	South Andes	Borrero 1999
54	Cerro Tres Tetas	11,560–10,260	Argentina	Paunero 2003
55	RS-168	11,555 ± 230	Brazil	Miller 1987; Dillehay 2000
56	Tagua-Tagua II	11,380 ± 320	Chile	Montane ⯑1968
57	El Tigre	11,355 ± 30	Uruguay	Suárez, Piñeiro, and Barceló 2018
58	San José	11,248–9,321	Ecuador	Dillehay 2000

References for South American Sites

Aceituno, F. J., N. Loaiza, M. E. Delgado-Burbano, and G. Barrientos. 2013. "The Initial Human Settlement Of Northwest South America during the Pleistocene/Holocene Transition: Synthesis and Perspectives." *Quaternary International* 301:23–33.

Aschero, C. A., J. G. Martínez, and J. E. Powell. 2013. "Una asociación cultural con megafauna extinta en el sitio Cacao 1A ca. 13.350/12.500 AP (Antofagasta de la Sierra, Catamarca)." Paper presented in the III Congreso Nacional de Zooarqueología, Tilcara, Jujuy.

Beltrao, M., C. R. Enriquez, J. Danon, E. Zuleta, and G. Poupeau. 1987. "Thermoluminescence Dating of Burnt Cherts from the Alice Boer Site (Brazil) (No. CBPF-NF-004/83)." In *The Origin of Man in America: Proceedings of a Symposium Held at the 10th Congress of the International Union of Prehistoric and Protohistoric Sciences*, Mexico City, October 19–24, 1981. Rio de Janeiro: Centro Brasileiro de Pesquisas Fisicas.

Beltrão, M. C. 1974. "Datações arqueológicas mais antigas do Brasil." *Anais da Academia Brasileira de Ciências* 46 (2): 211–51.

Boëda, E., R. Rocca, A. Da Costa, M. Fontugne, C. Hatté, I. Clemente-Conte, J. C. Santos, et al. 2016. "New Data on a Pleistocene Archaeological Sequence in South America: Toca do Sítio do Meio, Piauí, Brazil." *PaleoAmerica* 2 (4): 286–302.

Borrero, L. A. 1996. "The Pleistocene–Holocene Transition in Southern South America." In *Humans at the End of the Ice Age*, edited by L. G. Straus, B. V. Erlandson, and D. R. Yesner, 339–54. Boston: Springer.

———. 1999. "Human Dispersal and Climatic Conditions during Late Pleistocene Times in Fuego-Patagonia." *Quaternary International* 53:93–99.

Borrero, L. A., and N. V. Franco. 1997. "Early Patagonian Hunter-Gatherers: Subsistence and Technology." *Journal of Anthropological Research* 53 (2): 219–39.

Borrero, L. A., M. Zárate, L. Miotti, and M. Massone. 1998. "The Pleistocene–Holocene Transition and Human Occupations in the Southern Cone of South America." *Quaternary International* 49:191–99.

Bryan, A. L., and R. Gruhn. 1979. "The Radiocarbon Dates of Taima-Taima." In *Taima-Taima: A Late Pleistocene Paleo-Indian Kill Site in Northernmost South America; Final Reports of 1976 Excavations*, edited by Claudio Ochsenius and Ruth Gruhn, 53–58. N.p.: South American Quaternary Documentation Program.

Cardich, A. 1973. "Exploración en la caverna de Huargo, Perú." *Revista del Museo Nacional de Lima* 39:11–47.

———. 1978. "Recent Excavations at Lauricocha (Central Andes) and Los Toldos (Patagonia)." In *Early Man in America from a Circum-Pacific Perspective*, edited by Alan Lyle Bryan, 296–300. Occasional Papers of the University of Alberta 1. Edmonton: Archaeological Researchers International.

———. 1987. "Arqueología de Los Toldos y El Ceibo (Provincia de Santa Cruz, Argentina)." *Estudios Atacameños* 8:98–117.

Cardich, A., and A. D. Izeta. 1999. "Revisitando Huargo (Perú): Análisis cuantitativos aplicados a restos de Camelidae del Pleistoceno tardío." *Anales de Arqueología y Etnología* 54:29–40.

Cardich, A. R., V. Durán, M. E. Mansur-Franchomme, and M. Giesso. 1982. *Archeology of the Caves of El Ceibo, Santa Cruz*. Relations of the Argentine Society of Anthropology 14.

Dillehay, T. D. 2000. *The Settlement of the Americas: A New Prehistory*. New York: Basic Books.

Dillehay, T. D., S. Goodbred, M. Pino, V. F. V. Sánchez, T. R. Tham, J. Adovasio, M. B. Collins, et al. 2017. "Simple Technologies and Diverse Food Strategies of the Late Pleistocene and Early Holocene at Huaca Prieta, Coastal Peru." *Science Advances* 3 (5): e1602778.

Dillehay, T. D., C. Ocampo, J. Saavedra, A. O. Sawakuchi, R. M. Vega, M. Pino, M. B. Collins, et al. 2015. "New Archaeological Evidence for an Early Human Presence at Monte Verde, Chile." *PLoS ONE* 10 (11): e0141923.

Fariña, R. A., P. S. Tambusso, L. Varela, A. Czerwonogora, M. Di Giacomo, M. Musso, R. Bracco, and A. Gascue. 2014. "Arroyo del Vizcaíno, Uruguay: A Fossil-Rich 30-Ka-Old Megafaunal Locality with Cut-Marked Bones." *Proceedings of the Royal Society B* 281 (1774): 2013–2211.

Gnecco, C., and J. Aceituno. 2006. "Early Humanized Landscapes in Northern South America." In *Paleoindian Archaeology: A Hemispheric Perspective*, edited by Juliet E. Morrow and Cristóbal Gneco, 86–104. Gainesville: University Press of Florida.

Guidon, N., and G. Delibrias. 1986. "Carbon-14 Dates Point to Man in the Americas 32,000 Years Ago." *Nature* 321 (6072): 769.

Guidon, N., E. Peyre, C. Guérin, and Y. Coppens. 2000. "Resultados da datação de dentes humanos da Toca do Garrincho, Piauí, Brasil." *Clio Arqueológica* 14:75–86.

Jackson, D., C. Méndez, and P. De Souza. 2004. "Poblamiento Paleoindio en el norte-centro de Chile: Evidencias, problemas y perspectivas de estudio." *Complutum* 15:165–76.

Kipnis, R. 1998. "Early Hunter-Gatherers in the Americas: Perspectives from Central Brazil." *Antiquity* 72 (277): 581–92.

Lahaye, Christelle, Marion Harnendaz, Eric Boëda, Gisele D. Felice, Nième Guidon, Sirlei Hoeltz, Antoine Lourdeau, et al. 2013. "Human Occupation in South America by 20,000 BC: The Toca da Tira Peia Site, Piaui, Brazil." *Journal of Archaeological Science* 40 (6): xxx, 1–8.

Laming-Emperaire, A. 1979. "Missions archeologiques franco-bresiliennes en Lagoa Santa, Minas Gerais, Bresil: Le grand abri de Lapa Vermelha (P.L.)." *Revista de Pré-História* 1 (1): 53–89.

Lynch, T. F. 1978. "Late Pleistocene Adaptations: A New Look at Early Peopling of the New World as of 1976." *Journal of Anthropological Research* 34 (4): 475–96.

———. 1979. "The Early Man Remains from Pikimachay Cave, Ayacucho Basin, Highland Peru." In *Pre-Llano Cultures of the Americas: Paradoxes and Possibilities*, 1–48. Anthropological Society of Washington.

———. 1980. "Guitarrero Cave in Its Andean Context." In *Guitarrero Cave: Early Man in the Andes*, edited by Thomas F. Lynch, 293–320. New York: Academic Press.

Meggers, B. J., and E. T. Miller. 2003. "Hunter-Gatherers in Amazonia during the Pleistocene–Holocene Transition." In *Under the Canopy: The Archaeology of Tropical Rain Forests*, edited by Julio Mercader, 291–316. New Brunswick NJ: Rutgers University Press.

Miller, E. T. 1987. "Pesquisas arqueológicas paleoindígenas no Brasil Ocidental." *Estudios Atacameños* 8:37–61.

Miotti, L., and M. Salemme. 1998. "Hunting and Butchering Events during the Late Pleistocene and Early Holocene in Piedra Museo (Patagonia, Southernmost South America)." Paper presented at the Eighth International Congress of the International Council for Archaeology, Victoria.

Montané, J. 1968. "Paleo-Indian Remains from Laguna de Tagua Tagua, Central Chile." *Science* 161 (3846): 1137–38.

Nami, H. G. 2008. "Paleomagnetic Results from the Urupez Paleoindian Site, Maldonado Department, Uruguay." https://www.academia.edu/3629389/Nami_Hugo_G _2008_Paleomagnetic_Results_from_the_Urupez_Paleoindian_Site_Maldonado _Department_Uruguay.

Neves, W. A., and M. Hubbe. 2005. "Cranial Morphology of Early Americans from Lagoa Santa, Brazil: Implications for the Settlement of the New World." *Proceedings of the National Academy of Sciences* 102 (51): 18309–14.

Neves, W. A., A. Prous, R. González-José, R. Kipnis, and J. Powell. 2003. "Early Holocene Human Skeletal Remains from Santana do Riacho, Brazil: Implications for the Settlement of the New World." *Journal of Human Evolution* 45 (1): 19–42.

Núñez, L. 1983. *Paleoindio y Arcaico en Chile: Diversidad, secuencia y procesos.* Vol. 3. Escuela Nacional de Antropología e Historia, Mexico City.

Núñez, L., J. Varela, R. Casamiquela, and C. Villagrán. 1994. "Reconstrucción multidisiplinaria de la ocupación prehistórica de Quereo, centro de Chile." *Latin American Antiquity*, 99–118.

Ossa, P. 1978. "Paiján in Early Andean Prehistory: The Moche Valley Evidence." In *New Evidence for the Pleistocene Peopling of the Americas, University of Alberta, Edmonton*, edited by A. L. Bryan, 290–95. Orono ME: Center for the Study of Early Man.

Paunero, R. 2003. "The Cerro Tres Tetas (C3T) Locality in the Central Plateau of Santa Cruz, Argentina." In *Where the South Winds Blow: Ancient Evidence of Paleo South Americans*, edited by L. Miotti, M. Salemme, and N. Flegenheimer, 133–40. College Station: Center for the Study of the First Americans, Texas A&M University Press.

Politis, G. G., M. A. Gutiérrez, D. J. Rafuse, and A. Blasi. 2016. "The Arrival of *Homo sapiens* into the Southern Cone at 14,000 Years Ago." *PLoS ONE* 11 (9): e0162870.

Prouse, A. 1986. "Os mais antigos vestigios arqueollogicos no Brazil Central (Estados de Minas Gerais, Goiase e Bahia)." In *New Evidence for the Pleistocene Peopling of the Americas*, edited by A. L. Bryan, 15–26. Orono ME: Center for the Study of Early Man.

Rick, J. W. 1980. *Prehistoric Hunters of the High Andes.* New York: Academic Press.

Rouse, I., and J. M. Cruxent. 1963. "Some Recent Radiocarbon Dates for Western Venezuela." *American Antiquity* 28 (4): 537–40.

Santos, G. M., M. I. Bird, F. Parenti, L. K. Fifield, N. Guidon, and P. A. Hausladen. 2003. "A Revised Chronology of the Lowest Occupation Layer of Pedra Furada Rock Shelter, Piauí, Brazil: The Pleistocene Peopling of the Americas." *Quaternary Science Reviews* 22 (21–22): 2303–10.

Suárez, R., G. Piñeiro, and F. Barceló. 2018. "Living on the River Edge: The Tigre Site (K-87) New Data and Implications for the Initial Colonization of the Uruguay River Basin." *Quaternary International* 473:242–60.

Urrego Correal, G. 1986. "Apuntes sobre el medio ambiente pleistocénico y el hombre prehistórico en Colombia." In *New Evidence for the Pleistocene Peopling of the Americas*, edited by A. L. Bryan, 115–31. Orono ME: Center for the Study of Early Man.

Urrego Correal, G., and T. Van der Hammen, T. 1977. "Investigaciones arqueológicas en los abrigos rocosos del Tequendama." Biblioteca Banco Popular, Bogotá.

Van der Hammen, T., and G. C. Urrego. 2001. "Mastodontes en el humedal pleistocénico en el valle del Magdalena (Colombia) con evidencias de la presencia del hombre en el pleniglacial." *Boletín de Arqueología* 16:1.

Vialou, D., M. Benabdelhadi, J. Feathers, M. Fontugne, and A. V. Vialou. 2017. "Peopling South America's Centre: The Late Pleistocene Site of Santa Elina." *Antiquity* 91 (358): 865–84.

NOTES

INTRODUCTION

1. Holm and Reid, *Indian Art*, 7.
2. Canadian Museum of History, https://www.historymuseum.ca/cmc/exhibitions/aborig
   /fp/fpz2a22e.html.
3. Meltzer, "Peopling of North America."
4. Thorne and Wolpoff, "The Multiregional Evolution"; Pääbo, "The Diverse Origins."
5. Strasser et al., "Dating Paleolithic Sites"; Clarkson et al., "Human Occupation," 306.
6. Alfred and Corntassel, "Being Indigenous," 598.
7. Meltzer, *First Peoples*; Stanford and Bradley, *Across Atlantic Ice.*
8. Thomas, *Skull Wars.*
9. Proctor and Schiebinger, *Agnotology*, vii.
10. Dugassa, "Colonialism of Mind."
11. Deloria, *Red Earth, White Lies.* Vine Deloria Jr. critiqued archaeologists' use of "extinct
    people" to erase Indigenous people from the land.
12. Loewen, *Lies My Teacher Told Me.*
13. Clark et al., "The Last Glacial Maximum."
14. Gonzalez, "Indigenous Values"; Yellowhorn, "Awakening"; Atalay, *Community-Based
    Archaeology.*
15. Wagamese, *Embers*, 36.
16. Crazy Bull, "A Native Conversation."
17. Louis, "Can You Hear Us Now?," 131.
18. Wilson, *Research Is Ceremony*, 11.
19. Adovasio and Page, *The First Americans*; Dillehay, *The Settlement*; Deloria, *Red Earth,
    White Lies.*
20. Tafoya, "Finding Harmony," 12.
21. Bourgeon, Burke, and Higham, "Earliest Human Presence."
22. Halligan et al., "Pre-Clovis Occupation."
23. Tune et al., "Assessing," 47.

24. Battiste and Henderson, *Protecting Indigenous Knowledge*; Miller and Riding In, *Native Historians Write Back*; Wilson, *Research Is Ceremony*; Smith, *Decolonizing Methodologies*; Simpson, "Oshkimmadiziig."
25. Schmidt and Patterson, *Making Alternative Histories*.
26. Wylie, "Making Alternative Histories," 261.

1. DECOLONIZING INDIGENOUS HISTORIES

1. Deloria, *Red Earth, White Lies*.
2. Zhu et al., "Hominin Occupation," 608.
3. Dillehay, *The Settlement*.
4. Holm and Reid, *Indian Art*.
5. Bryan, *New Evidence*.
6. Hrdlička et al., *Early Man*.
7. Adovasio and Pedler, *Strangers in a New Land*, 315.
8. Adovasio and Pedler, *Strangers in a New Land*.
9. Dillehay, *The Settlement*.
10. Olsson, "Radiocarbon Dating History."
11. Waters and Stafford, "Redefining."
12. Dillehay, *The Settlement*.
13. Beck and Jones, "Clovis and Western Stemmed," 81.
14. Smith, *Decolonizing Methodologies*.
15. Turnbull, "Territorializing/Decolonizing."
16. Turnbull, "Territorializing/Decolonizing," 12.
17. Wilson, *Research Is Ceremony*.
18. Sinclair, "Indigenous Research," 122.
19. Rigney, "Internationalism"; Martin and Mirraboopa, "Ways of Knowing."
20. Kovach, *Indigenous Methodologies*.
21. Sprague and Frye, *The Genealogy*.
22. Denton, "Frenchman's Island"; Denton, *A Visit in Time*.
23. Hall, *Thunderbirds*; Reagan and Walters, "Thunderbird Fights."
24. Echo-Hawk, "Kara Katit Pakutu."
25. Flores and Acuto, "Pueblos originarios"; Politis and Curtoni, "Archaeology and Politics"; Kovach, *Indigenous Methodologies*.
26. Haynes, "Were Clovis Progenitors," 383.
27. Haynes, "Were Clovis Progenitors," 383.
28. Bryan, *Early Man*.
29. Beck and Jones, "Clovis and Western Stemmed."
30. Duk-Rodkin and Hughes, "Age Relationships."
31. Jennings, *Prehistory*, 68.

32. Adovasio and Pedler, *Strangers in a New Land*, 315; Dillehay, *The Settlement*; Holen et al., "A 130,000-Year-Old Archaeological Site," 479; Boëda et al., "A New Late Pleistocene."

33. Fiedel, "The Peopling"; Haynes, "The Cerutti Mastodon"; Braje et al., "Were Hominins in California"; Raghavan et al., "Genomic Evidence."

34. Tankersley, "The Concept of Clovis."

35. Clarke, *Analytical Archaeology*; Hurcombe, *Archaeological Artefacts*; Hodder, *Archaeological Theory Today*; Childe, *The Most Ancient East*.

36. Renfrew and Bahn, *Archaeology*, 407.

37. Childe, *The Most Ancient East*, 3.

38. Childe, *The Most Ancient East*.

39. Kay, "Microwear Analysis."

40. Adovasio and Pedler, *Strangers in a New Land*, 315.

41. Adovasio and Pedler, "Monte Verde."

42. Waters and Stafford, "Redefining"; Haynes, "Were Clovis Progenitors"; Agam and Barkai, "Elephant and Mammoth Hunting"; Devièse et al., "Increasing Accuracy"; Waguespack and Surovell, "Clovis Hunting Strategies."

43. Guidon and Arnaud, "The Chronology," 168.

44. Bryan, *New Evidence*.

45. Cavalli-Sforza, cited in Churchill, *Since Predator Came*.

46. Adovasio and Pedler, foreword.

47. Byrd, *The Transit of Empire*; Smith, *Decolonizing Methodologies*.

48. Sium and Ritskes, "Speaking Truth to Power," iii.

49. Niezen, *The Origins*; Robinson, "Psychological Decolonization."

50. Denton, "Frenchman's Island"; Nicholas and Markey, "Traditional Knowledge"; Atalay, "Indigenous Archaeology"; Gonzalez, Kretzler, and Edwards, "Imagining Indigenous and Archaeological Futures."

51. Pullar, "The Quikertarmiut."

52. Pullar, "The Quikertarmiut."

53. Brown, *The Spiritual Legacy*, 3.

54. Doxtator, "The Idea of Indianness."

55. Schmidt and Patterson, *Making Alternative Histories*.

56. Wylie, "Making Alternative Histories," 261.

57. Rathje, Shanks, and Witmore, *Archaeology in the Making*.

58. Watanabe, *Tensions*.

59. Smith, *Decolonizing Methodologies*.

60. Yellowhorn, "Awakening," iv.

61. Wilson, *Research Is Ceremony*.

62. Smith, *Decolonizing Methodologies*.

63. Wilson, *Research Is Ceremony*.

64. Nicholas, "Understanding the Present"; Atalay, "Indigenous Archaeology"; Smith and Wobst, *Indigenous Archaeologies*; Wilcox, "Saving Indigenous Peoples."

65. Bray, "Repatriation."

66. Wiseman, *Reclaiming the Ancestors.*

67. Preucel and Hodder, *Appropriated Pasts.*

68. Atalay, "Introduction."

69. Byrd, *The Transit of Empire.*

70. Kimmerer and Lake, "The Role of Indigenous Burning"; Mistry et al., "Indigenous Fire Management."

71. For more on this topic, see my dissertation, "Decolonizing Indigenous Histories."

72. Battiste, *Indigenous Knowledge*, 4.

73. Brown and Strega, *Research as Resistance.*

74. Gnecco and Ayala, *Indigenous Peoples.*

75. Wilson, "Indigenous Knowledge Recovery."

76. Wilson, "Indigenous Knowledge Recovery," 359.

77. Kovach, *Indigenous Methodologies*, 27. Sources in the block quote include Little Bear, "JaggedWorldviews Colliding"; Matthew King (1981), cited in Churchill, *Since Predator Came*, 62; Cajete, *Native Science*; Castellano, "Updating Aboriginal Traditions"; Battiste and Henderson, *Protecting Indigenous Knowledge*; Wilson, "What Is an Indigenous Research Methodology?"

78. Deloria, *Red Earth, White Lies.*

79. Momaday, *American Indian Authors.*

80. Doxtater, "Indigenous Knowledge," 620.

81. Wobst, "Power," 76.

82. Bruchac, Hart, and Wobst, *Indigenous Archaeologies.*

83. Churchill, *Fantasies.*

84. Mihesuah, *Natives and Academics.*

85. Colwell-Chanthaphonh, *Living Histories.*

86. Battiste, *Indigenous Knowledge*, 4, 5.

87. Augustine, "Preface," 2.

88. Cajete, *Native Science.*

89. Augustine, "Preface."

90. Wilson, *Research Is Ceremony.*

91. Echo-Hawk, "Ancient History."

92. Yellowhorn, "Awakening," 78.

93. Chilisa, *Indigenous Research Methodologies*, 25.

94. Holm and Reid, *Indian Art*, 7.

95. Mandryk, "Invented Traditions." See also Dincauze, "An Archaeological Evaluation."

1. Morgan, *Ancient Society*.
2. McGuire, "Archaeology."
3. Niezen, *The Origins of Indigenism*.
4. Browman, "The Peabody Museum."
5. Bernstein, "First Recipients."
6. Meltzer, "North American Archaeology"; Bernstein, "First Recipients."
7. Meltzer, "North American Archaeology."
8. Schultz, *Biographical Memoir*.
9. American Anthropology Association. On Madison Grant, see http://www .understandingrace.org/history/science/eugenics_physical.html.
10. Caspari, "From Types to Populations."
11. Giles, "Hooton, Earnest Albert."
12. Scupin and DeCorse, *Anthropology*.
13. Trigger, *A History*.
14. Caspari, "From Types to Populations."
15. Scarre and Scarre, *The Ethics of Archaeology*.
16. Hrdlička et al., *Early Man*; Cremo and Thompson, *Forbidden Archaeology*, 294.
17. Dillehay, *The Settlement*, 36.
18. Yazzie, "Indigenous Peoples"; Yellowhorn, "Awakening."
19. Justice, "Seeing (and Reading) Red."
20. Byrd, *The Transit of Empire*.
21. Colón and Hobbs, "The Intertwining."
22. Alsoszatai-Petheo, "An Alternative Paradigm," 16.
23. Fowler, "Uses of the Past"; Bruchac, Hart, and Wobst, *Indigenous Archaeologies*.
24. Morgan, *Ancient Society*.
25. Mason, "Sketch," 350.
26. Lame Deer and Erdoes, *Lame Deer*, xxvii.
27. Little and Kennedy, *Histories*.
28. Marsh, "Walking the Spirit Trail," 79.
29. Gulliford, "Bones of Contention."
30. Fine-Dare, *Grave Injustice*.
31. Rose, Green, and Green, "NAGPRA Is Forever."
32. National Park Service, American Indian Liaison Office, "Native American Graves Protection and Repatriation Act (NAGPRA): A Quick Guide for Preserving Native American Cultural Resources," https://www.nps.gov/history/tribes/documents /nagpra.pdf.
33. Meighan, "Burying American Archaeology," 68.

34. Rose, Green, and Green, "NAGPRA Is Forever," 81.

35. Dumont, "Contesting Scientists' Narrations."

36. Ryan Foley, "Retired US Official Charged with Stealing Ancient Remains," *Albuquerque Journal*, December 10, 2015.

37. Gonzalez, "Member Survey."

38. Alonzi, "SAA Repatriation Survey Analysis."

39. La Salle and Hutchings, "What Makes Us Squirm," 168, quoting Johnson, *Privilege*, 100, and Martindale and Lyons, "Community-Oriented Archaeology," 427.

40. Coleman and Herman, "Ways of Knowing."

41. F. P. McManamon, "Kennewick Man," May 2004, Archeology Program, National Park Service, https://www.nps.gov/archeology/kennewick/Index.htm.

42. Donald J. Barry, Assistant Secretary, Fish and Wildlife Service, memorandum, National Park Service, United States Department of the Interior.

43. Taylor et al., "Radiocarbon Dates."

44. Barry memorandum.

45. Deloria, *Marginal and Submarginal*, 20–21.

46. Smay and Armelagos, "Galileo Wept."

47. Deloria, *Marginal and Submarginal*.

48. Joseph F. Powell and Jerome C. Rose, "Report on the Osteological Assessment of the 'Kennewick Man' Skeleton" (CENWW.97.Kennewick), Archeology Program, National Park Service, https://www.nps.gov/archeology/kennewick/powell_rose.htm, quoting Buikstra and Ubelaker, *Standards*.

49. "Kennewick Man: The Untold Saga of Early Man in the Americas," *Time Magazine*, March 13, 2006.

50. Kasnot Medical Illustration, https://kasnot.com/.

51. Powell and Rose, "Report," 1.

52. Downey, *Riddle of the Bones*.

53. Fowler, "Uses of the Past," 22.

54. Gnecco, *Native Americans*, 251.

55. Gathercole and Lowenthal, *The Politics*.

56. Deloria, *Red Earth, White Lies*, 9.

57. Lomawaima, "Tribal Sovereigns."

58. Duran, *Healing the Soulwound*.

59. Yellow Horse Brave Heart and Debruyn, "The American Indian Holocaust."

60. "Two-Hundred-Year-Old Scalp Law Still on Books in Nova Scotia," *CBC News Canada*, January 4, 2000, https://www.cbc.ca/news/canada/200-year-old-scalp-law-still-on-nova-scotia-books-1.208320.

61. Newcomb, "The Doctrine of Discovery."

62. Chilisa, *Indigenous Research Methodologies*; Gnecco, "Native Histories."

63. Morgan, *Ancient Society*.

64. Dugassa, "Colonialism of Mind."

65. Silko, *Yellow Woman*.

66. Don Olson, "Educate First Nations to Be Modern Citizens," letter to the editor, *Nanaimo News*, March 27, 2013.

67. "'Racist' Newspaper Letter Sparks Nanaimo Protest," *CBC News Canada*, March 28, 2013, http://www.cbc.ca/news/canada/british-columbia/story/2013/03/28/bc-nanaimo-daily news-first-nations.html?cmp=rss.

68. Snuneymuxw blog site, Chief Douglas White, March 2013, http://snuneymuxw.blogspot.com/2013/03/the-nanaimo-daily-news-today-published.html.

69. "'Racist' Nanaimo Daily News Letter about First Nations Sparks Outrage" (TWEETS), March 28, 2013, http://www.huffingtonpost.ca/2013/03/28/racist-nanaimo-daily-news-first-nations-letter_n_2971956.html.

70. Judith Lavoie, "Letter Published in Nanaimo Newspaper Shows Need for Education, First Nations Leaders Say," *Times Colonist*, March 28, 2013, 1, http://www.timescolonist.com/news/local/letter-published-in-nanaimo-newspaper-shows-need-for-education-first-nations-leaders-say-1.100276.

71. Byrd, *The Transit of Empire*, 201.

72. Wenke and Olszewski, *Patterns in Prehistory*, 43.

73. Meltzer, *First Peoples*, 1.

74. Dillehay, "Probing Deeper."

75. Watkins, "Communicating Archaeology."

76. Deloria, *Red Earth, White Lies*, 73.

77. McNiven and Russell, *Appropriated Pasts*, 197.

78. Frank H. H. Roberts (1940), cited in Brennan, *No Stone Unturned*, 27.

79. Mayes, "These Bones Are Read."

80. Gnecco, "Native Histories."

81. Gnecco and Ayala, *Indigenous Peoples*, 14.

82. McNiven and Russell, *Appropriated Pasts*.

3. RELATIONS WHO OPENED THE WAY

1. Proctor and Schiebinger, *Agnotology*, 5.

2. Bryan, *New Evidence*.

3. Chlachula, "Geoarchaeology."

4. Haynes, "The Calico Site"; Payen, "Artifacts"; Meltzer, Adovasio, and Dillehay, "On a Pleistocene Human Occupation."

5. Lubinski, Terry, and McCutcheon, "Comparative Methods," 308.

6. Whitley and Dorn, "New Perspectives"; Erlandson, "After Clovis-First Collapsed"; Sarnthein et al., "Warmings."

7. Wallace and Hulbert, "A New Machairodont"; Heintzman et al., "Genomic Data"; Mihlbachler et al., "Dietary Change."

8. Graham, "Paleoclimates."

9. Herbert et al., "Late Miocene Global Cooling."

10. Proust, chapter 2, "The Verdurins' Quarrel with M. de Charlus," in *The Captive*, 160.

11. Chilisa, *Indigenous Research Methodologies*.

12. Smith, *Decolonizing Methodologies*.

13. Fladmark, "Routes."

14. Stanford and Bradley, *Across Atlantic Ice*.

15. Meltzer, *First Peoples*; Stanford and Bradley, *Across Atlantic Ice*; Mayes, "These Bones Are Read."

16. Mayes, "These Bones Are Read," 135.

17. Malhi et al., "Megafauna."

18. Mackie et al., "Locating Pleistocene-Age."

19. Muhs et al., "Quaternary Sea-Level History."

20. Muhs et al., "Quaternary Sea-Level History."

21. Ehlers and Gibbard, *Quaternary and Glacial Geology*.

22. Clark, "The Last Glacial Maximum," 710.

23. Meltzer, "Clocking the First Americans."

24. Madsen, *Entering America*.

25. Anderson and Lozhkin, "The Stage 3 Interstadial Complex."

26. Prothero, *The Evolution*.

27. Rybczynski et al., "Mid-Pliocene Warm-Period Deposits," 2.

28. Mukasa-Mugerwa, *The Camel*, 1, 3, 20–21, 65, 67–68.

29. Heintzman et al., "Genomic Data."

30. Wallace and Hulbert, "A New Machairodont," 6.

31. Radinsky, "Oldest Horse Brains."

32. Froese et al., "Fossil and Genomic Evidence."

33. Froese et al., "Fossil and Genomic Evidence," 3460.

34. MacFadden and Hulbert, "Calibration."

35. Lister and Sher, "Evolution."

36. Enk et al., "Mammuthus Population Dynamics."

37. Madden, "Earliest Isotopically Dated Mammuthus."

38. Marincovich and Gladenkov, "New Evidence."

39. Prothero, *The Evolution*, 182.

40. West, Dawson, and Hutchison, "Fossils"; Radinsky, "A Review."

41. Prothero, *The Evolution*.

42. Wang et al., "Earliest Known," 1.

43. "Meet Your Ancestors," *NOVA*, http://www.pbs.org/wgbh/nova/sciencenow/0303/02-mya-nf.html.

44. Chester et al., "Oldest Known Euarchontan Tarsals," 1487.

45. Bloch et al., "New Paleocene Skeletons."

46. Chester et al., "Oldest Known Euarchontan Tarsals," 1487.

47. Klein, *The Human Career*.

48. Fox and Craig, "A New, Early Puercan," 537.

49. Silcox et al., "Euarchonta"; Van Valen and Sloan, "The Earliest Primates."

50. Bloch et al., "New Paleocene Skeletons," 1159.

51. Meltzer, "Peopling of North America," 540, 542, 550.

52. Faith and Surovell, "Synchronous Extinction," 20641.

53. Hansford et al., "Early Holocene Human Presence."

54. "Ancient Bird Bones Re-date Human Activity in Madagascar by 6,000 Years," September 12, 2018, Zoological Society of London, https://www.sciencedaily.com/releases/2018/09/180912144434.htm.

55. Leakey, Tobias, and Napier, "A New Species."

56. Foucault, *The Archaeology of Knowledge*, 49; Gathercole and Lowenthal, *The Politics*.

57. Dugassa, "Colonialism of Mind," 57.

58. Bourgeon, Burke, and Higham, "Earliest Human Presence."

59. Dillehay et al., "New Archaeological Evidence."

60. Adovasio, Donahue, and Stuckenrath, "The Meadowcroft Rockshelter."

61. Bryan, *New Evidence*.

4. MINDS WIDE OPEN

1. Yellen et al., "A Middle Stone Age Worked Bone."

2. Krause et al., "Neanderthals."

3. Strasser et al., "Dating Paleolithic Sites."

4. Dominguez-Rodrigo, *Stone Tools*, 15.

5. Miller, *Anthropology*.

6. Sondaar et al., "The Human Colonization."

7. Strasser et al., "Dating Paleolithic Sites."

8. Clarkson et al., "Human Occupation," 306.

9. Fran Dorey, "The Spread of People to Australia," June 6, 2019, Australia Museum, https://australianmuseum.net.au/learn/science/human-evolution/the-spread-of-people-to-australia/.

10. Strasser et al., "Dating Paleolithic Sites."

11. Guidon and Arnaud, "The Chronology," 168.

12. Strasser et al., "Dating Paleolithic Sites."

13. Birney and Pritchard, "Archaic Humans."

14. Wilson and Cann, "The Recent African Genesis"; Thorne and Wolpoff, "The Multiregional Evolution."

15. Nei, "Genetic Support."

16. Thorne and Wolpoff, "The Multiregional Evolution."

17. Pääbo, "The Diverse Origins."

18. Liu et al., "The Earliest Unequivocally Modern Humans."

19. Thorne and Wolpoff, "The Multiregional Evolution"; quote from Wolpoff, Hawks, and Caspari, "Multiregional," 130.

20. Green et al., "A Draft Sequence."

21. Krause et al., "Neanderthals."

22. Trinkaus et al., "An Early Modern Human."

23. Bräuer, Broeg, and Stringer, "Earliest Upper Paleolithic Crania"; quote from Green et al., "A Draft Sequence," 721.

24. Higham et al., "The Timing," 306.

25. Pääbo, "The Diverse Origins," 314.

26. Pääbo, "The Diverse Origins," 313.

27. Hublin et al., "New Fossils."

28. Stringer and Galway-Witham, "Paleoanthropology."

29. Stringer, "Modern Human Origins"; Bräuer, "The Origin."

30. Stringer and Galway-Witham, "Paleoanthropology."

31. Hublin et al., "New Fossils," 289.

32. Stringer and Galway-Witham, "Paleoanthropology."

33. Smith et al., "Earliest Evidence."

34. Stringer and Galway-Witham, "Paleoanthropology."

35. Hublin et al., "New Fossils," 289.

5. PLEISTOCENE SITES IN NORTH AMERICA

1. Adovasio and Page, *The First Americans*, 89.

2. Deter-Wolf, Tune, and Broster, "Excavations."

3. Dillehay, *The Settlement*.

4. Dillehay, *The Settlement*, xviii.

5. Waters and Stafford, "Redefining," 315.

6. Barton et al., *The Settlement*; Waters and Stafford, "Redefining."

7. Anderson et al., "PIDBA."

8. Patterson et al., "Analysis"; Hopkins, *The Bering Land Bridge*, vol. 3; Humphrey and Stanford, *Pre-Llano Cultures*, 198–258, 296–321, 45–213.

9. Deloria, *Red Earth, White Lies*.

10. Carrie Wilson, personal communication with the author, 1998.

11. Deloria, *Red Earth, White Lies*.

12. Morrow and Gnecco, *Paleoindian Archaeology*.

13. National Park Service, National Historic Landmarks Program, https://www.nps.gov/nhl/.

14. Bryan, *Early Man*.

15. Chlachula, "Geoarchaeology," 68.

16. Reimer et al., "IntCal09"; Vries, "Variation"; Stuiver and Suess, "On the Relationship."

17. Reimer et al., "IntCal09."

18. Kuzmin and Keates, "Dates," 773.

19. Harmand et al., "3.3-Million-Year-Old Stone Tools"; Oakley, "Man the Skilled Tool-Maker"; Bordes, *The Old Stone Age*.

20. Waters and Stafford, "Redefining."

21. Yellowhorn, "Regarding."

22. Yellowhorn, "Regarding," 62.

23. Yellowhorn, "Regarding," 62.

24. B. W. Ife, "Introduction to the *Letters from America*," Research at King's College London: Early Modern Spain, 1992, http://www.ems.kcl.ac.uk/content/pub/b002 .html.

25. Yellow Bird, "What We Want to Be Called," 2.

26. Julien, Bernard, and Rosenmeier, "Paleo."

27. Deter-Wolf, Tune, and Broster, "Excavations."

28. Breitburg and Broster, "A Hunt for Big Game."

29. Breitburg and Broster, "A Hunt for Big Game."

30. Cannon and Meltzer, "Early Paleoindian Foraging," 1957.

31. Breitburg et al., "The Coats-Hines Site."

32. Cannon and Meltzer, "Early Paleoindian Foraging," 1970.

33. Adovasio and Pedler, *Strangers in a New Land*.

34. Waters et al., "Geoarchaeological Investigations."

35. Adovasio and Pedler, *Strangers in a New Land*.

36. Clausen et al., "Little Salt Spring."

37. Holman and Clausen, "Fossil Vertebrates."

38. Clausen et al., "Little Salt Spring."

39. Halligan et al., "Pre-Clovis Occupation."

40. Halligan et al., "Pre-Clovis Occupation," 5.

41. Gustafson, Gilbow, and Daugherty, "The Manis Mastodon Site."

42. Waters et al., "Pre-Clovis Mastodon Hunting."

43. Adovasio and Pedler, *Strangers in a New Land*.

44. Cressman, Williams, and Krieger, *Early Man*.

45. Jenkins et al., "Clovis Age."

46. Jenkins et al., "Geochronology."

47. Gilbert et al., "DNA."

48. Jenkins et al., "Geochronology."

49. Sistiaga et al., "Steroidal Biomarker Analysis."

50. Adovasio and Pedler, *Strangers in a New Land*.

51. Adovasio and Pedler, *Strangers in a New Land*.

52. Tankersley and Munson, "Comments."

53. Tankersley, Munson, and Smith, "Recognition."

54. Adovasio, Donahue, and Stuckenrath, "Never Say Never Again," 327.

55. Marshall, "Pre-Clovis Sites," 1732.

56. Adovasio and Pedler, *Strangers in a New Land*.

57. Feathers et al., "Luminescence Dating."

58. Feathers et al., "Luminescence Dating," 185.

59. Joyce, "Chronology."

60. Overstreet and Kolb, "Geoarchaeological Contexts."

61. Neiburger, "The Mammoth Eaters."

62. Holen, "Taphonomy."

63. Holen, "Taphonomy," 39.

64. Holen, "Taphonomy."

65. Morlan, "Current Perspectives."

66. Johnson, "Current Developments."

67. Holen, "Taphonomy," 40.

68. Holen, "Taphonomy."

69. Haynes and Krasinski, "Taphonomic Fieldwork," 185, 195.

70. Haynes and Krasinski, "Taphonomic Fieldwork," 198.

71. Waters et al., "The Buttermilk Creek Complex."

72. Jennings and Waters, "Pre-Clovis Lithic Technology," 26.

73. Morrow et al., "Pre-Clovis in Texas?"

74. Jennings and Waters, "Pre-Clovis Lithic Technology"; Driese et al., "Analysis of Site Formation"; Jennings, "Clovis, Folsom, and Midland Components"; Keene, "Site Formation Processes"; Lindquist, Feinberg, and Waters, "Rock Magnetic Properties."

75. Jennings and Waters, "Pre-Clovis Lithic Technology."

76. Demere, Cerutti, and Majors, "San Diego Natural History Museum."

77. Holen et al., "A 130,000-Year-Old Archaeological Site."

78. Haynes, "The Cerutti Mastodon," 196.

79. Holen et al., "Broken Bones," 9.

80. Gruhn, "Observations," 101.

81. Cinq-Mars, "Bluefish Cave 1."

82. Bourgeon, Burke, and Higham, "Earliest Human Presence."

83. Bourgeon, Burke, and Higham, "Earliest Human Presence," 1.

84. Adovasio and Pedler, *Strangers in a New Land*.

85. Weiner, *Microarchaeology*.

86. Camacho, *Vestiges*.

87. Irwin-Williams, "Summary."

88. Irwin-Williams et al., "Comments."

89. Clarkson et al., "Human Occupation," 306; Hublin et al., "New Fossils."

90. Haynes, "The Calico Site"; Payen, "Artifacts or Geofacts."

91. Patterson et al., "Analysis."

92. Leakey, Simpson, and Clements, "Archaeological Excavations," 160.

93. Bischoff et al., "Uranium-Series."

94. Payen, "Artifacts or Geofacts."

95. Patterson et al., "Analysis," 91.

96. Gruhn and Young, "The Burial," 499.

97. Leakey, Simpson, and Clements, "Archaeological Excavations"; Patterson et al., "Analysis."

98. Ardelean et al., "Evidence of Human Occupation."

99. Holen, "Taphonomy"; Dillehay, *The Settlement*; Adovasio and Pedler, *Strangers in a New Land*.

100. Chlachula, "Geoarchaeology."

101. MacNeish, "A New Look," 491.

6. PLEISTOCENE SITES IN SOUTH AMERICA

1. Arriaza et al., "Chinchorro Culture."

2. On Quebrada Jaguay, see Sandweiss, "Early Fishing Societies." On Quebrada Los Burros, see Arriaza et al., "Chinchorro Culture."

3. Jones et al., "Evidence."

4. Arriaza, *Beyond Death*.

5. Standen, "Temprana complejidad funeraria."

6. Gnecco and Aceituno, "Early Humanized Landscapes," 86.

7. Speth et al., "Early Paleoindian Big-Game Hunting."

8. Cannon and Meltzer, "Early Paleoindian Foraging."

9. Borrero, "Moving"; Speth et al., "Early Paleoindian Big-Game Hunting."

10. Gnecco and Aceituno, "Early Humanized Landscapes."

11. Borrero, "Moving"; Dillehay, *The Settlement*; Yesner, "Moose Hunters."

12. Dillehay and Rossen, "Plant Food," 237.

13. Dillehay and Rossen, "Plant Food."

14. *Encyclopaedia Britannica*, https://www.britannica.com/place/Western-Hemisphere.

15. Steele and Politis, "AMS ^{14}C Dating."

16. Steele and Politis, "AMS ^{14}C Dating," 428.

17. UNESCO, http://whc.unesco.org/en/list/606.

18. Watanabe et al., "Some Evidence."

19. Lahaye et al., "New Insights."

20. Kinoshita et al., "Electron Spin Resonance Dating," 636.

21. Guidon and Delibrias, "Carbon-14 Dates."

22. Santos et al., "A Revised Chronology."

23. Lahaye et al., "Human Occupation."

24. Parenti, Mercier, and Valladas, "The Oldest Hearths."

25. Meltzer, Adovasio, and Dillehay, "On a Pleistocene Human Occupation."

26. Lahaye et al., "Human Occupation."

27. Kinoshita et al., "Dating Human Occupation."

28. Kinoshita et al., "Dating Human Occupation," 186.

29. Kinoshita et al., "Dating Human Occupation," 193.

30. Guidon and Delibrias, "Carbon-14 Dates," 769.

31. Dillehay, *The Settlement*.

32. Watanabe et al., "Some Evidence."

33. Rowe and Steelman, comment, 1349.

34. Pessis and Guidon, "Dating Rock Art Paintings."

35. Bednarik, "The Evidence of Paleo Art."

36. Bednarik, "On the Pleistocene Settlement."

37. Lahaye et al., "New Insights."

38. Felice, "A controvérsia," 1.

39. Lahaye et al., "Human Occupation."

40. Parenti, "Old and New."

41. Lahaye et al., "Human Occupation."

42. Boëda et al., "New Data."

43. Boëda et al., "A New Late Pleistocene."

44. Beltrao et al., "Thermoluminescence Dating."

45. Dillehay, *The Settlement*.

46. Ochsenius and Gruhn, *Taima-Taima*.

47. Ochsenius and Gruhn, *Taima-Taima*.

48. Lynch, "The Antiquity"; Haynes, "Paleoenvironments"; Bryan, "Paleoenvironments."

49. Bryan, "Paleoenvironments: A Rejoinder."

50. Casamiquela, "An Interpretation."

51. Bryan, "The Stratigraphy."

52. Cruxent and Ochsenius, "Paleo-Indian Studies."

53. Correal Urrego, *Evidencias culturales*.

54. Dillehay, *The Settlement*, 120.

55. Lynch, "Lack of Evidence"; Gruhn, "The Ignored Continent."

56. Dillehay, *The Settlement*, 119.

57. Herrera et al., "Nuevas fechas"; Urrego and Van der Hammen, *Investigaciones*; Dillehay, *The settlement*.

58. MacNeish, *The Prehistory*, vol. 2.

59. MacNeish, *The Prehistory*, vol. 4.

60. Canales and Capcha, "New Analysis."

61. Rick, "The Character"; Lynch, "Zonal Complementarity."

62. Dillehay, "A Regional Perspective."

63. Canales and Capcha, "New Analysis."

64. MacNeish, *The Prehistory*, vol. 2.

65. Dillehay, *The Settlement*, 104.

66. Steele and Politis, "AMS ¹⁴C Dating."

67. Salemme, "Zooarqueología."

68. Fidalgo et al., "Investigaciones."

69. Barrientos et al., "The Craniofacial Morphology."

70. Politis, "The Pampas."

71. Gutierrez, "Tafonomía."

72. Steele and Politis, "AMS ¹⁴C Dating."

73. Steele and Politis, "AMS ¹⁴C Dating," 423.

74. Perez et al., "Peopling Time."

7. GENETICS, LINGUISTICS, ORAL TRADITIONS

1. Acosta, "Historia natural."

2. Merriwether, Rothhammer, and Ferrell, "Distribution"; Bonatto and Salzano, "A Single and Early Migration"; Goebel, Waters, and O'Rourke, "The Late Pleistocene Dispersal."

3. McGregor, *Since Time Immemorial.*

4. Arias et al., "High-Resolution"; Rasmussen et al., "The Genome."

5. Merriwether, "A Mitochondrial Perspective"; Mark Stoneking, personal communication, 2018.

6. Rasmussen et al., "The Genome."

7. Taylor, "The Wilsall Excavations."

8. Owsley and Hunt, "Clovis and Early Archaic Crania."

9. Arias et al., "High-Resolution."

10. Arias et al., "High-Resolution," 3.

11. Fagundes, Kanitz, and Bonatto, "A Reevaluation," 1.

12. Merriwether, "A Mitochondrial Perspective," 299.

13. Günther and Nettelblad, "The Presence," 1.

14. Arias et al., "High-Resolution Mitochondrial DNA," 3.

15. Arias et al., "High-Resolution Mitochondrial DNA," 2.

16. Torroni et al., "Asian Affinities."

17. Merriwether, "A Mitochondrial Perspective," 296.

18. Brown et al., "mtDNA Haplogroup X," 1852.

19. Malhi et al., "Mitochondrial Haplogroup M."

20. Malhi et al., "Mitochondrial Haplogroup M," 647.

21. Malhi et al., "Mitochondrial Haplogroup M," 642.

22. Arias et al., "High-Resolution Mitochondrial DNA," 2.

23. Kashani et al., "Mitochondrial Haplogroup C4c."

24. Stone and Stoneking, "mtDNA Analysis"; Merriwether, Rothhammer, and Ferrell, "Distribution"; Bonatto and Salzano, "Diversity"; Karafet et al., "Ancestral Asian Source(s)."

25. Lahr, "Patterns"; Skoglund et al., "Genetic Evidence"; Lell et al., "The Dual Origin"; Torroni et al., "Native American Mitochondrial DNA Analysis."

26. Greenberg et al., "The Settlement."

27. Schanfield, "Immunoglobulin Allotypes"; Horai et al., "Peopling of the Americas"; Torroni et al., "Asian Affinities"; Torroni et al., "Native American Mitochondrial DNA Analysis."

28. Ward et al., "Extensive Mitochondrial Diversity," 8720.

29. Lalueza et al., "Lack of Founding."

30. Lalueza et al., "Lack of Founding," 41.

31. Torroni et al., "Asian Affinities"; Shields et al., "Absence."

32. Bailliet et al., "Founder Mitochondrial Haplotypes"; Stone and Stoneking, "Ancient DNA."

33. Merriwether, Rothhammer, and Ferrell, "Distribution."

34. Cavalli-Sforza, cited in Churchill, *Since Predator Came*, 266.

35. Wallace and Torroni, "American Indian Prehistory."

36. Wang et al., "Genetic Variation."

37. Meriwether, "A Mitochondrial Perspective."

38. Denevan, "The Pristine Myth."

39. Tamm et al., "Beringian Standstill."

40. Llamas et al., "Ancient Mitochondrial DNA," 1.

41. Llamas et al., "Ancient Mitochondrial DNA," 1.

42. TallBear, *Native American DNA*.

43. Greenberg, *Language in the Americas*.

44. Nichols, "Linguistic Diversity," 476.

45. Denevan, "The Pristine Myth," 71.

46. Nichols, "Linguistic Diversity," 72.

47. Nichols, "Linguistic Diversity."

48. Clauge, Mathews, and Ager, "Environments."

49. Nichols, "Linguistic Diversity."

50. Augustine, "Preface"; Battiste, "Research Ethics"; Kovach, *Indigenous Methodologies*.

51. Augustine, "Preface," 5.

52. Kovach, *Indigenous Methodologies*.

53. Watkins, "Artefacts," 187.

54. Cultural Resources Protection Program, "A Review."

55. Montagu, "An Indian Tradition."

56. Mayor, *Fossil Legends*, 201.

57. Mayor, *Fossil Legends*, 208, 202.

58. Montagu, "An Indian Tradition."

59. Mayor, *Fossil Legends*.

60. Cruikshank, "Legend and Landscape."

61. Augustine, "Preface."

62. Montagu, "An Indian Tradition."

63. Cashman and Cronin, "Welcoming a Monster."

64. Pendergast and Meighan, "Folk Traditions."

65. Bahr et al., *The Short, Swift Time*; Dongoske, Jenkins, and Ferguson, "Understanding the Past"; Teague, "Prehistory"; Pendergast and Meighan, "Folk Traditions."

66. Sium and Ritskes, "Speaking Truth to Power," vii.

67. Trask, *From a Native Daughter*, 121.

68. Sium and Ritskes, "Speaking Truth to Power," i.

69. Cruikshank, "Legend and Landscape," 86.

8. REAWAKENING, RESISTING, REWRITING

1. Deloria, *Red Earth, White Lies*, 68; Balter, "DNA from Fossil Feces," 37; Toledo, "Geoarcheology," 27.

2. Moeke-Pickering et al., "Keeping Our Fire Alive," 2.

3. Smith-Tuhiwai, *Decolonizing Methodologies*; Dion, *Braiding Histories*.

4. Guidon and Arnaud, "The Chronology," 167.

5. Hoffecker, Elias, and O'Rourke, "Out of Beringia?"

6. Borrero, "Moving," 126.

7. Poupart, "The Familiar Face"; Whitbeck et al., "Conceptualizing."

8. Guidon and Arnaud, "The Chronology," 167.

9. Ferguson, "Native Americans"; McGuire, "Archaeology," 828.

10. Handsman, "Towards Archaeological Histories," 28.

11. Fowler, "Uses of the Past," 229.

12. Deloria, "Indians."

13. Smith, "Building."

14. Meiri et al., "Faunal Record."

15. Holen et al., "A 130,000-Year-Old Archaeological Site."

16. Dillehay, *The Settlement*; Holen et al., "A 130,000-Year-Old Archaeological Site"; Jenkins, "Distribution"; Waters et al., "Pre-Clovis Mastodon Hunting."

17. Mayes, "These Bones Are Read," 136.

18. Nicholas and Hollowell, "Ethical Challenges," 61.

19. Yellowhorn, "Awakening," 17.

20. Franklin, "Power to the People," 37.

21. Chilisa, *Indigenous Research Methodologies*, 55.

22. Wheat, "Survey."

23. Adovasio and Pedler, "Monte Verde."

24. Adovasio and Pedler, "Monte Verde."

25. Steve Holen, personal communication with the author, 2010.

26. Dillehay, *The Settlement*.

27. Steve Holen, personal communication with the author, 2010.

28. Holen, "Taphonomy."

29. Holen et al., "A 130,000-Year-Old Archaeological Site."

30. Battiste, "Indigenous Knowledge Foundations."

31. Battiste, "Indigenous Knowledge Foundations," 9.

32. Forbes, "Intellectual Self-Determination," 19.

33. Lambert, *Research for Indigenous Survival*; Smith-Tuhiwai, *Decolonizing Methodologies*.

34. Hodder, *Symbolic and Structural Archaeology*.

35. Duran, *Healing the Soulwound*.

36. Chandler and Lalonde, "Cultural Continuity"; Hallett, Chandler, and Lalond, "Aboriginal Language Knowledge."

37. Cree Cultural Institute, http://www.creeculturalinstitute.ca/en/about/mission-and -vision/.

38. Wilson, *Research Is Ceremony*; Bendremer and Richman, "Human Subjects."

39. Mallon, *Decolonizing Native Histories*, vii.

40. Miller and Riding In, *Native Historians*.

41. Bendremer and Richman, "Human Subjects Review," 114.

42. Gnecco and Ayala, *Indigenous Peoples*; Wilson, "Indigenous Knowledge Recovery."

43. Grande, *Red Pedagogy*, 5.

44. Matthew King, cited in Churchill, *Since Predator Came*, 62.

45. Silko, "Landscape, History."

46. Smith, *Decolonizing Methodologies*; Mihesuah, *Natives and Academics*.

BIBLIOGRAPHY

Acosta, José de. "Historia natural y moral de las Indias: En que se tratan las cosas notables del cielo, y elementos, metales, plantas y animales dellas y los ritos y ceremonias, leyes y gouierno y guerras de los Indios / compuesta por el Padre Ioseph de Acosta." 1590. In *Casa de Iuan de Leon*, edited by René Acuña. Seville, 1962.

Adovasio, J. M., J. Donahue, and R. Stuckenrath. "The Meadowcroft Rockshelter Radiocarbon Chronology 1975–1990." *American Antiquity* 55, no. 2 (1990): 348–54.

———. "Never Say Never Again: Some Thoughts on Could Haves and Might Have Beens." *American Antiquity* 57, no. 2 (1992): 327–31.

Adovasio, James, and Jake Page. *The First Americans: In Pursuit of Archaeology's Greatest Mystery*. New York: Random House, 2002.

Adovasio, James M., and David Pedler. Foreword to *Pre-Clovis in the Americas: International Science Conference Proceedings*, edited by Dennis Joe Stanford and Alison T. Stenger, 253–57. Washington DC: Smithsonian Institution Press, 2014.

———. "Monte Verde and the Antiquity of Humankind in the Americas." *Antiquity* 71 (1997): 573–80.

———. *Strangers in a New Land: What Archaeology Reveals about the First Americans*. Richmond Hill ON: Firefly Books, 2016.

Agam, Aviad, and Ran Barkai. "Elephant and Mammoth Hunting during the Paleolithic: A Review of the Relevant Archaeological, Ethnographic, and Ethno-historical Records." *Quaternary* 1, no. 1 (2018): 1–28.

Alfred, Taiaiake, and Jeff Corntassel. "Being Indigenous: Resurgences against Contemporary Colonialism." *Government and Opposition* 40, no. 4 (2005): 597–614.

Allen, Jim, and Peter Kershaw. "The Pleistocene–Holocene Transition in Greater Australia." In *Humans at the End of the Ice Age*, 175–99. Boston: Springer, 1996.

Allen, Jim, and J. Peter White. "The Lapita Homeland: Some New Data and an Interpretation." *Journal of the Polynesian Society* 98, no. 2 (1989): 129–46.

Alonzi, Elise. "SAA Repatriation Survey Analysis: Responses to Survey Results." *SAA Archaeological Record* 16, no. 4 (2016): 15–21.

Alsoszatai-Petheo, J. "An Alternative Paradigm for the Study of Early Man in the New World." In *New Evidence for the Pleistocene Peopling of the Americas*, edited by Alan L. Bryan, 15–26. Orono ME: Center for the Study of Early Man, 1986.

Ambrose, S. H. "Paleolithic Technology and Human Evolution." *Science* 291, no. 5509 (2001): 1748–53.

Anderson, D. G., D. S. Miller, S. J. Yerka, J. C. Gillam, E. N. Johanson, D. T. Anderson, A. C. Goodyear, and A. M. Smallwood. "PIDBA (Paleoindian Database of the Americas) 2010: Current Status and Findings." *Archaeology of Eastern North America* 38 (2010): 63–89.

Anderson, P. M., and A. V. Lozhkin. "The Stage 3 Interstadial Complex (Karginski / Middle Wisconsin Interval) of Beringa: Variations in Paleoenvironments and Implications for Paleo Climatic Interpretations." *Quaternary Science Reviews* 20 (2001): 93–125.

Ardelean, C. F., L. Becerra-Valdivia, M. W. Pedersen, J. L. Schwenninger, C. G. Oviatt, J. I. Macías-Quintero, J. Arroyo-Cabrales, et al. "Evidence of Human Occupation in Mexico around the Last Glacial Maximum." *Nature* (2020): 1–6.

Arias, L., C. Barbieri, G. Barreto, M. Stoneking, and B. Pakendorf. "High-Resolution Mitochondrial DNA Analysis Sheds Light on Human Diversity, Cultural Interactions, and Population Mobility in Northwestern Amazonia." *American Journal of Physical Anthropology* 165, no. 2 (2018): 238–55.

Arriaza, B. T. *Beyond Death: The Chinchorro Mummies of Ancient Chile*. Washington DC: Smithsonian Institution Press, 1995.

Arriaza, B. T., V. G. Standen, V. Cassman, and C. M. Santoro. "Chinchorro Culture: Pioneers of the Coast of the Atacama Desert." In *The Handbook of South American Archaeology*, edited by Helaine Silverman and William Isbell, 45–58. New York: Springer, 2008.

Atalay, Sonya. *Community-Based Archaeology: Research with, by, and for Indigenous and Local Communities*. Berkeley: University of California Press, 2012.

———. "Indigenous Archaeology as Decolonizing Practice." *American Indian Quarterly* 30, no. 3–4 (2006): 280–310.

———. "Introduction: Decolonizing Archaeology." Special issue, *American Indian Quarterly* 30, no. 3 (2006): 269–79.

Augustine, Stephen J. "Preface: Oral History and Oral Traditions." In *Aboriginal Oral Traditions: Theory, Practice, Ethics*, edited by Renee Hulan and Renate Eigenbrod. Halifax NS: Fernwood Publishing, 2008.

Bahr, D. M., J. Smith, W. S. Allison, and J. Hayden. *The Short, Swift Time of Gods on Earth: The Hohokam Chronicles*. Berkeley: University of California Press, 1994.

Bailliet, G., F. Rothhammer, F. R. Carnese, C. M. Bravi, and N. O. Bianchi. "Founder Mitochondrial Haplotypes in Amerindian Populations." *American Journal of Human Genetics* 542 (1994): 7–33.

Balter, Michael. "DNA from Fossil Feces Breaks Clovis Barrier." *Science*, April 4, 2008, 37.

Barrientos, G., H. Pucciarelli, G. Politis, S. Pérez, and M. Sardi. "The Craniofacial Morphology of Early- to Middle-Holocene Human Populations from the Pampean Region, Argentina:

Getting a New Insight into the Morphological Variability of Early Americans." In *Where the South Winds Blow: Ancient Evidence of Paleo South Americans*, edited by L. Miotti, M. Salemme, and N. Flegenheimer, 69–76. College Station: Center for the Study of the First Americans, Texas A&M University Press, 2003.

Barton, C. M., Geoffrey A. Clark, David R. Yesner, and Georges A. Pearson, eds. *The Settlement of the American Continents: A Multidisciplinary Approach to Human Biogeography*. Tucson: University of Arizona Press, 2004.

Battiste, M. *Indigenous Knowledge and Pedagogy in First Nations Education: A Literature Review with Recommendations*. Ottawa: Apamuwek Institute, 2002.

———. "Indigenous Knowledge Foundations for First Nations." *WINHEC: International Journal of Indigenous Education Scholarship* 1 (2005): 1–17.

———. "Research Ethics for Protecting Indigenous Knowledge and Heritage: Institutional and Research Responsibilities." In *Ethical Futures in Qualitative Research: Decolonizing the Politics of Knowledge*, edited by Norman Denzin and Michael D. Giardina, 111–32. Walnut Creek CA: Left Coast Press, 2007.

Battiste, M., and Y. Henderson, eds. *Protecting Indigenous Knowledge and Heritage: A Global Challenge*. Saskatoon SK: Purich Publishing, 2000.

Beck, Charlotte, and George T. Jones. "Clovis and Western Stemmed: Population Migration and the Meeting of Two Technologies in the Intermountain West." *American Antiquity* 75, no. 1 (2010): 81–116.

Bednarik, R. G. "The Initial Peopling of Wallacea and Sahul." *Anthropos* 92 (1997): 355–67.

———. "On the Pleistocene Settlement of South America." *Antiquity* 63, no. 238 (1989): 101–11. https://semioticon.com/sio/courses/cognition-symbolism-evolution/.

Bellomo, R. V. "A Methodological Approach for Identifying Archaeological Evidence of Fire Resulting from Human Activities." *Journal of Archaeological Science* 20 (1993): 525–53.

Beltrao, M., C. R. Enriquez, J. Danon, E. Zuleta, and G. Poupeau. "Thermoluminescence Dating of Burnt Cherts from the Alice Boer Site (Brazil) (No. CBPF-NF-004/83)." In *The Origin of Man in America: Proceedings of a Symposium Held at the 10th Congress of the International Union of Prehistoric and Protohistoric Sciences*, Mexico City, October 19–24, 1981. Rio de Janeiro: Centro Brasileiro de Pesquisas Fisicas, 1987.

Bendremer, J. C., and K. A. Richman. "Human Subjects Review and Archaeology: A View from Indian Country." In *The Ethics of Archaeology: Philosophical Perspectives on Archaeological Practice*, edited by G. F. Scarre and C. Scarre, 97–114. Cambridge: Cambridge University Press, 2006.

Bernstein, J. H. "First Recipients of Anthropological Doctorates in the United States, 1891–1930." *American Anthropologist* 104, no. 2 (2002): 551–64.

Bilosi, Thomas, and Larry Zimmerman. *Indians and Anthropologists: Vine Deloria, Jr., and the Critique of Anthropology*. Tucson: University of Arizona Press, 1997.

Birney, E., and J. K. Pritchard. "Archaic Humans: Four Makes a Party." *Nature* 505, no. 7481 (2014): 32–34.

Bischoff, J. L., R. J. Shlemon, T. L. Ku, R. D. Simpson, R. J. Rosenbauer, and F. E. Budinger Jr. "Uranium-Series and Soils-Geomorphic Dating of the Calico Archaeological Site, California." *Geology* 9, no. 12 (1981): 576–82.

Bloch, J. I., M. T. Silcox, D. M. Boyer, and E. J. Sargis. "New Paleocene Skeletons and the Relationship of Plesiadapiforms to Crown-Clade Primates." *Proceedings of the National Academy of Sciences* 104, no. 4 (2007): 1159–64.

Boëda, Eric, Ignacio Clemente-Conte, Michel Fontugne, Christelle Lahaye, Mario Pino, Gisele Daltrini Felice, Nide Guidon, et al. "A New Late Pleistocene Archaeological Sequence in South America: The Vale da Pedra Furada (Piauí, Brazil)." *Antiquity* 88, no. 341 (2014): 927–41.

Boëda, Eric, Roxane Rocca, Amélie Da Costa, Michel Fontugne, Christine Hatté, Ignacio Clemente-Conte, Janaina C. Santos, et al. "New Data on a Pleistocene Archaeological Sequence in South America: Toca do Sítio do Meio, Piauí, Brazil." *PaleoAmerica* 2, no. 4 (2016): 286.

Bonatto, S. L., and F. M. Salzano. "Diversity and Age of the Four Major mtDNA Haplogroups, and Their Implications for the Peopling of the New World." *American Journal of Human Genetics* 61, no. 6 (1997): 1413–23.

———. "A Single and Early Migration for the Peopling of the Americas Supported by Mitochondrial DNA Sequence Data." *Proceedings of the National Academy of Sciences* 94, no. 5 (1997): 1866–71.

Bordes, François. *The Old Stone Age*. World University Library. New York: McGraw-Hill, 1968.

Borrero, L. A. "Moving: Hunter-Gatherers and the Cultural Geography of South America." *Quaternary International* 363 (2015): 126–33.

Bourgeon, L., A. Burke, and T. Higham. "Earliest Human Presence in North America Dated to the Last Glacial Maximum: New Radiocarbon Dates from Bluefish Caves, Canada." *PLoS ONE* 12, no. 1 (2017): e0169486.

Braje, Todd J., Tom D. Dillehay, Jon M. Erlandson, Scott M. Fitzpatrick, Donald K. Grayson, Vance T. Holliday, Robert L. Kelly, et al. "Were Hominins in California ⊠130,000 Years Ago?" *PaleoAmerica* 3, no. 3 (2017): 200–202.

Bräuer, G. "The Origin of Modern Anatomy: By Speciation or Intraspecific Evolution?" *Evolutionary Anthropology: Issues, News, and Reviews* 17, no. 1 (2008): 22–37.

Bräuer, G., H. Broeg, and C. B. Stringer. "Earliest Upper Paleolithic Crania from Mladeč, Czech Republic, and the Question of Neanderthal-Modern Continuity: Metrical Evidence from the Fronto-Facial Region." In *Neanderthals Revisited: New Approaches and Perspectives*, edited by K. Harvati and T. Harrison, 269–79. Dordrecht, the Netherlands: Springer, 2006.

Bray, Tamara. "Repatriation and Archaeology's Second Loss of Innocence: On Knowledge, Power, and the Past." In *Opening Archaeology: Repatriation's Impact on Contemporary Research and Practice*, edited by Thomas W. Killion, 79–90. Santa Fe NM: School for Advanced Research Press, 2007.

Breitburg, Emanuel, and John Broster. "A Hunt for Big Game: Does the Coats-Hines Site Confirm Human Mastodon Contact?" *Tennessee Conservationist* 61, no. 4 (1995): 18–26.

Breitburg, Emanuel, John B. Broster, Arthur L. Reesman, and Richard G. Sterns. "The Coats-Hines Site: Tennessee's First Paleoindian-Mastodon Association." *Current Research in the Pleistocene* 13 (1996): 6–8.

Brennan, Louis A. *No Stone Unturned: An Almanac of North American Prehistory.* New York: Random House, 1960.

Browman, D. L. "The Peabody Museum, Frederic W. Putnam, and the Rise of U.S. Anthropology, 1866–1903." *American Anthropologist* 104, no. 2 (2002): 508–19.

Brown, J. *The Spiritual Legacy of the American Indian.* New York: Crosswood Publication, 1988.

Brown, L. A., and S. Strega, eds. *Research as Resistance: Critical, Indigenous, and Anti-oppressive Approaches.* Toronto: Canadian Scholars' Press, 2015.

Brown, Michael D., Seyed H. Hosseini, Antonio Torroni, Hans-Jürgen Bandelt, Jon C. Allen, Theodore G. Schurr, Rosaria Scozzari, et al. "mtDNA Haplogroup X: An Ancient Link between Europe / Western Asia and North America?" *American Journal of Human Genetics* 63, no. 6 (1998): 1852–61.

Brown, P. "LB1 and LB6 *Homo floresiensis* Are Not Modern Human (*Homo sapiens*) Cretins." *Journal of Human Evolution* 62, no. 2 (2012): 201–24.

Bruchac, M. M., S. M. Hart, and H. M. Wobst, eds. *Indigenous Archaeologies: A Reader on Decolonization.* Walnut Creek CA: Left Coast Press, 2010.

Bryan, Alan L. *Early Man in America from a Circum-Pacific Perspective.* Edmonton: Archaeological Researches International, 1978.

——. *New Evidence for the Pleistocene Peopling of the Americas.* Orono: University of Maine, Center for the Study of Early Man, 1986.

——. "Paleoenvironments and Cultural Diversity in Late Pleistocene South America." *Quaternary Research* 3, no. 2 (1973): 237–56.

——. "Paleoenvironments and Cultural Diversity in Late Pleistocene South America: A Rejoinder to Vance Haynes and a Reply to Thomas Lynch." *Quaternary Research* 5, no. 1 (1975): 151–59.

——. "The Stratigraphy of Taima-Taima." In *Taima-Taima: A Late Pleistocene Paleo-Indian Kill Site in Northernmost South America. Final Reports of 1976 Excavations,* edited by Claudio Ochsenius and Ruth Gruhn, 41–52. South American Quaternary Documentation Program, 1979.

Buikstra, J. E., and D. Ubelaker. *Standards for Data Collection from Human Skeletal Remains.* Arkansas Archeological Survey Research Series No. 44. Fayetteville, 1994.

Byrd, Jodi A. *The Transit of Empire: Indigenous Critiques of Colonialism.* Minneapolis: University of Minnesota Press, 2011.

Cajete, G. *Native Science: Natural Laws of Interdependence.* Santa Fe NM: Clear Light, 2000.

Cajune, Julie. *Montana Tribal Histories: Educators' Resource Guide and Companion DVD.* Montana Office of Public Instruction, 2011.

Camacho, J. A. *Vestiges of Human Labor in the Bones of Extinct Animals from Valsequillo, Puebla, Mexico.* Editorial Board of the Government of the State of Puebla, 1978.

Canales, E. L., and J. Y. Capcha. "New Analysis of Lithic Artifacts from the Ayacucho Complex, Peru. Archaeology: Latin America." *Current Research in the Pleistocene* 25 (2008): 34–37.

Cannon, M. D., and D. J. Meltzer. "Early Paleoindian Foraging: Examining the Faunal Evidence for Large Mammal Specialization and Regional Variability in Prey Choice." *Quaternary Science Reviews* 23, no. 18 (2004): 1955–87.

Casamiquela, R. M. "An Interpretation of the Fossil Vertebrates of the Taima-Taima Site." In *Taima-Taima: A Late Pleistocene Paleo-Indian Kill Site in Northernmost South America. Final Reports of 1976 Excavations,* edited by Claudio Ochsenius and Ruth Gruhn, 59–76. South American Quaternary Documentation Program, 1979.

Cashman, Katherine V., and Shane J. Cronin. "Welcoming a Monster to the World: Myths, Oral Tradition, and Modern Societal Response to Volcanic Disasters." *Journal of Volcanology and Geothermal Research* 176, no. 3 (2008): 407–18.

Caspari, R. "From Types to Populations: A Century of Race, Physical Anthropology, and the American Anthropological Association." *American Anthropologist* 105, no. 1 (2003): 65–76.

Castellano, M. B. "Updating Aboriginal Traditions of Knowledge." In *Indigenous Knowledges in Global Contexts: Multiple Readings of Our World,* edited by G. J. S. Dei, B. L. Hall, and D. G. Rosenberg, 21–36. Toronto: Published in Association with the University of Toronto Press, 2000.

Chandler, M. J., and Christopher E. Lalonde. "Cultural Continuity as a Protective Factor against Suicide in First Nations Youth." Special issue, "Youth, Hope, or Heartbreak: Aboriginal Youth and Canada's Future," *Horizons: Policy Research Initiative* 10, no. 1 (2008): 68–72.

Cherry, J. "The First Colonization of the Mediterranean Islands: A Review of Recent Research." *Journal of Mediterranean Archaeology* 3, no. 2 (1990): 145–221.

Chester, S. G., J. I. Bloch, D. M. Boyer, and W. A. Clemens. "Oldest Known Euarchontan Tarsals and Affinities of Paleocene Purgatorius to Primates." *Proceedings of the National Academy of Sciences* 112, no. 5 (2015): 1487–92.

Chilardi, S., D. W. Frayer, P. Gioia, R. Macchiarelli, and M. Mussi. "Fontana Nuova di Ragusa (Sicily, Italy): Southernmost Aurignacian Site in Europe." *Antiquity* 70, no. 269 (1996): 553–63.

Childe, V. G. *The Most Ancient East: The Oriental Prelude to European Prehistory.* New York: Knopf, 1929.

Chilisa, Bagele. *Indigenous Research Methodologies.* Los Angeles: Sage Publications, 2012.

Chlachula, Jiri. "Geoarchaeology of Paleo-American Sites in Pleistocene Glacigenic Deposits." In *Archaeology: New Approaches in Theory and Techniques,* edited by I. Ollich-Castanyer, 67–116. Rijeka, Croatia: InTech, 2012.

Churchill, Ward. *Fantasies of the Master Race: Literature, Cinema, and the Colonization of American Indians*. Monroe M E: Common Courage Press, 1992.

———. *Since Predator Came: Notes from the Struggle for American Indian Liberation*. Oakland C A: A K Press, 2005.

Cinq-Mars, J. "Bluefish Cave 1: A Late Pleistocene Eastern Beringian Cave Deposit in the Northern Yukon." *Canadian Journal of Archaeology / Journal Canadien d'Archéologie* 3 (1979): 1–32.

Clark, Peter, Arthur S. Dyke, Jeremy D. Shakun, Anders E. Carlson, Jorie Clark, Barbara Wohlfarth, Jerry X. Mitrovica, et al. "The Last Glacial Maximum." *Science* 325, no. 5941 (2009): 710–14.

Clarke, D. L. *Analytical Archaeology*. New York: Routledge, 2014.

Clarkson, Chris, Zenobia Jacobs, Ben Marwick, Richard Fullagar, Lynley Wallis, Mike Smith, Richard G. Roberts, et al. "Human Occupation of Northern Australia by 65,000 Years Ago." *Nature* 547, no. 7663 (2017): 306–10.

Clauge, J., R. Mathews, and T. Ager. "Environments of Northwest North America before the Last Glacial Maximum." In *Entering America, Northeast Asia, and Beringia before the Last Glacial Maximum*, edited by D. Madsen, 63–94. Salt Lake City: University of Utah Press, 2004.

Clausen, C. J., A. D. Cohen, C. Emiliani, J. A. Holman, and J. J. Stipp. "Little Salt Spring, Florida: A Unique Underwater Site." *Science* 203, no. 4381 (1979): 609–14.

Coleman, Cynthia-Lou, and Douglas Herman. "Ways of Knowing: 'Naked Science' or Native Wisdom." *National Museum of the American Indian*, Winter 2010–11, 28–33.

Colón, G. A. T., and C. A. Hobbs. "The Intertwining of Culture and Nature: Franz Boas, John Dewey, and Deweyan Strands of American Anthropology." *Journal of the History of Ideas* 76, no. 1 (2015): 139–62.

Colwell-Chanthaphonh, Chip. *Living Histories: Native Americans and Southwestern Archaeology*. Lanham M D: AltaMira Press, 2010.

Correal Urrego, G. *Evidencias culturales y megafauna pleistocénica en Colombia* (No. 560.178 C O R). Bogotá: Fundación de Investigaciones Arqueológicas Nacionales, Banco de la República, 1981.

Crazy Bull, C. "A Native Conversation about Research and Scholarship." *Tribal College Journal* 9, no. 1 (1997): 17–23.

Cremo, Michael A., and Richard L. Thompson. *Forbidden Archaeology: The Hidden History of the Human Race*. Los Angeles: Bhaktivedanta Book Publishing, 2005.

Cressman, L. S., H. Williams, and A. D. Krieger. *Early Man in Oregon: Archaeological Studies in the Northern Great Basin*. Eugene: University of Oregon Press, 1940.

Cruikshank, J. "Legend and Landscape: Convergence of Oral and Scientific Traditions in the Yukon Territory." *Arctic Anthropology* 18, no. 2 (1981): 67–93.

Cruxent, J., and C. Ochsenius. "Paleo-Indian Studies in Northern Venezuela. Brief Review." In *Taima-Taima: A Late Pleistocene Paleo-Indian Kill Site in Northernmost South*

America. Final Reports of 1976 Excavations, edited by Claudio Ochsenius and Ruth Gruhn, 9. South American Quaternary Documentation Program, 1979.

Cultural Resources Protection Program. "A Review of Oral History Information of the Confederated Tribes of the Umatilla Indian Reservation." Department of Natural Resources, Confederated Tribes of the Umatilla Indian Reservation, March 2000.

Dansie, A. "Early Holocene Burials in Nevada: Overview of Localities, Research, and Legal Issues." *Nevada Historical Quarterly* 40, no. 1 (1997): 4–14.

Davis, S. D., ed. *The Hidden Falls Site Baranof Island, Alaska.* Alaska Anthropological Association Monograph 5. Anchorage, Aurora, 1989.

Deloria, Vine, Jr. "Indians, Archaeologists, and the Future." *American Antiquity* 57, no. 4 (1992): 595–98.

———. "Marginal and Submarginal." In *Indigenizing the Academy: Transforming Scholarship and Empowering Communities*, edited by Devon Abbot Mihesuah and Angela Cavender Wilson, 16–30. Lincoln: University of Nebraska Press, 2004.

———. *Red Earth, White Lies: Native Americans and the Myth of Scientific Fact.* Golden CO: Fulcrum Publishing, 1997.

Demere, Thomas, Richard A. Cerutti, and Paul C. Majors. "San Diego Natural History Museum Hwy 54 Mastodon Site Final Report." Prepared for Caltrans District 11, 1995.

Denevan, W. M. "The Pristine Myth: The Landscape of the Americas in 1492." *Annals of the Association of American Geographers* 82, no. 3 (1992): 346–69.

Denton, David. "Frenchman's Island and the Naatuwaau Bones: Archaeology and Cree Tales of Culture Contact." In *At a Crossroads: Archaeology and First Peoples in Canada*, edited by G. P. Nicholas and T. D. Andrews, 105–24. Burnaby BC: Simon Fraser University Archaeology Press, 1997.

———. *A Visit in Time: Ancient Places, Archaeology and Stories from the Elders of Wemindji.* Nemaska QC: Cree Regional Authority Administration Régionale Crie, 2001.

Deter-Wolf, A., J. W. Tune, and J. B. Broster. "Excavations and Dating of Late Pleistocene and Paleoindian Deposits at the Coats-Hines Site, Williamson County, Tennessee." *Tennessee Archaeology* 5, no. 2 (2011): 142–56.

Devièse, T., T. W. Stafford Jr., M. R. Waters, C. Wathen, D. Comeskey, L. Becerra-Valdivia, and T. Higham. "Increasing Accuracy for the Radiocarbon Dating of Sites Occupied by the First Americans." *Quaternary Science Reviews* 198 (2018): 171–80.

Dillehay, T. D. "Probing Deeper into First American Studies." *Proceedings of the National Academy of Sciences* 106, no. 4 (2009): 971–78.

———. "A Regional Perspective of Preceramic Times in the Central Andes." *Reviews in Anthropology* 12, no. 3 (1985): 193–205.

———. *The Settlement of the Americas: A New Prehistory.* New York: Basic Books, 2000.

Dillehay, T. D., C. Ocampo, J. Saavedra, A. O. Sawakuchi, R. M. Vega, M. Pino, M. B. Collins, et al. "New Archaeological Evidence for an Early Human Presence at Monte Verde, Chile." *PLoS ONE* 10, no. 11 (2015): e0141923.

Dillehay, T. D., and J. Rossen. "Plant Food and Its Implications for the Peopling of the New World: A View from South America." In *The First Americans: The Pleistocene Colonization of the New World*, edited by N. G. Jablonski, 237–54. San Francisco: California Academy of Sciences, 2002.

Dincauze, D. F. "An Archaeological Evaluation of the Case for Pre-Clovis Occupations." *Advances in World Archaeology* 3 (1984): 275–323.

Dion, S. D. *Braiding Histories: Learning from Aboriginal Peoples' Experiences and Perspectives.* Vancouver: University of British Columbia Press, 2009.

Dixon, E. James. *Bones, Boats, and Bison: Archeology and the First Colonization of Western North America.* Albuquerque: University of New Mexico Press, 2000.

Dominguez-Rodrigo, Manuel. *Stone Tools and Fossil Bones: Debates in the Archaeology of Human Origins.* New York: Cambridge University Press, 2012.

Dongoske, K., L. Jenkins, and T. J. Ferguson. "Understanding the Past through Hopi Oral History." *Native Peoples* 6, no. 2 (1993): 24–31.

Downey, R. *Riddle of the Bones: Politics, Science, Race, and the Story of Kennewick Man.* New York: Springer Science and Business Media, 2000.

Doxtater, Michael G. "Indigenous Knowledge in the Decolonial Era." *American Indian Quarterly* 28, no. 3–4 (2004): 618–33.

Doxtator, D. "The Idea of Indianness and Once upon a Time: The Role of Indians in History." In *Racism, Colonialism, and Indigeneity in Canada: A Reader*, edited by M. J. Cannon and L. Sunseri, 31–35. Don Mills ON: Oxford University Press, 2011.

Driese, Steven G., Lee C. Nordt, Michael R. Waters, and Joshua L. Keene. "Analysis of Site Formation History and Potential Disturbance of Stratigraphic Context in Vertisols at the Debra L. Friedkin Archaeological Site in Central Texas, USA." *Geoarchaeology* 28, no. 3 (2013): 221–48.

Dugassa, B. F. "Colonialism of Mind: Deterrent of Social Transformation." *Sociology Mind* 1 (2011): 5–64.

Duk-Rodkin, A., and O. L. Hughes. "Age Relationships of Laurentide and Mountain Glaciations, McKenzie Mountains, Northwest Territories." *Géographie Physique et Quaternaire* 45 (1991): 79–90.

Dumont, C. W., Jr. "Contesting Scientists' Narrations of NAGPRA's Legislative History: Rule 10.11 and the Recovery of 'Culturally Unidentifiable' Ancestors." *Wicazo Sa Review* 26, no. 1 (2011): 5–41.

Duran, Eduardo. *Healing the Soulwound: Counseling with American Indians and Other Native Peoples.* New York: Teachers College Press, 2006.

Duvall, James G., and William T. Venner. "A Statistical Analysis of the Lithics from the Calico Site (SBCM 1500A), California." *Journal of Field Archaeology* 6, no. 4 (1979): 455–62.

Echo-Hawk, Roger. "Ancient History in the New World: Integrating Oral Traditions and the Archaeological Record in Deep Time." *American Antiquity* 65, no. 2 (2000): 267–90.

———. "Kara Katit Pakutu: Exploring the Origins of Native American Anthropology and Oral Traditions." Master's thesis, University of Colorado, 1990.

Ehlers, J., and P. L. Gibbard. *Quaternary and Glacial Geology*. New York: Wiley and Sons, 1996.

Enk, Jacob, Alison Devault, Christopher Widga, Jeffrey Saunders, Paul Szpak, John Southon, Jean-Marie Rouillard, et al. "Mammuthus Population Dynamics in Late Pleistocene North America: Divergence, Phylogeography, and Introgression." *Frontiers in Ecology and Evolution* 4 (2016): 1–13.

Erlandson, Jon M. "After Clovis-First Collapsed: Reimagining the Peopling of the Americas." In *Paleoamerican Odyssey*, edited by Kelly E. Graf, Caroline V. Ketron, and Michael R. Waters, 127–31. College Station: Texas A&M University Press, 2013.

———. "Anatomically Modern Humans, Maritime Voyaging, and the Pleistocene Colonization of the Americas." In *The First Americans: The Pleistocene Colonization of the New World*, edited by N. G. Jablonski, 59–92. San Francisco: California Academy of Sciences, 2002.

Fagundes, N. J., R. Kanitz, and S. L. Bonatto. "A Reevaluation of the Native American mtDNA Genome Diversity and Its Bearing on the Models of Early Colonization of Beringia." *PLoS ONE* 3, no. 9 (2008): e3157.

Faith, J. Tyler, and Todd A. Surovell. "Synchronous Extinction of North America's Pleistocene Mammals." *PNAS* 106, no. 49 (2009): 20641–45.

Fanon, Frantz. *The Wretched of the Earth*. Translated by Constance Farrington. New York: Grove Press, 1963.

Feathers, J. K., E. J. Rhodes, S. Huot, and J. M. McAvoy. "Luminescence Dating of Sand Deposits Related to Late Pleistocene Human Occupation at the Cactus Hill Site, Virginia, USA." *Quaternary Geochronology* 1, no. 3 (2006): 167–87.

Fedje, Daryl W., and Tina Christensen. "Modeling Paleoshorelines and Locating Early Holocene Coastal Sites in Haida Gwaii." *American Antiquity* 64, no. 4 (1999): 635–52.

Felice, G. D. "A controvérsia sobre o sítio arqueológico Toca do Boqueirão da Pedra Furada, Piauí, Brasil." *FUMDHAMentos* 2 (2002): 143.

Ferentinos, G., M. Gkioni, M. Geraga, and G. Papatheodorou. "Early Seafaring Activity in the Southern Ionian Islands, Mediterranean Sea." *Journal of Archaeological Science* 39, no. 7 (2012): 2167–76.

Ferguson, T. J. "Native Americans and the Practice of Archaeology." *Annual Review of Anthropology* 25 (1996): 63–79.

Fidalgo, F., L. Meo Guzmán, G. Politis, M. Salemme, E. P. Tonni, J. Carbonari, G. J. Gómez, et al. "Investigaciones arqueológicas en el sitio 2 de Arroyo Seco (Pdo. de Tres Arroyos, Pcia. de Buenos Aires, República Argentina)." In *New Evidence for the Pleistocene Peopling of the Americas*, edited by Alan L. Bryan, 221–69. Orono ME: Center for the Study of Early Man, 1986.

Fiedel, S. J. "The Peopling of the New World: Present Evidence, New Theories, and Future Directions." *Journal of Archaeological Research* 8, no. 1 (2000): 39–103.

Fine-Dare, Kathleen. *Grave Injustice: The Native American Repatriation Movement and NAGPRA*. Lincoln: University of Nebraska Press, 2002.

Fladmark, Kurt. "Routes: Alternate Migration Corridors for Early Man in North America." *American Antiquity* 44, no. 1 (1979): 55–69.

Flores, C., and F. A. Acuto. "Pueblos originarios y arqueología argentina: Construyendo un diálogo intercultural y reconstruyendo la arqueología." *Intersecciones en Antropología* 16, no. 1 (2015): 179–94.

Fonda, Marc. "Towards Cultural Well-Being: Implications of Revitalizing Traditional Aboriginal Religions." *Canadian Issues*, March 2009, 73–79.

Forbes, J. D. "Intellectual Self-Determination and Sovereignty: Implications for Native Studies and for Native Intellectuals." *Wicazo Sa Review* 13, no. 1 (1998): 11–23.

Foucault, Michel. *The Archaeology of Knowledge*. Translated by A. M. Sheridan Smith. London: Tavistock, 1972.

Fowler, D. "Uses of the Past: Archaeology in the Service of the State." *American Antiquity* 52, no. 2 (1987): 229–48.

Fox, Richard, and Craig Scott. "A New, Early Puercan (Earliest Paleocene) Species of *Purgatorius* (Plesiadapiformes, Primates) from Saskatchewan, Canada." *Journal of Paleontology* 85, no. 3 (2011): 537–48.

Franklin, N. "Power to the People: Sociopolitics and the Archaeology of Black Americans." *Historical Archaeology* 31 (1997): 36–50.

Fredericksen, Clayton, Matthew Spriggs, and Wal Ambrose. "Pamwak Rockshelter: A Pleistocene Site on Manus Island, Papua New Guinea." *Sahul in Review: Pleistocene Archaeology in Australia, New Guinea and Island Melanesia* 24 (1993): 144–54.

Froese, D., M. Stiller, P. D. Heintzman, A. V. Reyes, G. D. Zazula, A. E. Soares, M. Meyer, et al. "Fossil and Genomic Evidence Constrains the Timing of Bison Arrival in North America." *Proceedings of the National Academy of Sciences* 114, no. 13 (2017): 3457–62.

Gathercole, P. W., and D. Lowenthal. *The Politics of the Past*. London: Routledge, 1990.

Gilbert, M. T. P., D. L. Jenkins, A. Götherstrom, N. Naveran, J. J. Sanchez, M. Hofreiter, P. F. Thomsen, et al. "DNA from Pre-Clovis Human Coprolites in Oregon, North America." *Science* 320, no. 5877 (2008): 786–89.

Giles, E. Hooton. "Hooton, Earnest Albert." *American National Biography* 11 (1999): 147–49.

Gnecco, Cristóbal. *Native Americans and Archaeologists: Indigenous People and Archaeology*. Calgary AB: Chacmool, 2003.

———. "Native Histories and Archaeologists." In *Indigenous Peoples and Archaeology in Latin America*, edited by Cristóbal Gnecco and Patricia Ayala. Walnut Creek CA: Left Coast Press, 2011.

Gnecco, Cristóbal, and Javier Aceituno. "Early Humanized Landscapes in Northern South America." In *Paleoindian Archaeology: A Hemispheric Perspective*, edited by Juliet E. Morrow and Cristóbal Gnecco. Gainesville: University Press of Florida, 2006.

Gnecco, Cristóbal, and Patricia Ayala, eds. *Indigenous Peoples and Archaeology in Latin America*. Walnut Creek CA: Left Coast Press, 2011.

Goebel, T., M. R. Waters, and D. H. O'Rourke. "The Late Pleistocene Dispersal of Modern Humans in the Americas." *Science* 319, no. 5869 (2008): 1497–1502.

Gonzalez, Diane Gifford. "Member Survey: Repatriation and SAA's Relationship to NAG-PRA." *SAA Archaeological Record* 16, no. 4 (2016): 15.

Gonzalez, S. L. "Indigenous Values and Methods in Archaeological Practice: Low-Impact Archaeology through the Kashaya Pomo Interpretive Trail Project." *American Antiquity* 81, no. 3 (2016): 533–49.

Gonzalez, S. L., I. Kretzler, and B. Edwards. "Imagining Indigenous and Archaeological Futures: Building Capacity with the Confederated Tribes of Grand Ronde." *Archaeologies* 14, no. 1 (2018): 85–114.

Goodyear, Albert C. "Update on Research at the Topper Site." *Legacy* 13, no. 1 (2009): 8.

Graham, Russell W. "Paleoclimates and Late Pleistocene Faunal Provinces in North America." In *Pre-Llano Cultures of the Americas: Paradoxes and Possibilities*, edited by Robert L. Humphrey and Dennis Stanford. Washington DC: Anthropological Society of Washington, 1979.

Grande, Sandy. *Red Pedagogy: Native American Social and Political Thought*. Lanham MD: Rowman and Littlefield, 2004.

Green, R. E., J. Krause, A. W. Briggs, T. Maricic, U. Stenzel, M. Kircher, N. Patterson, et al. "A Draft Sequence of the Neandertal Genome." *Science* 328, no. 5979 (2010): 710–22.

Greenberg, Joseph H. *Language in the Americas*. Stanford CA: Stanford University Press, 1987.

Greenberg, Joseph H., Christy G. Turner II, Stephen L. Zegura, Lyle Campbell, James A. Fox, W. S. Laughlin, Emöke J. E. Szathmary, et al. "The Settlement of the Americas: A Comparison of the Linguistic, Dental, and Genetic Evidence [and Comments and Reply]." *Current Anthropology* 27, no. 5 (1986): 477–97.

Groube, Les, John Chappell, John Muke, and David Price. "A 40,000-Year-Old Human Occupation Site at Huon Peninsula, Papua New Guinea." *Nature* 324, no. 6096 (1986): 453–55.

Gruhn, R. "The Ignored Continent: South America in Models of Earliest American Prehistory." In *Paleoamerican Origins: Beyond Clovis*, edited by R. Bonnichsen, 199–208. College Station: Center for the Study of the First Americans, Texas A&M University Press, 2005.

———. "Observations Concerning the Cerutti Mastodon Site." *PaleoAmerica* 4, no. 2 (2018): 101–2.

Gruhn, R., and D. Young. "The Burial of Calico Is Premature: A Critique of Duvall and Venner." *Journal of Field Archaeology* 7, no. 4 (1980): 499–500.

Guidon, N., and B. Arnaud. "The Chronology of the New World: Two Faces of One Reality." *World Archaeology* 23, no. 2 (1991): 167–78.

Guidon, N., and G. Delibrias. "Carbon-14 Dates Point to Man in the Americas 32,000 Years Ago." *Nature* 321, no. 6072 (1986): 769–71.

Gulliford, A. "Bones of Contention: The Repatriation of Native American Human Remains." *Public Historian* 18, no. 4 (1996): 119–43.

Gunnarsdóttir, E. D., M. Li, M. Bauchet, K. Finstermeier, and M. Stoneking. "High-Throughput Sequencing of Complete Human mtDNA Genomes from the Philippines." *Genome Research* 21, no. 1 (2011): 1–11.

Günther, T., and C. Nettelblad. "The Presence and Impact of Reference Bias on Population Genomic Studies of Prehistoric Human Populations." *PLOS Genetics* 15, no. 7 (2019): e1008302.

Gustafson, C., D. Gilbow, and R. Daugherty. "The Manis Mastodon Site: Early Man on the Olympic Peninsula." *Canadian Journal of Archaeology / Journal Canadien d'Archéologie* 3 (1979): 157–64.

Gutierrez, M. A. "Tafonomía del área interserrana bonaerense." PhD dissertation, Facultad de Ciencias Naturales y Museo, National University of La Plata, Argentina, 2004.

Hall, M. A. *Thunderbirds: America's Living Legends of Giant Birds.* New York: Cosimo, 2004.

Hallett, Darcy, Michael J. Chandler, and Christopher E. Lalond. "Aboriginal Language Knowledge and Youth Suicide." *Cognitive Development* 22 (2007): 392–99.

Halligan, J. J., M. R. Waters, A. Perrotti, I. J. Owens, J. M. Feinberg, M. D. Bourne, B. Fenerty, et al. "Pre-Clovis Occupation 14,550 Years Ago at the Page-Ladson Site, Florida, and the Peopling of the Americas." *Science Advances* 2, no. 5 (2016): e1600375.

Handsman, R. G. "Towards Archaeological Histories of the Nipmuc Indian Community in the 'Lost Century' (1820–1920)." In *Indigenous People and Archaeology: Honouring the Past, Discussing the Present, Building for the Future; Proceedings of the 32nd Annual Chacmool Conference*, edited by T. Peck, E. Siegfried, and G. Oetelaar, 28–42. Archaeological Association of the University of Calgary, Saskatchewan, 2003.

Hansford, J., P. C. Wright, A. Rasoamiaramanana, V. R. Pérez, L. R. Godfrey, D. Errickson, T. Thompson, and S. T. Turvey. "Early Holocene Human Presence in Madagascar Evidenced by Exploitation of Avian Megafauna." *Science Advances* 4, no. 9 (2018): eaat6925.

Harmand, S., J. E. Lewis, C. S. Feibel, C. J. Lepre, S. Prat, A. Lenoble, X. Boës, et al. "3.3-Million-Year-Old Stone Tools from Lomekwi 3, West Turkana, Kenya." *Nature* 521, no. 7552 (2015): 310–15.

Haynes, Gary. "The Calico Site: Artifacts or Geofacts?" *Science* 181 (1973): 305–10.

———. "The Cerutti Mastodon." *PaleoAmerica* 3, no. 3 (2017): 196–99.

———. "Were Clovis Progenitors in Beringia?" In *Paleoecology of Beringia*, edited by David M. Hopkins, John V. Matthews, and Charles E. Schweger, 383–98. Waltham MA: Academic Press, 1982.

Haynes, Gary, and Kathryn Krasinski. "Taphonomic Fieldwork in Southern Africa and Its Application in Studies of the Earliest Peopling of North America." *Journal of Taphonomy* 8, no. 2–3 (2010): 181–202.

Haynes, Vance. "Paleoenvironments and Cultural Diversity in Late Pleistocene South America: A Reply to A. L. Bryan 1." *Quaternary Research* 4, no. 3 (1974): 378–82.

Heintzman, P. D., D. Froese, J. W. Ives, A. E. Soares, G. D. Zazula, B. Letts, T. D. Andrews, et al. "Bison Phylogeography Constrains Dispersal and Viability of the Ice Free Corridor in Western Canada." *Proceedings of the National Academy of Sciences* 113, no. 29 (2016): 8057–63.

Heintzman, P. D., G. D. Zazula, J. A. Cahill, A. V. Reyes, R. D. MacPhee, and B. Shapiro. "Genomic Data from Extinct North American Camelops Revise Camel Evolutionary History." *Molecular Biology and Evolution* 32, no. 9 (2015): 2433–40.

Herbert, T. D., K. T. Lawrence, A. Tzanova, L. C. Peterson, R. Caballero-Gill, and C. S. Kelly. "Late Miocene Global Cooling and the Rise of Modern Ecosystems." *Nature Geoscience* 9, no. 11 (2016): 1–7.

Herrera, L., W. Bray, M. Cardale, and P. Botero. "Nuevas fechas de radiocarbono para el precerámico de la Cordillera Occidental de Colombia." In *Archaeology and Environment in Latin America*, edited by O. Ortiz-Troncoso and T. van der Hammen, 145–63. Amsterdam: Instituut voor Pre- en Protohistorische Archeologie Albert Egges van Giffen, Universiteit van Amsterdam, 1992.

Hidy, Alan J., and Mike Buckleyet. "Mid-Pliocene Warm-Period Deposits in the High Arctic Yield Insight into Camel Evolution." *Nature Communications* 4, no. 1550 (2013): 1–9. https://www.nature.com/articles/ncomms2516.

Higham, T., K. Douka, R. Wood, C. B. Ramsey, F. Brock, L. Basell, M. Camps, et al. "The Timing and Spatiotemporal Patterning of Neanderthal Disappearance." *Nature* 512, no. 7514 (2014): 306–9.

Hodder, Ian, ed. *Archaeological Theory Today*. Cambridge: Polity Press, 2012.

——, ed. *Symbolic and Structural Archaeology*. Cambridge: Cambridge University Press, 1982.

Hoffecker, J. F., S. A. Elias, and D. H. O'Rourke. "Out of Beringia?" *Science* 343, no. 6174 (2014): 979–80.

Holen, S. "Taphonomy of Two Last Glacial Maximum Mammoth Sites in the Central Great Plains of North America: A Preliminary Report on La Sena and Lovewell." *Quaternary International* 142 (2006): 30–43.

Holen, S. R., T. A. Deméré, D. C. Fisher, R. Fullagar, J. B. Paces, G. T. Jefferson, J. M. Beeton, et al. "A 130,000-Year-Old Archaeological Site in Southern California, USA." *Nature* 544, no. 7651 (2017): 479–83.

——. "Broken Bones and Hammerstones at the Cerutti Mastodon Site: A Reply to Haynes." *PaleoAmerica* 4, no. 1 (2018): 8–11.

Holen, S. R., and K. Holen. "The Mammoth Steppe Hypothesis: The Middle Wisconsin (Oxygen Isotope Stage 3) Peopling of North America." In *Paleoamerican Odyssey*, edited by K. E. Graf, C. V. Ketron, and M. R. Waters, 429–44. College Station: Texas A&M University Press, 2014.

Holm, Bill, and Bill Reid. *Indian Art of the Northwest Coast*. Seattle: University of Washington Press, 1976.

Holman, J. A., and C. J. Clausen. "Fossil Vertebrates Associated with Paleo-Indian Artifacts at Little Salt Spring, Florida." *Journal of Vertebrate Paleontology* 4, no. 1 (1984): 146–54.

Hooton, E. A. *Up from the Ape*. New York: Macmillan, 1946.

Hopkins, D. M. *The Bering Land Bridge*. Stanford CA: Stanford University Press, 1967.

Horai, S., R. Kondo, Y. Nakagawa-Hattori, S. Hayashi, S. Sonoda, and K. Tajima. "Peopling of the Americas, Founded by Four Major Lineages of Mitochondrial DNA." *Molecular Biology and Evolution* 10, no. 1 (1993): 23–47.

Hou, Y., and L. X. Zhao. "An Archaeological View for the Presence of Early Humans in China." *Quaternary International* 223–24 (2010): 10–19.

Hrdlička, A., W. H. Holmes, B. Willis, F. E. Wright, and C. N. Fenner. *Early Man in South America*. Smithsonian Bureau of American Ethnology Bulletin No. 52. Washington DC: US Government Printing Office, 1912.

Hublin, J. J., A. Ben-Ncer, S. E. Bailey, S. E. Freidline, S. Neubauer, M. M. Skinner, I. Bergmann, et al. "New Fossils from Jebel Irhoud, Morocco and the Pan-African Origin of *Homo sapiens*." *Nature* 546, no. 7657 (2017): 289–92.

Humphrey, Robert L., and Dennis Stanford, eds. *Pre-Llano Cultures of the Americas: Paradoxes and Possibilities*. Washington DC: Anthropological Society of Washington, 1979.

Hurcombe, L. *Archaeological Artefacts as Material Culture*. New York: Routledge, 2014.

Irwin-Williams, C. "Summary of Archaeological Evidence from the Valsequillo Region, Puebla, Mexico." In *Cultural Continuity in Mesoamerica*, edited by D. L. Browman, 7–22. The Hague: Mouton Publishers, 1978.

Irwin-Williams, C., R. S. MacNeish, F. A. Petersen, and H. M. Wormington. "Comments on the Associations of Archaeological Materials and Extinct Fauna in the Valsequillo Region, Puebla, Mexico." *American Antiquity* 34, no. 1 (1969): 82–83.

Jenkins, Dennis L. "Distribution and Dating of Cultural and Paleontological Remains at the Paisley Five Mile Point Caves in the Northern Great Basin." In *Paleoindian or Paleoarchaic? Great Basin Human Ecology and the Pleistocene/Holocene Transition*, edited by Kelley E. Graf and Dave N. Schmitt, 57–81. Salt Lake City: University of Utah Press, 2007.

Jenkins, D. L., L. G. Davis, T. W. Stafford Jr., P. F. Campos, T. J. Connolly, L. S. Cummings, M. Hofreiter, et al. "Geochronology, Archaeological Context, and DNA at the Paisley Caves." In *Paleoamerican Odyssey*, edited by K. E. Graf, C. V. Ketron, and M. R. Waters, 485–510. College Station: Texas A&M University Press, 2013.

Jenkins, D. L., L. G. Davis, T. W. Stafford Jr., P. F. Campos, B. Hockett, G. T. Jones, L. S. Cummings, et al. "Clovis Age Western Stemmed Projectile Points and Human Coprolites at the Paisley Caves." *Science* 337, no. 6091 (2012): 223–28.

Jennings, J. D. *Prehistory of North America*. Mountain View CA: Mayfield Publishing Company, 1989.

Jennings, T. A. "Clovis, Folsom, and Midland Components at the Debra L. Friedkin Site, Texas: Context, Chronology, and Assemblages." *Journal of Archaeological Science* 39, no. 10 (2012): 3239–47.

Jennings, T. A., and M. R. Waters. "Pre-Clovis Lithic Technology at the Debra L. Friedkin Site, Texas: Comparisons to Clovis through Site-Level Behavior, Technological Trait-List, and Cladistic Analyses." *American Antiquity* 79, no. 1 (2014): 25–44.

Johnson, Allan G. *Privilege, Power, and Difference*. 2nd ed. New York: McGraw Hill, 2006.

Johnson, E. "Current Developments in Bone Technology." *Advances in Archaeological Method and Theory* 8 (1985): 157–235.

Johnson, John R., Thomas W. Stafford Jr., Henry O. Ajie, and Don P. Morris. "Arlington Springs Revisited." In *Proceedings of the Fifth California Islands Symposium* 5:541–45. Santa Barbara CA: Santa Barbara Museum of Natural History, 2002.

Jones, J., T. F. Higham, R. Oldfield, T. P. O'Connor, and S. A. Buckley. "Evidence for Prehistoric Origins of Egyptian Mummification in Late Neolithic Burials." *PLoS ONE* 9, no. 8 (2014): e103608.

Joyce, D. J. "Chronology and New Research on the Schaefer Mammoth (? *Mammuthus primigenius*) Site, Kenosha County, Wisconsin, USA." *Quaternary International* 142 (2006): 44–57.

Julien, Donald M., Tim Bernard, and Leah Morine Rosenmeier. "Paleo Is Not Our Word: Protecting and Growing a Mi' Kmaw Place." In *Indigenous Archaeologies: A Reader on Decolonization*, edited by M. Bruchac, S. M. Hart, and H. M. Wobost. Walnut Creek CA: Left Coast Press, 2010.

Justice, D. H. "Seeing (and Reading) Red: Indian Outlaws in the Ivory Tower." In *Indigenizing the Academy: Transforming Scholarship and Empowering Communities*, edited by D. A. Mihesuah and A. C. Wilson, 100–123. Lincoln: University of Nebraska Press, 2004.

Karafet, T. M., S. L. Zegura, O. Posukh, L. Osipova, A. Bergen, J. Long, D. Goldman, et al. "Ancestral Asian Source(s) of New World Y-Chromosome Founder Haplotypes." *American Journal of Human Genetics* 64, no. 3 (1999): 817–31.

Kashani, B. H., U. A. Perego, A. Olivieri, N. Angerhofer, F. Gandini, V. Carossa, H. Lancioni, et al. "Mitochondrial Haplogroup C4c: A Rare Lineage Entering America through the Ice-Free Corridor?" *American Journal of Physical Anthropology* 147, no. 1 (2012): 35–39.

Kay, M. "Microwear Analysis of Some Clovis and Experimental Chipped Stone Tools." In *Stone Tools: Theoretical Insight into Human Prehistory*, edited by G. H. Odell, 315–44. Boston: Springer, 1996.

Keene, Joshua L. "Site Formation Processes at the Buttermilk Creek Site (41BL1239), Bell County, Texas." PhD dissertation, Texas A&M University, 2010.

Kimmerer, R. W., and Frank K. Lake. "The Role of Indigenous Burning in Land Management." *Journal of Forestry* 99, no. 11 (2001): 36–41.

Kinoshita, A., A. M. G. Figueiredo, G. D. Felice, M. C. S. M. Lage, N. Guidon, and O. Baffa. "Electron Spin Resonance Dating of Human Teeth from Toca da Santa Shelter of São Raimundo Nonato, Piauí, Brazil." *Nuclear Instruments and Methods in Physics Research Section B: Beam Interactions with Materials and Atoms* 266, no. 4 (2008): 635–39.

Kinoshita, A., A. R. Skinner, N. Guidon, E. Ignacio, G. D. Felice, C. D. A. Buco, S. Tatumi, et al. "Dating Human Occupation at Toca do Serrote das Moendas, São Raimundo Nonato, Piauí-Brasil by Electron Spin Resonance and Optically Stimulated Luminescence." *Journal of Human Evolution* 77 (2014): 187–95.

Klein, Richard G. *The Human Career: Human Biological and Cultural Origins*. Chicago: University of Chicago Press, 1989.

Kovach, M. *Indigenous Methodologies: Characteristics, Conversations, and Contexts*. Toronto: University of Toronto Press, 2009.

Krause, J., L. Orlando, D. Serre, B. Viola, K. Prüfer, M. P. Richards, J.-J. Hublin, et al. "Neanderthals in Central Asia and Siberia." *Nature* 449, no. 7164 (2007): 902–4.

Kuzmin, Y. V. "Obsidian as a Commodity to Investigate Human Migrations in the Upper Paleolithic, Neolithic, and Paleometal of Northeast Asia." *Quaternary International* 442 (2017): 5–11.

Kuzmin, Y. V., and S. G. Keates. "Dates Are Not Just Data: Paleolithic Settlement Patterns in Siberia Derived from Radiocarbon Records." *American Antiquity* 70, no. 4 (2005): 773–89.

Lahaye, C., G. Guérin, E. Boëda, M. Fontugne, C. Hatté, M. Frouin, I. Clemente-Conte, et al. "New Insights into a Late-Pleistocene Human Occupation in America: The Vale da Pedra Furada Complete Chronological Study." *Quaternary Geochronology* 30 (2015): 445–51.

Lahaye, C., M. Hernandez, E. Boëda, G. D. Felice, N. Guidon, S. Hoeltz, A. Lourdeau, et al. "Human Occupation in South America by 20,000 BC: The Toca da Tira Peia Site, Piauí, Brazil." *Journal of Archaeological Science* 40, no. 6 (2013): 2840–47.

Lahr, M. M. "Patterns of Modern Human Diversification: Implications for Amerindian Origins." *American Journal of Physical Anthropology* 38, no. S21 (1995): 163–98.

Lalueza, Carlos, Alejandro Pérez-Pérez, Eva Prats, Luís Cornudella, and Daniel Turbón. "Lack of Founding Amerindian Mitochondrial DNA Lineages in Extinct Aborigines from Tierra del Fuego, Patagonia." *Human Molecular Genetics* 6, no. 1 (1997): 41–46.

Lambert, L. *Research for Indigenous Survival: Indigenous Research Methodologies in the Behavioral Sciences*. Pablo MT: Salish Kootenai College Press, 2002.

Lame Deer, John (Fire), and Richard Erdoes. *Lame Deer, Seeker of Visions*. New York: Simon and Schuster, 1994.

La Salle, Marina, and Richard Hutchings. "What Makes Us Squirm: A Critical Assessment of Community-Oriented Archaeology." *Canadian Journal of Archaeology* 40, no. 1 (2016): 164–80.

Leakey, L. S. B., R. D. Simpson, and T. Clements. "Archaeological Excavations in the Calico Mountains, California: Preliminary Report." *Science* 160, no. 3831 (1968): 1022–23.

Leakey, Louis S. B., Phillip V. Tobias, and John Russell Napier. "A New Species of the Genus *Homo* from Olduvai Gorge." *Nature* 202, no. 4927 (1964): 7–9.

Lell, J. T., R. I. Sukernik, Y. B. Starikovskaya, B. Su, L. Jin, T. G. Schurr, P. A. Underhill, and D. C. Wallace. "The Dual Origin and Siberian Affinities of Native American Y Chromosomes." *American Journal of Human Genetics* 70, no. 1 (2002): 192–206.

Lindquist, Anna K., Joshua M. Feinberg, and Michael R. Waters. "Rock Magnetic Properties of a Soil Developed on an Alluvial Deposit at Buttermilk Creek, Texas, USA." *Geochemistry, Geophysics, Geosystems* 12, no. 12 (2011).

Lister, A. M., and A. V. Sher. "Evolution and Dispersal of Mammoths across the Northern Hemisphere." *Science* 350, no. 6262 (2015): 805–9.

Little, M. A., and K. A. Kennedy. *Histories of American Physical Anthropology in the Twentieth Century.* Lanham M D: Lexington Books, 2010.

Little Bear, Leroy. "Jagged Worldviews Colliding." In *Reclaiming Indigenous Voice and Vision*, edited by M. Battiste. Vancouver: University of British Columbia Press, 2000.

Liu, W., M. Martinón-Torres, Y. J. Cai, S. Xing, H. W. Tong, S. W. Pei, M. J. Sier, et al. "The Earliest Unequivocally Modern Humans in Southern China." *Nature* 526, no. 7575 (2015): 696–99.

Llamas, B., L. Fehren-Schmitz, G. Valverde, J. Soubrier, S. Mallick, N. Rohland, S. Nordenfelt, et al. "Ancient Mitochondrial D N A Provides High-Resolution Time Scale of the Peopling of the Americas." *Science Advances* 2, no. 4 (2016): e1501385.

Loewen, James W. *Lies My Teacher Told Me: Everything Your American History Textbook Got Wrong.* New York: New Press, 2008.

Lomawaima, K. Tsianina. "Tribal Sovereigns: Reframing Research in American Indian Education." *Harvard Educational Review* 70, no. 1 (2000): 1–23.

Louis, Renee Pualani. "Can You Hear Us Now? Voices from the Margin: Using Indigenous Methodologies in Geographic Research." *Geographical Research* 45, no. 2 (2007): 130–39.

Lubinski, Patrick M., Karisa Terry, and Patrick T. McCutcheon. "Comparative Methods for Distinguishing Flakes from Geofacts: A Case Study from the Wenas Creek Mammoth Site." *Journal of Archaeological Science* 52 (2014): 308–20.

Lynch, T. F. "The Antiquity of Man in South America." *Quaternary Research* 4, no. 3 (1974): 356–77.

———. "Zonal Complementarity in the Andes: A History of the Concept." In *Networks of the Past*, Proceedings of the 12th Annual Chaacmool Conference, edited by P. Framcis, F. Kense, and P. Duke, 221–31. Alberta: University of Calgary, 1981.

MacFadden, B. J., and R. C. Hulbert. "Calibration of Mammoth (Mammuthus) Dispersal into North America Using Rare Earth Elements of Plio-Pleistocene Mammals from Florida." *Quaternary Research* 71, no. 1 (2009): 41–48.

Mackie, Quentin, Loren Davis, Daryl Fedje, Duncan McLaren, and Amy Gusick. "Locating Pleistocene-Age Submerged Archaeological Sites on the Northwest Coast: Current Status of Research and Future Directions." In *Paleoamerican Odyssey*, edited by Kelly E. Graf, Caroline V. Ketron, and Michael R. Waters, 133–47. Center for the Study of the First Americans, 2013.

MacNeish, R. S. "Early Man in the Andes." *Scientific American* 224, no. 4 (1971): 36–47.

———. "The Early Man Remains from Pikimachay Cave, Ayacucho Basin, Highland Peru." In *Pre-Llano Cultures of the Americas: Paradoxes and Possibilities*, edited by R. Humphrey and D. Stanford, 1–48. Washington DC: Anthropological Society of Washington, 1979.

———. "A New Look at Early Peopling of the New World as of 1976." *Journal of Anthropological Research* 34, no. 4 (1978): 475–96.

———. *The Prehistory of the Ayacucho Basin, Peru*, vol. 2, *Excavations and Chronology*. Ann Arbor: University of Michigan Press, 1981.

———. *The Prehistory of the Ayacucho Basin, Peru*, vol. 4, *The Preceramic Way of Life*. Ann Arbor: University of Michigan Press, 1983.

Madden, C. T. "Earliest Isotopically Dated Mammuthus from North America." *Quaternary Research* 13, no. 1 (1980): 147–50.

Madsen, David B., ed. *Entering America: North East Asia and Beringia before the Last Glacial Maximum*. Salt Lake City: University of Utah Press, 2004.

Malhi, R. S., B. M. Kemp, J. A. Eshleman, J. Cybulski, D. G. Smith, S. Cousins, and H. Harry. "Mitochondrial Haplogroup M Discovered in Prehistoric North Americans." *Journal of Archaeological Science* 34, no. 4 (2007): 642–48.

Malhi, Y., C. E. Doughty, M. Galetti, F. A. Smith, J. C. Svenning, and J. W. Terborgh. "Megafauna and Ecosystem Function from the Pleistocene to the Anthropocene." *Proceedings of the National Academy of Sciences* 113, no. 4 (2016): 838–46.

Mallon, F. E. *Decolonizing Native Histories: Collaboration, Knowledge, and Language in the Americas*. Durham NC: Duke University Press, 2012.

Mandryk, C. A. "Invented Traditions and the Ultimate American Origin Myth." In *The Settlement of the American Continents: A Multidisciplinary Approach to Human Biogeography*, edited by C. M. Barton et al., 113–22. Tucson: University of Arizona Press, 2004.

Marincovich, L., Jr., and A. Y. Gladenkov. "New Evidence for the Age of Bering Strait." *Quaternary Science Reviews* 20 (2001): 329–35.

Marsh, G. A. "Walking the Spirit Trail: Repatriation and Protection of Native American Remains and Sacred Cultural Items." *Arizona State Law Journal* 24 (1992): 79–96.

Marshall, E. "Pre-Clovis Sites Fight for Acceptance." *Science*, n.s., 291, no. 5509 (2001): 1730–32.

Martin, K., and B. Mirraboopa. "Ways of Knowing, Being and Doing: A Theoretical Framework and Methods for Indigenous and Indigenist Re-search." *Journal of Australian Studies* 27, no. 76 (2003): 203–14.

Martin, Paul Schultz, and Herbert Edgar Wright. *Pleistocene Extinctions: The Search for a Cause.* New Haven CT: Yale University Press, 1967.

Martindale, A., and N. Lyons. "Community-Oriented Archaeology." *Canadian Journal of Archaeology* 38, no. 2 (2014): 425–33.

Mason, O. T. "Sketch of North American Anthropology in 1879." *American Naturalist* 14, no. 5 (1880): 349–56.

Matsu'ura, S. "A Chronological Review of Pleistocene Human Remains from the Japanese Archipelago." In *Interdisciplinary Perspectives on the Origins of the Japanese,* edited by K. Omoto, 181–96. Kyoto: International Research Center for Japanese Studies, 1999.

Mayes, Arion T. "These Bones Are Read." *American Indian Quarterly* 34, no. 2 (2010): 131–56.

Mayor, Adrienne. *Fossil Legends of the First Americans.* Princeton NJ: Princeton University Press, 2005.

McAvoy, J. M., and L. D. McAvoy. *Archaeological Investigations of Site 44SX202, Cactus Hill, Sussex County, Virginia (No. 2).* Department of Historic Resources, 1997.

McGregor, S. *Since Time Immemorial: "Our Story"; The Story of the Kitigan Zibi Anishinàbeg.* Kitigan Zibi Education Council, 2004.

McGuire, Randall H. "Archaeology and the First Americans." *American Anthropologist* 94, no. 4 (1992): 816–36.

McNiven, I. J., and L. Russell. *Appropriated Pasts: Indigenous Peoples and the Colonial Culture of Archaeology.* Walnut Creek CA: AltaMira Press, 2005.

Meighan, C. W. "Burying American Archaeology." *Archaeology* 47, no. 6 (1994): 64–68.

Meiri, M., A. M. Lister, M. J. Collins, N. Tuross, T. Goebel, S. Blockley, G. D. Zazula, et al. "Faunal Record Identifies Bering Isthmus Conditions as Constraint to End-Pleistocene Migration to the New World." *Proceedings of the Royal Society B, Biological Sciences* 281, no. 1776 (2014): 2013–167.

Meltzer, D. "Clocking the First Americans." *Annual Review of Anthropology* 24, no. 1 (1995): 21–45.

———. *First Peoples in a New World: Colonizing Ice Age America.* Berkeley: University of California Press, 2009.

———. "North American Archaeology and Archaeologists, 1879–1934." *American Antiquity* 50, no. 2 (1985): 249–60.

———. "Peopling of North America." *Development in Quaternary Science* 1 (2003): 539–63.

Meltzer, D. J., J. M. Adovasio, and T. D. Dillehay. "On a Pleistocene Human Occupation at Pedra Furada, Brazil." *Antiquity* 68, no. 261 (1994): 695–714.

Merriwether, D. A. "A Mitochondrial Perspective on the Peopling of the New World." In *The First Americans: The Pleistocene Colonization of the New World,* edited by N. G. Jablonski, 295–310. San Francisco: California Academy of Sciences, 2002.

Merriwether, D. A., F. Rothhammer, and R. E. Ferrell. "Distribution of the Four Founding Lineage Haplotypes in Native Americans Suggests a Single Wave of Migration for the New World." *American Journal of Physical Anthropology* 98, no. 4 (1995): 411–30.

Mihesuah, D. A., ed. *Natives and Academics: Researching and Writing about American Indians*. Lincoln: University of Nebraska Press, 1998.

Mihlbachler, M. C., F. Rivals, N. Solounias, and G. M. Semprebon. "Dietary Change and Evolution of Horses in North America." *Science* 331, no. 6021 (2011): 1178–81.

Miller, B. *Anthropology*. 2nd ed. Boston: Pearson Education, Inc., 2008.

Miller, S. A., and J. R. Riding In. *Native Historians Write Back: Decolonizing American Indian History*. Lubbock: Texas Tech University Press, 2011.

Milner, R. "Time Traveler." *Scientific American* 306, no. 4 (2012): 70–73. http://www.jstor.org/stable/26014329.

Mistry, J., A. Berardi, V. Andrade, T. Krahô, P. Krahô, and O. Leonardos. "Indigenous Fire Management in the Cerrado of Brazil: The Case of the Krahô of Tocantíns." *Human Ecology* 33, no. 3 (2005): 365–86.

Moeke-Pickering, T., S. Hardy, S. Manitowabi, A. Mawhiney, E. Faries, K. Gibson-van Marrewijk, N. Tobias, et al. "Keeping Our Fire Alive: Towards Decolonising Research in the Academic Setting." *WINHEC (World Indigenous Higher Education Consortium) Journal* (2006): 1–8. http://citeseerx.ist.psu.edu/viewdoc/download?doi=10.1.1.532.5368&rep=rep1&type=pdf.

Momaday, N. Scott. *American Indian Authors*. New York: Houghton, Mifflin, 1971.

Montagu, Ashley M. F. "An Indian Tradition Relating to the Mastodon." *American Anthropologist*, n.s., 46, no. 4 (1944): 568–71.

Morgan, Lewis H. *Ancient Society: Or Research in the Lines of Human Progress from Savagery to Barbarism to Civilization*. New York: William Holt and Company, 1877.

Morlan, R. E. "Current Perspectives on the Pleistocene Archaeology of Eastern Beringia." *Quaternary Research* 60, no. 1 (2003): 123–32.

Morrow, J. E., S. J. Fiedel, D. L. Johnson, M. Kornfeld, M. Rutledge, and W. R. Wood. "Pre-Clovis in Texas? A Critical Assessment of the 'Buttermilk Creek Complex.'" *Journal of Archaeological Science* 39, no. 12 (2012): 3677–82.

Morrow, Juliet E., and Cristóbal Gnecco, eds. *Paleoindian Archaeology: A Hemispheric Perspective*. Gainesville: University Press of Florida, 2006.

Morwood, M. J., P. B. O'Sullivan, F. Aziz, and A. Raza. "Fission-Track Ages of Stone Tools and Fossils on the East Indonesian Island of Flores." *Nature* 392, no. 6672 (1998): 173.

Muhs, D. R., J. F. Wehmiller, K. R. Simmons, and L. L. York. "Quaternary Sea-Level History of the United States." *Developments in Quaternary Sciences* 1 (2003): 147–83.

Mukasa-Mugerwa, E. *The Camel (Camelus dromedarius): A Bibliographical Review*. International Livestock Centre for Africa Monograph 5. Addis Ababa, Ethiopia: International Livestock Centre for Africa, 1981.

Nakagawa, R., N. Doi, Y. Nishioka, S. Nunami, H. Yamauchi, M. Fujita, S. Yamazaki, et al. "Pleistocene Human Remains from Shiraho-Saonetabaru Cave on Ishigaki Island, Okinawa, Japan, and Their Radiocarbon Dating." *Anthropological Science* 118, no. 3 (2010): 173–83.

Nei, M. "Genetic Support for the Out-of-Africa Theory of Human Evolution." *Proceedings of the National Academy of Sciences* 92, no. 15 (1995): 6720–22.

Neiburger, E. J. "The Mammoth Eaters: Very Early Man in America." *Central States Archaeological Journal* 57, no. 1 (2010): 6–11.

Newcomb, S. "The Doctrine of Discovery." In video of presentation, the Indigenous Peoples' Forum on the Doctrine of Discovery, Arizona State Capitol, House of Representatives, Phoenix, March 2012.

Nicholas, G. P. "Understanding the Present, Honoring the Past: Indigenous People and Archaeology." In *Indigenous People and Archaeology: Honoring the Past, Discussing the Present, Building for the Future; Proceedings of the 32nd Annual Chacmool Conference,* edited by T. Peck, E. Siegfried, and G. A. Oetelaar, 11–27. Archaeological Association of the University of Calgary, Saskatchewan, 2003.

Nicholas, G. P., and J. J. Hollowell. "Ethical Challenges to a Postcolonial Archaeology." In *Archaeology and Capitalism: From Ethics to Politics,* edited by Y. Hamilakas and P. Duke, 59–82. Walnut Creek CA: Left Coast Press, 2007.

Nicholas, G. P., and N. Markey. "Traditional Knowledge, Archaeological Evidence, and Other Ways of Knowing." In *Material Culture as Evidence: Best Practices and Exemplary Cases in Archaeology,* edited by R. Chapman and A. Wylie, 287–307. New York: Routledge, 2014.

Nichols, Johanna. "Linguistic Diversity and the First Settlement of the New World." *Language* 66, no. 3 (1990): 475–521.

Niezen, R. *The Origins of Indigenism: Human Rights and the Politics of Identity.* Berkeley: University of California Press, 2003.

Oakley, K. P. "Man the Skilled Tool-Maker." *Antiquity* 43, no. 171 (1969): 222–24.

Oar, P. C. *The Prehistory of Santa Rosa Island.* Santa Barbara CA: Santa Barbara Museum of Natural History, 1968.

Ochsenius, Claudio, and Ruth Gruhn, eds. *Taima-Taima: A Late Pleistocene Paleo-Indian Kill Site in Northernmost South America. Final Reports of 1976 Excavations.* South American Quaternary Documentation Program, 1979.

Oda, Shizuo. "A Review of Archaeological Research in the Izu and Ogasawara Islands." *Man and Culture in Oceania* 6 (1990): 53–79.

Olson, Don. "Educate First Nations to Be Modern Citizens." Letter to the editor, *Nanaimo News,* March 27, 2013.

Olsson, I. U. "Radiocarbon Dating History: Early Days, Questions, and Problems Met." *Radiocarbon* 51, no. 1 (2009): 1–43.

Ortiz, Simon J. *from Sand Creek.* New York: Thunder's Mouth Press, 1981.

Overskaug, Kistian. "Homage to Marcel Proust: Aspects of Dissemination and Didactic in a Museum and a Science Center; Science Communication Visions for the Third Generation Museums." In *Archaeology: New Approaches in Theory and Techniques*, edited by Imma Ollich-Castanyes, 279–92. Rijeka, Croatia: InTech, 2012.

Overstreet, D. F., and M. F. Kolb. "Geoarchaeological Contexts for Late Pleistocene Archaeological Sites with Human Modified Woolly Mammoth Remains in Southeastern Wisconsin, U.S.A." *Geoarchaeology* 18, no. 1 (2003): 91–114.

Owsley, D. W., and D. R. Hunt. "Clovis and Early Archaic Crania from the Anzick Site (24PA506), Park County, Montana." *Plains Anthropologist* 46, no. 176 (2001): 115–24.

Pääbo, S. "The Diverse Origins of the Human Gene Pool." *Nature Reviews: Genetics* 16, no. 6 (2015): 313–14.

Parenti, F. "Old and New on the Same Site: Putting Vale Da Pedra Furada into a Wider Context; A Comment to Lahaye et al." *Quaternary Geochronology* 30, pt. A (2015): 48–53.

Parenti, F., M. Fontugue, and C. Guérin. "Pedra Furada in Brazil and Its 'Presumed' Evidence: Limitations and Potential of the Available Data." *Antiquity* 70, no. 268 (1996): 416–21.

Parenti, F., N. Mercier, and H. Valladas. "The Oldest Hearths of Pedra Furada, Brasil: Thermoluminescence Analysis of Heated Stones." *Current Research in the Pleistocene* 7 (1990): 36–38.

Patterson, L. W., L. V. Hoffman, R. M. Higginbotham, and R. D. Simpson. "Analysis of Lithic Flakes at the Calico Site, California." *Journal of Field Archaeology* 14, no. 1 (1987): 91–106.

Payen, L. A. "Artifacts or Geofacts at Calico: Application of the Barnes Test." In *Peopling of the New World*, edited by J. E. Ericson, R. Berger, and R. E. Taylor, 193–201. Los Altos CA: Ballena Press, 1982.

Pedersen, M. W., A. Ruter, C. Schweger, H. Friebe, R. A. Staff, K. Kjeldsen, M. L. Z. Mendoza, et al. "Postglacial Viability and Colonization in North America's Ice-Free Corridor." *Nature* 537, no. 7618 (2016): 45–49.

Pendergast, David M., and Clement W. Meighan. "Folk Traditions as Historical Fact, a Paiute Example." *Journal of American Folklore* 72, no. 284 (1959): 128–33.

Perez, S. I., M. B. Postillone, D. Rindel, D. Gobbo, P. N. Gonzalez, and V. Bernal. "Peopling Time: Spatial Occupation and Demography of Late Pleistocene–Holocene Human Population from Patagonia." *Quaternary International* 425 (2016): 214–23.

Pessis, Anne-Marie, and Niède Guidon. "Dating Rock Art Paintings in Serra de Capivara National Park." *Adoranten* 1 (2009): 49–59.

Politis, G. "The Pampas and Campos of South America." In *The Handbook of South American Archaeology*, edited by Helaine Silverman and William Isbell, 235–60. New York: Springer, 2008.

Politis, G., and R. P. Curtoni. "Archaeology and Politics in Argentina during the Last 50 Years." In *Comparative Archaeologies: A Sociological View of the Science of the Past*, edited by L. R. Lozny, 495–525. New York: Springer, 2011.

Politis, G., M. A. Gutierrez, and C. Scabuzzo. *Current State of the Investigations at Site 2 of Arroyo Seco (Pampas Region, Argentina)*. Monographic Series INCUAPA 5. Olavarría: INCUAPA, 2014.

Poupart, Lisa M. "The Familiar Face of Genocide: Internalized Oppression among American Indians." *Hypatia* 118, no. 2 (2003): 87–100.

Preucel, Robert, and Ian Hodder. *Appropriated Pasts: Indigenous People and the Colonial Culture of Archaeology*. Walnut Creek CA: AltaMira Press, 2005.

Proctor, Robert, and Londa Schiebinger. *Agnotology: The Making and Unmaking of Ignorance*. Stanford CA: Stanford University Press, 2008.

Prothero, Donald R. *The Evolution of North American Rhinoceros*. Cambridge: Cambridge University Press, 2005.

Proust, Marcel. *Remembrance of Things Past*. Vol. 5, *The Captive*. Translated by C. K. Scott Moncrieff. New York: Random House, 1982. Originally published in 1923.

Pullar, Gordon L. "The Quikertarmiut and the Scientist." In *Reckoning with the Dead: The Larson Bay Repatriation and the Smithsonian Institution*, edited by Tamara Bray and Thomas Killion. Washington DC: Smithsonian Institution Press, 1994.

Radinsky, Leonard Burton. "Oldest Horse Brains: More Advanced Than Previously Realized." *Science*, n.s., 194, no. 4265 (1976): 626–27.

———. "A Review of the Rhinocerotoid Family Hyracodontidae (Perissodactyla)." *Bulletin of the AMNH* 136 (1967): 5–43.

Raghavan, M., M. Steinrücken, K. Harris, S. Schiffels, S. Rasmussen, M. DeGiorgio, A. Albrechtsene, et al. "Genomic Evidence for the Pleistocene and Recent Population History of Native Americans." *Science* 349, no. 6250 (2015): aab3884.

Rasmussen, M., S. L. Anzick, M. R. Waters, P. Skoglund, M. DeGiorgio, T. W. Stafford Jr., and S. Rasmussen. "The Genome of a Late Pleistocene Human from a Clovis Burial Site in Western Montana." *Nature* 506, no. 7487 (2014): 225–29.

Rathje, William L., Michael Shanks, and Christopher Witmore. *Archaeology in the Making: Conversations through a Discipline*. London: Routledge, 2013.

Reagan, Albert B., and L. V. W. Walters. "Thunderbird Fights Mimlos-Whale, in Tales from the Hoh and Quileute." *Journal of American Folklore* 46, no. 182 (1933): 297–346.

Reimer, P. J., E. Bard, A. Bayliss, J. W. Beck, P. G. Blackwell, C. B. Ramsey, and C. E. Buck. "IntCal13 and Marine13 Radiocarbon Age Calibration Curves 0–50,000 Years Cal BP." *Radiocarbon* 55, no. 4 (2013): 1869–87.

Reimer, R. W., D. A. Richards, J. R. Southon, S. Talamo, C. S. M. Turney, J. van der Plicht, and C. E. Weyhenmeyer. "IntCal09 and Marine09 Radiocarbon Age Calibration Curves, 0–50,000 Years Cal BP." *Radiocarbon* 51, no. 4 (2009): 1111–50.

Renfrew, Colin, and Paul G. Bahn. *Archaeology: Theories, Methods, and Practice*. London: Thames and Hudson, 1991.

Rick, J. W. "The Character and Context of Highland Preceramic Society." In *Peruvian Prehistory: An Overview of Pre-Inca and Inca Society*, edited by Richard W. Keatinge, 3–40. Cambridge: Cambridge University Press, 1988.

Rigney, Lester-Irabinna. "Internationalism of an Aboriginal or Torres Strait Islander Anticolonial Cultural Critique of Research Methodologies: A Guide to Indigenist Research Methodology and Its Principles." *Wicazo Sa Review* 14, no. 2, special issue, "Emergent Ideas in Native American Studies" (1999): 109–21.

Roberts, F. H. H. *Developments in the Problem of the North American Paleo-Indian*. Washington DC: Smithsonian Institution Press, 1940.

Roberts, R. G., R. Jones, and M. A. Smith. "Thermoluminescence Dating of a 50,000-Year-Old Human Occupation Site in Northern Australia." *Nature* 345 (1990): 153–56.

Robinson, M. "Psychological Decolonization: Getting Back My Indian Soul." Paper presented at the American Academy of Religion, Eastern International Regional, Ottawa, ON, 2010.

Rose, Jerome C., Thomas J. Green, and Victoria D. Green. "NAGPRA Is Forever: Osteology and the Repatriation of Skeletons." *Annual Review of Anthropology* 25, no. 1 (1996): 81–103.

Rowe, M. W., and K. L. Steelman. Comment on "Some Evidence of a Date of First Humans to Arrive in Brazil." *Journal of Archaeological Science* 30, no. 10 (2003): 1349–51.

Rybczynski, N., J. C. Gosse, C. R. Harington, R. A. Wogelius, A. J. Hidy, and M. Buckley. "Mid-Pliocene Warm-Period Deposits in the High Arctic Yield Insight into Camel Evolution." *Nature Communications* 4, no. 1 (2013): 1–9.

Salemme, M. "Zooarqueología y paleoambientes en la región pampeana: Sitio 2 de Arroyo Seco." In *Estado actual de las investigaciones en el sitio 2 de Arroyo Seco (región pampeana, Argentina)*, edited by G. Politis, M. Gutierrez, and C. Scabuzzo. Serie Monográfica INCUAPA 5. Olavarría, 2009.

Sandweiss, D. H. "Early Fishing Societies in Western South America." In *The Handbook of South American Archaeology*, edited by Helaine Silverman and William Isbell, 145–56. New York: Springer, 2008.

Santos, G. M., M. I. Bird, F. Parenti, L. K. Fifield, N. Guidon, and P. A. Hausladen. "A Revised Chronology of the Lowest Occupation Layer of Pedra Furada Rock Shelter, Piauí, Brazil: The Pleistocene Peopling of the Americas." *Quaternary Science Reviews* 22, no. 21 (2003): 2303–10.

Sarnthein, M., T. Kiefer, P. M. Grootes, H. Elderfield, and H. Erlenkeuser. "Warmings in the Far Northwestern Pacific Promoted Pre-Clovis Immigration to America during Heinrich Event 1." *Geology* 34, no. 3 (2006): 141–44.

Scarre, C., and G. Scarre. *The Ethics of Archaeology*. Cambridge: Cambridge University Press, 2006.

Schanfield, M. S. "Immunoglobulin Allotypes (GM and KM) Indicate Multiple Founding Populations of Native Americans: Evidence of at Least Four Migrations to the New World." *Human Biology* 64, no. 3 (1992): 381–402.

Schmidt, Peter R., and Thomas C. Patterson, eds. *Making Alternative Histories: The Practice of Archaeology and History in Non-Western Settings*. Sante Fe NM: School of American Research Press, 1995.

Schultz, A. H. *Biographical Memoir of Aleš Hrdlička, 1869–1943*. National Academy of Sciences, Biographical Memoirs, vol. 23, 1945.

Scupin, R., and C. R. DeCorse. *Anthropology: A Global Perspective*. Boston: Pearson, 2015.

Shields, G. F., K. Hecker, M. I. Voevoda, and J. K. Reed. "Absence of the Asian-Specific Region V Mitochondrial Marker in Native Beringians." *American Journal of Human Genetics* 50, no. 4 (1992): 758–65.

Silcox, M. T., J. I. Bloch, E. J. Sargis, and D. Boyer. "Euarchonta (Dermopetra, Scandentia, Primates)." In *The Rise of Placental Mammals*, edited by Rose Kenneth and J. Davis Archibald, 127–44. Baltimore MD: Johns Hopkins University Press, 2005.

Silko, Leslie Marmon. "Landscape, History, and the Pueblo Imagination." In *The Ecocriticism Reader: Landmarks in Literary Ecology*, edited by Cheryll Glotfelty and Harold Fromm, 264–75. Athens: University of Georgia Press, 1996.

———. *Yellow Woman and a Beauty of the Spirit: Essays on Native American Life Today*. New York: Simon and Schuster, 1997.

Simpson, Leanne. "Oshkimmadiziig, the New People." In *Lighting the Eighth Fire: The Liberation, Resurgence, and Protection of Indigenous Nations*, edited by Leanne Simpson, 13–17. Winnipeg MB: Arbeiter Ring Publishing, 2008.

Sinclair, Raven Peltier. "Indigenous Research in Social Work: The Challenge of Operationalizing Worldview." *Native Social Work Journal* 5 (2003): 117–39.

Sistiaga, A., F. Berna, R. Laursen, and P. Goldberg. "Steroidal Biomarker Analysis of a 14,000 Years Old Putative Human Coprolite from Paisley Cave, Oregon." *Journal of Archaeological Science* 41 (2014): 813–17.

Sium, Aman, and Eric Ritskes. "Speaking Truth to Power: Indigenous Storytelling as an Act of Living Resistance." *Decolonization, Indigeneity, Education and Society* 2, no. 1 (2013): i–x.

Skoglund, P., S. Mallick, M. C. Bortolini, N. Chennagiri, T. Hünemeier, M. L. Petzl-Erler, F. M. Salzano, et al. "Genetic Evidence for Two Founding Populations of the Americas." *Nature* 525, no. 7567 (2015): 104.

Smay, D., and G. Armelagos. "Galileo Wept: A Critical Assessment of the Use of Race in Forensic Anthropology." *Transforming Anthropology* 9, no. 2 (2000): 19–29.

Smith, C., and G. Jackson. "Decolonizing Indigenous Archaeology: Developments from Down Under." *American Indian Quarterly* 30, no. 3 (2006): 311–49.

Smith, C., and H. M. Wobst, eds. *Indigenous Archaeologies: Decolonising Theory and Practice*. New York: Routledge, 2004.

Smith, D. G., C. M. Vullo, and D. C. Wallace. "Asian Affinities and Continental Radiation of the Four Founding Native American mtDNAs." *American Journal of Human Genetics* 53 (1993): 563–90.

Smith, Linda Tuhiwai. "Building Research Capability in the Pacific, for the Pacific, and by Pacific Peoples." In *Researching the Pacific and Indigenous Peoples: Issues and Perspectives*, edited by Tupeni L. Baba et al., 4–16. Auckland: Centre for Pacific Studies, the University of Auckland, 2004.

————. *Decolonizing Methodologies: Research and Indigenous Peoples*. London: Zed Books. 1999.

Smith, T. M., P. Tafforeau, D. J. Reid, R. Grün, S. Eggins, M. Boutakiout, and J. J. Hublin. "Earliest Evidence of Modern Human Life History in North African Early *Homo sapiens*." *Proceedings of the National Academy of Sciences* 104, no. 15 (2007): 6128–33.

Sondaar, P. Y. "Faunal Evolution and the Mammalian Bio Stratigraphy of Java: The Early Evolution of Man with Special Emphasis on Southeast Asia and Africa." *Courier Forschungsinstitut Senckenberg, Frankfurt am Main* 69 (1984): 219–35.

Sondaar, P. Y., R. Elhurg, G. K. Holmeijer, F. Martini, M. Sanges, A. Spaan, and H. de Visser. "The Human Colonization of Sardinia: A Late Pleistocene Human Fossil from Corbeddu Cave." *Académie de Science*, Library of France, 1995.

Speth, J. D., K. Newlander, A. A. White, A. K. Lemke, and L. E. Anderson. "Early Paleoindian Big-Game Hunting in North America: Provisioning or Politics?" *Quaternary International* 30, no. 285 (2010): 111–39.

Sprague, D. N., and R. P. Frye. *The Genealogy of the First Metis Nation: The Development and Dispersal of the Red River Settlement, 1820–1900*. Winnipeg MB: Pemmican, 1983.

Standen, V. G. "Temprana complejidad funeraria de la cultura Chinchorro (norte de Chile)." *Latin American Antiquity* 8, no. 2 (1997): 134–56.

Stanford, Dennis J., and Bruce A. Bradley. *Across Atlantic Ice: The Origin of America's Clovis Culture*. Berkeley: University of California Press, 2012.

Steele, J., and G. Politis. "AMS ^{14}C Dating of Early Human Occupation of Southern South America." *Journal of Archaeological Science* 36, no. 2 (2009): 419–29.

Steeves, P. F. "Clovis and Folsom, Indigenous Occupation Prior To." In *Encyclopedia of Global Archaeology*, 2nd ed., edited by Claire Smith, 1508–13. New York: Springer, 2019.

————. "Decolonizing Indigenous Histories: Pleistocene Archaeology Sites of the Western Hemisphere." PhD dissertation, State University of New York at Binghamton, 2015.

————. "Decolonizing the Past and Present of the Western Hemisphere (the Americas)." *Archaeologies* 11, no. 1 (2015): 42–69.

Stone, A. C., and M. Stoneking. "Ancient DNA from a Pre-Columbian Amerindian Population." *American Journal of Physical Anthropology* 92, no. 4 (1993): 463–71.

————. "mtDNA Analysis of a Prehistoric Oneota Population: Implications for the Peopling of the New World." *American Journal of Human Genetics* 62, no. 5 (1998): 1153–70.

Strasser, T. F., C. Runnels, K. Wegmann, E. Panagopoulou, F. Mccoy, C. Digregorio, P. Karkanas, et al. "Dating Palaeolithic Sites in Southwestern Crete, Greece." *Journal of Quaternary Science* 26, no. 5 (2011): 553–60.

Stringer, C. "Modern Human Origins: Progress and Prospects: Philosophical Transactions of the Royal Society of London B." *Biological Sciences* 357, no. 1420 (2002): 563–79.

Stringer, C., and J. Galway-Witham. "Palaeoanthropology: On the Origin of Our Species." *Nature* 546, no. 7657 (2017): 212–14.

Stuiver, M., and H. E. Suess. "On the Relationship between Radiocarbon Dates and True Sample Ages." *Radiocarbon* 8, (1966): 534–40.

Tafoya, T. "Finding Harmony: Balancing Traditional Values with Western Science in Therapy." *Canadian Journal of Native Education* 21 (1995): 7–27.

TallBear, Kim. *Native American DNA: Tribal Belonging and the False Promise of Genetic Science*. Minneapolis: University of Minnesota Press, 2013.

Tamm, E., T. Kivisild, M. Reidla, M. Metspalu, D. G. Smith, C. J. Mulligan, C. M. Bravi, et al. "Beringian Standstill and Spread of Native American Founders." *PLoS ONE* 2, no. 9 (2007): e829.

Tankersley, K. B. "The Concept of Clovis and the Peopling of North America." In *The Settlement of the American Continents: A Multidisciplinary Approach to Human Biogeography*, edited by C. Michael Barton, Geoffrey A. Clark, David R. Yesner, and Georges A. Pearson, 49–63. Tucson: University of Arizona Press, 2004.

Tankersley, K. B., and C. A. Munson. "Comments on the Meadowcroft Rockshelter Radiocarbon Chronology and the Recognition of Coal Contaminants." *American Antiquity* 57, no. 2 (1992): 321–26.

Tankersley, K. B., C. A. Munson, and D. Smith. "Recognition of Bituminous Coal Contaminants in Radiocarbon Samples." *American Antiquity* 52, no. 2 (1987): 318–30.

Taylor, D. C. "The Wilsall Excavations: An Exercise in Frustration." *Proceedings of the Montana Academy of Sciences* 29, no. 14 (1969): 7–150.

Taylor, R. E., D. L. Kirner, J. R. Southon, and J. C. Chatters. "Radiocarbon Dates of Kennewick Man." *Science* 280, no. 5637 (1998): 1171–72.

Teague, L. S. "Prehistory and the Traditions of the O'odham and Hopi." *Kiva* 58, no. 4 (1993): 435–54.

Thomas, D. H. *Skull Wars: Kennewick Man, Archaeology, and the Battle for Native American Identity*. New York: Basic Books, 2001.

Thorne, A., R. Grün, G. Mortimer, N. A. Spooner, J. J. Simpson, M. McCulloch, L. Taylor, et al. "Australia's Oldest Human Remains: Age of the Lake Mungo 3 Skeleton." *Journal of Human Evolution* 36, no. 6 (1999): 591–612.

Thorne, A. G., and M. H. Wolpoff. "The Multiregional Evolution of Humans." *Scientific American* 266, no. 4 (1992): 76–83.

Tierney, P. *Darkness in El Dorado: How Scientists and Journalists Devastated the Amazon*. New York: W. W. Norton and Company, 2001.

Toledo, M. J. "Geo-archeology of the Pleistocene–Holocene Transition in the Northeastern Pampan (Buenos Aires, Argentina): Historical, Stratigraphic and Taphonomic

Revision, Perspectives for the First Settlement." PhD dissertation, Muséum national d'histoire naturelle, Paris, 2009.

Torroni, A., T. G. Schurr, M. F. Cabell, M. D. Brown, J. V. Neel, M. Larsen, D. G. Smith, et al. "Asian Affinities and Continental Radiation of the Four Founding Native American mtDNAS." *American Journal of Human Genetics* 53, no. 3 (1993): 563.

Torroni, A., T. G. Schurr, C. C. Yang, E. J. Szathmary, R. C. Williams, M. S. Schanfield, G. A. Troup, et al. "Native American Mitochondrial DNA Analysis Indicates That the Amerind and the Nadene Populations Were Founded by Two Independent Migrations." *Genetics* 130, no. 1 (1992): 153–62.

Trask, Haunani-Kay. *From a Native Daughter: Colonialism and Sovereignty in Hawai'i.* Revised edition. Honolulu: University of Hawai'i Press, 1999.

Trigger, B. G. *A History of Archaeological Thought.* Cambridge: Cambridge University Press, 1989.

Trinkaus, E., O. Moldovan, S. Milota, A. Bîlgăr, L. Sarcina, S. Athreya, S. E. Bailey, et al. "An Early Modern Human from the Peştera cu Oase, Romania." *Proceedings of the National Academy of Sciences* 100, no. 20 (2003): 11231–36.

Tsutsumi, T. "The Dynamics of Obsidian Use by the Microblade Industries of the Terminal Late Palaeolithic." *Quaternary Research* (Japan Association for Quaternary Research) 46, no. 3 (2007): 179–86.

Tune, J. W., M. R. Waters, K. A. Schmalle, L. R. DeSantis, and G. D. Kamenov. "Assessing the Proposed Pre–Last Glacial Maximum Human Occupation of North America at Coats-Hines-Litchy, Tennessee, and Other Sites." *Quaternary Science Reviews* 186 (2018): 47–59.

Turnbull, D. "Territorializing/Decolonizing South American Prehistory: Pedra Furada and the Cerutti Mastodon." *Tapuya: Latin American Science, Technology and Society* 2, no. 1 (2019): 127–48.

Underhill, P. A., G. Passarino, A. A. Lin, P. Shen, M. M. Lahr, R. A. Foley, P. J. Oefner, et al. "The Phylogeography of Y Chromosome Binary Haplotypes and the Origins of Modern Human Populations." *Annals of Human Genetics* 65, no. 1 (2001): 43–62.

Urrego, G. C., and T. Van der Hammen. "Investigaciones arqueológicas en los abrigos rocosos del Tequendama: 12.000 años de historia del hombre y su medio ambiente en la altiplanicie de Bogotá; With an Extensive English Abstract, Archaeological Investigations in the Tequendama Rock Shelters: 12,000 Years of History of Man and His Environment on the High Plain of Bogotá." *Fondo de Promoción de la Cultura del Banco Popular* (1977).

Van Valen, L. M., and R. E. Sloan. "The Earliest Primates." *Science* 150, no. 3697 (1965): 743–45.

Vries, Hessel de. "Variation in Concentration of Radiocarbon with Time and Location on Earth." *Proceedings of the Koninklijke Nederlandse Akademie van Wetenschappen Series B* 61 (1958): 94–102.

Wagamese, R. *Embers: One Ojibway's Meditations.* Madeira Park BC: D and M Publishers, 2016.

Waguespack, N. M., and T. A. Surovell. "Clovis Hunting Strategies, or How to Make Out on Plentiful Resources." *American Antiquity* 68, no. 2 (2003): 333–52.

Wallace, Douglas C., and Antonio Torroni. "American Indian Prehistory as Written in the Mitochondrial DNA: A Review." *Human Biology* 64, no. 3 (1992): 403–16.

Wallace, Steven C., and Richard C. Hulbert. "A New Machairodont from the Palmetto Fauna (Early Pliocene) of Florida, with Comments on the Origin of the Smilodontini (Mammalia, Carnivora, Felidae)." *PLoS ONE* 8, no. 3 (2013). https://journals.plos.org/plosone/article?id=10.1371/journal.pone.0056173.

Wang, H., B. Bai, J. Meng, and Y. Wang. "Earliest Known Unequivocal Rhinocerotoid Sheds New Light on the Origin of Giant Rhinos and Phylogeny of Early Rhinocerotoids." *Scientific Reports* 6, no. 39,607 (2016): 1–9.

Wang, S., C. M. Lewis Jr., M. Jakobsson, S. Ramachandran, N. Ray, G. Bedoya, W. Rojas, et al. "Genetic Variation and Population Structure in Native Americans." *PLOS Genetics* 3, no. 11 (2007): e185.

Ward, R. H., B. L. Frazier, K. Dew-Jager, and S. Pääbo. "Extensive Mitochondrial Diversity within a Single Amerindian Tribe." *Proceedings of the National Academy of Sciences* 88, no. 19 (1991): 8720–24.

Watanabe, S., W. E. F. Ayta, H. Hamaguchi, N. Guidon, E. S. La Salvia, S. Maranca, and O. Baffa Filho. "Some Evidence of a Date of First Humans to Arrive in Brazil." *Journal of Archaeological Science* 30, no. 3 (2003): 351–54.

Watanabe, S. L. *Tensions in Rhetorics of Presence and Performance.* Publication No. 3522607, University of Utah, 2012.

Waters, M. R., S. L. Forman, T. A. Jennings, L. C. Nordt, S. G. Driese, J. M. Feinberg, J. L. Keene, et al. "The Buttermilk Creek Complex and the Origins of Clovis at the Debra L. Friedkin Site, Texas." *Science* 331, no. 6024 (2011): 1599–1603.

Waters, M. R., S. L. Forman, T. W. Stafford, and J. Foss. "Geoarchaeological Investigations at the Topper and Big Pine Tree Sites, Allendale County, South Carolina." *Journal of Archaeological Science* 36, no. 7 (2009): 1300–1311.

Waters, M. R., and T. W. Stafford. "Redefining the Age of Clovis: Implications for the Peopling of the Americas." *Science* 315, no. 5815 (2007): 1122–26.

Waters, M. R., T. W. Stafford, H. G. McDonald, C. Gustafson, M. Rasmussen, E. Cappellini, J. V. Olsen, et al. "Pre-Clovis Mastodon Hunting 13,800 Years Ago at the Manis Site, Washington." *Science* 334, no. 6054 (2011): 351–53.

Waters, Michael R., Thomas W. Stafford, H. Gregory McDonald, Carl Gustafson, Morten Rasmussen, Enrico Cappellini, Jesper V. Olsen, et al. "Pre-Clovis Mastodon Hunting 13,800 Years Ago at the Manis Site, Washington." *Science* 334, no. 6054 (2011): 351–53.

Watkins, J. E. "Artefacts, Archaeologists and American Indians." *Public Archaeology* 4 (2005): 187–91.

———. "Communicating Archaeology: Words to the Wise." *Journal of Social Archaeology* 6, no. 1 (2006): 100–118.

Watson, T. "News Feature: Is Theory about Peopling of the Americas a Bridge Too Far?" *Proceedings of the National Academy of Sciences* 114, no. 22 (2017): 5554–57.

Weiner, S. *Microarchaeology: Beyond the Visible Archaeological Record.* Cambridge: Cambridge University Press, 2010.

Wenke, Robert J., and Deborah Olszewski. *Patterns in Prehistory: Humankind's First Three Million Years.* New York: Oxford University Press, 2007.

West, R. M., M. R. Dawson, and J. H. Hutchison. "Fossils from the Paleogene Eureka Sound Formation, NWT, Canada: Occurrence, Climatic and Paleogeographic Implications." *Paleontology and Plate Tectonics.* Milwaukee Public Museum Special Publications in Biology and Geology 2 (1977): 77–93.

Wheat, A. D. "Survey of Professional Opinions Regarding the Peopling of the Americas." *SAA Archaeological Record* 12, no. 2 (2012): 10–14.

Whitbeck, L. B., G. W. Adams, D. R. Hoyt, and X. Chen. "Conceptualizing and Measuring Historical Trauma among American Indian People." *American Journal of Community Psychology* 33, no. 3–4 (2004): 119–30.

Whitley, D. S., and R. I. Dorn. "New Perspectives on the Clovis vs. Pre-Clovis Controversy." *American Antiquity* 58, no. 4 (1993): 626–47.

Wilcox, M. "Saving Indigenous Peoples from Ourselves: Separate but Equal Archaeology Is Not Scientific Archaeology." *American Antiquity* 75, no. 2 (2010): 221–27.

Wilke, P. J., J. J. Flenniken, and T. L. Ozbun. "Clovis Technology at the Anzick Site, Montana." *Journal of California and Great Basin Anthropology* 13, no. 2 (1991): 242–72.

Wilson, A. C., and R. L. Cann. "The Recent African Genesis of Humans." *Scientific American* 266, no. 4 (1992): 68–75.

Wilson, A. C., and E. Taylor. *Remember This! Dakota Decolonization and the Eli Taylor Narratives.* Lincoln: University of Nebraska Press, 2005.

Wilson, Shawn. *Research Is Ceremony: Indigenous Research Methods.* Halifax NS: Fernwood Publishing, 2008.

———. "What Is an Indigenous Research Methodology?" *Canadian Journal of Native Education* 25, no. 2 (2001): 175–79.

Wilson, Waziyatawin Angela. "Indigenous Knowledge Recovery Is Indigenous Empowerment." *American Indian Quarterly* 28, no. 3–4 (2004): 359–72.

Wiseman, Frederick. *Reclaiming the Ancestors: Decolonizing a Taken Prehistory of the Far Northeast.* Hanover NH: University Press of New England, 2005.

Wobst, Martin H. "Power to the Indigenous Past and Present, or, The Theory and Method behind Archaeological Theory and Method." In *Indigenous Archaeologies: A Reader on Decolonization,* edited by M. Bruchac, S. M. Hart, and H. M. Wobst, 17–27. Walnut Creek CA: Left Coast Press, 2010.

———. "The Three 'R's,' Rights, Respect, and Representation: Understanding the Present, Honoring the Past; Indigenous People and Archaeology." In *Indigenous People and Archaeology: Honouring the Past, Discussing the Present, Building for the Future;*

Proceedings of the 32nd Annual Chacmool Conference, edited by T. Peck, E. Siegfried, and G. Oetelaar. Archaeological Association of the University of Calgary, Saskatchewan, 2003.

Wolpoff, M. H., J. Hawks, and R. Caspari. "Multiregional, Not Multiple Origins." *American Journal of Physical Anthropology* 112, no. 1 (2000): 129–36.

Wylie, Alison. "Making Alternative Histories: Epistemic Disunity and Political Integrity." In *Making Alternative Histories: The Practice of Archaeology and History in Non-Western Settings*, edited by Peter R. Schmidt and Thomas C. Patterson, 225–72. Sante Fe NM: School of American Research Press, 1995.

Yazzie, Robert. "Indigenous Peoples and Postcolonial Colonialism." In *Reclaiming Indigenous Voice and Vision*, edited by M. Battiste, 39–49. Vancouver: University of British Columbia Press, 2000.

Yellen, J. E., A. S. Brooks, E. Cornelissen, M. J. Mehlman, and K. Stewart. "A Middle Stone Age Worked Bone Industry from Katanda, Upper Semliki Valley, Zaire." *Science* 268, no. 5210 (1995): 553–56.

Yellow Bird, Michael. "What We Want to Be Called: Indigenous Peoples' Perspectives on Racial and Ethnic Identity Labels." *American Indian Quarterly* 23, no. 2 (1999): 1–21.

Yellowhorn, Eldon. "Awakening Internalist Archaeology in the Aboriginal World." PhD dissertation, McGill University, 2002.

———. "Regarding the American Paleolithic." *Canadian Journal of Archaeology / Journal Canadien d'Archéologie* 27, no. 1 (2003): 62–73.

Yellow Horse Brave Heart, Maria, and Lemyra M. Debruyn. "The American Indian Holocaust: Healing Historical Unresolved Grief." *American Indian and Alaska Native Mental Health Research* 8, no. 2 (1998): 60–82. American Indian and Alaska Mental Health Programs, University of Colorado at Denver and Health Sciences Center.

Yesner, D. R. "Moose Hunters of the Boreal Forest? A Re-examination of Subsistence Patterns in the Western Subarctic." *Arctic* 42, no. 2 (1989): 97–108.

Yokoyama, Y., K. Lambeck, P. De Deckker, P. Johnston, and L. K. Fifield. "Timing of the Last Glacial Maximum from Observed Sea-Level Minima." *Nature* 406, no. 6797 (2000): 713.

Zhu, Z., R. Dennell, W. Huang, Y. Wu, S. Qiu, S. Yang, Z. Rao, et al. "Hominin Occupation of the Chinese Loess Plateau Since about 2.1 Million Years Ago." *Nature* 559, no. 7715 (2018): 608–12.

Zilhão, J., and E. Trinkaus. "Portrait of the Artist as a Child: The Gravettian Human Skeleton from the Abrigo do Lagar Velho and Its Archaeological Context." *Trabalhos de Arqueologia* 22 (2002): 609.

INDEX

Page numbers in italics indicate illustrations.

American Antiquity, 113, 118

the Ancient One (Kennewick Man): burial site, 37; embedded colonialism seen in treatment of, 37–45; facial reconstructions of, 37, 39–45; images of, *41*, *42*, *43*, *44*, *46*, *47*; lawsuit attempting to block repatriation of, 38–40, 45; NAGPRA tribal repatriation claims filed for, 37–38; radiocarbon dating of, 38

Anderson, P. M., 65

anthropology: burial sites protection and repatriation, 32–36; changes needed in, 53–54, 57, 182–83; cognitive imperialism of, 180; decolonizing, 182–83; development of, 28–31; discrimination and racism in, 27–32, 36–45; erasing and dehumanizing identities and histories, 28, 30–31, 48–49, 51–53, 57, 187; Indigenous scholars critiquing, 180; lack of Indigenous voices in, 31; molecular anthropology, 152–60; ongoing colonialism within, 36–45, 51–54, 180, 187; repercussions for scholars supporting pre-Clovis dates, 52; social and political power of, 48–54, 187; subfields of, 29. *See also* academia

Anzick site (MT), 152–53

Appropriated Pasts (McNiven and Russell), 27

archaeological sites: areas of study informing, 59, 86; material remains, 12–13, 59, 79, 81, 85, 91, 104, 163; methods for determining human presence at, 79, 81; methods of discovery, 91; naming practices, 112; reevaluating and retesting of, 93–94; scientific criteria for legitimizing, 91–94, 104; scientific critiquing process, 94, 119–21, 172; stories told by, xxii, 9–10, 91. *See also* dating methods

archaeological sites (Pleistocene): areas of study informing, 59, 86; bias against pre-Clovis dates for, 2–5, 59–60, 85, 90, 94–98, 119–21, 126, 127, 172, 175, 177–79; biases impacting interpretations of, 14, 59–60; changing attitudes regarding pre-Clovis sites, 12, 13; databases of, 95, 98–99; in the Eastern Hemisphere, 31, 79–80, 81–85, 100–102, 192–94; expanding understanding of, 81; funding for, 126, 127, 179; further research needed in, 127–28, 180–81, 191–92; maps of, *84*, *92*, *132*; needed framing on global scale, 58–59, 95, 98–99; reevaluating and retesting of, xxii–xxiii, 93–94; role of oral traditions in understanding, 162–63; scientific criteria for legitimizing, 91–94, 104; stories told by, xxii, 9–10, 16, 91, 186–87

archaeological sites (Pleistocene, North America), 199–207; Bluefish Caves site (YT), 75, *93*, 99, 121–22, 201; Cactus Hill site (VA), *93*, 113–15, 177–78, 202; Calico site (CA), *92*, 100, 124–26, 200; Cerutti Mastodon site (CA), xxiii, *92*, 100, 118–21, 126, 179–80, 200; Coats-Hines-Litchy site (TN), xxiii, *93*, 99, 104–6, 163, 204; Debra L. Friedkin site (TX), *93*, 117–18, 203; Hebior Mammoth site (WI), *93*, 115–16, 205; Little Salt Springs site (FL), *93*, 107–8, 204; Manis Mastodon site (FL), *93*, 99, 109–10, 114, 205; maps of, *92*; Meadowcroft Rockshelter site (PA), 75–76, *93*, 112–13, 114, 177–78, 202; mummification practices at, 131–33; needed framing on global scale, 58–59, 98–99; Page-Ladson site (FL), *93*, 99, 108, 109, 205; Paisley Caves site (OR), *93*, 110–12, 177–78, 205; reevaluating and retesting of, 93–94, 99;

La Sena site (NE), xxiii, *93*, 116–17, 163, 179, 202; Topper site (SC), *92*, 99, 107, 177–78, 200; Valsequillo Reservoir site (Mexico), *92*, 122–24, 199, 200

archaeological sites (Pleistocene, South America), xxiv–xxv, 214–17; Alice Boer site (Brazil), *132*, 136, 141–42, 215; Arroyo Seco 2 site (Argentina), *133*, 147–48, 216; map of, *132–33*; Monte Verde sites (Chile), xxiv–xxv, 75, *132–33*, 145–47, 177–78, 179, 214, 216; mummification practices, 131–33; needed framing on global scale, 58–59, 98–99; Pedra Furada site (Brazil), *132*, 136, 137–39, 140, 214; Pikimachay site (Peru), *132*, 144–45, 214; possible regional areas, 135–36; reevaluation and retesting of, 99; Sítio do Meio site (Brazil), *132*, 136, 141, 214; Taima-Taima site (Venezuela), *133*, 142–43, 215; Tibitó site (Colombia), *133*, 143–44, 217; Toca de Tira Peia site (Brazil), *132*, 136, 137, 140, 214; Vale da Pedra Furada site (Brazil), *132*, 136, 139–40, 214

archaeology: academic training, 54, 58; archaeological cultural complexes, 12–13; bias against pre-Clovis dates in, 2–5, 59–60, 94–98, 119–21, 127, 129, 175, 177–79; burial sites protection and repatriation, 32–36; changes needed in, 53–54, 57, 74, 181–85; community-centered research, xx, 36, 53; critical discussions needed in, 169, 172, 182–85; decolonizing frameworks, xxiv, xxv–xxvi, 18, 167, 176–80, 182–85; dehumanizing and erasing Indigenous people, 27–28, 30–31; development of, 28–31; differentiating artifacts from geofacts, 59; discrimination and racism in, xx, xxiii, 27–32, 36–45; erasing and dehumanizing identities and histories,

xviii–xx, xxiii, 48–49, 51–53, 57, 96–97, 158–59, 174–76, 187; erasing Indigenous ancestral homeland links, xix–xx, xxiii, 61, 96–97, 174–76, 186; future areas of study in, 127–28; holistic approach to, 167, 185; Indigenous voices expanding, 16, 18, 19–24, 34, 53, 162–63; lack of Indigenous voices in, 31, 35–36, 54, 98, 174; ongoing colonialism within, 36–45, 129, 171, 175–80, 183–84, 187; open-mindedness needed in, 85, 99–100, 121, 127, 163, 170; oral traditions broadening, 10, 16, 19, 162–63, 167; Paleolithic studies needed in, 58–59, 99; protests against NAGPRA in, 34–35; pyroepistemology cleansing, 184; relation to anthropology, 29; repercussions for supporting pre-Clovis dates, 14–15, 52, 90, 119–21, 170, 172, 178–79; scientific critiquing process, 119–21, 152, 172; social and political power of, 20, 45–54, 171, 173–74, 176–77, 187; terminology changes needed in, 102–3; use of modern place names, 61–62

Ardelean, Ciprian, 127

Arias, Leonardo, 153–55, 156

Arnaud, B., 82

Arroyo del Vizcaíno site (Uruguay), *132*, 214

Arroyo Seco Sitio 2 site (Argentina), *133*, 147–48, 216

artifacts: differences in interpretation of, 163; holistic framework needed for interpreting, 163; in material culture, 12–13; method of differentiating geofacts from, 59; signaling human presence, 79, 81; used to legitimize archaeological sites, xxiv, 79, 81, 91, 104; varying concentrations of, 85. *See also* bone tool technologies; stone tool technologies

Brown, Michael D., 155
Bruwelheide, Karin, 40, 42
Bryan, Alan, 2, 17, 99, 142, 149
Buikstra, J. E., 40
burial sites: Anzick site, 152–53; Arroyo
    Seco 2 site, 147; Chinchorro mummies,
    131–33; in Egypt, 131, 133; Little Salt
    Springs site, 108; mummification sites,
    131–33; protection of, 32–36; Spirit Cave
    site, 131, 133
Burke, A., 75, 121–22
Burnham site (OK), *92*, 201
Burning Tree site (OH), *93*, 205
Bush, George H. W., 34
Bush-Steeves, Reva Leona (Native
    American-European), xvii
butchering sites: Arroyo Seco 2 site
    (Argentina), 147–48; Bluefish Caves
    (YT) site, 121–22; Coats-Hines (TN)
    site, 105–6; Hebior (WI) site, 115–16;
    Manis Mastodon (WA) site, 110; Monte
    Verde (Chile) sites, 146; Page-Ladson
    (FL) site, 109; Paisley Caves (OR) site,
    111; Schaefer (WI) site, 115–16; Tibitó
    site (Colombia), 143; Vale da Pedra
    Furada site (Brazil), 139; Valsequillo
    Reservoir (Mexico) sites, 123. *See also*
    hunting
Buttermilk Creek Complex site (TX), *93*,
    117–18, 203
Byrd, Jody (Chickasaw), 15
Byzovaya site (Russia), *84*, 194

Cactus Hill site (VA), *93*, 113–15, 177–78, 202
Cajune, Julie, 174
Caldeirão de Rodrigues site (Brazil), *132*, 214
calibrated radiocarbon dating, 100, *101*
Calico site (CA), *92*, 100, 124–26, 200
Callao Cave site (Philippines), *84*, 193
Camacho, Armenta, 123

camelid species: intercontinental migrations
    of, 65–67; at the Page-Ladson (FL) site,
    109; at the Paisley Caves (OR) site, 111;
    in Pleistocene landscapes, 10, 67, 70; at
    Valsequillo Reservoir sites, 123
Canales, Leon, 145
Cann, R. L., 85–86
Cannon, M. D., 105
Capcha, Yataco, 145
carbon dating technique. *See* radiocarbon
    dating techniques
Cashman, Katherine, 166–67
Cators Cove site (MD), *93*, 202
Caulapan site (Mexico), *92*, 201
Cavalli-Sforza, Luca, 157
Cayuse people, 164–65
El Ceibo site (Argentina), *133*, 216
Cerro Tres Tetas site (Argentina), *133*, 135, 217
Cerutti, Richard A., 119
Cerutti Mastodon site (CA), xxiii, *92*, 100,
    118–21, 126, 179–80, 200
cervid fossils *(Blastocerus dichotomus)*,
    137–38
Channel Islands (CA), *83*
Charlie Lake site (BC), 155
Chatters, James, 39–40, *41*, 45
Chauvet Cave site (France), *84*, 194
Cheh, Jiwoong, *44*
Chesrow site (WI), *93*, 206
Chester, S. G., 71
Childe, Gordon, 12
Chilisa, Bagele, 23, 177
Chinchihuapi site (Chile), *132*, 215
Chinchorro mummies (Atacama Desert,
    Chile), 131–33
Chiquihuite cave site (Mexico), 127
Chishaawaamishtikushiiyuu, 7
Chlachula, Jiri, 58, 99
Cincinnati Museum of Natural History, 3
Cinmar site (VA), *93*, 202

Demere, Thomas, 118–19

Denisovan Cave site (Siberia), 87

Denisovans, xviii, 1, 87–88, 89

Denton, David, 7

Deter-Wolf, Aaron, 106

diatoms, 123

Dillehay, Tom: on Aleš Hrdlička's legacy, 30; on the Alice Boer site, 141–42; on the Beringia migration route, 52; on bias against pre-Clovis sites, 94–95; on the Clovis First hypothesis, 146; on earlier time frames for initial peopling, 2, 17, 134, 149; on the Monte Verde sites, 75, 146; *The Settlement of the Americas*, 95; on the Tibitó site, 143–44

Dincauze, D. F., 24

Diring Yuriakh site (Siberia), *84*, 193

discrimination and racism: within academia, xxv, 15, 18, 55; within anthropology, 27–32, 37–45; within archaeology, xx, xxiii, 27–32, 36–45; decolonization confronting, xxv, 15, 18, 55, 182, 183; within physical anthropology, 37–45; social and political impacts of, 15, 18, 48–52, 171; within Western knowledge production, xxiii, 15, 48–52, 171

Dixon, James, 95

Dmanisi site (Georgia), *84*, 192

Dolni Vestonice site (Czech Republic), *84*, 194

Dominguez-Rodrigo, Manuel, 81

Donahue, J., 75, 113

Downing, Roger, 45

Doxtater, Michael, 22

Driese, Steven G., 118

Duran, Eduardo, 181

Dutchess Quarry Cave site (NY), *93*, 205

Dutton site (CO), *93*, 116, 203

Duvall, James, 126

eco-functional theory, 134

Effigy Mounds National Monument, 34

Eighth Fire, xxv, 26, 184, 188, 189

environments and ecosystems: during glacial events, 64–65; impacts on cultural identities, 11, 58; impacts on cultural practices, 11, 58, 135; impacts on migrations, xxi, 11, 58, 60, 171, 174–75; during interglacial events, 63–65, 75, 175; during the Pleistocene, 60, 63–65, 75, 174–75; relationality of, xx–xxi, 23, 58; subsistence patterns adapted to, 11, 133–34. *See also* land (ancestral homelands)

Eocene period, 67, 70–72

epistemologies: of agnotology, xix, 184; in archaeological studies, 23, 162–63; definition of Indigenous, 21; impact of decolonization on, 20, 167, 180, 185–86; pyroepistemology, xxv, 20, 184, 188; role of critical thinking, 9. *See also* knowledge production; worldviews

Eppley Rock Shelter site (OH), *93*, 205

Erodes, Richard, 31

Erq El-Ahmar site (Israel), *84*, 192

ESR (electron spin resonance) dating technique, 138

eugenics movement, 29, 32

Eve of Naharon site (Mexico), *93*, 206

extinct species: at the Arroyo Seco 2 site, 147; extinctions of, 74; images of, *68, 69, 70, 73*; intercontinental migrations of, 65–67; linked to oral traditions, 10, 163–66; at the Little Salt Springs site, 108; at the Page-Ladson site, 109; at the Paisley Caves site, 111; "Riddle Me This," 77–78; at the Taima-Taima site, 142–43; understanding initial peopling through, 73–74; at the Valsequillo Reservoir sites, 123. *See also* mammoths; mastodons

human evolution: and emergence of behavior, 79; expanding understandings of, 30–31; knowledge gaps, 89; multiregional theory, 85, 86–90; other truths, 4–5; out-of-Africa replacement theory, 85–86. *See also* migrations (human)

humans (archaic): Denisovans, xviii, 1, 87–88, 89; dispersal of, 1, 70, 75, 79–80, 82–85; diverse ecosystems adapted to, xviii, 75; evolutionary debates, 71, 72, 85–90; gene flow between other hominins and, 86–88; *Homo erectus*, xviii, 1, 75, 85; morphology of, 89; Neanderthals, xviii, 1, 79–80, 85–89

humans (early modern): archaeological bias concerning, 57; dispersal of, 1, 70, 75, 79, 81–85; diverse ecosystems adapted to, xviii, 63–64, 75, 133–34; evolutionary debates, 30–31, 71, 72, 85–90; expanding evolutionary time frames, 30–31, 124; gene flow between other hominins and, 86–88; open-water crossings, 14, 80, 81–83, 90. *See also* migrations (human)

humans (modern): behavior traits identifying, 80–81; dispersal of, 79, 81–85; diverse ecosystems adapted to, 133–34; emergence of behavior traits, 79; evolutionary debates, 30–31, 85–90; gene flow between other hominins and, 86–88; morphology of, 87, 89. *See also* migrations (human)

hunter-gatherer subsistence strategy, xx, 11, 133, 134

hunting: assumptions regarding, xx, 11, 73–74, 134; big game hunting, 11, 73–74, 110, 134; in the "Clovis hunter overkill" hypothesis, 73–74; Clovis tools as technology for, 3, 13; in linear evolution,

29. *See also* butchering sites; mammoths; mastodons; stone tool technologies

Hutchings, Richard, 36

Idle No More movement, 50

Illinoisan glaciation, *66*

Indigenous Methodologies (Kovach), 18

Indigenous Paleolithic Database of the Americas (IPDBA), 99, 101, 127

Indigenous people: ancestral links to homelands, xvii, 5–8, 16, 25–26, 31, 48–53, 96–97, 187–88; commonalities in worldviews and cultures, xx–xxi, 15; defined, xxvii, 15; disease and genocide decimating populations, 158, 159, 161; diversity in subsistence patterns, 133–34; diversity in worldviews and culture, xx; genetic diversity among, 154–56, 158–59; genetic links between ancient and contemporary, 151; genetic sampling datasets, 151–52, 153–54; linguistic diversity among, 161–62; lobbying for burial sites protection, 32–36; misrepresentations of, 49–52; of the Northwest Amazon, 154–55; relationality, xx–xxi, 16, 22–23, 31, 58, 163, 186, 189; settler identifiers for, 102–3. *See also* colonialism and colonization; cultural identity; cultural practices; histories (Indigenous); oral traditions

Indigenous scholars: community-centered research of, xx, 36, 53; expanding Western archaeology, 22–24, 54, 163; holistic approach, 163, 185; increasing numbers of, 53; opportunities of genetics for, 160; privileging Indigenous knowledge, xviii, 2; and pyroepistemology, 20; role in decolonizing, 15–16, 18, 19–22, 180, 182, 183, 184. *See also* research (Indigenous)

Inouye, Daniel K., 33

interglacial events: Beringia landmass during, *63*, 65, *66*, 75; environmental conditions during, 63–65, 75; map of, *63*; migration routes during, 90, 191; overview of, *65*; Sangamon interglaciation, 64, *66*, 123

Iowa repatriation claims, 32

Irtysh River site (Siberia), *84*, 194

Irwin-Williams, Cynthia, 124

Jackson, Gary, 91

Jack Wade Creek site (AK), *92*, 201

Jaguar Cave site (ID), *93*, 206

James Bay Cree, xvii, 6, 7

Jantz, Richard L., 38

Jebel Faya site (UAE), *84*, 193

Jebel Irhoud site (Morocco), 89

Jenkins, Dennis, 111–12

Jennings, T. A., 118

Jensen site (NB), *93*, 203

El Jobo stone tool technology, 142–43

Johnson, Michael, 114

Johnson site (TN), *93*, 204

Jones, George, 4

El Jordan site (Colombia), *133*, 215

Journal of Archaeological Science, 118

Joyce, Daniel, 115

Julien, Donald (Mi'kmaq), 103

Jwalapuram site (India), *84*, 193

Kadar site (Ethiopia), *84*, 192

Kanorado site (KS), *93*, 204

Kansan glaciation, *66*

Kara-Bom site (Siberia), *84*, 193

Kashani, B. H., 156

Kasnot, Keith, 40, 42

Katanda site (Zaire), 79

Keats, S. G., 100

Kidder, Alfred, 3

Kimmswick site (MO), 166

Kinoshita, A., 136, 137–38

knowledge production: changes needed in, 48, 51, 53–54; cognitive imperialism of, 180; decolonization of, xxv–xxvi, 19–22, 167, 180, 181–83, 187–88; discrimination and racism within, xxiii, 15, 48–52, 171; erasing and dehumanizing identities and histories, 15–18, 48–53, 72–73, 173, 176, 186, 187; ongoing colonialism within, xviii, xxiv, 9, 15, 169–70, 180, 187; pyroepistemology cleansing, 20, 184; social and political power of, 45–54, 173, 179, 182, 187; worldviews formed through, 172–73. *See also* academia

Koch, Albert, 166

Koobi Fora site (Kenya), *84*, 192

Kovach, Margaret (Cree), 6, 15, 18, 21

Kozushima Island (Japan), *83*

Krajacic site (PA), 112

Krasinski, Katherine, 117

Krause, Johannes, 79–80

Krems Wachtberg site (Austria), *84*, 194

Kroeber, Alfred, 28

Kuzmin, Y. V., 100

Lahaye, C., 139–40

Laibin site (China), *84*, 194

Lake Mungo site (Australia), *84*, 193

Lalueza, Carlos, 157

Lamb site (NY), *93*, 207

Lamb Springs site (CO), *93*, 204

Lame Deer, John (Fire), 31

Lampang site (Thailand), *84*, 193

land (ancestral homelands): decolonization rebuilding links to, xxvi, 2, 6–7, 176, 181, 183; erasure of Indigenous links to, xvii, xviii–xx, 6–7, 16, 49, 61, 171, 176, 183, 186, 187; importance of links to, 5–6, 186; Indigenous links to impacting genetic diversity, 153–55; linked to

oral traditions, 58, 163, 165–66, 167, 168; pyroregeneration cleansing, 20, 184; relationality of, xx–xxi, 16, 23, 58, 163, 186; role in Indigenous research, 5; stories left on, xx, 9–10, 16, 81, 91, 186–87; Western knowledge of, 163. *See also* environments and ecosystems
Lapa do Boquete site (Brazil), *133*, 136, 216
Lapa dos Bichos site (Brazil), 136
Lapa Mortuaria site (Brazil), *133*, 217
Lapa Vermelha site (Brazil), *133*, 136, 217
Largo Santa site (Brazil), 136
Larhen, L., 153
LaRocque, Emma (Cree-Metis), 15
La Salle, Marina, 36
Laurasia, 65, 71
laurel-leaf stone tools, 61
Leakey, Louis S. B., 124–25, 126
Lee, Thomas, 17
legislation: NAGPRA, 32, 33–35; normalizing genocide, 49; protecting burial sites, 32–36
Lehner site (AZ), *93*, 205
Levins Morales, Aurora, 129
Levi site (TX), *93*, 204
LGM (Last Glacial Maximum): Beringia landmass during, *66*, 76, 175; maximum ice extent during, 64–65; time frame of, xx, *66*; viable migration routes during, 65
Libby, Willard, 4
Lies My Teacher Told Me (Loewen), 16–17
Lindquist, Anna K., 118
Lindsay site (MT), *93*, 205
linear evolutionary framework, 30
linguistics: Eastern Hemisphere linguistic stocks, *161*; initial migrations timing based on, xxi, 160–62; rates of language spread, 160; Western Hemisphere linguistic stocks, *161*
lithic technologies. *See* stone tool technologies

Little Salt Spring site (FL), *93*, 107–8, 204
Liu, W., 86
Liujiang site (China), *84*, 193
Llamas, B., 159
Loewen, James, 16–17
Lomawaima, K. Tsianina (Creek), 48
Longgupo Cave site (China), *84*, 192
Louis, Renee Pualani, xxi
Lovewell sites (KS), xxiii, *93*, 116–17, 202
Lozhkin, A. V., 65
LT Brazil site (Venezuela), *132*, 215
LT Ji-Paraná-Rolim de Moura site (Brazil), *132*, 215
Lubbock Lake site (TX), *93*, 204
Lubinski, Patrick, 59
Lucy site (NM), *93*, 204
Lynch, Thomas, 142

MacNeish, Richard Scotty, 2, 17, 128, 131, 144–45, 149
Madagascar, 74
Madjedbebe rockshelter site (Australia), 81
Madsen, David, 65
Majors, Paul C., 119
Majuangou III site (China), *84*, 192
Mak, Kam, 40, 42, *43*
Malhi, R. S., 155–56
mammoths: at the Blackwater Draw (NM) site, 3; at the Cerutti Mastodon (CA) site, 180; evidence of Indigenous interactions with, 110, 163; at the Hebior (WI) site, 115–16; images of, *70*; at the Kimmswick (MO) site, 166; at the Little Salt Springs (FL) site, 108; at the Lovewell (KS) sites, 116–17; migrations of, 69–70; in oral traditions, 163, 165; in Pleistocene landscapes, 10; at the Schaefer (WI) site, 115–16; at the La Sena (NE) site, 116–17, 179. *See also* mastodons

157–58; lines of evidence clarifying patterns of, 86; maintaining openness to possibilities of, 4–5, 59–60, 75–76, 79–85, 90, 170–71; mammalian migrations showing possibilities for, xxi, xxiv, 60, 90; oral traditions regarding, 151; theories erasing Indigenous identities and histories, xviii–xx, 52, 61, 170, 174–76, 187; theories supporting colonial doctrines, 5, 15, 52–53, 75, 174–76, 179, 187; time frames based on linguistic diversity, 160–62; viewing on a global scale, xviii, 60, 61–62, 79–80. *See also* Clovis First hypothesis

migrations (mammalian): Atlantic connection route, 70; Beringia landmass route, 65, 67, 69–70, 75, 175; of bison species, 67–69; of camel species, 65–67; environmental factors in, 58, 60, 64, 175; intercontinental examples, 65–74; of mammoths, 69–70; of primate species, 72–73; of rhinoceros species, 70–71; of saber-toothed cats, 67; showing human migration possibilities, xxi, xxiv, 60, 90; timing of intercontinental, 67–69

Mihesuah, Devon (Choctaw-Chickasaw), 15, 22

Miles Point site (MD), *92*, 201

Miller, Albert, 112

Miller projectile points, 112

Mill Iron site (MT), *93*, 206

Minatogawa site (Japan), *84*, 194

Miocene, 60, 67, 70

El Mirador site (Valsequillo, Mexico), *92*, 122–24, 200

Mojokerto site (Indonesia), *84*, 192

molecular research. *See* genetics (molecular) research

Momaday, Scott, 22

Montagu, Ashley, 165–66

Montana Tribal Histories (Cajune), 174

Monte Verde sites (Chile), xxiv–xxv, 75, *132–33*, 145–47, 177–78, 179, 214, 216

Moore, Marcia K., *46*

Moose Creek site (AK), *93*, 206

Morgan, Lewis Henry, 29

Morro Furado site (Brazil), *132*, 214

Morrow, Juliet, 118

Mousterian stone tool technologies, 89

Muaco site (Venezuela), *132*, 215

Mud Lake site (WI), *93*, 115, 204

Mugnai Farm site (PA), 112

multiregional human evolution theory, 85, 86–90

mummification practices, 131–33

Munson, C. A., 113

NAGPRA (Native American Graves Protection and Repatriation Act): and the Ancient One repatriation controversy, 37–45; archaeologists protesting, 34–35; background of, 32–34; passage of, 32, 34; Quapaw tribe's repatriation claim, 97

Nanaimo News, 50

NARF (Native American Rights Fund), 32

National Museum of the American Indian Act (1989), 33

National Park Service (NPS): and the Ancient One repatriation controversy, 37–38; managing the Calico (CA) site, 126; NHL and NRHP listing criteria, 99

National Register of Historic Places (NRHP), 94, 99, 105, 126

Native American Graves Protection and Repatriation Act (NAGPRA). *See* NAGPRA (Native American Graves Protection and Repatriation Act)

Native American Rights Fund (NARF), 32

Nature, 119

Nazi Germany, 29, 32

archaeological sites (Pleistocene); bone tool technologies; migrations; stone tool technologies

El Palto site (Peru), *133*, 217

Parenti, F., 140

Parsons Island site (MD), *93*, 203

The Passing of the Great Race (Grant), 28–29

Patagonia, 148

Patterns in Prehistory (Wenke and Olszewski), 51–52

Patterson, Leland W., 125–26

Paviland site (Wales), *84*, 194

Pawnee people, 32

Peabody Museum (Harvard), 28

Pearson, Maria (Lakota Sioux), 32

Pedler, David, 14, 95, 112, 115, 122, 178

Pedra Furada site (Brazil), *132*, 136, 137–39, 140, 214

Pendejo Cave site (NM), *92*, 200

Pendergast, David, 167

Perez, S. I., 148

Perez, Ventura, 37, 74

perissodactyls, 65. *See also* horse species; rhinoceros species

Perry Mastodon site (IL), *93*, 206

Pessis, A. M., 138–39

Peştera cu Oase site (Romania), *84*, 194

petroglyphs, xx, 23, 139, 163

Petronila Creek site (TX), *93*, 202

physical anthropology, 28–29, 32, 36–45

PIDBA (Paleoindian Database of the Americas), 95

Piedra Museo site (Argentina), *133*, 215

Pikimachay site (Peru), *132*, 144–45, 214

Plato, 57

Pleistocene epoch: defined, xxvii; environments during, 60, 63–65, 75, 174–75; in European archaeology, 99; global comparisons, 58–59; maps of, *62*, *63*;

open-water crossings during, 14, 80, 81–82, *82–83*, 90; plant and animal species during, 63–64; subsistence strategies during, 133–34. *See also* archaeological sites (Pleistocene); extinct species; glacial events; migration routes

plesiadapiforms (basal primates), 71–72

Pokrovka 2 site (Russia), *84*, 194

Politis, G., 135, 147–48

Powell, Joseph, 40

Preucel, Robert, 20

primates, 71–73

Proctor, Robert, 57

Prothero, Donald, 70

protoprimates, 71–73

Proust, Marcel, 60

Pubenza site (Colombia), *132*, 215

Putnam, Frederick Ward, 28

pyroepistemology, xxv, 20, 184, 188

pyroregeneration, xxv, 20, 184

Quapaw tribe, 96–97

Quaternary Period, 64, 99

The Quaternary Period in the United States (Meltzer), 73–74

Quebrada El Membrillo site (Chile), *132*, 215

Quebrada Los Burros site (Peru), 133

Quebradas Tacahuay Quebrada Jaguay site (Peru), 133

Quereo 1 site (Chile), *133*, 216

Quirihuac site (Peru), *133*, 216

racism. *See* discrimination and racism

radiocarbon dating techniques: as an absolute dating method, 4; of the Ancient One, 38; at the Cactus Hill site, 114–15; calibrating, 100, *101*; invention of, 4; at the Manis Mastodon site, 110; at Meadowcroft Rockshelter site, 113; at the Monte Verde sites, 146; at the

Los Toldos site (Argentina), *133*, 216

Toluquilla site (Mexico), *92*, 200

tool technologies. *See* bone tool technologies; stone tool technologies; technologies (human)

Topper site (SC), *92*, 99, 107, 177–78, 200

El Toro site (Mexico), *93*, 202

Torroni, Antonio, 155, 157

tortoise species, 108

Trask, Haunani-Kay, 167

Tres Arroyos site (Argentina), *133*, 217

Tune, Jesse W., 105, 106

El Tunel site (Mexico), *93*, 202

Turnbull, David, 5

Turtle Island, defined, xxvii

turtle species, 106, 108

Ubeidiya site (Israel), *84*, 192

Ubelaker, D., 40

Ucko, Peter, 31

Umatilla Indian Reservation, Confederated Tribes of, 37, 163–65

underwater archaeological sites, 64; Little Salt Springs (FL) site, 108; Page-Ladson (FL) site, 109

Union Pacific Mammoth site (WY), *93*, 206

University of California at Berkeley, 28

University of Chicago, 28

Up from the Ape (Hooten), 29

uranium-series dating technique, 123, 125

Urupez site (Uruguay), *133*, 217

U/Th (uranium-thorium) dating technique, 123, 125

Vale da Pedra Furada site (Brazil), *132*, 136, 139–40, 214

Vallparadis site (Spain), *84*, 193

Valsequillo Reservoir sites (Mexico), *92*, 122–24, 199, 200

Van Walsum, Saskia, *47*

Varsity Estates site (Alberta), *93*, 202

Venner, William, 126

Vero Beach site (FL), *93*, 205

Vertesszölös site (Hungary), *84*, 193

Villa Grove site (CO), *92*, 201

Vinteuil (composer), 60

WAC (World Archaeological Congress), 31, 54

Wagamese, Richard (Anishinaabe), xx–xxi

Wakulla Springs site (FL), *93*, 202

Walker Road site (AK), *93*, 207

Wallace, Douglas, 157

Wallace, Steven, 67

Walton, Christie, 119

Walton, John, 119

Wanapum people, 38

Wang, H., 70–71

Ward, R. H., 156–57

Warm Mineral Springs site (FL), 108

Watanabe, S., 138

Waters, Michael R., 107, 110, 118

Watkins, Joe, 163

Wenke, Robert J., 51–52

Western Stemmed points, 4, 103, 111–12

Whally Beach site (AB), *93*, 207

Wheat, Amber, 177–78

White, Doug (Snuneymuxw), 50, 51

Wilson, Allan, 85–86

Wilson, Angela Cavender (Dakota), 15

Wilson, Carrie, 37, 96–97

Wilson, Shawn (Cree), xxi, 5, 15, 19

Wilson, Waziyatawin Angela, 21

Wilson Butte Cave site (ID), *93*, 203

Winnepaigoraquai (Cree), 7

Wisconsin glaciation, 64–65, *66*, 76

Wiseman, Frederick (Abenaki), 20

Wobst, Martin, 22

World Archaeological Congress (WAC), 31, 54

worldviews: circularity of time in, 16; decolonizing, 176; diversity of, 24; impact of education on, 172–73; impacts of colonialism on, 169–71; impacts of Eurocentric on histories, xviii, 17–18, 27, 49, 172–74, 180; privileging other-than-Western, xxii, 162–63; relationality within, xx–xxi, 22–23. *See also* epistemologies; oral traditions

Wylie, Alison, xxv–xxvi

Wyman, Jeffries, 28

Xiaochangliang site (China), *84*, 192

Xihoudu site (China), *84*, 193

Yakama Nation of Washington State, 37–38

Yamashita-cho cave site (Japan), *83*

Yana River Valley site (Siberia), *84*, 194

Yarmouth interglaciation, *66*

Yellow Bird, Michael (Mandan-Hidatsa-Arikara), 103

Yellowhorn, Eldon (Piikani), 19, 23, 102

Yellow Horse Brave Heart, Maria (Hunkpapa-Oglala Lakota), 49

Yiron site (Israel), *84*, 192

Young, David, 126

Zhoukoudian site (China), *84*, 194

CPSIA information can be obtained
at www.ICGtesting.com
Printed in the USA
LVHW031738030323
740869LV00003B/218

9 781496 234704